A

# COLLECTION

OF ALL

# THE WILLS,

NOW KNOWN TO BE EXTANT,

OF THE

KINGS and QUEENS of ENGLAND,

PRINCES and PRINCESSES of WALES,

AND EVERY BRANCH OF THE BLOOD ROYAL,

FROM THE REIGN OF WILLIAM THE CONQUEROR,
TO THAT OF HENRY THE SEVENTH EXCLUSIVE.

WITH EXPLANATORY NOTES, AND A GLOSSARY.

THE LAWBOOK EXCHANGE, LTD.
Clark, New Jersey

ISBN 9781886363878 (hardcover)
ISBN 9781616192822 (paperback)

Lawbook Exchange edition 1999, 2012

*The quality of this reprint is equivalent to the quality of the original work.*

## THE LAWBOOK EXCHANGE, LTD.
33 Terminal Avenue
Clark, New Jersey 07066-1321

*Please see our website for a selection of our other publications and fine facsimile reprints of classic works of legal history:*
www.lawbookexchange.com

**Library of Congress Cataloging-in-Publication Data**

A collection of all the wills, now known to be extant, of the kings and queens of England, princes and princesses of Wales, and every branch of the blood royal, from the reign of William the Conqueror, to that of Henry the Seventh exclusive : with explanatory notes and a glossary.
    p. cm.
  Originally published : London : Printed by J. Nichols, 1780.
  Includes bibliographical references.
  ISBN 1-886363-87-0 (cloth : alk. paper)
  1. Great Britain—Kings and rulers—Biography—Sources.  2. Great Britain—History—Medieval period, 1066-1485—Sources.  3. Great Britain—History—Henry VII, 1485-1509—Sources.  4. Princesses— Great Britain—Biography—Sources.  5. Princes—Great Britain—Biography—Sources.  6. Queens—Great Britain—Biography—Sources.  7. Wills—Great Britain.  I. Lawbook Exchange, Ltd.
    DA28.1 .C65   1999
      942'.009'9—dc21                           99-17114
                                                  CIP

*Printed in the United States of America on acid-free paper*

A

# COLLECTION

OF ALL

# THE WILLS,

NOW KNOWN TO BE EXTANT,

OF THE

KINGS and QUEENS of ENGLAND,

PRINCES and PRINCESSES of WALES,

AND EVERY BRANCH OF THE BLOOD ROYAL,

FROM THE REIGN OF WILLIAM THE CONQUEROR,

TO THAT OF HENRY THE SEVENTH EXCLUSIVE.

WITH EXPLANATORY NOTES, AND A GLOSSARY.

---

LONDON:
PRINTED BY J. NICHOLS,
PRINTER TO THE SOCIETY OF ANTIQUARIES:
SOLD BY H. PAYNE, PALL-MALL; C. DILLY, IN THE POULTRY;
J. WALTER, CHARING-CROSS; N. CONANT, FLEET-STREET;
AND E. BROOKE, BELL-YARD, TEMPLE-BAR.
MDCCLXXX.

Printed in U.S.A.

# PREFACE.

WHEN the great Sobieſki, to whoſe valour, not only Vienna, but the German empire, owed its preſervation from the Turkiſh power, was aſked in extremity to make his will, he laught in the face of the biſhop, who had been obliged to take the moſt round-about method to make the propoſal. "The misfortune of royalty," ſaid the King, recollecting himſelf, "is, that we are not obeyed while we are alive: and can it be expected we ſhould be obeyed after we are dead?"

Elective kings have not the power, and the kings of uncultivated northern nations have not the idea, of making proviſion for heirs, even though they are to ſink at once into a private rank.

The kings of England wanted no ſuch monitor: but, either from motives of juſtice or contrition, or in a miſtaken zeal to ſave their ſouls by a momentary good deed, we find moſt of them ready enough to engage in "the laſt great act of a wiſe man's life." The utmoſt of their ability was to diſpoſe of their great treaſures among their relations, ſervants, or eccleſiaſtics. The Conqueror bequeathed kingdoms; Henry II. money to monks and nuns; Henry I.

iv PREFACE.

and III. Edward I. and III. money, jewels, houſehold furniture, and charitable legacies; the unhappy Richard II. in whoſe reign it ſeems to have been firſt allowed by authority of parliament to our kings, their heirs and ſucceſſors, to make their wills, and have them duly executed *, makes his teſtament in the ſpirit of the times, and at the eve of a revolution which he little ſuſpected, while the uſurper confeſſes his ſins with all the contrition he had need of. Henry V. expreſſes all the anxiety of a wealthy country gentleman about his lordſhips and manors; and his monkiſh ſon devotes his teſtament intirely to found and plan two colleges.

If from ROYAL we turn our eyes to NOBLE teſtaments, we ſhall find them conceived in nearly the ſame ſentiments. The care of ſepulture, debts, legacies, and charitable foundations, fill up the common outline †. Lady Clare, the foundreſs of Clarehall, Cambridge, ſeems to have completed that pious foundation in her life-time, only a

* " Fait a remembr', Qe les Prelatz, Seigñrs Temporels, & Communes, ſ'aſſenterent en plein Parlement, q̃ ñre Sr̃ le Roi & ſes heirs & ſucceſſours Roys d'Engleterre purront franchement faire lour Teſtamentz, & q̃ execution purra eſtre faite d'icelles." Rot. Parl. 16 Ric. II. vol. III. n. 10. p. 301.

† The French biſhops, in the ſixteenth century, claimed a right to refuſe burial to perſons dying inteſtate, or without leaving a legacy to the church; and the relations of the deceaſed were obliged to make amends for the omiſſion. Saintfoix, Eſſais Hiſt. ſur Paris, I. 50.

legacy

legacy of £.40 to it appearing in her will. The gallant Prince of Wales enlarges on his tomb and his bed-furniture, within a month of his lingering death, as much as his brother of Gaunt does on his wardrobe, or the rich Cardinal of England on his plate. Henry Duke of Lancaster and Edward Duke of York founded colleges which have long since given way to diffolution, while thofe two founded by Henry VI. with thofe which claim the " venerable Margaret" for their foundrefs furvive and flourifh as much as they furpafs them in utility, for the " increafe of virtue, and dilatation " of conning, and ftablifhment of Chriftian faith." Richard Earl of Arundel affords a ftriking picture of human vanity in the troublefome reign of Richard II. and Edward IV's queen a perfect portrait of royal poverty.

This feries of mifcellaneous and different wills prefents us with many curious particulars. We learn from them more of the manners and private life of our illuftrious anceftors, fome new facts in their public hiftory, and feveral new defcents in their pedigrees. The profpect of death fets their lives in a new point of light. Such is the force of fuperftition, however the prefent age thinks itfelf above its reach, that the recommendation of the foul to half a dozen faints was fet up as a palliative for a thoufand crimes. Men left their good
works

# PREFACE.

works to their last moments, died in the midst of their sins, with every vicious impression deeply stampt on their souls, till purgatory or papal indulgence should wear it out.

The language of these wills is the common language of the times, here attempted to be rendered intelligible by the help of those excellent compendious Glossaries of old French, published by Monf. Borel\*, Monf. Laccombe, and Mr. Kelham, and the more extensive Latin one of Du Cange †.

The forms of the bequests are precise and nervous, unincumbered with the trusts and devises of modern times, more advantageous to lawyers than testators. They breathe the spirit of an age when the most important grants and charters were comprised in slips of parchment not six inches square, attested by a croud of witnesses who seldom wrote their names.

The prerogative of the archbishop of Canterbury in testamentary matters extends to the probate of granting administrations, and all causes thereon depending, where the parties deceased were possessed of *bona notabilia* (that is, effects to the value of five pounds) in different dioceses, within his province,

\* Trefor de Recherches et Antiquitez Gauloifes et Françoifes, 4to, Paris, 1655.
† In the will of Philippa Duchefs of York, 1330, fome words abfolutely Englifh have crept in.

except

except in the diocese of London, where it is ten pounds by antient composition, and this will account for so many of the wills here printed being extant in the Archiepiscopal Registry at Lambeth.

These and the registers of the different sees, which have hitherto been generally considered as mere records of institution, endowments, or other ecclesiastical matters, have in various instances preserved many curious particulars of our national history. The Black Prince's letter to the Bishop of Worcester, published from his register in Archæol. I. p. 212. may be considered as a Gazette account of the battle of Poitiers. Innumerable wills, of which this small sample is here presented to the curious, deserve to be published\*, at least in abstract; as Sir William Dugdale has done †, throughout his Baronage. Le Neve mentions two recorded upon the Clause Rolls ‡, where great numbers are preserved.

Abusing the sacred trust of testamentary disposition was one of the aggravated crimes of that egregious plagiarist and libeller Edmund Curll,

---

\* See one of lady Eliz. Fitz Hugh, 1427, Ant. Rep. N° xxix.

† Sir William Dugdale supposes the will of Clifford implies a recantation of the errors, as he calls them, of Lollardism. He would have formed a judgment more candid, as well as more just, had he said the testator only spoke the general penitential language of wills.

‡ Blomefield's Norfolk, J. p. 677. Mr. Becket the surgeon observed more wills in the Prerogative Office, relating to the county of Lincoln, than any other county. Stukeley's Itin. Cur. I. p. 25.

PREFACE.

who overleapt all bounds that opposed the interest of the moment. The present Editor violates no confidence which the revolution of seven centuries has not made the property of the publick. Ambitious to contribute his mite to that spirit of historic investigation that distinguishes the present age, he is conscious of the incompetency of his subject to yield him much beyond the fame of an Antiquary, while he presents his countrymen with a series of wills made by our Sovereigns, or the several collateral branches of the royal families; some taken from the parliamentary registers and public records, and most * of the others transcribed from the archiepiscopal registers at Lambeth under the immediate inspection of the present librarian, by whom the proof-sheets were in part revised, and the whole illustrated with notes and a glossary by other learned friends.

*March* 27, 1780.                                          J. N.

* The will of John of Gaunt, having been deposited at Lincoln, is faithfully copied from the register of his son Bp. Beaufort, who enjoyed that see from 1397 to 1405, when he was translated to Winchester, which he held till 1447.

# ROYAL AND NOBLE WILLS.

|  | Page |
|---|---|
| William the Conqueror, | 1 |
| William Rufus [inteſtate], | 4 |
| Henry the Firſt, | 5 |
| Stephen [inteſtate], | 6 |
| Henry the Second, | 7 |
| ———— Tranſlation into old Engliſh verſe, | *10 |
|  | 11 |
| Richard the Firſt, | 13 |
| John, | 15 |
| Henry the Third, | 18 |
| Edward the Firſt, | 21 |
| Edward the Second [inteſtate], | 22 |
| Elizabeth de Burgh, lady Clare, | 44 |
| Humfray de Bohun, ninth Earl of Hereford and Eſſex, | 57 |
| Humfray de Bohun, tenth earl of Hereford and Eſſex, | 59 |
| Edward the Third, | 66 |
| Edward the Black Prince, | 78 |
| Joan Princeſs of Wales, | 83 |
| Henry Duke of Lancaſter, | 88 |
| Lionel Duke of Clarence, | 92 |
| John Earl of Pembroke, | 98 |
| Philippa Counteſs of March, | 104 |
| Edmund Earl of March, | 118 |
| Thomas Earl of Kent, | 120 |
| Richard Earl of Arundel, | 145 |
| John of Gaunt, Duke of Lancaſter, | 177 |
| Eleanor Bohun, Ducheſs of Glouceſter, | 187 |
| Edmund duke of York, | 191 |
| Richard the Second, | 203 |
| Henry the Fourth, | 208 |
| John Beaufort Earl of Somerſet, | 212 |
| Elizabeth de Juliers, Counteſs of Kent, | Edward |

Edward Duke of York, — — — 217
Philippa de Bohun Duchess of York, — 224
Thomas Duke of Clarence, — — — 230
Henry the Fifth, — — — 236
Katherine Queen of Henry the Fifth, — — 244
Thomas Beaufort Duke of Exeter, — — 250
John Mowbray Duke of Norfolk, — — 266
John Duke of Bedford, Regent of France, — 270
Anne Countess of Stafford, — — 278
John Holland Duke of Exeter, — — 282
Henry the Sixth, — — — 291
Cardinal Beaufort, Bishop of Winton, — — 321
King Edward the Fourth, — — 345
Elizabeth wife of Edward the Fourth, — 350
Edward VI. } [intestate], 355
Richard III. }
Margarate Countess of Richmond [extracted from the Prerogative Court of Canterbury], — — 356

---

*Lately published,*
The Will of King Henry the Seventh; with an Historical Preface, by Thomas Astle, Esq.

# ROYAL WILLS.

## WILLIAM THE CONQUEROR.

THE Conqueror's will consisted only of a distribution of all his wealth among the churches, clergy, and the poor, the precise sums which he bequeathed to each being set down by notaries from his mouth, on his death-bed, where he made a long and pathetic speech about his affairs and successors in his different dominions. He was particularly liberal to the clergy of Mantes, whose churches he had burnt. To his younger son Henry he left 5000 £. of silver; to his eldest son Robert, Normandy\*; and to his second son William, the crown of England.

"Sapiens heros in futurum sibi multisque commoda facere non distulit, omnesque thesauros suos ecclesiis et pauperibus, Deique ministris distribui præcepit. Quantum vero singulis dari voluit callide taxavit, & coram se describi a notariis imperavit. Clero quoque Mandantensi supplex ingentia dona misit, ut inde restaurarentur ecclesiæ quas combusserat."

\* See Lord Lyttelton's observations in this bequest in his History of Henry II. vol. I. p. 77, 8vo.

## WILLIAM THE CONQUEROR.

" Ducatum Normanniæ antequam in epitumo * Senlac contra Heraldum certaffem Roberto filio conceffi quia primogenitus eft. Conceffus honor nequit abftrahi.—Robertus habebit Normanniam, et Gulielmus Angliam.

Henricus junior filius ut nihil fibi de regalibus gazis dari audivit mœrens cum lacrymis ad regem dixit, Et mihi, pater, quid tribuis? Cui rex ait, quinque millia libras argenti de thefauro meo tibi do."

Ord. Vitalis, l. vii. p. 656. 659.

ANNO 1087. Rex Gulielmus regnum devaftans Franciæ, caftrum nobile quod vocatur Maante combuffit, et ecclefias quæ ibi erant et plebem multam et duos fanctos anachoritas igni tradidit; quibus vifum non fuit & in tanto periculo deferere cellas fuas. Sed in ipfo redditu dirus dolor vifcerum apprehendit illum. Cum autem diem fibi mortis imminere fenfiffet, fratrem fuum Odonem Bajocenfem epifcopum et omnes quos in Anglia vel Normannia tenebat in vinculis relaxabat. Terras vero fuas fic divifit. Roberto primogenito fuo Normanniam; Gulielmo fecundo filio fuo Angliæ monarchiam. Henrico thefauri copiam. Pro quo cum Robertus vendidiffet ei partem Normanniæ, thefauro habito, quod ei vendiderat abftulit. Rex igitur Gulielmus poftquam genti Anglorum præ-

---

* *Epitumum, epitimium,* are terms peculiar to Ordericus Vitalis for a *field.* Du Cange, in voc. *Senlac,* or *Sang Lac,* was the name given to the fpot where the decifive battle was fought between Harold and William., Camden *Brit. Suffex.*

fuiffet viginti * annis, decem menfibus et 27 diebus, quinto idus Septembris die Jovis regnum cum vita reliquit, et Cadomi in ecclefiam S. Stephani quam ipfe a fundamentis conftruxerat fepultus requiefcit. Uxor vero fua Matildis abbaciam fanctimonialium ibidem conftruxit, ubi et ipfa requiefcit.

Walfingham Ypodigma Neuftriæ, p. 440. in Camdeni Anglica Normannica fol. Francfort. 1603.

The difpofal of his eftates between his three fons, is recorded in thefe few old rhimes; in the continuation of Robert of Glocefter, p. 335.

> He gaf his eldeft fon Normandy,
> And to the fecund Engelond truly,
> To the thridde his goods menable;
> This was holde ferme and ftable.

Du Moulin † fays he divided his treafure among the churches, the religious, the fecular clergy, and the poor, fpecifying the exact fums to each; fent to the clergy of Mantes a confiderable fum of money for the repair of the churches which he had burnt, with fome lines which fhewed the reality of his repentance, and his earneft defire to be remembered in their prayers.

* In the 22d year, according to Malmfbury.
† Hift. Gen. de Norm. VII. p. 234.

WILLIAM THE CONQUEROR.

The stately monuments of the Conqueror and of his queen (destroyed by the Huguenots in the civil wars of France, A.D. 1562) are succeeded by modern altar tombs, which are engraven in Dr. Ducarel's Anglo-Norman Antiquities, plates VI. and VII. where also (at p. 51.) is a particular description of the original monument erected for the Conqueror by his son William Rufus.

---

THE immature death of WILLIAM RUFUS, A. D. 1000. did not give him time to make any testamentary disposition. His tomb in Winchester cathedral met with the same treatment as his father's in our late civil wars [*]. It is engraven in Sandford, p. 23. edit. 1677. and in Gale's Antiquities of Winchester.

[*] Mr. Warton says, that "his tomb was opened by the rebels in the "civil wars, who stole from thence the remains of a cloth of gold, a ring "set with rubies, said to be worth £. 500, and a small silver chalice." *Description of Winchester,* p. 90.

HENRY

[ 5 ]

# HENRY THE FIRST.

HENRY I. ordered his natural son Robert * to take £.60,000. out of his treasure in his custody at Falaise, and to distribute gratuities and pay among his servants and soldiers; and directed his body to be carried to Reading, where he had founded an abbey.

" Roberto filio suo de thesauro quod idem servabat Falesiæ sexaginta millia libras jussit accipere famulisque suis atque stipendiariis militibus mercedes et donativa erogare. Corpus vero suum Reddingas deferri præcepit ubi cœnobium cc monachorum in honore sanctæ et individuæ Trinitatis condiderat." Ord. Vit. l. vii. p. 901.

This king died at St. Denys, in the castle and forest of Lions, in Normandy, Dec. 4, 1135; and was buried at Reading abbey, where there are not now the smallest memorials of him.

* Earl of *Gloucester*, the guardian of the kingdom, and able defender of the title of his sister and nephew against Stephen. He died in November, 1146. See his character admirably drawn by Lord Lyttelton, Vol. II. p. 148, &c.

STEPHEN

STEPHEN was too much of a foldier of fortune to have it in his power to make any bequefts. The kingdom was fettled for him the moment the right heir was able to affert his claim. He died at Dover, Oct. 25, 1154. His own and his queen's bodies * were torn out of their graves at Feverfham abbey, at the diffolution, for the fake of the lead of their coffins.

* *Weever* and *Stow*, the latter as quoted by *Lewis*, fpeak only of the king's body. *Lewis*, however, fpeaks of it as probable, that the bodies of the queen and Euftace their fon fhared the fame fate. Euftace died at St. Edmondfbury, Aug. 10, 1152. Maud, Stephen's queen, May 3, 1151. *Weever.*

# HENRY THE SECOND.

"HENRICUS Dei gratia rex Angliæ, Dux Normanniæ et Aquitaniæ, comes Andegaviæ, Henrico regi, et Ricardo, et Galfrido, et Johanni filiis suis; archiepiscopis, episcopis, abbatibus, archidiaconis, decanis, comitibus, baronibus, justiciariis, vicecomitibus, ministris, & omnibus hominibus & fidelibus suis tam clericis quam laicis tocius terræ suæ citra mare & ultra, salutem. Notum vobis facio, quod apud Waltham, præsentibus episcopis R. Wintoniensi et J. Norwicensi, & G. * cancellario filio meo, et magistro Waltero [de] Constantiis archidiacono Oxon. et Godefrido de Luci archidiacono de Derebi, & Ranulfo de Glanvilla, et Rogero filio Reimfridi, et Hugone de Morewic, & Radulfo filio Stephani camerario, et Willelmo Rufo, feci divisam meam de quadam parte pecuniæ meæ in hunc modum: domui militiæ templi Jerusalem MMMMM marcas argenti, domui hospitali Jerusalem MMMMM marcas argenti; et ad communem defensionem terræ Jerosolimitanæ MMMMM marcas argenti, per manum magistrorum templi et hospitalis Jerusalem & visum eorundem habendas; præter pecuniam illam quam prius prædictis domibus templi et hospitalis commiseram custodiendam; quam similiter dono ad defensionem ipsius terræ Jerosolimitanæ, nisi eam in vita mea repetere voluero; et aliis domibus religiosis tocius Jerosolimæ, et leprosis et

---

* Geoffrey son of Henry II. by fair Rosamond. He was archdeacon and bishop of Lincoln, chancellor of England, and archbishop of York 21 years. He died 1213. Sandford, p. 71, 72.

inclusis

inclufis et heremitis ejufdem terræ MMMMM marcas argenti, dividendas per manum patriarchæ Jerufalem, & vifum epifcoporum terræ Jerofolimæ, et magiftrorum templi et hofpitalis; domibus religiofis Angliæ, monachorum, canonicorum, fanctimonialium, & leprofis, et inclufis, & heremitis ipfius terræ MMMMM marcas argenti, dividendas per manum et vifum [1]R. archiepifcopi Cant. et [2]R. Winton' et [3] B. Wigorn' et [4] G. Elycn' et [5] J. Norwic' epifcoporum, et Ranulfi de Glanvilla jufticiarii Angliæ; domibus religiofis Normanniæ, monachorum, canonicorum fanctimonialium, et inclufis, et heremitis ejufdem terræ MMM marcas argenti, dividendas per manum et vifum archiepifcopi Rothomagenfis, et Baiocenfis, et Abrincenfis, et Sagienfis, et Ebroicenfis epifcoporum; domibus leproforum ipfius CCC marcas argenti per manum et vifum prædictorum dividendas; monialibus Moretoniæ C marcas argenti; monialibus de Viliers extra Faleifiam C marcas argenti; domibus religiofis terræ comitis Andegaviæ patris mei, exceptis fanctimonialibus de ordine fontis Ebraldi, M marcas argentis per manus epifcoporum Cenomannenfis et Andegavenfis dividendas; ipfis autem fanctimonialibus Fontis Ebraldi, et domibus ipfius ordinis, MM marcas argenti, dividendas per manum et vifum abbatiffæ Fontis Ebraldi; fanctimonialibus fancti Sulpicii Britanniæ C marcas argenti; domui et toti ordini Grandis Montis

[1] Richard prior of Dover, immediate fucceffor of Thomas Becket.
[2] Richard Topclive, al. More, al. de Ivelchefter.
[3] Baldwin abbot of Ford.
[4] Galfridus Rydall, archdeacon of Canterbury,
[5] John Oxford, archdeacon of Salifbury.

MMM marcas argenti; domui & toti ordini de Chartusa MM marcas argenti; domui Cistertii et omnibus domibus ipsius ordinis, exceptis domibus ejusdem ordinis quæ in terra mea sunt quibus divisam meam feci, MM marcas argenti, dividendas per visum et manum abbatis Cistertii et Clarevallis; domui Cluniaci M marcas argenti, præter hoc quod eidem domui accommodavi, quod ei perdono nisi in vita mea repetere voluero; domui Majoris Monasterii\* perdono M marcas argenti quas ei commodavi, nisi eas in vita mea repetere voluero; sanctimonialibus de Maitilli c marcas argenti; domui de Præmonstrato et toti ordini, exceptis domibus ejusdem ordinis quæ in terra mea sunt, CC marcas argenti; domui de Arrodis et toti ordini, exceptis domibus ejusdem ordinis terræ meæ, C marcas argenti; ad maritandas pauperes et liberas fœminas Angliæ quæ carent auxilio, CCC marcas auri, dividendas per manum et visum R. Wintoniensis, et B. Wigorn', et G. Elyensis, et J. Norwicensis episcoporum, et Ranulfi de Glanvilla; ad maritandas pauperes et liberas fœminas Normanniæ quæ carent auxilio, C marcas auri, dividendas per manum et visum Rothomagensis archiepiscopi, et Baiocensis et Abrincensis, et Sagiensis, et Ebroicensis episcoporum; ad maritandas [pauperes] et liberas fœminas de terra comitis Andegaviæ patris mei C marcas auri, per manum et visum Cenomannensis et Andegavensis episcoporum dividendas. Hanc autem divisam feci imprædicto loco anno incarnationis Domini MCLXXXII. Quam

\* Marmonstier.

vobis filiis meis per fidem quam mihi debetis et facramentum quod mihi juraftis, præcipio ut firmiter et inviolabiliter teneri faciatis; et quod fuper eos qui ipfam fecerint manum non apponatis; et quicunque contra hoc venire prefumpferit, indignationem et iram omnipotentis Dei, et maledictionem ipfius Dei et meam incurrat. Vobis etiam archiepifcopis et epifcopis mando, ut per facramentum quod mihi feciftis, et fidem quam Deo et mihi debetis, in fynodis veftris follempniter accenfis candelis excommunicetis et excommunicare faciatis omnes illos qui hanc divifam meam infringere præfumpferint: et fciatis quod dominus papa hanc divifam meam fcripto et figillo fuo confirmavit fub interminatione anathematis."

Ex antiquo Cod. MS. Feodorum militum Angliæ penes Remem. Regis, fol. 1. Habet hunc titulum five rubricam,

"Hoc eft Teftamentum illuftriffimi Regis Henrici Se-
"cundi Angliæ."

Printed in Madox's Formulare Anglicanum, p. 421.

This king died before the altar in the church at Chinon, July 7, 1189; and was buried at Font Evrauld in Anjou. See his monument, and that of his queen Eleanor, in Sandford, p. 64. and Montfaucon, Monumens de la Monarchie Françoife, II. pl. xv. Alfo by G. Vertue, in Rapin's Hiftory of England.

# RICHARD

[ 10* ]

Since this Will was printed, we have difcovered a clofe Tranflation of it into old Englifh in PETER LANGTOFT's Rhyming Chronicle, publifhed by HEARNE, Vol. I. p. 135—137. The Author lived about the Time of Edw. I. or II.

THAN faid Sir Henry, nedes burd him wende [a]
To France & Normundie, to witte a certeyn ende.
At Parys [b] wild he be, at ther parlement.
Ther wille wald [b] he fe, to what thei wild [b] confent.
At the duzepers [c] the fothe wild he wite,
And on what maners, & wharto he fuld lite,
And whedir thei wild to werre, or thei wild nouht,
Or alle in luf fperre [d] that thing that thei had wrouht.
He fauh wele bi figne, he drouh [e] faft tille [f] elde [g],
Long myght he not regne, ne on his lif belde [h].
Wherfor Henry faid he wild, or he went,
That the fumme wer laid of his teftament.
Lifte & I falle rede the parcelles what amountes,
If any man in dede wille kefte in a countes [i].

*De teftamento Henrici fecundi, facto apud Waltham, per totum.*
SEX thoufand marke tille Acres did he fend.
Ageyn his comyng thidere, bi marchandz fo he wend [k].
Fifty thoufand marcs had he lent abbeis,
That wer in pouerte, up tham forto reife.
Alle that was gyuen, & befor hand lent,
That was not in cofre, whan he mad teftament.

[a] Go. [b] Would. [c] The 12 peers. [d] In peace examine. [e] Drew. [f] To. [g] Old age. [h] Build, reckon. [i] Caft up the account. [k] Weened, thought.

[ 11* ]

Of that that was in cofre, & in his cotines <sup>l</sup>,
He mad his teſtament, als did other pilgrimes.
To Waltham gede the kyng, his teſtament to make,
And thus quathe <sup>m</sup> he his thing, for his ſoule ſake.
To temples * in Acres he quath.<sup>m</sup> fiue thouſand marke,
And fiue thouſand to the hoſpitale †, for thei were in karke <sup>n</sup>.
To the folk that duelled, Acres for to fende <sup>o</sup>,
Other fiue thouſand marke he gaf tham to ſpende.
Tille other houſes <sup>p</sup> of the cuntre fiue thouſand marke he gaf,
Tille heremites & tille ſeke <sup>q</sup> men, & other of ſuilk raf <sup>r</sup>.
Tille monkes & to chanons <sup>s</sup>, that were in Inglond,
Fiue <sup>t</sup> thouſand marke reſceyued thei of his hond.
To tho of that religion, that were in Normundie,
Fiue thouſand mark unto ther treſorie.
And to meſelle <sup>u</sup> houſes of that ſame lond,
Thre thouſand mark unto ther ſpenſe he fond <sup>x</sup>.
To ladies of habite, Vilers & Mortayn <sup>y</sup>,
He gaf tuo hundreth mark, I trowe thei were fayn <sup>z</sup>.
To tho religiouſes that were in Gaſcoyne <sup>a</sup>,
He gaf a thouſand mark, withouten eſſoyne <sup>b</sup>.
To tham of Founz Eberard <sup>c</sup>, ther his body lis,
He gaf tuo thouſand mark, tho ladies of pris <sup>d</sup>.

<sup>l</sup> *Cophinus*, cheſt. <sup>m</sup> Bequeathed. * The knights templars. † The knights hoſ-pitalers. <sup>n</sup> In charge. Hearne. <sup>o</sup> Defend. *Ad communem defenſionem terræ Jeroſo-limitanæ.* Latin Will. *Acres* in this poetical will is ſynonymous with Jeruſalem or the Holy Land. <sup>p</sup> Religious houſes in Jeruſalem and the Holy Land. <sup>q</sup> *Leproſis.* <sup>r</sup> Such mean condition. Hearne. <sup>s</sup> And to other religious houſes and hoſpitals, adds the Latin Will. <sup>t</sup> Three. Lat. Will: perhaps to be corrected from this. <sup>u</sup> Houſes of *lepers.* <sup>x</sup> Found. <sup>y</sup> To the Nuns of Viliers and Mortayne each 200 marks. See Alien Priories, II. 49. I. 156. The latter of theſe houſes was founded by Henry's great uncle, Robert earl of Mortain, 1082. <sup>z</sup> Glad. <sup>a</sup> *Monialibus terræ comitis Andegaviæ patris mei.* <sup>b</sup> Excuſe. <sup>c</sup> Fontevrauld. <sup>d</sup> Though the religious in it were women of rank or fortune. See Alien Priories, II. 69.

To

To the ladies of Bretayn, men calle Seynt Suplice [e],
He gaf a hundreth mark, to mend ther office [f].
To the houſes of Chartres [g] tuo thouſand mark bi counte,
And thre thouſand mark to the ordre of Grant mounte [h].
To the ordre of Ciſteaus [i] he gaf tuo thouſand mark,
The ordre of Clony [k] a thouſand, to lay up in arke [l].
The ordre of Premonſtere [m] tuo hundreth mark thei had.
To the ladies of Markayne [n] a hundreh mark thei lad [o].
To the houſes of Arroys [p], that ere bigond the ſe,
Tuo [q] hundreth mark thorgh [r] teſtament gaf he.
To women of Inglond, of gentille lynage [s],
A hunderth mark of gold, to ther mariage.
To gentille, & tille other [s], that were in Normundie,
A hundreth mark of gold thei had to ther partie [t].
To gentille women of Aniowe [u], of non auancement [x],
A hundreth mark of gold unto tham was ſent.
Withouten this teſtament that he did writen,
And the grete treſore tille Acres was witen,
And that he lent religiouſe to bring tham aboue [y],
Fourty thouſand mark [z] he gaf for Gode loue.

Whan the kyng Henry had mad his teſtament,
He dight his oſte redy [a], & to Parys went.

[e] St. Sulpice in Brittany. [f] Stock, income. [g] Charter-houſe. [h] Grandmont near Rouen, founded by this prince. See Alien Priories, II. 30. [i] *Citeaux*, Ciſtercians. [k] Clugni. [l] *Arca*, coffer. [m] Premonſtratenſes. [n] Marmoutier *Majoris Monaſterii*. Alien Priories, II. 131. Why called *Markayne* does not appear. [o] They carried, *on porta*. This was money lent and forgiven them. Lat. Will. [p] *Domibus de Arrodis & toti ordini*. Q. Canons of Arroaſia, a reform of the Auguſtin order by St. Nicholas of Arroaſia in Artois about 1090, of which there were five houſes in England. See Stevens, Mon. II. 149. Tanner, Not. Mon. pref. p. xviii. [q] One. Lat. Will. [r] By. [s] *Pauperes & liberæ*. Lat. Will. [t] Portion, ſhare. [u] Anjou. [x] Poor. [y] To raiſe them. [z] The total amount is 45,000 marks. [a] Made his army ready.

# ELEANOR

## QUEEN OF HENRY II.

IT appears by the Patent Rolls of her son John that this Queen had licence to make a will. Whether she made it has not yet appeared.

Quod Alienora regina Angliæ faciat testamentum suum.
Pat' de anno 4° Johannis, p. 29.

Rex omnibus ad quos presentes literæ pervenerint salutem. Sciatis quod concessimus dominæ Alienoræ reginæ Angliæ matris nostræ quod ipsa faciat racionabile testamentum suum de reditu suo ad terminum Sancti Michaelis proximo futuro regni nostri anno quarto. Teste meipso apud Rothomagum vicesimo secundo die Julii [a].

This Princess was eldest daughter and heir of William 9th duke of Aquitaine, by Eleanor of Chastelheraut, the divorced wife of Lewis VII. king of France. She was the prime cause of those bloody wars which continued so long

---

[a] Ex libro pen. Tho. Astle arm; de transcriptu Rotulor. Pat. et Claus. necnon aliorum munimentorum Regum Angliæ. Printed at the end of the second edition of the Liber Niger Scaccarii, 1771. vol. II. p. 805.

between England and France; and after having seen three of her sons succeffively enjoy the crown of England, she died in the caftle of Mirabel in Anjou, June 26, 1202, and was buried at Font Evraud, where her figure is ftill to be feen, lying by her hufband, as before defcribed. Sandford, p. 60.

RICHARD.

# RICHARD THE FIRST.

WHEN Richard I. was pronounced paſt recovery of his wound, 1199, he bequeathed to his brother John his kingdom of England, and all his other territories, and made all preſent take the oath of allegiance to him. He ordered that his caſtles ſhould be delivered to him, and three parts of his treaſure: and all his jewels he deviſed to his nephew * Otho emperor of Germany, and directed that the remaining fourth of his treaſures ſhould be diſtributed among his ſervants and the poor. He directed that his brains, his blood, and his entrails, ſhould be buried at Charrou [Chaluz], his heart at Rouen, and his body at Font Evraud, at the feet of his father.

"Cum autem rex de vita deſperaret, diviſit Johanni fratri ſuo regnum Angliæ et omnes alias terras ſuas; et fecit fieri prædicto Johanni fidelitates ab illis qui aderant; et præcepit ut traderentur ei caſtella ſua et tres partes theſauri ſui, et omnia baubella ſua diviſit Othoni nepoti ſuo regi Alemannorum, et quartam partem theſauri ſui, præcepit ſervientibus ſuis et pauperibus diſtribui. Deinde præcepit rex ut cerebrum et ſanguis et viſcera ſua ſe-

* Otho IV. emperor of Germany was ſon of Maud ſiſter of Richard I. married to Henry V. ſurnamed the Lion, duke of Saxony and Bavaria. Sandford, p. 69.

pelirentur apud Charrou, et cor fuum apud Rothomagum, et corpus fuum apud Fontem Ebraudi ad pedes patris fui."

Hoveden, Annal. p. 449, 450. 1596.

This king died at Gizors, April 6, 1199. His body was buried at Font Evraud in Anjou; fee his monument in Sandford, p. 64. and in Montfaucon, Mon. de la Monarchie, Franc. II. pl. xv. Alfo by G. Vertue, in Rapin's Hiftory of England. His heart was buried at Rouen; his monument, and that of his fecond wife Elizabeth, is engraven in Montfaucon, ubi fupra, and copied in Dr. Ducarel's Anglo-Norman Antiquities, pl. 2. as is alfo the effigies of Berengera his wife, taken from her tomb in the abbey of L'Efpan near Mons. where fhe is interred.

# KING JOHN.

EGO J. Dei gratia rex Anglie, dominus Hibernie, dux Norm' et Aquit', Com' Andegav', gravi infirmitate preventus, nec sufficiens ad tempus infirmitatis mee currere per singula, ut testamentum meum de singulis rebus meis condam; ordinationem et dispositionem testamenti mei fidei et dispositioni legitime committo fidelium meorum subscriptorum, sine quorum consilio etiam in bono statu constitutus nullatenus impresentia eorum ordinarem: ut quod ipsi fideliter ordinaverint et disposuerint de rebus meis, tam in satisfactione facienda Deo et sancte ecclesie de dampnis et injuriis eis illatis, quam in succursu faciendo terre Jerosolimitane, et sustentatione prestanda filiis meis pro hereditate sua perquirenda et defendenda, et in remuneratione facienda illis qui fideliter nobis servierunt, et in distributione facienda pauperibus et domibus religiosis pro salute anime mee, ratum sit et firmum. Peto etiam, ut qui consilium et juvamen eis fecerit ad testamentum meum ordinandum, gratiam Dei percipiat et favorem. Qui autem ordinationem et dispositionem suam infregerit, maledictionem et indignationem omnipotentis Dei et beate Marie, et omnium sanctorum incurrat. Imprimis igitur volo, quod corpus meum sepeliatur in ecclesia Sancte Marie et Sancti Wulstani de Wigorn.

gorn. Ordinatores autem et dispositores tales constituo: dominum G. Dei gratia titulo Sancti Martini presbiterum cardinalem apostolice sedis legatum, dominum [1] P. Winton' episcopum, dominum [2] R. Cicestrensem episcopum, dominum [3] S. Wigorn' episcopum, fratrem Aimericum de Sancta Maura, W. Marescallum comitem Penbroc', R. Com. Cestr', Willielmum Comitem de Ferrarris, Willielmum Bruwne, Walterum de Lasey, et Johannem de Monemut, Savaricum de Malo Leone, Falkesium de Breante.

Ex Originale penes Dec. et Cap. Wigorn'.

Printed in Thomas's Survey of the Cathedral of Worcester, Appendix, N° 33.

He died at Newark, Oct. 19, 1216, and was buried in Worcester cathedral. See his Monument in Sandford, p. 85. Thomas's Survey of Worcester cathedral, p. 36. and Stukeley's Itinerary, I. pl. XVIII. and by G. Vertue, in Rapin's History of England. His bowels were buried at Croxton-abbey. Green's Survey of Worcester, p. 67.

[1] Peter de Rupibus.
[2] Richard Poore, afterwards bp. of Sarum.
[3] Silvester de Evesham, prior of Evesham.

HENRY

## HENRY THE THIRD.

IN nomine Patris et Filii et Spiritus Sancti, Ego Henricus, Dei gratia, Rex Angliæ, et Dominus Hiberniæ, Dux Normanniæ, Aquitanniæ, et Comes Andegaviæ, die Martis proxime post festum apostolorum Petri et Pauli, anno gratiæ millesimo ducentesimo quinquagesimo tercio, apud Suthwyk proponens transfretare in Vasconiam, hujusmodi condo testamentum meum. In primis, animam meam lego et commendo Deo, et * beatæ virgini matri suæ, et † omnibus sanctis. Sepulturam corpori meo eligo apud ecclesiam beati Edwardi Westmonasterii, eo non obstante, quod prius eligeram sepulturam apud Novum Templum Londoniæ. Custodiam vero Edwardi primogeniti filii mei et hæredis, et aliorum puerorum meorum, et ‡ regni mei Angliæ, et omnium aliarum terrarum mearum Walliæ et Hiberniæ et Vasconiæ, lego et committo illustri reginæ meæ Alionoræ, usque ad legitimam ætatem hæredum meorum; et totum aurum meum, præter § jocalia, lego in subsidium terræ sanctæ, deportandum cum cruce mea per viros strenuos et fide dignos, per prædictam reginam et executores meos subscriptos eligendos. Et fabricam ecclesiæ beati Edwardi West-

\* Beati, MS.      † Et et omnibus, MS.
‡ Reginæ mei MS.      § Jacalia, MS.

monasterii lego et committo præfato Edwardo primogenito meo perficiendum; ad feretrum vero ipsius Edwardi beati perficiendum lego quingentas marcas argenti, percipiendas de * jocalibus meis per manus prædictorum reginæ et executorum meorum. Et de debitis meis sic volo et ordino, quod regina mea, hæredibus meis infra ætatem et in custodia ipsius reginæ existentibus, cum prædictis terris meis debita mea acquietet, quatenus potest, de exitibus prædictarum terrarum, salvis statu et continencia propriorum hæredum. Cum vero † idem hæredes ad ætatem legitimam pervenerint, totum residuum sive remanens eorundem debitorum acquietabunt. Satisfactionem vero obsequiorum militum, serviencium, et aliorum, quibus teneor, committo et injungo præfatis reginæ et Edwardo primogenito meo, ut eis, juxta merita obsequiorum, respondeant et retribuant. Crucem autem, quam dedit michi comitissa Canciæ, cum vestimento capellæ meæ albo, et cum imagine beatæ virginis ‡ argentea, parvo tabernaculo lego predictæ ecclesiæ beati Edwardi Westmonasterii; et aliam crucem auream, et vestimentum capellæ meæ, cum lapidibus preciosis et aliis pertinentibus ad capellam et imaginem beatæ Virginis auream, lego prædicto Edwardo primogenito et hæredi meo. Alia autem, in hoc testamento non expressa, committo et relinquo dispocissioni executorum meorum subscriptorum † videliced prefatæ

* Jacalibus, MS.        † Sic.
‡ Argentei, MS.

Reginæ

HENRY THE THIRD.

Reginæ meæ, Bonefacii Cantuariæ archiepifcopi; [1] Adomari Wintoniæ electi, et Ricardi comitis Cornubiæ, fratrum meorum; Petri de Sabaudia, Johannis Maunfelle præpofiti Beverlye, †Petri Chiceporm ‡ archediaconi Walliæ, Johannis prioris de Novoburgo, capellanis meis; Johannis de Gray fenefcalli mei, et Henrici de Wengham clerici mei. Ita quod ifti de fingulis, hic non expreffis, difponant, fecundum quod faluti meæ viderint expedire. Et in hujus rei majorem evidenciam et firmitatem, figillum noftrum præfenti fcripto in modum cirographi confecto una cum figillis præfcriptorum fecimus apponi.

Printed in Liber Niger Scaccarii, vol. II. p. 532. publifhed by Hearne.

He died at his palace at Weftminfter, Nov. 16, 1272. His heart was buried at Font Evraud in Anjou; his body in Weftminfter Abbey. See his Monument in Sandford, p. 92. and by G. Vertue, in Rapin's Hiftory of England.

[1] Aymer de Valence, own brother to H. III. by the fecond marriage of his mother with Hugh earl of March. He was elected by the king's intereft; but not confecrated till the year before his death, which happened 1261. Godwin.

† Petro, MS.          ‡ Sic.

EDWARD

# EDWARD THE FIRST.

EN nun du Pere, du Fitz, e du Seynt Efprit, Amen. Nus Edward, einfne filz au noble Roy d'Engleterre, fefoms noftre teftament, en noftre bon fen, e en noftre bone memorie, le Samedis procheyn apres la Pentecoufte, en le an de noftre feygnur mil, deu cent, feptfaunt fecund, en cefte manere. En primes, nus divifoms a Deu, e a noftre dame Seinte Marie, e a tuz feyns noftre alme; et noftre cors enfeuelir, ou nos effeketurs, ceo eft a faver, fire Johan de Bretayne, fire William de Valence, fire Rog. de Clifford, fire Payn de Chautros, fire Roberd Tiletot, fire Otes de Grauntfon, Robert Burnett, et Antoyne Bek, o oukuns de eus aurunt deviffe: As queus nus donoms et grauntoms plener poer, ke il pufint ordiner por noftre alme, de tuz nos beyns, moebles e noun moebles, cum en rendre nos dettes, e redrecher les tort ke nus avoms fet par nus ou par nos baliz, et rendre a noftre gent' lur fervife, fulom ceo ke il verrunt ke bon feyt.

E por ceo ke nus favoms ben, ke noz moebles ne purrunt pas fuffire a ceo vulums e otroms ke noz avaunt diz exfeketurs eyent plener poer, le quel nus les grauntoms fi avaunt ke nus pouns, de ordiner, et eftablir de tutes nos teres d'Engleterre, de Irelaunde, de Gafcoine, e de tutes nos autres teres, ke il en pufent ourir en memes la manere ke nus feymes quant eles furent en noftre meign, faunt

# EDWARD THE FIRST.

wendre ou doner, e en lur meyns tenir enfemblement o la garde de nos enfaunz, ufque au plener age de eus, pur noftre teftament acomplir, et nos aumones fere en Engletere, et aillurs fulum ceo ke nos effeketurs verrunt ke feyt a fere; as queus fere, nus ordinoms ceynt mille marcs.

Et, apres noftre devis fet, et nos aumons acomplies, volums ke les iffues des avaunt dites teres, turnent au profit de noz enfaunz, e demurgent en les meyns des avaunt diz exeketurs, jufkes a l'age de noz enfaunz avaunt nomes.

Et, fi aventure avenge ke noftre feygnur rey, noftre pere, murge dedenz le age de nos enfauns (ke Deu defende) nos volums ke le reaume d'Engletere, et tutes les autres teres ke porrunt efchair a noz enfaunz, demorgent en les meyns de nos effeketurs avaunt nomes, enfemblement ovefque noftre cher piere le Erceuefk de Everwyk, * e fire Rog. e ovefk autres prodes homes du reaume, ke il akondrunt fi meftier feyt, jufkes al plener age de nos enfaunz fus nomez, e ke les iffues avaunt dites teres feyent cuilliz, e gardez, per les meyns de nos exfeketures avauntdiz, e liverez a nos enfaunz, quant il ferrunt de plener age a lur profift.

E, fur ceo nus volums e ordinoms ke deus, ou plus de noz effeketurs, eyent poer de oyr nos acuntes, e de receyvere de tuz nos baliz, ou ke il feyent, devaunt noftre departir d'Engletere.

E puis, fe il ne poent mufter ke il eyent leal acunte rendue, et fi nul de noz baliz feyt mort, ke fes heirs feyent tenuz a rendre la cunte pur luy.

* Walter Giffard, 1265—1279.

Endreyt de dowarie de noſtre chere femme Alianore, volums ke ele eyt pleynement ceo ke fuſt nome quant nus les puſams, e ſi de ceo ne ſe tent pas a pae, nus voloms ke ele eyt ceo ke dreyt e ley la dorra, ſulom les uſages e le leys d'Engletere.

E voloms auſi ke la ou tuz noz effeketurs ne poirunt eſtre pur fere le execution de noſtre teſtament avaunt dit, ke quatre ou plus, en num des autrys, eyent poer pur eus, e pur les autrys, pur acomplir les choſes ſuſdites.

E pur ceo, priums a noſtre ſeynt pere l'apoſtle, ke il voyll ceſte choſe tenir, et fere tenir, e confirmer; e ke il voyle prier noſtre cher pere, ke il voyle tenir eſtable, e fere tenir, par tut ſon reaume, e tot ſon poer, quel part ke il ſeyt, les choſes avaunt nomes.

En teſtimoniaunce de la queu choſe, a ceo teſtament avoms fet mettre noſtre ſel, et avoms prie ſire Johan erceveſke de Sur, et vicarie de la ſeinte egliſe de Jeruſalem, et les honurables pers, frere Hue Revel, meſtre de l'Hoſpital, et frere Thomas Berard, meſtre du Temple, ke a ceſt eſcrit meis ent auſi lur ſeus, les quieus ſi le vut fet enſemblement, o nos effeketurs avaunt nomes en teſmoiſnaunce des choſes ſus dites.

Done a Acre, le Samedy avaunt nome, le diſutime jur de Juen, l'an du regne le roy noſtre pere cinkaunt e ſinc *.

RYMER's Fœdera, tom. I. p. 885.

* Edward was at Acres 1271, the fifty-*ſixth* and laſt year of his father's reign. Rapin III. 488, 489.

## EDWARD THE FIRST.

Whether the military tranfactions, and the revenge this great Prince was preparing to execute on the Scotch, when death overtook him at Burgh on Sands, in Cumberland, July 7, 1307, prevented him from making any teftamentary difpofition after he came to the crown; no other will of his has yet come to light. He was buried at the head of his father in Weftminfter-abbey. See his Monument in Sandford, p. 136. and by G. Vertue in Rapin's Hiftory of England, vol. I.

See alfo Sir Jofeph Ayloffe's account of his body, as it appeared on opening his tomb in the year 1774. Archæologia, vol. IV. p. 376.

It is more eafy to account for the want of a will of his unhappy fon and fucceffor EDWARD THE SECOND, who was murdered on the 25th of January, 1326, and buried in the monaftery (now the cathedral) of St. Peter at Gloucefter. See his monument in Sandford, p. 151. and by G. Vertue in Rapin's Hiftory of England, vol. I.

ELIZ.

# ELIZABETH DE BURGH, LADY CLARE.

Third daughter of Gilbert de Clare, laſt earl of Glouceſter and Hereford of that name, and Joan of Acres, daughter of Edward I.

She was foundreſs of Clare-hall, Cambridge, and married firſt to John de Burgh, who was ſon and heir of Richard earl of Ulſter; and died 1313. ſecondly, 1315, to Theobald lord Verdon, who died next year, 10 E. II *. and laſtly to Roger Damory, baron of Armoy in Ireland, who was attainted for taking part with Thomas earl of Lancaſter, 15 E. II. but his life was ſpared, and he died the ſame year. Elizabeth ſurvived him, and died Nov. 4, 1360. 34 E. III. leaving for heir Elizabeth her grandaughter, by William de Burgh, her ſon by her firſt huſband, who died in her life-time. She was buried in the middle aile of Ware church, c. Herts, with her third huſband. Weever (p. 544) has preſerved this epitaph over them:

" Hic jacet Rogerus Damory, baro, tempore Edwardi
" Secundi, et Elizabetha, tertia filia Gilberti Clare,
" comitis Glouceſtriæ, et Johannæ uxoris ejus, filiæ
" Edwardi primi vocat. Johan de Acris ———†"

* Leaving her with child of a daughter, afterwards named Iſabel. Dugd. Bar. I. 474.
† Sandford, p. 141, 142. Chauncy, p. 216, 217.

Mr.

Mr. Salmon (Hertfordſhire, p. 247) ſays, that in his
time there remained only the coronet; but there is now
no memorial at all.

EN noun du Pere, du Fitz, et du Seint Eſpirit, Amen.
Je Elizabeth de Burg, dame de Clare, ordeine et face
mon teſtament et ma darreine volunte en ma pleine memoire le xxv jour de Septembr' l'an de l'Incarnation noſtre
Seign'r I'hu Criſt' M.CCC.LV. en la fourme et maniere
q'enſuyt. A de primes jeo deviſe m'alme a Dieu et a ſa
douce miere Seinte Marie et a touz les Seintz du Ciel; et mon
corps a la terre d'eſtre enterre a les ſoeres Menureſſes hors
de Algate en Loundres. It'm je deviſe pur lumiere entour
mon corps la veille et le jour de mon enterrement II C lb.
de cire des queux jeo voel et ordeine q tut le ſurplus de la
lumiere qe ſerra deſpendue graunt * gree ſurra part a la
place ſus dite ſoit departi as povres eſgliſes environ ſolonc
la diſcretion de mes executours. It'm je deviſe et ordeine
en toles maneres deſpenſes afaire pur mon corps enterer
la veille et le jour de mon enterrement et pur la departiſon
des povres meſme le jour II C li. Et voel et ordeine q'
mon corps ne demoerge de ſeu terre outre quinſ'ze jours
apres mon deces, deinz queu temps je voel q' la ſolempnite
de mon enterrement ſe face ſans plus outre delai. Et
apres mon enterrement je voel et ordeine q' mes dettes

\* Sic Orig.

ſoient

LADY CLARE.

foient primerement paies, et apres mes dites dettes renduz et paies je voel a de primes qe les fervices de mes fervants foient paies en manere q' enfuit; primerement a Monf'r Nichol Dammory vi chargeours<sup>a</sup>, xii efqueles<sup>b</sup>, i godet<sup>c</sup> d'argent ove covercle et i faler <sup>d</sup> d'argent. A Rob't Marefchal xii efqueles d'argent et ii cruet d'argent p'celle furorre<sup>e</sup>. A Sufanne de Neketon, xii efqueles d'argent ii cruets novels d'argent, i mors<sup>f</sup> d'argent amaille<sup>g</sup> de mes armes, et ma meillour robe ove touz les garnementz. A Anne de Lexeden xx li defterlinges, i chaliz, i mors d'argent et maille <sup>g</sup> de mes armes, xii efqueles d'argent, et ma robe de noir ove touz les garnementz. A Elizabeth Torel un godet <sup>h</sup> d'argent ove covercle kernelle, et ii bacyns d'argent ove tuelle<sup>i</sup> amaillez en founs, et ma feconde meillure robe ove les garnements. A Margarete Banchon iiii ewers d'argent et ma tirce meillure robe ove touz les garnemens. A Colmet de Morlee et a Ifabel fa femme i godet d'argent furorre ove covercle kernelle, viii grant faufers, xxxvi meindres faucers, et a la dite Ifabel ma quartre mellure robe ove touz les garnements. A Joh'n de Southam' et a Agnes fa femme iiii pootz <sup>k</sup> d'argent, i godet d'argent i hanap' <sup>l</sup> d'alabaftre h'noife <sup>m</sup> d'argent furorre, i petit bacyn d'argent du tour

<sup>a</sup> chargers.
<sup>b</sup> porringers.
<sup>c</sup> *godet*, a mug.
<sup>d</sup> faltfeller.
<sup>e</sup> *furdorre*, gilt.
<sup>f</sup> F. *morceau*.
<sup>g</sup> *emaille*, enamelled.
<sup>h</sup> cup.
<sup>i</sup> *tuyau, conduit*, pipe.
<sup>k</sup> pots.
<sup>l</sup> *coupe a boire*, cup.
<sup>m</sup> *harnoife*, mounted.

d'une

d'une esquele; et a la dite Agneis trois garnements de ma quinte meillure robe, c'est assavoir cote, surcote, et mantel de Paone<sup>n</sup>. A Alison de Wodeham VI plates d'argent, I poudrer d'argent, et tut le remenant de ma sisme meillurs robe outre ce q'est devise a Johan de Horselee come piert p' anal. A Johanette Drueys VI plates d'argent, et II quillers<sup>o</sup> d'argent surorrez, et I quiller d'argent blank. It'm a departir entre les dites Alason et Johanette mes deux robes de tyrteyne. * A Sire Johan' de Lenne I maser<sup>p</sup> ove covercle hernoise d'argent surorre et kernelle, I chaliz d'argent I vestiment pur confessours d'un drap de soye chekere<sup>q</sup> ove surrore, l'apparail. A Sire Piers de Ereswell I boeste d'argent surorre amaille, I chaliz, L poire des chaundelabres, II bacyns, I benoit' ove esperge, <sup>r</sup> I seyn <sup>s</sup> et I mors d'argent surorre ove perrie<sup>t</sup> mes deux antiphoners d'un volum vieux, II grayels d'un volum vieux, I vestiment d'un camoka<sup>u</sup> rouge et ynde<sup>x</sup> ove tut l'apparail, et VI surplis de ma chapelle des meillurs q'il voudra eslire. A Sire Henry Motelot VI bacyns, I plate d'argent ove pee, I vestiment d'un camoke rouge tanne ove tut l'apparail, et I maser ove covercle hernoise d'argent surorre. A Sire William de Mantonz III pootz d'argent, XV pieces d'argent, et I escalop d'argent. A frere John de

---

<sup>n</sup> Purple.   <sup>o</sup> Q *esquiles*, bells.
* *Sorte de mauvaise ctoffe qui a pris son nom de Tyre, et dont on habille la milice.* Laccombe, Dict. du vieux langage François.
<sup>p</sup> A bowl.   <sup>q</sup> F. Chequer'd.
<sup>r</sup> Holy water pot, with a sprinkler.
<sup>s</sup> *cloche*, bell.   <sup>t</sup> Q *pierres*, precious stones.
<sup>u</sup> Sorte d'etoffe riche.   <sup>x</sup> blue.

Hafelbech v marcs. A frere Rob't de Wifebech v mars. A Sire William Albon le meillure de deux fengles veftiments de blank camoka. A Sire John de Chiph'm l'autre fengle veftiment de blank camoka. A Sire Edward Sothword c s. A Sire Joh'n de Huntyngdon c s. A Sire William de Berkwey un veftiment d'un camoca, le champ noir tanne ove tut l'apparail. A Sire William de Wykkewane II quillers d'argent, un poire de chandelabres d'argent ove vyz, et I hanap de beril h'noife d'argent furorre. A Sire William Ailmare c s. A Sire William de Ditton I boeft d'argent blank, I chaliz d'argent furorre, II cruets, I pees, I chandeler d'argent pur la feinte chaundele, I veftiment de camoca le champ noir. A Sire Henri Palmer I pees d'argent furorre, XXXIIII quillers d'argent, II chargeours d'argent, un veftiment palee de deux camocas ove tut l'apparel. A Sire William Coke LX s. A frere John L'eremyte I petit feyn d'argent, I quiller d'or et II ervers d'argent. A Sire John de Kireby LX s. A Richard de Waterden, LX s. A Joh'n de Clare XX li. d'efterlings. A John Bataile II cruets d'argent furorrez, II grant poots, et II meindres poots d'argent, et XII efqueles d'argent. A Rob't Flemengs, II ervers d'argent, et I efquele pur l'aumerie d'argent ove le pee bien lee ʸ. A Johan de Horfelee, III garnements de ma fifme meillure robe c'eft affavoir coté, furcote, et mantel de paone. A Wauter de Kireby, I poire de bacyns d'argent, I benoiter, et I efperge d'argent furorre. A Ni-

ʸ broad.

cholas Nowers x li. A John Gough 1 ewer d argent p'-
celle furorre, et IIII godets d'argent. A Humfrei de Waleden, II. chargeours d'argent, II plates ove pees p'celle
amailles d'une fuyte. A Thomas Charman, 1 ewer et XII
efqueles d'argent. A Richard de Kingefton, 1 petit poot
d'argent, 1 coupe de jafpre, 1 hanap d'argent plat. A Alifaundre Charman III. poire) des bacyns. A Richard de
Bufkeby 1 tablet, II. chaufe poynts d'argent dont l'un furorre et 1 grant poot d'argent. A John le Meffag' c s. a
meftre Philip Lichet x marcs. A Eftephene Derby LX s.
A John de Knarefburgh xx marcs. A William Beneyt
II chargeours d'argent. A Richard de Wodeham c s. A
John Motelot 1 chandelabre p'tie d'argent, II benoiters, et
II efperges. It'm, a Thomas de Lynton LX s. It'm, a
Firmyn de Shropham XL s. A John de Henle XL s. A
Wauter de Colefhull c s. A William de Stone IIII li. A
Eftephene le Pelleter L s. A William de Coleceftre VI
godets d'argent. A Thomas Montjoye c s. A Thomas Scot
1 bacyn et III ervers d'argent. A John le Lardiner x
marcs. A Hugh le Pullitier x marcs. A Richard le Paf-
teler LX s. A John de Dunmowe LX s. A Henri le Pul-
letier v marcs. A Cok Haveryngs IIII li. A John Brian
c s. A John Whitehened c s. A Joh'n Braceour c s. A
John de Rufhton c s. A John le Chaundeler 1 hanap
plat d'argent furorre, 1 ewerot ᶻ d'arg'. A Richard le Gayte

ᶻ Q. Little Ewer.

LX S.

LX s. A Richard le Charer IIII li. et le char as damoifeles ove le houce a ce appurtinant. A Joft'an Forefter v marcs. A Richard Forrider LXX s. A Joh'n de Kent LX s. A Joh'n de Rinefhale XL s. A Joh'n le Venour jadis demorant ovefq' moi XL s. A Richard de Waltham LX s. A Joh'n Parker de Southfrith XX s. A John Parker baillif de Erbury XL s. A Roger Garbedons C s. A Richard Segor C s. A Richard atte Pole XL s. A William Edward XL s. A Symon Parker de Trillek XL s. A Adam le Baker XL s. A William Gruffuth LX s. A Thomas Aylmer XX s. A Efmon Edward de Farnham XL s. A Joh'n Bacon baillifs de Burton XX s. A Nicholas Artour baillifs de Craneburn LX s. A John Goffe baillifs de Wyke XL s. A Thomas Palmer provoft de Stoke Verdon C s. A Adam ap Wyllym baillif de Novelgraunge XL s. A Richard Cook baillif de Lifwyry LX s. A Richard Toyere provoft de Troye XL s. It'm a Rob't de la Chambre XL s. a Joh'n de Wardon II pieces d'argent. A Nichol le Ewer et a Ifabel fa femme v marcs. A John de Redyngs XL s. A Thomas de Henham XLVI s. VIII. A John Teftepyn II marcs. A Richard garceon de la chambre II marcs. A Thomas le Purtreour II marcs. A Richard de Lanyngton XL s. A John garceon de la Botellerie II marcs. A Adam de la Peftriue C s. A William Bacon XL s. A Rob't Wolwy XX s. A Perot de Holand XXXIII s. IIII d. A Joh'n Caton LX s. A Joh'n Lucefon LX s. A Rob't Lucefone LX s. A Henri Cnappyngs LX s. A Richard de la la Forge ii marcs. A Rob't de la Chaundelerie ii marcs. A Wauter Hunte ii marcs. A William Joliffe ii marcs. A John le Seller xx s. A touz le pages de mon hoſtel q' portent ma liveree a departir entre eux x li. ſolent la diſpoſition de mes executours. It'm je deviſe pur meſſes chauntre pur les almes Monſ'r John de Bourgs, Monſ'r Theobaud de Verdon, et Monſ'r Roger Dammory mes Seignours *, m'alme, et pur les almes de touz mes bons et loials ſervants qe murrerent ou murront en mon ſervice cxl li. Et voel qe ceſte choſe ſoit faite le primer an apres mon deces a plus en haſte qe honi purra bonement en les places plus convenables ſolont l'ordinance de mes executors ſuſdits. It'm je deviſe pur trover v homes d'armes a la terre ſeinte c marcs a bailler a aſcun qe loil ſoit et covenable qe voudra enprendre la charge ſi comune viage ſe face dedeins les ſept anns p'chains apres mon deces de les deſpendre en la ſervice Dieu et deſtruction de ſes enemys pur les almes mes Seignours Monſ'r John, Monſ'r Thebaud, Monſ'r Roger ſuſdits et la moie. Et eſt ma volunte et ma entention darreine tiele q' ſi nulle comune voiage ſe face devers la dite terre dedeins les ans ſuſdits q' les avant dits c marcs ſoint meyntendant apres les anns ſus nomes departiz et dones as autres aumoſnes et oevres de charite come en partie de relevement des meſons des religious et religiouſes poſſeſſioners q' ſount eſcheuz en poverte per cheance de miſfortunies diverſes de prier pur les almes ſuſditz les almes de touz mes bienfeſours et de tous creſtiens.

* Her third huſband.

It'm,

It'm, Je devife a la terre feinte en eide des creftiens pur la loy Dieu meignteign di marc. It'm, Je devife a la mefon des foeres menoreffes hors de Algate en Loundres xx li. 1 reliqer de criftal, 1 grant chaliz d'argent furorre, et 11 cruets cofteles [a], 1 veftiment de blank drap door [b] ove qantq' au dit veftiment app'ent, et 111 mors ove M l'res †de perles, enfemblement ove ma robe de ruffet ove tous les garnementz. I'tm, Je devife a mefme la place pur un memorial le veftiment d'un noir drap door ove quantq' a ce app'ent. v draps door, 1 lit de noir tartaryn, ove VIII tapitz et qantq' appent a mefme le lit, dont les IIII tapits foient atticles a noir veftiment fufdit. It'm, a mefme la place, VI tapits grants de delie leyne d'un de mes autres lits noirs, et XII tapits grants de delie leyne d'un de mes autres lits noirs et XII tapits vert'z ove la bordure * m're poudre des Huans. It'm, a Soer Katerine de Ingham abbeffe de mefme le lieu xx li. It'm a chefcune foer de mefme l'abbeye le jour de mon enterrement XIII s. IIII d. It'm, as qatres freres de mefme le lieu au dit jour a chefcun di marc. I'tm, Je devife a ma fale appelle Clarehall en Cantebrig' XL li. en deniers, 1 encenfer d'ergent furorre, VI chargeours, XXXIX faufers, 1 nief pur l'aumerie en eide de les edifier. It'm, Je devife a ma fale fufdite pur un perpetuel memorial al oeps [c] de mes chapelleins en le collegie deux chalix d'argent furorrez ove deux petites quillers,

---

[a] Q. coftly.  [b] d'or.
† Dugd. Bar. I. 475. tranflates this a thoufand pearls.
* Sic Orig.  [c] *oeps*, volonte.

## LADY CLARE. 31

II. cruets, 1 boefte fyrorre et amaille oye le hernoife [d] pur le corps noftre feign'r, et un encenfer ove un mef d'argent pur encens. It'm, a mefme la place un veftiment de rouge camoka embroide dymagerie door ove qantq' a dit veftiment app'ent, 1 veftiment de noir camoka pur requiem ove une chape et qantq' au dit veftiment attient, 1 veftiment de blank tartayn raie door pur quarifme ove tut l'apparail, et un atir pur le fepulcre, un veftiment d'un camoka plunket diapre de noir tanne ove deux aubes et qantq' au dit veftiment atient, un veftiment d'un blank famyt [f] auxint pur quarefme, et touz les fuppliz de ma chapelle forfpris ceux qe fount devifes a Sire Pieres et le griender efp'uer des deux pur le corps n're feign'r. It'm, Je devife a ma fale fufdits deux bons antiphoners chefcun ove un grayel en mefme le volum, 1 bone legende, 1 bone meffale bien note, 1 autre meffal covert de blank quir, [g] 1 bone Bible covert de noir quir, 1 hugucion [h], 1 legende fanctorum, 1 poire de decretals, 1 livre des queftions, et xxxii quaiers d'un livre appelle, de caufa Dei contra Pelagianos. It'm, Je devife al eglife cathedrale de Seint Paul, un veftiment novel de blank camoca ove qantq' a ce ap'p'ent pur un memorial. It'm, Je devife a Seint Thomas de Hereford un ymage de n're dame d'argent furorre d'eftre tache [i] fur fon

---

[d] furniture.
[e] fhip for incenfe; fee churchwardens of Abingdon's accounts, Archæol. I.
[f] Fine ftuff or linen.     [g] *cuir*.
[h] Hugutio or Hugh de Vercellis bifhop of Terrara, a great writer on the Decretals. Hoffman Lex.
[i] faften'd, *attache*: *tache* in old French and Spanifh is a nail.

fiertre,

fiertre [k], et al eglife cathedrale illoeq' [l], I veftiment dynde fatyn c'eft affavoir chefible, II tonicles, I chape broides de ymagerie et d'archangeles poudres. I'tm, Je devife a l'overaigne [m] de l'eglife de Walfingham, I godet d'argent furorre et amaille ove un trepar, et IIII lb. en deniers, et II draps door. It'm, a la mefon de Stokes, XII quillers d'argent furorrez, et I drag' ove pee d'argent p'celle furorre, et II draps door. It'm, a la mefon de Anglefeye x marcs, et le veftiment d'un rouge drap door de Raffata [n] ove III creftes p'argent furorres pur les chapes. It'm, a la mefon de Croiz Roeis [o] LX s. et II draps door. It'm, a la mefon de Teukefbirs deux reliqers, I crois ove Marie et Joh'n, et II draps door. A la mefon de Ambrebirs x li. et II draps door. A la mefon de Cranebourne xx s. et II draps door. A la mefon de Tonebriggs c s. et II draps door. A la mefon de Tynterne I veftiment d'un drap faeryn blanks ove qantq' a ce app'ent, et II draps door. A la mefon des dames de Ufk x marcs, et II draps door. A la mefon de Crokefden [p] c s. et II draps door. A la mefon de Chirpelee [q] XL s. et I drap door. A la mefon de Seint Efmon [r] III draps door. A l'hofpital de Seint John en Cantebrigg XL s. A la mefon des moignes en Thetford x marcs, et I drap door. A la mefon des dames en Swafham, XII efqueles d'argent, et II draps door. A l'eglife parochiale de

---

[k] *fierte*, feretory, fhrine.     [l] there.
[m] *ouvrage*, work.    [n] Q. Taffeta.    [o] Royfton.
[p] c. Stafford, where her fecond hufband was buried.
[q] Q. Chipley, a priory of Auftin Canons in Suffolk. Tan. N. M. 525.
[r] Q. *St. Edmund*, fcil. Bury.

## LADY CLARE.

Clare LX s. et I drap door. A l'efglife paro'hiale de Berdefeld ˢ, LX s. et I drap door. A l'efglife p'ochiale de Stanndon ᵗ LX s. et I drap door. A l'eglife parochiale de Bode-
kefham ᵘ, XL s. et un drap door. It'm, a les freres de feynt
Auguftyn de Clare x li. A les freres menours de Babewell
c s. As freres precheours de Thetford XL s. As qatre
ordres des freres de Norwiz' VIII li. As freres menours de
Walfingham c s. A qatre ordres des freres en Jernem' ʷ
VIII li. A freres de Seint Auguftyn en Oreford ˣ XL s. As
freres precheours de Donwiz ʸ XL s. As freres menours de
Gipwy ᶻ XL s. A freres menours de Coleceftre XL s. As
freres precheours de Subirs ᵃ x marcs. As freres precheours
de Chelmesford XL s. As freres menours de Ware XL s.
As freres des Carmes de Maldon, as quatre ordres des freres
en Loundres VIII li. As trois ordres des freres en Canter-
biris VI li. As freres menours de Canterbrugg' XL s. It'm
a mefmes les freres pur lour overaigne c s. et les autres
trois des freres en Cantebrugg' VI li. As freres menours
de Bedeford XL s. As freres de Seint Auguftyn de Hun-
tyndon XL s. As quatre ordres des freres de Northampton
VIII li. As quatre ordres des freres en . . . . . . VIII li.
As deux ordres de freres de Caerdit VI li. As quatre
ordres de freres de Glouceftre VIII li. As freres precheours
et menours de Salefbirs IIII li. As freres menours de Dor-

ˢ Q. Berdwell, c. Suffolk.  ᵗ Standon, c. Herts.
ᵘ Q. Botteſham, c. Cambridge.  ʷ Yarmouth.
ˣ Orford.  ʸ Dunwich.
ᶻ Ipſwich.  ᵃ Sudbury.

F                                    cheftre

cheſtre XL s. It'm, Je deviſe a dame Elizabeth ma fille counteſſe d'Ulveſtier[b] tote la dette qe mon filz' ſon piere me devoit le jour q'il moruſt. It'm, Je deviſe a ma dite fille pur ſemail[c] ſur les manoirs de mon heritage en la baillie de Clare c'eſt aſſavoir Staundon, Berdefeld, Clarete, Erbury, Hoveden, Wodehalle, Bricham, et Walſingham: en la baillie de Dorſete c'eſt aſſavoir Cranebourne, Tarent, Pimperne, Stupel, Wykes, et Portlonde: et en Gales c'eſt aſſavoir Troye, Trillek, Lancombe, Novelle Graunge, Lantſan, et Tregruke, de furment, ſegle et mixtilon[d] pur la ſeſon yvernaille en les manoirs ſuſditz CCCC. VII qartres. It'm de feves, pois, et veſces en meſmes les manoirs pur la ſeſon quaremele[e], LXI qartres. It'm, d'orge et draget[d] pur meſme la ſeſon CCIIII quartres. It'm aveignes pur meſme la ſeſon V C XXIX qartres. It'm, des chivaux chareterres pur les manoirs ſuſditz XXIII. It'm des affres[f] XXIIII. XIII. des boefs pur les carves[g] IIC XLVIII. enſemblement ove le mort eſtor[h] deinz[i] les ditz manoirs come charettes, carves, chare as boefs, feur[k] et paille. It'm, Je deviſe a ma fille Bardolf[l], mon lit de vert velvet raie de rouge ove qantq'

[b] Ulſter. Maud, daughter of Henry earl of Lancaſter, and ſiſter to Henry duke of Lancaſter, married to her ſon William de Burgh earl of Ulſter. Sandford, p. 142.     [c] Seed corn.
[d] Monk, meſlin, or mixt corn.     [e] Lent.
[f] *Averia*, beaſts.     [g] carts, whence *carvage*.
[h] dead ſtock, or *ſtore*.     [i] *dedans*.
[k] Laccombe makes *feur* ſynonymous with *paille*, elſewhere *hay*, *forrage*.
[l] Elizabeth, her daughter by Roger Damory, married, 10 E. III. to John Bardolf, who died 45 E. III. Dugd. Bar. I. 682.

a ce attient enfemblement ove une coverture d'un drap m're ove la paane ᵐ de menever puree, une dymy coverture de la feute, et une coverchief d'ynde famyt ove la paane de Bla . . . . . . . . et 1 coverture de tanne medle ove la paane de grys. It'm, Je devife a ma dite fille une grant fale de worftede le champ tanne ove papejayes ⁿ, et cokerele de blu et qantq' a ce ap'p'ent. It'm, Je devife a ma ditte fille mon grant char ove les houces, tapets, et quiffyns, et qantqʳ a ce appendent. It'm, Je devife a Monfʳ John de Bardolf et a ma ditte fille fa compaigne joyntement en mes manoirs de Cathorp et Clapton, de furment pur le femail come appertient a fefon yvernaille xxvi qartres, de mixtilon et fegle vii qartres, iiii bs. ᵒ It'm, pur la fefon quaremele des pois xvii qartres iiii bs. d'erge ᵖ xxxvii quart iiii b. de draget ᑫ ix qartres iiii b. des aveignes xxii qartres, i b. des chivaux chare heres iiii. des affres, xii des boefs xxii. enfeffiblement ove ʳ mes charettes et carves qe as ditz manoirs ap'ptinent et tut lur apparail. It'm, Je devife a ma joefne ˢ fille ᵗ Ifabell Bardolf en eide de lui marier, un hanap' plat door, ii grant dragners amaillez en parcelle et xii groffes faufers d'argent, mon lit de fandal m're—ove une coverture de cendryn medle ove la paane de menever. It'm, a Agneis ᵗ fa foer en

ᵐ *pane,* parcel, fkirt.  
ᵒ *boiffeaux,* bufhels.  
ᑫ *dragee,* meflin.  
ˢ *joëne,* jeune.  
ⁿ popinjays, parrots.  
ᵖ *orge,* barley.  
ʳ *enfemblement,* together.  
ᵗ Q. If her *grandaughters,* daughters of John and Elizabeth Bardolf, not mentioned by Dugdale.

eide le lui marier, 1 croiz d'argent, 11 chaundelabres, 11 falers, 1 godet, 1 grant eſquele pur l'aumerie, 1 hanep' d'argent pounſone, 1 nief pur encens, 1 encenſer, 1 mors de l'annuntiation, et vi chargeours novelles d'argent. It'm a la ditte Agneis un lit d'ynde dont la chemcere et cutepoint d'un tamelot de tripe ove les appurtenances, et 1 coverture de blu, ove la pane de gris. It'm, Je deviſe a Monſ'r William de Ferrers ᵘ en mon manoir de Litleworth, ſemail pur le dit manoir, c'eſt aſſavoir de furment xi qartres, vi b's. de ſegle vi qartres, iiii b. de mixtillon ii qartres. de fieves et pois xiii qartres, d'orge, xiii qartres, de draget ii qartres, de aveïgnes xxix qartres; des chivaux charettres iiii, des affres vi, des boefs xviii, enſemblement ove les charettes et carves et tut l'apparaile. It'm, Je deviſe a Monſ'r Thomas Furnivall ſur mes manoirs de Farnham, Sere, Stoke, Verdon, et Wyneleford de ble pur ſemail, c'eſt aſſavoir de furment xxxv qartres, ii b's. de ſegle et mixtilon xii qartres iiii b's. d'eſpois ˣ et veſtes ʸ z qartres, vi b's. d'orge et draget xlv qartres, iiii b's. des aveïgnes xxxiiii qartres, vii b's. des chivaux charettres ii, des affres xvi. des boefs xxviii, enſemblement ove les charettes, carves, et tut l'apparail. It'm, Je diviſe a ma fille counteſſe D'Atthelles mes deux litz de tanne le grant et le petit enſemblement ove qantq' a ceux appertienent. It'm, 1 coverture d'un bruſ-

---

ᵘ Richard Damory, ſuppoſed by Dugdale nephew to Elizabeth's huſband Roger, had the cuſtody of lands of ſome of the Ferrers, temp. E. II. Dugd. Bar. II. 100.

ˣ *pois*.     ʸ *veſſes*, vetches.

kyn [z] en greyn [a] ove la paane demy puree, et 1 coverchief d'un camoka noir tanne ove la paane demy puree. It'm, Je divife a mon feign'r le Roi pur fa collegie de Wynde-fore une coupe door ove pee pur le corps n're feign'r, et un d'argent furorre ove trois anngelets pur mefme le coupe. It'm, Je devife a mon feign'r le prince un tabernacle door, ove l'ymage de noftre dame, et 11 anngeletz entaille door, 1 grant crois ove Marie et Joh'n d'argent furorre, et 11 grant pees d'argent furorrez et amailles, et 1 anel door ove un rubie. It'm, Je devife au duc de Lancaftre mon petit fauter covert d'arcail door, et 1 cruis quarre ove une peice de la verroie cruis q'eft en 1 cas door amaille. It'm, Je devife a dame Marie de Seint Poul countefle Penibrok une petit croiz d'or ove un faphir en my lieu, et 1 anel door ove un faphir en my lieu, et 1 anel door ove un diamant. It'm, Je devife a dame Johanne de Bars countefle de Garenne [b] une ymage door de Seint John le Baptiftre efteant en defert. Et je voel et ordeine q' fi je face nul regard as afcunes des perfones fufnomes come en gardes, mariages, donns des terres, rents, donns en deniers, afcune fume drapeft [c] ou autre bienfait outre la certeine covenant des mes fervantz fus dits, c'eft affavoir entre la date de ceftes et le jour de mon deces; qe mefme le regard des gardes, mariages, donns des terres, rentes, donns en deniers, et la fumme dapreft, fi nulle y foit eftoife [d] en partie du

[z] *Brufq* is old French for *green*.   [a] in grain.
[b] Wife of John laft earl of Warren. She died 1361. 35 E. III. Dugd. Bar. I. 82.
[c] Q. *dapreft,* loans.   [d] fubject, *eftoifer a la ley,* fubir a la loi.

paiement

paiement de cest mon divis, nulle persone sorsprise, sans soulement ceuz q' imprendront la charge et execution de cest mon testament, le regard des queux ensemblement ove l'ur nouns et la sume des deniers en gros qe je vouchsauf a chescune persone serront trovez en une remembrance ensealee de mon seal, en lieu de quele sume des deniers susditz, les parcelles d'or et d'argent sont as avantdits persones et diverses mesons assignes. It'm, Je voel et ordeine qe de totes les parcelles, parament nomeez et divises, sauve soulement de monoye, la liveree se face per mes executours solonc ce qe jai mesmes les dites parcelles declaree et article a chescune persone en la remembrance susdite, qe les parcelles je voel qe soient eues [e] et tenues pur encloses et comprises dedeins cestes, et de mesme l'effect et value, come elles susent escrites de parole en parole en cest mon dit testament. Et s'il aveigne qe nulles des parcelles door ou d'argent a ma meignee [f] parameont divises apres la date de cestes soient en ascun autre oeps ordinees moi vivante, issuit qe mesmes les parcelles ne soient trovees apres mon deces per cause de la chaunge per moi faite; je voel qe a mesme la persone due satisfaction soit fait en deniers ou en autre parcelle de mes biens a la value. Et sachent totes gents qe cest ma volente et ordinance darreinere [g] qe chescun a qi jai devise ma vessele ou autre parcelle d'argent sorspris monoye, soit la sume meindre ou greindre [h] eit solonc sa

[e] *eues*, had.
[g] *dernier*.
[f] famille, menage.
[h] plus grande.

partion

partion diſſept livres per pois d'orfieure en lieu de xx li. d'eſterlings, et ſi per cas la portion d'aſcune perſone paſſe la ſumme des deniers a lui deviſes, face la dit perſone ſatiſ-faction a mes executours du ſurplus, et ſi nulle perſone eit meyns pur ſa portion du pois ſuſditz, je voel qe gree lui ſoit fait pur la defaute. Et ſi aviſe ſoit a mes executours qe je neye pas fait plein ſatisfaction a mes ſervants ſuſdits, et as autres mes ſervants nient compris en ceſt mon teſti-ment pur lur travail du temps du temps paſſe, et de temps a venir, je voel et ordeine qe de la reſidue de ma veſſele d'argent de ma chapelle et de ma garderobe, outre ce q'eſt diviſee en certein lur ſoit fait un regard reſonable ſo-lonc la bone diſcretion de mes executours ſuſditz et qe la reſidue ſuſdite ne ſoit mys autre oeps, vendu, ne per nulle part delivery tantq' c'eſt ma darraine volunte ſoit pleine-ment perfourmie. Et ſi per cas aviegne, qe Dieu defend, qe nul de mes precheins, amys, ou nul autre a qi jai rien diviſe, ou nul autre en lour noun mettent empeſchement a mes executours de les deſturbir q'ils ne purrount peiſible-ment aminiſtrer tous mes biens moebles et nient moebles ſolonc l'ur charge et le purport de ceſte ma darreine vo-lente, je voil et ordeigne qe le devis a les dites perſones de qele condition q'elles ſoient ſoit pur nul et de tut avienti iſſint q'ils n'eyent de ceſt mon devis ne de mes autres biens ſuſditz parte ne parcelle forſq' a peril qe appent a torcenous[i] occupours des biens de mortz et deſtourbours de

[i] wrongful.

lur darreines voluntees. It'm fi defalcation doit eftre fait pur neceffite, je voel qelle foit faite fi bien des biens qe jai divifee as ditz dame Elizabeth ma fille d'Ulveftier, Monf'r John Bardolf, et ma fille fa compaigne, Monf'r William de Ferrers, Monf'r Thomas de Furnivall, et ma fille d'Athelles, come a touz autres contenuz dedeins ceft mon teftament. Et pur ce qe diverfes empefchementz fe fount fovent per malice, et fubtilite de home eft plus qe ne foleit avant ces heures, je voel et ordeine qe touz ceux as queux jai devife afcune chofe in ceft mon teftament, facent a mes executours aquitances fi bien des totes maneres d'actions, quereles, et demandes, queux ils ount ou avre purrount encontre mes executours come divis as eux fait et paie per les executours avantditz. Et fi les ditz legataires recufent et ne voillent tieles aquitances faire folonc le purport de cefte ma ordinance, voel et ordeine qe les divis a moi faites as cieux foient tenuz pur nulles et pur nonnefcrites. It'm, Je ordeine qe mes executours facent aquitance et pleine liberation a Sire Johan Leche de mille marcs en quels il m'eft tenuz per fon fait obligatorie, iffint q'il face general acquitance a mes executours de totes maneres d'actions queles il ad ou avre purra devers eux come executours. Et de la refidue de touz mes biens et chatelx qe demurront apres l'execution faite de ceft mon teftament, je voel et ordeine qe une diftribution foit fait par mes executours fufditz en la manere q'enfuyt, ceft affavoir de relever les povres religious poffeffioners [k] fi bien des dames come des

[k] Q. houfekeepers.

autres

## LADY CLARE.

autres qe font efcheuz en mefchiefs, partie povres gentiles femmes qe fount charges des enfantz, eider povres fglifes parochiales, et lour furnementz redrefcer et amender, partie pur povres efcolers a lefcole trover et fuftenir, pounts et caufes [j] redrefcer, povres gentz q' foleient tenir hoftiel, povres marchantz qe pur cheantz fount anientiz, & povres prifoners regarder et eider, remenant foit fait en autres oevres de charite par avifement a bone difcretion de mes executours folonc ce q'ils verront mieltz [k] faire pur le falvation de malme. Et pur cefte ma darreine volunte et mon teftament pleynement et loialement performir et accomplir, jeo ordeine, face et noeme mes executours fouchefcrites; ceft affavoir Monf'r Nichol Dammory [l], Sire John de Lenne, Sire Henri Motelot, John Bataille, Sire Piers de Erefwell, Rob't Marefchal, et Sire William de Manton, principaus et chiefs; Sire Henri Palmer, Richard de Bufkeley, Thomas Charman, Alifaundre Charman, Humfrei de Waleden, Richard de Kyngefton, John Motelot, et Sire Will'x de Berkevoy, fecundaires. Et voel et ordeine qe les avant ditz Monf'r Nichol, Sire John, Sire Henri Motelot, John Bataile, Sire Pieres, Rob't, Sire William de Manton, Sire Henri Palmer, Richard, Thomas, Alifaundre, Humfrei, Richard de Kingefton, John Motelot, et Sire William de Berkewey, aminiftrent touz mes biens et chateux tochantz

---

[j] bridges and caufewvays.     [k] *mieux.*
[l] Q. A brother of her hufband. Dugd. Bar. II. 100.

ceſt mon teſtamont en les forme et manere qe enſuyent, et noun pas autrement; ceſt aſſavoir qe de mes biens qe ſurront venduz totes pars pour ma dite volunte perfourmir ſoient les vendours en les countees de Suff. Norff. et Eſſex, Sire Will' de Manton, Humfrey de Waleden, et Thomas Charman. It'm, en la ſeignourie d'Uſk, et aillours es parties de Gales, Sire Henri Motelot, et Aliſaundre ſuſditz; en les countees de Dorſet, Wilts, et Chilterne, Sire Henri Motelot, Ric' de Kyngeſton, et John Motelot. Item, en les counties Nichole [m], Leyc, & Warr', Richard de Buſkeley, & Sire Will' de Berkweye. Et ſoient les deniers levees de touz mes biens & chateux ſuſditz liveriees per endenture a Sire William de Manton, Sire Henry Palmer, et Richard de Buſkeley, et qe meſmes ceux Sire William, Henri, et Ric' ſoyent acountables de lour receite a les avant ditz Monſ'r Nichol, Sire John, Sire Henry Motelot, et a mes autres executours principaus, & qe per l'ordinance des avantditz Monſ'r Nichol, Sire John, Sire Henri Motelot, John Bataille, & les autres principaus & chiefs executours ſoient touz les divis faitz de ceſt mon teſtament, autres deſtributions qe ent ſerront faitez, & toutes autres choſes qe charge porterount perfourmis & eſtablis. En teſmoignance de qele choſes a ceſte ma darreine volunte ay mys mon ſeal. Don a Clare, les jour & an ſuſditz.

[m] Lincoln.

Probatio

Probatio dicti testamenti coram Simone Islip Cantuar' Archiep' in ecclesia Sororum Minorassarum ordinis Sancte Clare extra Elgate London, 3 non Decembris, Anno Domini 1360.

Register Islep. fol. 164, b. 165, a. b. 166, a. b. in the Archiepiscopal Registry at Lambeth.

# HUMFERY DE BOHUN,

NINTH OF THAT NAME, AND

EARL OF HEREFORD AND ESSEX.

He died unmarried, in his caftle of Pleffey in Effex, 1361. 35 Edw. III. and was buried in the church of the Auftin Friars, London, which he rebuilt 1354\*.

EN le noun du Piere, del Fuiz, et du Seint Esp'it, Amen. Le dymenge<sup>a</sup> lendemeyn de Seint Denys en Octobr', l'an de Incarnation n're Seign'r I'hu Crift mil troiz centz feyffauntifme p'mier nous Humfray de Bohun counte de He'ford et D'Eez<sup>b</sup>, et Seign'r de Breken en fancte et bone memoire fefoms n're teftament en cefte man'e. Ade-p'mes nous devifmes n're alme a dieux a la rev'ence de la T'inite, et de feint Auguftyn a qi nous ovons grant affection, et p' la refonn q' dieux nous ad p'ftez richeffez et honour en cefte feicle q' neft a la p'fyn q' ueyne gloire nous devifoms n're corps de gefier<sup>c</sup> et d'eftr' enfevely entre les pov's freres de l'ordre de Seint Auguftyn ceft affavoir en le quoer de lour efglife a Loundres devant le haut autier. Et ne voloms point q' nos executours facent pur nous le jour de n're enterement nule comune dep'tifonn as pov's

---

\* Dugd. Bar. I. 185. Vincent on Brooke, p. 244. Stowe's Survey of London, p. 185.

<sup>a</sup> *Dimanche*.      <sup>b</sup> *Effex*.      <sup>c</sup> lye.

gentz,

gentz, ne q'il p'ent granz feignours ne un ne autr', ne q'il facent nule mang'ie le jour de n're enterrement forfq' tant foulement a un evefq' q' s'ra prie de nous enterrer et as poevres freres et a n're meyfnee, ne q'il facent nule herce<sup>d</sup> entour n're corps fofq' de trerfe cierges, chefcun del pois de v lb. et q'il ordeinent n're toumbe folonc ceo q'il v'rount q' foit afaire et en qiconq' lieu q'il nous eftov<sup>e</sup>'a morir; nous devifoms a la parfone de la efglife pochiale de cele place xx li, fi q'il prie pur nous et nous affoile fi riems<sup>f</sup> eioms in efpris v's fa efglife en difmes offrendres ou autre chofe, et q'il releffe totes man'es dactions et chalanges q'il purra avoir p' caufe de n're fepulture et entrement riens, et fi ceft come n're alme f'ra a dieux comande, nous volons q' nos executours mandent le corps tout priveement a Londres ove n're confeffour et autres gentz des queux foient tout le plus chapelains, et foit entr' illoq'es priveement, nos devifoms auxint<sup>g</sup> et voiloms q' une huche<sup>h</sup> foit faite auxi com' pur n're corps, et demoere en certaine place la ou n're meifnee demurra tantq' n're ent'rement foit ordeine, et q' chefcun jour y foit fait pur nous placebo et dirige et meffes et cierges entour cele huche pur nous, chefcun de troiz lb. tantq' l'enterrement foit fait, et chefcune noet p' chemyn ou cele houche en lieu de n're corps covendra repofer, nous

<sup>d</sup> *herfe*, or frame of wood-work, to put over the body while it lay in ftate.
<sup>e</sup> eftovoir, *neceffité.* eftoyer, *etre.*
<sup>f</sup> *rien:* in old French this word has a pofitive fenfe, and means *any thing*.
<sup>g</sup> *auffi*, fometimes *aufinc*. Laccombe.
<sup>h</sup> Laccombe explains this *couvrechef, voile, coffre, coeffe*. Here it means a pall over an empty coffin reprefenting the real one.

voloms

voloms q' ceux trerſe cierges de cire ſoient ardanns entour cele huche tant com' placebo, dirige, et lendemeyn la meſſe avant n're departir ſoient adire, et ceux cierges demoerent a l'eſgliſe, ou le ſervice s'ra dit, ſil ne y ſoit q' une eſgliſe en la ville, & ſi deux ou pluſurs y ſoient, les cierges ſoient departiz entr' eles ſolonc le ordinance de n're confeſſour ap'er p' nous. Nous deviſoms auxint, et voloms q' tantoſt apres n're deces q' totes nos dettes, auxi bien celes q' nos ovoins charges de bouche q' ſont p'vees com les autres ſoient paiez, et q' gre et ſatisfactioun ſoit faite a totes gentz as queux nos executours poent ſavoir q' nos eioms meſpris ou t'paſſe p' qiconq' voie, nous voloms auxint, et diviſoms q' tote n're meiſnee demoerge enſemble a nous coſtages[1] tantq' cheſcun ſoit paie de ceo q' nous lui avoins deviſe, ſolom ceo q'eſt contenu p'deſoutz, et q' cheſcun ſoit charge quant il p'ndra ſa paie a prier pur nous. Nos deviſoms auxint, et voloms q' tantoſt apres n're detes nous executours deliverent a frere William de Monkeland n're confeſſour, a frere William Wilhale meſtre de divinite, et frere Geffrey de Berdefeld troiz centz marcs d'argent, dont ordein et aſſign' p' la ou il v'ront q' mieux ſoit afaire cinq'nte freres de meſme le ordre q' ſoient de bone et feinte vie a chaunter meſſes a dire placebo et dirige, comendation et autres devoutes priers pur nous cheſcun jour p'tot le p'mer an q' nous demeroins, et q' cheſcun de eux chante pur nous meſme l'an un plen' trental de meſſes, et q' trerſe de

[1] coſtages, Laccombe; frais, depenſes.

meſme

mefme les cinq'nte freres veillent jour et noet en quele place q'il foient affignez p' la difcreffioun de troiz freres avant nomes, les uns a repofer les autres p' tout l'an avantdit, et dient placebo et dirige, fauters et autres devoutes priers et q' les freres avantdiz foient jures de cefte n're voluntie p'faire leaument folent l'ordinance de n're confeffour et des autres deux freres defus nomes p' vewe de noz executours. Et fi l'un de troiz freres demye, choifent les deux un autre en foen lieu p' vewe de noz executours. Nos devifoms a l'ordre des freres avantdiz une fepultre ove tabernacles et finols[k], et ove pierres pur mettre eviz le corps n're feignour, fi la dite fepultre nous demoere apres n're deces, et a mefme l'ordre une coupe d'or affaire ent un chaliz, et un blank veftiment de n're chapele, et un noir veftiment dont les bordours font des armes d'Engleterre. Et voloms q' ceftes chofes demoerent en l'ordre pur fervir ou il v'rount q' mieux foit afaire. Et voloms q' ceftes chofes foient p'fees p' nos executours, et q' nre dit confeffour nous ordeine chaunteries annuels en l'ordre a la value des joiaux avantditz affaire mefme l'an. Nos devifoms auxint a les troiz ordres de mendinanz en Londres, ceft affavoir a les freres prechours, menours, et carmes, a chefcune maifonn x li. a prier pur nous. Nos devifoms auxint a les eftudinanz de q'tre ordres des mendinanz en Oxenford et Cantebrigg', ceft affavoir freres prechours, menours, carmes, et de feint Auguftyn,

---

[k] *finials*: a term of Gothic architecture for the little ornaments that terminate pinnacles.

a chefcun maifon x li. a prier pur nous. Nos devifoms auxint a n're abbeye de Walden c li. d'argent a departier entre les moignes et al proffit de la maifonn a prier pur nous en cieu manere q'il nos p'donnent et affoilent de q'ntq' nous avoins mefpris dev's eux fi rienz y foit. Nos devifoms auxint a n're a la dite abbeye de f'vir en la chapele de n're dame illoeq's une tixt[l] d'argent, et une veftment de rouge velvet, ove q'tre garnemens. Et p'r ceo q" nos fumes tenuz p' avow d'offrier en leon'ance de n're dame al ymage de n're dame en la dite chapele de Walden une g'unt corone d'argent doire, une doubletz & p'let en le frount, et de une efpaume de haut, nous voloms qe nos executours la facent faire, et l'offrent illoeq' a demurer fur la tefte le dit ymage en p'petuel memoire de nos. Nous devifoms auxint a n're priorie de l'Anthony[m] pres de Glouceftr' xl marcs a dep'tier entr' les chanoyns illoeq's et al p'ffit de la maifonn et q'il prient pur nous. Nous devifoms auxint, et voloms q' nous executours facent faire un chalys d'argent doire del pois de feiffaunte foutz pur fervir en la chapele de la Trinite, q" f'ra faite par nous a l'Anthony, & q'il facent achat a cella deux poire de veftiment, ceft affavoir deux aubres, deux amys, ove la tier q'il apent, deux chefibles de diverfe fewte de drap d'or, ove la tyr de l'autier de la fewte double et curtyns, l'une paire p'r jours

[l] Q. pix.
[m] Lantoni priory, founded 1136, by Milo earl of Hereford, whofe daughter was married to Humphrey de Bohun, firft earl of Hereford.

nous,

ferials et l'autre paire pur jours festivals, et l'offrent tout ensemble en la dite chapele de la Trinite, q' le priour et le covent de n're dite maisonn ferront faire pur nous en lour dite maisonn pres de la novele chaumbre le dit priour, a demurrer en la dite chapele en p'petuel memoire de nous. Et si la dite chapele soite commence et nemye p'faite a n're deces, nos volums, q' nous executours la facent p'faire entierrement a nous costages. Et si la dite chapele ne soit de riens commencie avant n're deces nos veloms q' nous executours facent faire illoeq' une bele chapele de la Trinite tout a nos costages. Nos devisoms auxint a n're priorie de Breken' cent marcs a dep'tier entr' les moignes et a profit de la mayson, si q'il nous p'dounent et assoillent de q'ntq' nous avoins mespris dev's eux, et a prier pur nos. Nos devisoms a les freres preceours de Breken x li. a prier pur nous, et a les freres p'cheours de Chemesford x li. a prier pur nous. Nous devisoms a n're priorie de Farlegh[n] xl. marcs a dep'tier entre les moignes a p'er pur nous, et a n're priorie de Hurlle [o] xx li. a dep'tier entr' les moignes a p'er pur nous, et a n're priorie de Notele [p] xx marcs a dep'tier entre les chanoignes a prier pur nous, et a n're priorie de Scoule xx marcs a prier pur nous. Nous devisoms auxint a

[n] In Wilts, founded by Humphrey de Bohun the Second. Dugd. Bar. I. 179. Tanner, Not. Mon. p. 596.
[o] Henley priory, Berks, founded by Geoffrey de Magnaville, temp. Wm. Conq. and subject to Walden Abbey, whence it came under the patronage of the earls of Essex. Tan. ib. p. 13.
[p] Notley abbey, c. Bucks. It does not appear what connexion the earl of Essex, or the Bohun family, had with it.

n're chapele deinz n're chaftel de Pleffy, un chaliz et un veftiment de vert ove les garnementz, un miffal, et un antiphoner pur fervir en la dite chapele a falu de n're alme pur touz jours. Nous devifoms auxint a frere William de Monkelane n're confeffour c li. d'argent et un plat hanap' d'argent deint nous foloms boire, un petit poot d'argent, vi efqueles, et vi faufers d'argent, q'il demoere la ou il purra plus fpecialment prier pur nous. Et prions devoutement al priour provincial et a tout l'ordre avantdit q'il voeillont grentier q' le dit frere William y puiffe demorer a touz jours, et q'il eyt fa chaumbre bele et honefte, et foit cione* com' une meftre de divinite. Nous devifoms auxint a frere Johan de Teye n're luminour ᑫ x li. a prier pur nous. Nous volons auxint et devifoms q' noz executours facent faire XIII chalys en noun de Dieux et de fes douce apoftres, et v chaliz d'argent en noun de v joyes de n're dame, et q'il les facent ailler ᵖ as diverfes efglifes poevres, a chefcune efglife un chaliz, fi q' nous foions en les proiers de genz converfanz as dite efglefe a touz jours. Nous devifoms auxint a l'abbeffe et as noneynes de Caam en Normandye xxx li. a prier pur nous. Nous devifoms auxint a n're cher neveu Humfray de Bohun une noche ˢ dor environne de groffes perles ove un ruby en my lieu affys entre qartre perles, troiz diamaunz entre troiz perles et troiz emerandes, et une poire de Paternoftres d'or de cin-

---

* Sic Orig.
ᑫ Adminiftrateur ou Marguillier de l'eglife. Laccombe. Q. chaplain, or chapel clerk.
ᵖ Nuns of Caen. ˢ *ouch*, or *nouche*, a gold ftud, or fetting, for jewels.

# EARL OF ESSEX.

q'nte pieces ove les [t] gaudez [u] q'errex et ovez une croiz d'or enquele eſt une piece de la v'roie croz n're ſeignour. Nous deviſoms auxint a Elizab't n're niece de Northampton [x] n're liht des armes d'Englet'e ove ceel et curteyns et dys tapitez. Nous deviſoms a n're niece dame Katerine Dengayn [y] XL li. pur ſa chambre. Nous deviſoms auxint a n're ſoer counteſſe Doremant [z] deux pots d'argent, XII eſqueles, et XII ſaucers d'argent pur ſon hoſtel. Nous deviſoms auxint a n're frere Monſ'r Hugh de Courtenay count de Deveniſshire un graunt ſaphir quarre de fyne colour dynde [a]. Nous deviſoms auxint a n're ſoer Counteſſe de Devenſhire n're liht vert poudre de roſes vermailles ove tout l'apparail, et un chapelet gobonne de g'nz ſaphirs et groſſes perles, et un bacyn darrein, en quel nous ſumes acouſtumez a laver n're teſte, et qe fuit a Madame ma miere. Nous deviſoms auxint a l'abbe de Walden XL li. A Sire Nichol de Neuton C marcs. A Sire Thomas de Walmesford XL li. A Sire Stiefne atte Roche XX li. A Sire Williem Agodeſhalf X li. A Wauter Blount et a Marionn ſa feme C marcs, et n're meillure robe ove mauntel furre

---

[t] Q. Ornaments.    [u] Q. *quarres.*

[x] Only daughter of his brother William, earl of Northampton, married to Richard ſon and heir to Edmund earl of Arundel. Dugd. Bar. I. 186.

[y] Daughter of Hugh earl of Devon, married to Thomas lord Engayn, who died 41 E. III. Dugd. Bar. I. 467.

[z] Eleanor his eldeſt ſiſter, maried James Botiler, earl of Ormond. Vincent on Brooke, p. 241. makes her youngeſt of the two. Dugdale, Bar. I. p. 184. makes her his ſecond ſiſter; but ſays nothing of her marriage. Margaret, the other ſiſter, married Hugh Courtney earl of Devonſhire, mentioned afterwards.

[a] blue.

de meniver, et la dite Marionn furra charges de lyverer entierrement a noz executours touz nous joiaux, et totes nos autres chofes, qele ad en garde forfpris, lyntheux et keverches, les queux nous voillons q'il foient dep'tiez entre nos damoyfels a prier p'r nous. Nous devifoms auxint a Letice de Maffendon xx li. A Helen Smyth x marcs. A Thomafine Belle xl marcs, pur fon mariage, ou plus fi qele foit bien mariee. A Joh'n de Chertefeye xl marcs, fi q'il foit aidant et entendant a nous executours. Nous devifoms a Rob't Nobet, et a Katerine fa femme xl marcs. A Symond Peiche xx li. A William Nobet x li. A Johan Maundeville xx marcs. A Ine de Sandhurft xx marcs. A frere William Belle x li. A Joh'n Atteford x marcs. A Thomas Docking xx li. f'il ne foit avance devant n're deces; et f'il foit avance, nous voloms q'il ne eit forfq' x li. A Joh'n atte Roche xl s. A Joh'n Bonnallet' x li. A Williem de la garderobe x li. et une robe, ove un mantel pur tout fon fee. A Henri Skynnere c foutz. A Joh'n Middleton x li. A Richard Maldon, c s. A Piers Peyn x marcs. A William Hurle xx marcs et une robe. A Watekyn Potter c s. A Waut" de la Chaumbre xx marcs et une robe. A Raunde de la Chaumbre c s. A Henri de la Chaumbre xl s. A Joh'n Rolf v marcs. A Joh'n Luminour xl s. A Joh'n rouge [b]Potager xl s. A Williem de Barton haftiler xl s. A Joh'n Ufsher xl s. A Willlem Gamage xl s. A Joh'n Ralgh venour xl s. A un garfon pur le ferour xx s. A Joh'n Ravenefton xl s. et un viel

[b] *Potagier* is in Laccombe, officier qui a foin du potage du Roi.

robe,

robe, cest assavoir cote et surcote. A Rob't de Legh'es II marcs. A Salkyn Wystok II marcs. A Benoyt de la Quisine I marc. A Whitenod I marc. A Gibbe Parkere I marc. A Perimant I marc. A Rog' Hergest XL s. pur laveurye I garson XX s. A VI charetters, chescun de eux v marcs, cest assavoir a ceux q' suict lungement demurrez ovesq' nous: et a les autres meynes solom lour demoere p' avisament de nos executours. A mestre Thomas le Ferour v marcs. A Davy q'est Barber et Ewer XL s. A un garson feurer [c] I marc; et q' null ne soit paie de nous gens avantditz, s'il ne soit en vie apres n're deces, et demorraunt ovesq' nous. Nous devisoms auxint a les executours Sire Stevene de Greveshende [d] jadys evesq' de Londres XX marcs les queux nous luy devoms. Et voloms auxint qe totes les depenses q' nos executours ferrount p' eux ou p' autres entour le executioun de n're testament q'ils les p'gnent de nous beins; et tout le remenant de nous biens a chateux q' ne sont pas devises ne paiez, sicom' d'ist est p' amont nous voloms q'il soient vendus, et les deniers quillies [e] ensemble et menex a Loundres, et illoeq's p' avisement de nos executours et des plus sages des freres illoeq's soit ordeine a paier nous dettes, si nuls soient aderere; et tout le remeneant voloms q' soit dep'tie et despendeu en diverses aumosnes, et nomeement en VII oev'es de charite, et en messes chauntiez p' les plus seintes gens q' q' hounne p'ra espier et autre aumosnes q' mieux et plus tost puissent proffit a n're alme.

[c] *fuere*, artisan, ouvrier: Laccombe. It is not easy to explain the offices of the several domestics here mentioned, such as *Hastiler*, *Ferour*, &c.
[d] He died 1338. [e] receuillez.

Nous voloms auxint q' par avifement de n're confeffour et de nous executours gre [f] foit fait a totes les efglifes p'ochials ou nous avoins demurres, fi riens foit arare [g] de difmes, ou d'offrendes, ou de nule autre chofe qap'tenoit a la droite de la efglife quele qele foit. Nous voloms auxint q' tous nos joiaux q' nous demoerent ap's n're detes par refoun q' nous avoins ew graunt delig't de eux regarder, q'il foient touz venduz, et les deniers dep'tiz en diverfes aumofnes per avifement n're confeffour, et p' nous executours. De ceft n're teftament nous ordenons et fefoms noz executours frere Williem Abbe de Walden, frere Williem Monkeland n're confeffour, Sire Nichoel de Neuton, et Sire Thomas de Walmesford, et Sire Eftiefnes atte Roche nos clers. Et prioms n're tres honourable piere in Dieu, q' totes ceftes chofes foient faites folom n're volentie. Nous voloms auxint et devifoms q' nous executours facent lewer un chapeleyn q' foit de bone condition daler a J'hrl'm principalment pur ma dame ma miere & pur mon feignour mon piere as queux Dieux face v'rore mercy et pour nous, et qe le chapelayn foit charge a dire meffes p' chemeyn a totes les fois q'il p'ra conement p'r les almes. Et auxint q' nous executours lowent un bon home et loial daler a Caunt'birs, et offrer illoeq's p'r nous XL s. d'argent. Et un autre tiel home daler a Pountfreyt, et offrir illoeq's a la toumbe Thomas jadys Counte de Lancaftre XL s [h]. Nous

[f] *gré*, allowance.¹
[g] *arere*, a rear, as *aderere* before.
[h] See Dugd. Bar. I. p. 782. and Walfingham, p. 167. The teftator's father loft his life by adhering to Thomas earl of Lancafter, in his rebellion againft Edward II. being flain on the bridge at Burroughbridge, 1321. Lancafter's popularity made him pafs for a martyr.

voloms

voloms auxint q' si nous eioms ubliez de mettr' en n're testament ascun de nous servans q' nous executours les facent trov' cynk chapelains tout un an a chaunter pur l'alme de nous et pur les almes de ceux q' nous ont servy et a prier pur nos. Nous devisoms auxint et ordenoms q' nos executours p'ignent c li. et achatent une p'celle de terre et enfeffent John de Mortimer et ses enfans de son corps engendre, et qe la terre soit taille, si qele ne puisse estre aliene si le dit Johan soit en vie adunq's, et s'il soit a dieux, comande q'il enheritient ses enfans a touz jours apper [i] pur nous. Nous voiloms auxint et ordenoms q' tantost apres n're deces noz executours et n're confessour ordeignent chapelains les plus seintes gentz q'il purrount trov', auxi bien des seculers com' de religious, a prier pour nous. En tesmoignance de queu chose a cescuy n're testament avoins mys n're seal estre [k] en n're presence en n're chastel de Plessy; le jour et l'an de susditz. Et pour ceo q' nous sumes en volientie affaire une chaunterie de certains chapelayns en l'onour de Dieux et de n're dame et de Seinte Anne a prier pur nous en manere q' s'ra ordeine, queu chose fuit enp'tie comences et puis destourbe p' la mort n're ch' frere counte de Northampton [l] q' dieux assoile, nous voloms q' si la dite chaunterie ne soit p'fourme en n're vie q' nos executours achatent tant de terre a la v'roie value del manoir de Dunmawe, et p'fourner la dite chaunt'ie a la priorie de Scoule, s'il p'ount acorder, ou ailleurs si com'

[i] Q. a prier. [k] *propre*, own, Laccombe.
[l] He died 1360, and was buried at Walden abbey. Dugd. ubi sup. See his wife's will. Ib.

il v'rount q' meux foit affaire. Nous voloms auxint et devifoms q' apres totes ceftes chofes faites contenues en n're teftament p' amount q' nos executours p'ignent dys-mill' marcs, et les defpendent per confaile et avifement des freres defuznomes en chaunt'ies et un autres fept oev'es de charite, folont ceo q'il poont mieux accorder q' mieux foit pur l'alme de nous, et auxient pur paier dettes fi nules foient aderere. Et tout le remenant foit defpendu com' eft avant devife en n're dit Teftament.

> Probatio dicti Teftamenti coram Simon. archiep' Cant' dat. 13 Kal. Novembr' Anno D'ni 1361. apud Novum Templum, London.

Extracted from the regifter of Simon Iflip, fol. 178. b. 179. a. b.

In the Archiepifcopal Regiftry at Lambeth.

**HUMFREY**

# HVMPHREY DE BOHVN.

### TENTH EARL OF HEREFORD AND ESSEX,

Nephew to the foregoing. He died 1371. 46 E. III. having married Joan daughter of Richard Fitz Alan earl of Arundel, by whom he left only two daughters, Eleanor, married to Thomas of Woodſtock duke of Glouceſter, and Mary, to Henry duke of Lancaſter, afterwards king Henry IV *.

EN noun de Dieu, Jeo Humfr' de Bohun, conte de Hereford, d'Eſſex, et de Northampton, et coneſtable d'Engleterre, de bone et ſaine memoire, face mon teſtament le xii jour de Decembr', en l'an de grace mil ccc ſeptant ſecond' en manere q'enſuit. Primerement, Jeo deviſe m'alme a Dieu tout puiſſant, a la bennye virge Seinte Marie, et a touz Seints du Ciel, et mon corps d'eſtre enterres en l'egliſe de l'abbeye de Walden. Et jeo doigne et deviſe touz mes biens et chateaux, vifs et morts moebles, et nient moebles q'cunq' p't q'ils ſoient a meſtre Simon † p' la grace de Dieu eveſq' de Londres, Monſ'r Gy de Bryane, Monſ'r John de Moulton, Monſ'r Rob't de Tye, Joh'n de Gyldeſ-burgh, et a S'r Ph. de Melreth, p'r mon corps enterrer, et

---

* Dugd. and Vincent ut ſup. Sandford, p. 143.
† Simon Sudbury, afterwards abp. of Canterbury, beheaded by Wat Tyler's mob, 1381.

p'r

p'r les dettes mon treſhonē' Seign'r et Piere q' Dieu aſſolle, et auſſint pur mes dettes propres entierement paier, et jeo deviſe q' mon dit corps enterrez, & les dettes mon dit treſhonē' Seign'r et Piere, et auſſint mes dettes propres paiez, qe le reſidue de touz mes biens et chateux ſoit fait p'r m'alme et p'r les almes de ceux as queux jeo ſui tenuz ſolonc la diſpoſition des ayaunditz eveſq', Monſ'r Gy, Monſ'r Joh'n, Monſ'r Rob't, John, et S'r Ph. quels jeo face et ordeigne mes executours de ceſt mon teſtament, et ceo p' la ſurveue Monſ'r Richard conte d'Arundell et de Surr' Johanne ma treſchere compaigne et Adam Fraunceys citezein de Londres. Don' a Pleſſiz le jour et l'an ſuſdits.

Probatio dicti Teſtamenti coram d'no Willielmo Wittleſey archiep' Cant', apud Lambeth, Id. Maii, Anno D'ni 1373.

Regiſt. Witleſey, fol. 127. a. b. In the Archiepiſcopal Regiſtry at Lambeth.

EDWARD

# EDWARD THE THIRD.

IN nomine fumme et individue trinitatis, Patris, et Filii et Spiritus Sancti, gloriofe virginis Marie matris Dei, et totius celeftis curie, amen. Cafus mortiferus parentis primi de ftatu labentis innocencie immortalitatem mortalitate infelici commercio commutavit, et adeo dire infectionis rivulos derivavit in pofteros ut genus humanum ab infectis radicib' propagatum racione ipfius originalis contagii exinde refolutionis patetur difcrimina, et divina volente jufticia de ceto' per mortis femitas incedere cogeretur. Quod nos Edwardus Dei gra', qui feptra regnorum Anglie et F'ncie, regis regum nobis affiftente clemencia, per nonnulla tenuimus tempora, in regalis difcretionis examine revolventes, ac confiderantes q'd permiffa mortis fentencia eft tam cont' maiores q'm infimos generaliter promulgata, cum juxta fapientis proverbium omnes morim' et dilabim' velud aqua, volentes que propterea dum recenti gaudemus memoria de n'ris anima et corpore ac bonis mobilib' nobis adeo collatis taliter ordinare, q'd n'ra difpoficio effe poterit deo placita, mundo accepta, ac liberis, miniftris et familiarib' n'ris fidelib', qui nedum nobis, fet toto regno n'ro, multa gratuita impenderunt obfequia, in aliqualem recompenfationem laborum fuorum admodum p'futura, ad teftamentum n'rm folempnit' condendum, et voluntatem n'ram ultimam regaliter declarand', procedere decrevimus, in

hunc

hunc modum. In primis siquidem, in puritate et sinceritate fidei catholice existentes, omnipotenti deo plasmatori n'ro animam n'ram quam suo cruore p'cioso redimit legamus, et eam sibi intensiori devotione qua possumus commendamus; p' corpore vero n'ro in eccl'ia Sancti Petri Westmonast'ii int' clare memorie p'genitores n'ros reges Anglie regalem eligimus sepulturam, seu funeris nostri exequias more regio volumus celebrari, cum tali tamen moderamine ut preter torcheas cereas in numero condecenti sint tantum circa corpus nostrum in ipsis exequiis, quinq' ceree seu luminaria cerea in quantitate competenti, cum sex mortariolis cereis absq' pluri; deinde vero volumus, et in hac ultima voluntate n'ra specialiter ordinamus, q'd monasterium n're d'ne de gracia jux'a Turrim n'ram London' al' p'nos fundatum quoad dotem sufficientem et alia incumbencia augmentetur juxta n'ram intentionem primevam. Volum' etiam, et exp'sse ordinamus, q'd collegium n'rm lib'e capelle n're Sancti Stephani apud Westmonast'm' p' nos fundatum p'ficiat', et omnib' debite de bonis n'ris compleat'r jux'a ordinacionem primeve fundacionis ejusdem. Item volum', et exp'sse ordinamus q'd in conventu fratrum predicatorum de Langele n're fundacionis construant' et fiant domus et edificia n'ris sumptib', prout per nos alias fuerat ordinatum: volum' insup' q'd conventus dictorum fr'm de num' viginti p'sonarum ejusd'm ordinis augmentetur, et q'd novi redditus de bonis n'ris adquirantur, qui ad solvendu' singulis ipsorum viginti fratrum annis singulis decem marcas sufficere poterunt

runt annuatim, qui omnes pro statu n're salubri dum vivimus, et pro anima n'ra cum ab hac luce subtracti fuerimus, ac anima clare memorie Philipe quondam regine Anglie consortis n're carissime, necnon pro bono statu om'ium liberorum n'rorum sup'stitum, et animabus extinctoru', apud Deum in missis et aliis oracionib' et devocionib' suis sp'ialit' intercedere p'petuo teneant'. Consequenter damus et legamus heredi n'ro futuro, cui Deus conferat graciam salutarem, Ricardo videlicet filio recolende memorie Edwardi nup' principis Wallie primogeniti n'ri, unu' lectum integrum cum toto apparatu suo de integris armis n'ris Anglie et F'nc' apud palacium n'rm Westmonast'ii existentem. Item damus & legamus eid'm quatuor alios lectos qui solebant extendi in quatuor cameris inferiorib' palacii sup'dicti eciam cum apparatu integro eorundem. Item damus et legamus eid'm dupplicem apparatum pro aula sua, quorum unus sit magnus et nobilis, reliquus vero lenis et tenuis pro cariagio ordinatus. Item damus et legamus eidem duos apparatus integros p' capella. Item damus et legamus Johanne nup' conjugi celebris memorie Edwardi primogeniti n'ri sup'dicti mille marcas in quibus nobis ex mutuo tenebatur, volentes quod jocalia sua nobis propterea impignorata lib'e restituant' eid'm. Item damus et legamus carissime filie n're Isabelle [a] comitisse Bedefordie pro subvencione sua et exhi-

---

[a] Isabel, eldest daughter of Edward III. was married 1365 to Ingelram de Coucy earl of Soissons, whom the king created earl of Bedford next year. He died at Barre in Apulia 1397. She died
and was buried at the Friars minors, without Aldgate. Sandford, p. 178. Vincent on Brooke.

bicione filie[b] fue trefcentas marcas annuas annuatim provenientes feu exeuntes de t'ris et redditib' filii et heredis bone memorie comitis Oxonie ultimo defuncti, [c] quas Thomas Tirell' miles tenet de nobis, quamdiu intra etatem fuerit idem heres. Refiduum vero omniu' bonorum n'rorum mobilium in quibufcumq' rebuz exiftenciu', eciam fi in cuftodia t'rarum et tenementor. maritagiis heredum, arreragiis firmarum', reddituu', vel in debitis, feu nominib' debitorum a retro quomodolib' exiftenciu' extiterint damus et legamus, ac omnib' viis et modis quib' melius pot'imus concedimus executoribus n'ris inferius nomi'atis, ip'orumq' bonoru' poffeffionem exnunc in ip'os executores in quantum poffumus transferimus, ut de illis debita n'ra, contemplacione p'fone n're dumtaxat, non racione regni feu guerrarum n'rarum contracta, ad que heredem et fucceffo- rem n'rm, ip'iusq' heredes et fucceffores, ex lege Dei et confciencie fore intendimus obligatos, et ideo ip'os execu- tores n'ros ad ea folvenda aftringi volumus vel artari, qua- tenus ip'a bona fe extendere potuerint jufte p'folvant, et alias p' animo n'ra ea difponant, p'ut voluerint coram fummo judice in ultimo examine refpondere. Habita femp' con- fideracione quod fideles miniftri et familiares n'ri qui hucufq' a nobis non fuerunt debite premiati, ex dicto refiduo bono-

[b] Philippa, youngeft daughter of the earl and countefs of Bedford before mentioned, was married to Robert de Vere earl of Oxford, afterwards duke of Ireland and marquis of Dublin, who forfook her for a foreigner. He died 1392. having been attainted in Parl. 11. Ric. II. The parliament allowed her lands, 2 H. IV. She was living 5 H. IV. and ftiled marchionefs of Ireland. MS. note of St. L. Kniveton on Vincent on Brooke, p. 404. This legacy was a further provifion for her, out of her hufband's eftate, after fhe was deferted by him.

[c] Thomas de Vere eighth earl of Oxford, father of Robert.

rum n'ror', quatenus juxta discrecionem dictorum executorum n'rorum fieri pot'it, debitam remuneracionem t'neant, et debite renumerati datis a nobis plene gaudeant, quod heredi n'ro futuro sub paterne benedictionis plenitudine judicamus. Hujus siquid'm testamenti n'ri regii executores nom'iamus, facim', et deputamus p'clarum videl't, filium n'rm Johannem ᵈ regem Castelle et Legionis, ac ducem Lancastrie illustrem, ven'abilesq' p'res ᵉ Joh'em ep'm Lincolinen', ᶠ Henricum ep'm Wigornien', ᵍ Johannem ep'm Hereforden', ac dilectos et fideles n'ros Will'mu' dnm' Latymer ʰ, Johannem Knyvet cancellariu', Rob'tum de Asheton thesaurarium, Rogerium de Bello Campo camerariu', Johannem de Ipre senescallum n'ros milites, ac Nich'm de Caren custodem privati sigilli Quos omnes et singulos oneramus ut hanc voluntatem n'ram ultimam debite exequi et adempleri faciant, prout superius ordinavim', et prout ad partem sunt de n'ris intentione et voluntate plenius et magis specifice informati; supervisores autem hujusmodi n'ri testamenti creamus, facimus, ordinamus et constituimus rev'endos in xp'o patres Simonem ⁱ archiep'm Cantuarien' et ᵏ Alexandrum archiep'm Eboracen', quos quantum ad nos attinet in d'no requi-

ᵈ John of Gaunt.
ᵉ John Buckingham, keeper of the privy seal, died 1397.
ᶠ Henry Wakefield, lord treasurer, died 1395.
ᵍ John Gilbert, lord treasurer, died 1398.
ʰ He died 4 R. II. Dugd. Bar. II. 32.
ⁱ Simon Sudbury.
ᵏ Alexander Neville, banisht 1387, died at Lovain 1391. Godwin.

rimus et rogamus quatenus ipsi tamquam regni n'ri Anglie primates sup'iores omnia hanc ultimam voluntatem n'ram concernencia quatenus opus fuit sup'videant, ipsamque executioni debite demandari faciant, resistentes vero eccli'astica censura p'ut eorum officin' exigit debite coherceant et compescant, p'ut coram Deo reddere volu'nt racionem. In quorum omnium et singulorum testimonium atq' fidem p'sentem paginam seu p'sens testamentum voluntatem n'ram ultimam continens superscriptam in scriptis redigi, ac sigillo privato et signeto n'ris includi, et signari, ac n'ri magni sigilli appensione fecimus roborari. Datum, scriptum, et ordinatum fuit p'sens testamentum in man'io n'ro regali de Haveryngge atte boure, in cam'a n'ra inferiori, septima die mens' Octobr', Anno D'ni mill'imo trecentesimo septuagesimo sexto, ac regni n'ri Anglie quinquagesimo, regni vero n'ri Francie tricesimo septimo. Presentibus dilectis et fidelib' n'ris Johanne de Bureleye, Ric'o Sturreie, et Ph'p la Vache militib'; Will'mo Strete controtulare hospicii n'ri, Johanne de Bev'rle, Walt'o et Johanne de Salesburi, scutiferis camere nostre, et aliis quampluribus, cum Wal'to de Skirlawe[1] decretorum doctore canonico una Eboracen' ad audiendum hanc ultimam voluntatem n'ram specialiter evocatis in solempnius testimoniu' p'missor'.

Probatio dicti Testamenti coram D'no Simone Cant' Archiep' apud Lamheth, 25 June 1377.

---

[1] Dean of St. Martin's, bp. of Litchfield and Coventry, 1385; Bath and Wells, 1386; Durham, 1388; died 1406. Godwin.

Regist.

Regift. Sudbury, fol. 97. b. 98. a. b. in the Archiepifcopal Regiftry at Lambeth.

King Edward the Third died at his manor of Shene, (now Richmond) in Surrey, June 21, 1377; and was buried in Weftminfter Abbey. See his monument engraven in Sandford's Genealog. Hiftory, p. 176. and by Vertue, for Rapin's Hift. of England.

# EDWARD, PRINCE OF WALES.

EN noun de Pere, du Fitz, et de Saint Efpirit, Amen. Nous Edward, eifne fitz du Roy d'Engletere et de Fraunce, prince de Gales, duc de Cornwaill, et count de Ceftre, le vii jour de Juyn, l'an de grace mil troifcentz feptantz et fifme, en n're chambre dedeyns le palois de n're trefredote S'r et pere le Roy a Weftm' efteantz en bon et fain memoire, et eiantz confideration a le brieve duree de humaine freletee, et come non certein eft le temps de la refolution a la divine volunte, et defiranz toutjourz d'eftre preft ove l'eide de dieu a fa difpoficioun, ordenons et fefons n're teftament en la maner qe enfuyt. Primeriment nous devifons n're alme a Dieu n're Creatour, et a la feinte benoite Trinite, et a la glorieufe virgine Marie, et a touz les fainz ; et n're corps d'eftre enfeveliz en l'eglife cathedrale de la Trinite de Canterbire, ou le corps du veray martir monf'r Seint Thomas repofe en mylieu de la chapelle de n're dame Undercrofte [a], droitement devant l'autier, fiq' le bout

de

---

[a] This is the chapel called by Mr. Somner "The Lady Undercroft," in the middle of which Becket was buried. Neither he nor Mr. Goftling, had they feen this will, would have entertained any doubt about the place of that prelate's interment. (Canterbury Walk, p. 220. 2d edit.). The Black Prince does not mean to be buried in the fame chapel with the faint; that would have been too great an intrufion. He only means to be laid in the fame church, directly before the altar; from which his tomb was to be ten feet diftant. He founded a chantry in this chapel, 1363, with licence of his father, king Edward III. and made a very confiderable alteration in the Gothic tafte, with ribs curioufly moulded, and having carved ornaments at their interfections, among which one has his arms. This was called the *Black Prince's Chapel*. The endowment of the chantry was

*Vauxhall*

## EDWARD PRINCE OF WALES.

de n're tombe devers les pees soit dix peez loinz de l'autier, et qe mesme la tombe soit de marbre de bone masonerie faite. Et volons qe entour la ditte tombe soient dufze escuchons de laton, chacun de la largesse d'un pie, dont les syx seront de noz armez entiers, et les autres six des plumez d'ostruce, et qe sur chacun escuchon soit escript, c'est assaveir' sur cellez de noz armez et sur les autres des plumes dostruce, houmout[b]. Et paramont[c] la tombe soit fait un tablement de laton suzorrez de largesse a longure de meisme la tombe, sur quel nouz voloms q'un ymage d'ov'eigne[d] leve[e] de latoun suzorrez soit mys en memorial de nous, tout armez de fier de guerre de nous armes quartillez & le visage mie, ove notre heaume du leopard mys dessous la teste de l'ymage, et volons qe sur n're tombe en lieu ou leu[f] le purra plus clerement lire et veoir soit escript ce qe ensuit en la maner qe sera mielz aviz a noz executours[g]:

Tu qe passez ove bouche close par la ou cist corps repose,
Entent ce qe te dirray, sicome te dire le say.

*Vauxhall* manor, near London, now belonging to the Dean and Chapter of Canterbury. The houses for the priests belonging to it were at the bottom of Best's-lane, where a stone door-way remains; and the place is or was lately privileged, under the board of Green-cloth. Ib. p. 218, 219. 62.

[b] This word in the German language signifying a *haughty spirit*, might represent him as an intrepid warrior. Gostling, p. 267. Whatever occasioned the alteration from his order here recited, the shields with the ostrich feathers have his motto *Ich dien.*

[c] *On the top of the tomb.*
[d] *Of work in relief of copper gilt.*
[e] Sic Orig. *i.e.* washed over with latyii, &c.
[f] Orig. *leu,* or *len.* Q. *l'on.*
[g] This epitaph is given in Sandford and in Dart's Canterbury, with some little variations, and some incorrectness. It is written on the edge of the brass table, in double lines, the lines of each couplet following one another. There is added an epitaph in prose, setting forth the Prince's titles, the day of his death, &c.

Tiel come tu es, je autiel fu; tu feras tiel come je fu;
De la mort ne penfay je mie, tant come javoy la vie.
En terre avoy grand richeffe, dont je y fys grand nobleffe,
Terre, mefons, et grand trefhor, draps, chivalx, argent, et or,
Mes ore fu je povres et cheitifs, profond en la terre gys.
Ma grand beaute eft tout alee, ma char eft tout gaftee.
Moult eft etroite ma mefon. En moy na fi verite non.
Et fi ore me veiffez, je ne quide pas qe vous deiffez,
Qe je euffe onqes hom efte, fi fu je ore de tout changee.
Pur Dieu pries au celeftien roy, qe mercy eit de l'alme de moy.

Tout cil qi pur moi prieront, ou a Dieu m'acorderont,
Dieu les mette en fon paradys, ou nul ne poet eftre chetifs."
Et volons qe a quele heure qe notre corps foit amenez parmy la ville de Canterbire tantq'[h] a la priore, q' deux deftrez[i] covertz de noz armez et deuz homez armez en noz armez et en noz heaumes voifent[k] devant dit n're corps, c'eft affavoir, l'un pur la guerre de noz armez entiers quartellez, et l'autre pur la paix de noz bages des plumes d'oftruce ove quartre baneres de mefme la fute, et qe checun de ceux q' porteront les ditz baneres ait fur fa tefte un chapeu de noz armes. Et qe celi qe fera armez pur la guerre ait un home armez portant apres li un penon de noir ove plumes d'oftruce. Et volons q' le herce[l] foit fait entre le haut autier et le cuer, dedeyns le quel nous voloms q' n're corps foit pofee, tantq'[h] les vigiliez, meffes, et les divines fervices foient faiftes; lefquelx fervices enfi faitez, foit n're corps portes en l'avant

[h] unto, until. [i] *deftriers*, horfes. [k] voifent. Q. fhall walk before our Lady.
[l] See before, p. 45.

dite

dite chappelle de notre dame ou il sera ensevillez. Item nous donnons et devisoms al haut autier de la dite eglise n're vestement de velvet vert enbroudez d'or avec tout ce q' appertient au dit vestement. Item deux bacyns d'or, un chalix avec le patyn d'or noz armez graves sur le pie, et deux cruetz d'or, et un ymage de la Trinite a mettre sur le dit autier, et n're grande croix d'argent suzorrez et enamellez, c'est assavoir la meliour croix qe nous avons d'argent; toutes lesqueles chosez nouz donnons et devisons au dit autier a y servir perpetuelement, sainz jammes le mettre en autre oeps[m] pur nul mischiefs[n]. Item nous donnons et devisons al autier de n're dame en la chappelle surdite n're blank vestiment tout entier diappree d'une viue dazure et auxi le frontel qe l'evesqe d'Excestre nous donna, q'est de l'assumption de n're dame en mylieu sev'er d'or et d'autre ymagerie, et un tabernacle de l'assumpcioun de n're dame qe le dit evesq' no' donna auxi, et deux grandez chandelabres d'argent q' sont tortillez, et deux bacyns de noz armez, et un grand chalix suzorre et enameillez des armes de Garrenne[o] ove deux cruetz taillez come deux angeles, pur servir a mesme l'autier perpetuelment, sainz jamez le mettre en autre oeps p' nul meschief. Item, noz donnons et devisons notre sale des plumes d'ostruce de tapiterie noir et la bordure rouge ove cignes ove testez de dames, cest assavoir un dossier, et huyt pieces pur les costs et deux banqueres[p] a la dit eglise de Canterbire. Et volons q' le dossier soit taillez ensi come mielz sera

---
[m] use, work.
[n] *to prevent prejudice being done to them*; or, *on no account.* [o] *Warren.*
[p] A back piece, and eight pieces for the sides and two benches.

avis a noz executours pur fervir devant et entour le haut autier, et ce q' ne befoignera a fervir illec du remenant du dit doffier, et auxi lez ditz banqueres volons q' foit departiz a fervir devant l'autier la ou Monf'r Saint Thomas gift, et l'autier la ou la tefte eft, et a l'autier la ou la poynte de l'efpie[q], et ento'r n're corps en la dite chappelle de n're dame Undercrofte, fi avant come il purra fuffiere. Et voloms q' les coftres[r] de la dit fale foient pur pendre en le quer tout du long paramont les eftallez[s] ; et en cefte maniere ordenons a fervir et eftre ufez en memorial de noz a la fefte de la Trinite, et a toutz les principales feftes de l'an, et a lez feftes et jours de Monf'r Saint Thomas et a toutez les feftes de n're dame, et les jours auxi de n're anniv'faire perpetuelement, tant come ils purront durer fainz james eftre mys en autre oeps. It'm nous donnons et devifons a n're chap-

[q] At the altar where St. Thomas lies, at the altar where the crown of his fkull which was cut off at his death was preferved, and at the altar where was kept the piece of Richard Brito's fword, which was broken off by the violence of his blow againft the arfhbifhop's head and the pavement. See Fitz Stephen's account of his death in Sparke's Hift. Anglic. Script. p. 87. Gervaife inter X. Script. p. 1416. The firft was called *altare tumbæ B. Thomæ martyris* (Somner p. 98. Battel. p. 28.) The fecond was probably in that part of the cathedral called *Becket's Crown*. (Ib. p. 94. Goftl. p. 124.) The third was dedicated to the Virgin Mary, and commonly called the altar of the martyrdom of St. Thomas. Erafmus fays it was of wood, and a very fmall one, and that there was laid upon it the point of the fword which cut off the crown of the archbifhop's head, and was ftirred about in his brain. At this altar he breathed his laft invocations on the Bleffed Virgin. Batteley, p. 27, fays, Roger who was chofen abbot of St. Auftin's 1176, and carried with him from it a piece of the fkull, and good part of the blood and brains of St. Thomas, was keeper of *this* altar; but Thorn (int. X. Script. p. 1819) fays, he was keeper of the altar *ad quod S. Thomas fuit martyrizatus*. This was *St. Benedict's* altar. Fitz Stephen. In the windows of the Library at Trinity College, Oxford, is a figure with a mitre and crofier, and *the point of a fword fticking in his forehead*, which from this circumftance the late Mr. Huddesford fuppofed to reprefent Becket.
[r] *coftes*, fide pieces. It feems to refer to the hangings of his hall.
[s] above the ftalls.

pelle de ceſte n're dite dame Undercrofte en laquele nous avoins fondes une chant'ie de deux chapellayns a chanter pur noz perpetuelement n're miſſal et n're portehors [t], leſquelx noz meſmez avons fait faire et enlumyner de noz armez en diverſez lieux, et auxi de noz bages dez plumes doſtruce, et ycelx miſſal et portehors ordenons a ſervir perpetuelement en la dite chappelle, ſainz james les mettre en autre oeps pur nul meſchiefs, et de toutez ceſtes choſes chargeons les almes des priour et convent de la d'te egliſe, ſicome ils vorront reſpondre devant Dieu. Item, nous donnons et deviſons a la dite chappelle deux veſtementz ſengles, ceſt aſſavoir, aube, amyt, cheſyble, eſtole, et fanon [u], avec towaill, covenables a chacun des ditz veſtementz a ſ'vir auxi en la dite chapelle perpetuelement. Item, nos donnons et deviſons notre grand table d'or & d'argent tout pleyn dez precieuſes reliques, et en mylieu un croiz de ligno ſanɔte crucis, et la dite table eſt garniz de pierres et de perles ceſt aſſavoir vingt cynk balois [x], trentquartre ſafirs, cinqaunt perles groſſes et pluſo's outres ſafirs, emeraudes, et perles petitz, a la haut autier de n're meſon d'Aſsheruggey q'eſt de n're fundatioun, a ſervir perpetuelement au dit autier, ſanz james le mettre en autre oeps pur nul meſchiefs, et de ee chargeons

[t] *Portiforium*, with which the French word is ſynonymous.

[u] *manipule*. Laccombe.

[x] ballaſs. This is the name of a ſpecies of rubies, of a vermeil roſe colour. Chambers's Dict.

[y] Aſhridge, in Buckinghamſhire. Edmund earl of Cornwall, ſon of Richard king of the Romans, founded this college of Bonhommes, 1283. Edward III. confirmed his charter, a. r. 5. What concern the Black Prince had in this foundation no further appears.

les almes du rectour et du convent de la d'te meson a respondre devant Dieu. Item, nous donnons et devisons le remenant de touz noz vestimentz, draps d'or, le tab'nacle de la resurrection, deux cixtes [z] d'argent suzorrez et enameillez d'une sute [a], croix, chalix, cruetz, chandelabres, bacyns, liveres, et touz noz autrez ornements appertenantz a seinte eglise a n're chapelle de Saint Nicholas [b] dedenz n're chastel de Walyngforde, a y s'vir et demurer perpetuelement, sanz james le mettre en autre oeps, et de ceo chargeons les almes des doien et souzdoyen de la dite chapelle a respondre devant Dieu, horspris toutesfois le vestement blu avec rosez d'or a plumes dostruce, lequel vestement tout entier, avec tout ce qe appertient a ycell noz donnons & devisons a n're fitz Richard, ensemble avec le lit q' nous avons de mesme la sute & tout l'apparaill du dit lit lequele n're tres redotes seignour & pere le Roy nous donna. Item, nous donnons et devisons a n're dit fitz n're lit palee de baudekyn et de camaka rouge qest tout novel, avec tout ce q' app'tient au dit lit. Item, noz donnons et devisons a n're dit filz n're grand lit des angeles enbroudes avec les quissins, capitz [c] cov'ture, lintaux, et tout ent'rement l'autre app'all app'tienant au dit lit. Item, nous donons et devisons a n're dit filz la sale [d] darras du pas de Saladyn, et auxi la sale de

---

[z] Q. *cistes*, little boxes.     [a] of one pattern.

[b] This chapel subsisted in the beginning of John's reign; if not before; was augmented by Edmund earl of Cornwall, 10 E. I. and again by the Black Prince and Henry VI. so that before the dissolution its revenues amounted to £. 147. 8s. per annum. Tan. Not. Mon. p. 19.

[c] cushions, tester, coverlets, sheets, &c.

[d] *Sale* sems to be used here, and in other wills, for the *hangings* of a *hall*.

worstede

worſtede embroudez avec mermyns de mier ͤ et la bordure de rouge et de noir pales et embroudez de cignes avec teſtes de dames et de plumes d'oſtruce, leſqueles ſales noz volons qe notre dit filz ait avec tout ce q' appartient a ycell. Et quant a n're veſſelle d'argent porte, q' nous penſons q' nos receumes avec n're compaigne la princeſſe au temps de n're mariage, juſqes a la value de ſept centz marcs d'eſt'lingesᶠ de la veſſelle de n're dit compaigne; nous volons q' elle ait du notre tantq' a la dite value. Et en remenant de n're dit veſſelle noz volons q' n're dit filz ait une partie covenable pur ſon eſtat, ſolonc l'avis de noz executours. Item, nous donnons et deviſons a n're dit compaigne la princeſſe la ſale de worſtede rouge d'egles et griffons embroudez avec la bordure de cignes ove teſtes de dames. Item, noz deviſoms a ſire Rog' de Claryndon ᵍ un lit de ſoie ſolonc l'avis de noz executours, avec tout ce q' app'tient au dit lit. Item, noz donnons & diviſons a ſire Rob't de Walſham n're confeſſour un grand lit de rouge camoca avec nos armes enbroudes a checun cornere, & le dit camaka eſt diapreez enlimines des armes de Hereford avec le celure ʰ entiere, curtyns, quiſſins, trav'ſin ͥ, capitz, de tapit'ee et tout entierment l'autre apparaill'. Item, nous donons et deviſons

ͤ mermaids of the ſea.  ᶠ ſterling.

ᵍ He was a natural ſon of the Prince of Wales, probably born at and named from Clarendon. He was made one of the knights of the chamber to king Richard II. his half brother, who Oct. 1, a. r. 13, granted him an annuity of 100l. during life, out of the iſſues of the ſubſidies in divers counties. He was attainted in the reign of Henry IV. and is thought to have been anceſtor of a family of Smith in Eſſex. Sandf. p. 189.

ʰ *coverlet*. Kelham. Q. if not rather *teaſter*, from *ciel*. In the following will, p. 79. we have *ciel integrum*.

ͥ *traverſin*, croſs piece, whatever that means here. In the next will is *tranſverſia*.

a Monſʳ Alayn Cheyne nʼre lit de camoka blank poudres dʼegles[k] dʼazure, ceſt aſſavoir, quilte[l], doſſier[m], celure entiere, curtyns, quiſſyns, travʼſyn, capitz, et touť entierment lʼautre apparaillʼ. Et tout le remenant de noz biens et chateux auxi bien veſſel dʼor et jocalx come touz autres biens, ou qʼils ſoient outre ceux qʼ nous avons deſſuz donnes et deviſez come dit eſt, auxi toutez maneres des dettes a nous due, en queconqʼ manere qʼ ſe ſoit, enſemble avec touz les iſſuez et profitz qʼ purront ſoudre[n] & avenir de touz nos terrez & ſeignouris par trois ans apres ce qe dieux aura fait ſa volunte de nous, leſ- quelx profitz nʼre dit ſeignour & pere nos a ottriez pʼ paier noz dettez, Nous ordenons et deviſoms ſi bien pur les deſpenz funʼales qʼ conveneront neceſſairement eſtre faites pur noſtre eſtat, come pʼ acquiter toutez noz dettez per les mains de noz executours, ſiqʼ ils paient primerement les dis deſpentz fu- nʼales, et apʼs acquitent principalement toutez les debtes par noz lyialement dehues[o]. Et ceſtes choſes perfourmez com dit eſt ſi rien remenit de noz ditz biens et chateux nous volons qe adonqes noz ditz executours, ſelonc la quantite enguerdonnent[p] noz povres ſervantz egalement ſelonc leur degreez et deſertes ſi avant come ils purront avoir informa- tion de ceux qʼ en ont melliour cogniſſante, ſi come ils en vorront reſpondre devant Dieu au jour de juggement, ou nul ne ſera jugge qʼ un ſeul. Et quant a les annuytes qʼ nous

---

[k] *with eagles.*
[l] *quilte* is not a modern French word, and yet occurs not in old gloſſaries.
[m] back piece.
[n] *ſouder, ſurder,* to ariſe. Kelham.
[o] due.  [p] reward.

avons

avons donnes a noz chivalers, efquiers, et autres noz fervitours en gueredon[q] des fervices q'ils nous ont fait et des travalx q'ils ont eu entour nous, n're entiere et darriene volunte eft q' les dictes annuytees eftoifent[r], et q' touz ceux afquelx nous les avons donnes en foient bien et loialement ferviz et paiez, folonc le purport de n're doun et de noz letres quels eu ont de noz. Et chargeoms n're filz Richard fur n're benefon de tenir et confermer a chefcun quant nous lour avons enfi donnez; et fi avant come Dieu nous a donnes pour[s] fur n're dit filz nous lui donnons n're malifon [t] fil empefche ou foeffre[u] eftre empefches en quantq' en il eft n're dit doun. Et de ceft n're teftament lequel nous volons eftre tenuz et perfourmez pur n're darreine volunte, fefons et ordenons noz executors n're tres cher et tres ame frere d'Efpaigne[x] duc de Lancaftre, les reverenz peres en Dieu William[y] evefq' de Wynceftre Johan[z] evefq' de Bath, William[a] evefq' de Saint Afaph, n're t'fch' en Dieu S. Rob't de Walfham n're confeffour, Hugh de Segrave fenefcal de noz terres, Aleyn de Stokes, et Johan de Fordham lefquelx nous prioms, requerons, et chargeoms de executer et accomplir loialment toutez les chofes fuf-

[q] *guerdon*, reward.
[r] *eftoier*, to ftand to, to abide. Kelham.
[s] power.  [t] or *malichon*, malediction.  [u] fuffer.
[x] *d'Efpaigne*. John of Gaunt, third brother of the Black Prince, married in 1372, Conftance eldeft daughter of Peter king of Caftile and Leon, in whofe right he claimed the kingdom of Spain, in re-eftablifhing Peter on which throne two years before the Black Prince contracted the ficknefs of which he died, 1376. Sandf. p. 250, 251.
[y] William Wyckham, died 1405.
[z] John Harewell, chancellor of Gafcoigne, chaplain to the Black Prince, died 1386.
[a] William de Spridlington advanced to the fee from the deanry this year.

dites. En tefmoignance de toutez et chefcuns les chofes fufdites nous avons fait mettre a ceft n're teftament et darreine volunte noz prive et fecree fealz, et avons auxi commandez notre notair deffous efcript de mettre n're dite darreine volunte & teftament en forme publiq', et de foy fouz efcriere et le figner et marcher [b] de fon figne acuftumez en tefmoignance de toutes et chefcuns les chofes deffuz dites.

Et ego Joh'nes de Ormefheved cl'icus Karliolen' dioc' publicus autoritate ap'lica notarius, p'miffis omnib' et fingulis dum fic ut premittittur fub anno D'ni Mill'imo ccc feptuagefimo fexto, Indictione quarta decima, pontificatus fanctiffimi in Xp'o p'ris et d'ni n'ri d'ni Gregorii divina providentia pape $xi^{mi}$ anno fexto, menfe, die et loco predictis predictum metuendiffimum d'num meum principem agentur et fierent, p'fentib' reverendo in X'po p're domino Johanne Hereforden' ep'o, d'nis Lodewico de Clifford, Nich'o Bonde et Nich'o de Scharnesfeld militib', et d'no Will'mo de Walfham cl'ico, ac aliis pluribus militib', cl'icis, & fcutiferis, unacum ipfis prefens fui, eaque fic fieri vidi et audivi, & de mandato dicti d'ni mei principis fcripfi, et in hanc publicam formam redegi, fignoq' meis et nomine confuetis fignavi rogatus in fidem et teftimonium omnium premifforum, conftat michi notario pred'co de interlinear' harum dictionum *tout eſt* per me fact' fup'ius approbando.

[b] *marquer.*

Probatio

# EDWARD PRINCE OF WALES.

Probatio dicti Testamenti coram Simone Cant' Archiep', 4 Idus Junii, 1376, in camera infra scepta domus fratrum prædicatorum conventus London. Nostre Translationis anno secundo.

Regist. Sudbury, fol. 90. b. 91. a. b. in the Archiepiscopal Registry at Lambeth.

Edward Prince of Wales, commonly called the Black Prince, died in the Royal Palace at Westminster, on Trinity Sunday, July 8, A. D. 1376; and was buried in Canterbury Cathedral. His monument is engraven in Sandford's Genealogical History, p. 187; in Dart's Antiquities of Canterbury; and by Vertue, in Rapin's History of England.

JOAN

## JOAN PRINCESS OF WALES.

IN nomine Sancte et individue Trinitatis, Patris et Filii et Spiritus Sancti. Anno ab incarnacione D'ni fecundum curfum et computac'oem ecclefie Anglic. mill'mo ccclxxxv, Regni vero cariffimi filii mei Ricardi Regis Anglie et Francie nono, menfis Augufti die feptimo in castro meo Walyngford Sar' dioc', Ego Johanna principiffa Wallie, duciffa Cornub', comitiffa Ceftr', et d'na Wake, habens integram fanitatem mentis mee, et fidem catholicam firmiter proficiendo, facio, ordino et conftituo teftamentum meum five ultimam voluntatem meam in hunc modum qui fequitur. Inprimis ego Johanna principiffa lego animam meam omnipotenti Deo falvatori meo, et beatiffime Virgini Marie fue genetrici, et omnibus fanctis ejus; Corpufq' meum ad fepeliend' in capella mea apud Stanford puxta monumentum ven' D'ni noftri et mariti comitis Kanjc' defuncti[a]. Item volo et ordino quod debita mea omnia et fingula celeri modo quo fieri potuerint perfolvantur. Item lego precariffimo filio meo regi fupradicto lectum meum de velvet rubrum novum operat' in broderia cum pennis oftric' argent' et cum capit' leopardor, de auro' cum ramis et foliis argenteis procedentibus ex utraque parte quolibet ore ipfor'· cum apparatu prout eft in cuftodia cuftodis garderobe mee London'. Item lego predilecto filio meo Thome comiti Kancie unum lectum

[a] He died Dec. 28, 34 E. III. Dugd. Bar. II, 74.

## JOAN PRINCESS OF WALES.

de camaca pallata in camaca rub' et radiata de auro cum apparatu, videlicet, cum dorsor' ciel integro, uno quilt quolibet operat' in broderia de v hachements in compass, III curtins de Tarteren rub' verberat' I transversiam de syndone, I materat'[b] de sindone rub', II fustian', I canevas de carde rub', XVIII capet' de tapisteria, II quiffin' long de camaca rub' I coopertor'[c] de scarlet furr' de meum purat'[d]. Item lego filio meo carissimo Johanni de Holand'[e] unum lectum de camaca rub' pulverizat' cum paniers, cum apparatu, videlicet, I dorsor', I ciel integr', I quilt quolibet operat' in broderia de v compass, III curtin de syndone rub' plan', I materat' de sindone ex utraque parte, XII quiffin', II fustian', XXIIII capit' de tapisteria, I cannevas de carde blod. Item unum coopertorium de scarlet furr' cum Meum purat' I coverchief de camaca sive furrura. Residuum vero omnium bonor' meor' p'sencium et futuror' ubicumq' existencium, ac omnes et singulos fructus, redditus et provent', necnon jura et dominia quecumq' quos et que carissimus filius meus Ricardus Rex Anglie et Francie michi et executoribus meis concessit et dedit, post mortem meam per unum annum habend' prout litteris suis inde confectis plenius continetur, do, lego, et concedo, meis executoribus subscriptis, viis et modis quibus de jure melius possum ad solvendum primitus de eisdem bonis et catallis meis debita mea supradicta, & deinde ad remunerandum servientes meos secundum qualitatem et merita personarum michi serviencium, et ad disponendum pro ani-

[b] mattras.   [c] coverlet.
[d] *Furra de Meum* is a particular sort of furr, not explained by the glossaries. It may be also read *furratum de* or *cum Meum*. Du Cange explains *puratus* for *purpuratus*, and applies it to a Byzantine coin.
[e] Her third son by the earl of Kent, beheaded by the mob at Pleshy, where he was buried I Henry IV.

ma mea ſicut eiſdem executoribus meis utilius, ſanius et ſalubrius videbitur expedire. Quibus executoribus meis do et concedo poteſtatem generalem et mandatum ſpeciale teſtamentum meum et ultimam voluntatem meam hujuſmodi exequendi et plenarie adimplendi ſecundum modum et formam ſuperius expreſſat'. Ad quod quidem teſtamentum meum ſive ultimam voluntatem hujuſmodi bene, fideliter et plenarie exequend' et adimplend' facio' ordino, conſtituo executores meos generales et ſpeciales venerabiles in Chriſto patres et amicos meos cariſſimos D'nos Rob'tum[f] conſanguineum meum Dei gr'a London', et Will'm[g] ead'm gr'a Wynton' ep'os, ac providos et circumſpectos viros michi predelictos. Dn'm Joh'nem Dn'm de Cobham, Dn'm Will'm de Beauchamp, Dn'm Will'm de Nevyll, Dn'm Simonem de Burlee, Dn'm Lodowycum Clyfford, Dn'm Ricardum Abberbury, Dn'm Joh'm Clanvowe, Dn'm Ricardum Stury, Dn'm Joh'nem de Worthe ſeneſcallum terrarum mearum et Dn'm Joh'em le Vache milites, ac cariſſimos clericos meos d'nos Will'm de Fulburn' et Joh'nem de Yernemouth, et dilectos armigeros meos, Will'm Harpele & Henr' de Norton, ipſoſque omnes et ſingulos executores meos rogo & per viſcera Jeſus Chriſti firmiter obſecro et requiro quatinus premiſſa omnia et ſingula ſecundum Deum et juſtam conſcienciam fideliter adimpleant, adimplerive faciant et procurent pro poſſe eorundem, et ſicut ante tribunal' eterni judicis in ſuo terribili judicio voluerint et debeant rendere preterea omnibus premiſſis ſecundum

[f] Robert Braybroke.   [g] William Wykeham.

pro-

## JOAN PRINCESS OF WALES.

propositum, vim et effectum presentis mei testamenti sive ultime mee voluntatis fideliter et plenarie ad bonam deliberacionem et conscientiam predictor' executor' meor' complet' omnia et singula bona mea insuper remanencia committo in potestatem et disposicōem predilicti filii mei Thome comit' Kancie et dictorum venerabil' in X'po patrum episcopor' London' et Wynton.' In quorum omnium testimonium, ac testamenti mei et ultime voluntatis mee hujus fidem pleniorem, presentes literas meas testimoniales et ultimam voluntatem huj' continentes sigilli mei apposic'one signavi et feci communiri. Dat. anno, mense, die, et loco supradictis. Hiis testib'. Priore Walyngfordie, et Joh'ne James.

> Probatio dicti testamenti coram Will'm Cantuar' archiep' in capella privata manerii n'ri de Lamhith, 9 die mensis Decemb' anno D'ni 1385, et n're translationis 5to.

> Regist. Courteney, fol. 213. b. 214. a. b. in the Archiepiscopal Registry at Lambeth.

This princess (called the Fair Maid of Kent) was the only daughter of Edmond of Woodstock earl of Kent, son of king Edward I. She was married first to Thomas Montacute, earl of Salisbury, from whom the pope divorced her[g], and gave her to her gallant Sir Thomas Holland, knight of the garter, who was created in her right earl of Kent, and lord Wake of Lidell, and died 34 E. III. She

[g] Dugd. Bar. I. 648, II. 75, 94. Sandford 184.

was thirdly married the year after to Edward the Black Prince, whom she outlived, and died at Wallingford castle, July 8, 1385, of grief for the king her son's just resentment to her son John Holland, for killing lord Stafford in a fray, and was buried in the church of the Friars minors at Stamford, which has long since been demolished [h].

[h] See in Peck's Annals of Stamford, book XII. p. 11, 12, an account of her death. Mr. Peck imagined a female bust set in the western outwall of the inclosure there, which he has engraved, belonged to her monument.

HENRY

## HENRY DUKE OF LANCASTER.

EN le noun del Piere, del Fitz, et del Seint Espirit. Nous Henry, Duc de Lancastre, Counte de Derby, de Nichol[a] et de Leicestr, Seneschal d'Engletere, Seigneur de Bruggerak[b], et de Beufort, le xv jour del mois de Marz l'an de grace mill ccc. et LX. a n're chastel de Leic' devisons et fesons n're testament en manere qe s'ensuit. Enprimes nous recommaundons et devisons n're alme a Dieu, et devisons n're corps a estre ensevellitz en l'eglise collegiale[c] del annunciation n're Dame de Leicestr' dautrepart[d] le autiere ou le corps n're seign'r et piere qe dieu assoile est enterrez. Et volums q' n're corps ne demeorge desenterrez outre trois symaynes apres le departir del alme. Et volons q' si nous devions[e] a Leic' que n're corps soit porte a l'eglise parochiele le tiers jour devant l'enterrement, et q' illoeq's soient faites les divines services, tiels come appartient, ove XXIII torches, et qe les douze torches demoergent a l'eglise et deux draps d'or; les cureez de la dite eglise aient n're melior chivall ou les pris en noun de

[a] Lincoln.
[b] Brigerak is a strong town in Gascoigne, which he reduced with many more in king Edward's French wars, 18 E. III. Froissart and Walsingham. in Dugd. Bar. I. 785.
[c] Founded by his father, Henry earl of Lancaster, 4 E. III.
[d] On the other side.
[e] *devier*, or *devoyer*, to die.

principal[f], et q' n're corps soit porteez d'illeoqes tanqe a l'eglise collegial de n're Dame avant dite, et illoqes enterrez come desus est dit; issint[g] q'il ny ait chose voine[h] ne de bobaunce[i], come des homes armeez, ne des chivals couvertz, ny autres choses veines, mes une herce ove cynk cierges, chescune cierge de centz lb, et IIII grauntz mortiers[k], et C torches entour les corps. Et qe cynqainte poures soient vestus, vint et cynk de blank et xxv de blew, portant les ditz torches. Et volons q' n're Seign'r le Roy et ma Dame le Reyne soient garniz de n're ent'rement[l], et Mons'r le Prince, et mes seign'rs ses freres, et madame Dame Isabell[m], et nos seors[n] et nos freres lo'r seigneurs, et les autres grauntz de n're saunk[o]. Et devisons cynqaunt linges[p] por departir as poures bosoignouses en temps environ n're enterement en manere come nous avons charge de bouche les unz de nos executors, si tauntz des poures y soeint. Et ne volons unc[q] q' nulles costages soeint faitz le jour de n're enterrement pour pestre les gentz del pais nes les coes[r] de la ville, et volons q' religiouses soient bien regardez. Et volons q' si nous devions

[f] The curates of that church to have our best horse, or his value, in the name of the principal. Dugdale.

[g] *ainsi*, so.  [h] vain.

[i] *bobans, bobanitè*, sumptuosité. Laccombe. extravagant.

[k] lamps.

[l] be warned or invited to the funeral.

[m] his wife.

[n] There were six of them; all married except the fourth, who was abbess of Ambresbury. Dugd. ubi sup. p. 783.

[o] great people of our blood or lineage.

[p] Quære, *sheets*.  [q] *oncques*, by no means.

[r] To amuse the country folks nor the common people. Les communes de la ville.

aillors

aillors qu'a Leic' q'. n're corps foit menez al eglife de n're dame collegial avauntdite et illeoqes enfterrez en manere come defus eft dit. Et volons et devifons q' toute la cire et touz les drapes d'or demoergent a la dite eglife collegial, et devifons a la dite eglife entierement n're chapele ove touz les aournementz<sup>s</sup> et touz nos reliqes. Et devifons touz nos biens, veffell d'argent, et touz lez autres moebles a aquiter noz dettes et guerdoner <sup>t</sup> noz poures fervauntz, qe ne fount mie ungore<sup>u</sup> guerdone, chefcun folom lour deffert, et folom lour eftat, a la difpoficion de nos executors, et a perfaire<sup>x</sup> la dite eglife collegial<sup>y</sup> et touz les autres maifons devifez et ordeignez entour la dite eglife. Et volons qe fi nos executours puiffent eftre enfourmes en verite qe nous tenoins terre qe fuift d'autruy, et qe nous ne avoins tiel eftat qe nos heires puiffent de bone foi le tenir, q'il perfuent a nos heires de rendre les terres a ceux ou a cely a queux ou a qy eles devient ou doit eftre de droit. Et auxint qe fi nos executours puiffent eftre enforme qe nous eions ewz d'autri a tort, q'ils facent gree en defcharge de n're alme. E a toutes ceftes chofes pleniement perfaire et acumplir folom n're volunte et devys fufditz, nous ordeignouns et fefons nos executors le rev'rent piere en Dieu John <sup>z</sup> evefq' de Nichol, le honorable home de feinte reli-

---

<sup>s</sup> *ornemens.*    <sup>t</sup> to reward.    <sup>u</sup> *encore.*    <sup>x</sup> finifh.

<sup>y</sup> The church and buildings were not compleated until long after this time. The fubfequent dukes of Lancafter granted an annual fum towards carrying on and finifhing the fame for feveral ages after the death of this Duke.

<sup>z</sup> John Gynwell, or Geneville, bifhop of Lincoln, 1351—1363.

gion William[a] abbe de Leic', n're trefchiere foer la Dame Wak[b], n're tres chiere cofyne de Walkynton, Monfieur Rob't la Mare, Monſ' John de Bokelonde, Sire John de Charnele, Sire Waut' Power, Sinkyn Simeon, et John de Neumarche; donaunt pleine poer a eux et a chefcun de eux toutes les chofes fufdites pleinement perfaire et acomplir en la manere fufdite. Et en cas qe nulle chofe foit endoubte et nemye defclare en le dit teftament, eient nos ditz executors pleine poer totes chofes en mefme le teftament defclarer folom ceo qils fenterent qe foit plus a pleifance de Dieu, al profit de n're alme, accordaunt a n're volunte et a refoun. Item nous devifons touz noz biens qe remenent outre noz dettes et outre ceo qe ferra donez pur reward a noz fervauntz, et a perfaire n're dite eglife collegial de Leic' et en eide de performir et accomplir les maifons qe nous avoins ordeignez iHoeqes, d'eftre mys al profit de n're alme par l'avis et affent denoz ditz executors. En tefmoigne de queles chofes nous avions a ceft n're teftament mys n're feal enfemblement ove n're fignet; efcript le jour, lu, et an fufditz.

Probatio dicti Teftamenti 3 Kal. April. A. D. 1361. in caftro Leyceftr' coram Johanne Lincoln Ep'o.

Alia probatio dict' Teftamenti coram D'n'm Will'mum de Witlefeye, Official' Cur' Cant'. Dat' London 7 Idus Maii, A. D. 1361.

[a] William Knight was dean of the duke's college, and refigned 1322. Quære if he was chofen abbot of Leicefter abbey afterwards.
[b] Blanche, his fecond fifter, married to Thomas lord Wake.

Regift'

## HENRY DUKE OF LANCASTER.

Regiſt' Iſlip. fol. 172. a. b. in the Archiepiſcopal Regiſtry at Lambeth.

This Henry, ſurnamed Griſmond, from the place of his birth, being Griſmond-caſtle, or Caſtrum de Groſſo Monte, in Monmouthſhire, and called alſo Tort-Col, or Wry Neck, was the only ſon of Henry earl of Lancaſter, the ſecond ſon of king Henry the Third. He was created earl of Derby in his father's life, 11 E. III. earl of Lincoln, 23 E. III. and duke of Lancaſter, 25 E. III. and married Iſabel, daughter of Henry lord Beaumont, by whom he had iſſue two daughters, of whom Blanche, the younger, being married to John of Gaunt, brought him the eſtate and title of Lancaſter. Henry died at Leiceſter of the plague, 35 Edw. III. 1360, and was buried in the collegiate church of Our Lady, at Leiceſter, where Leland[c] ſaw his monument, on the S. ſide of the altar, and at his head that of his wife. But theſe, with the church itſelf, were completely demoliſhed at the diſſolution; but the hoſpital of the ſame foundation ſtill ſubſiſts in part. See his ſeal in Sandford, p. 102.

[c] Itin. I. 17.

## LIONEL.

## LIONEL DUKE OF CLARENCE.

IN Dei nomine, Amen. Ego Leonellus, Dux Clarencie, fanus mente licet eger corpore, volenfque debitum mortis prevenire, teftamentum meum condo in hunc modum. In primis lego animam meam Deo et beate Marie et omnibus fanctis, et corpus meum ad fepeliend' in eccl'ia fratrum Auguftinenfium de Clare in choro ante magnum altare. It'm lego eccl'ie eorundem fratrum nigrum veftimentum meum cum toto apparatu. It'm lego eid'm eccl'ie pannum meum nigrum brondatum[a]. It'm Violente uxori mee rubeum veftimentum meum cum coronis aureis cum toto apparatu. It'm eidem uxori mee omnia jocalia mea exceptis fubfcriptis. It'm d'no Joh'i de Bromwych militi unum dextrarium qui vocatur Gerfacon'[b]. It'm lego d'no Ric'o Mufard militi unam zonam de auro cum uno dextrario qui vocat' Maungeneleyn. It'm lego Barthe'o Pycot duas zonas de argento & deaurat'. It'm lego D'no Joh'i de Capell capellano meo unam zonam de auro ad faciend' unum calicem in memoriam anime mee. It'm eidem D'no Joh'i melius portiforium meum notatum[c]. It'm eidem Joh'i unum par veftimentorum pauleatum[d] cum

[a] embroidered.
[b] A courfer named Gerfalcon. Another named Maungeneleyn.
[c] My beft portiforium, with mufical notes.
[d] paled.

albo

albo & rubeo. It'm lego mag'ro Nich'o de Haddeleye unum parvum portiforium non notatum. It'm lego D'no Joh'i Wayte capellano unum portiforium notatum. It'm lego Thomæ Waleys unum circulum aureum, quo circulo frater meus et dominus creabatur in principem[e]. It'm Edmundo Mone lego illum circulum quo in ducem fui creatus. It'm lego mag'ro Nich'o de Haddeley supradicto duo monilia de auro, blodio & viridi colore anamalat'[f]. It'm lego Nich'o Bekennesfeld unum monile de auro cum duabus manibus inclusis. Item lego eidem Nich'o decem marcas annui redditus in manerio de Bremmesfeld[g] ad totam vitam suam percipiend'. Et lego Rob'to Bardulf unum monile de auro ad modum cordis factum. It'm volo quod omnes annuli distribuantur inter valetos camere mee secundum disposicionem executor' meor'. It'm volo & executoribus meis injungo q'd nulla fiat bonorum meorum seu terrarum mearum saltim quas vendere seu donare possum aliquibus deliberacio seu diffipacio[h] exceptis legatis supradictis, quousque debita mea secundum quod facultates mee ad hoc suppetunt plene persolvantur, et si quod residuum fuerit, volo quod sit in disposic'one executorum meorum. Hos vero constituo & facio hujus testamenti mei seu ultime voluntatis mee executores, videlicet Violentam uxorem meam, Barth'm Pycot et D'n'm

[e] Edward the Black Prince.
[f] enamelled with red and green. *blodius*, color sanguineus. Du C.
[g] Brimsfield c. Gloc.
[h] This word is not in the glossaries.

Joh'm de Capell' capellanum, quibus adjungo D'n'm Joh'em de Bromwyche militem coadjutorem non tanquam executorem. Acta funt hec anno ab incarnacione D'ni millefimo tricentefimo fexagefimo octavo, indictione feptima, menfis Octobr' die tercia, pont' fanctiffimi in Xp'o patris ac d'ni n'ri d'ni Urbani divina providencia pape quinti anno fexto, in camera ip'ius d'ni ducis, infra muros civitatis Albanen' fituat'; prefentibus Nich'o de Bekennesfeld, Rob'to Bradwaye, Joh'e Bray, et aliis.

Et ego Nich'us de Haddeleye, clericus Miden'[i] dioc' publicus auctoritate apoftolica notarius premiffis omnibus et fingulis fupradictis dum fic ut premittit" agerent' et fierent una cum prenominat" teftibus prefens interfui, eaq' omnia et fingula fic fieri vidi et audivi, fcripfi, publicavi, et in hanc publicam formam redegi, fignoq' meo confueto fignavi rogat' in fidem et teftimonium premiffor".

Probatio dicti Teftamenti coram Will'mo Cant' Archiep' 6to Idus Junii 1369, apud Lambeth.

Regift' Witlefey, fol. 100. a. b. in the Archiepifcopal Regiftry at Lambeth.

Lionell duke of Clarence was third fon of Edward III. born 12 E. III. married firft Elizabeth de Burgh, and fecondly, 42 E. III. Violenta, daughter of Galeas, prince of Milan, within five months after which fecond marriage

---

[i] Meath.

he died, not without suspicion of poison, in her father's house, at Alba Pompeia, called also Longueville, in the marquisite of Montferrat, in Piemont, on the 17th of October, A. D. 1368, having made this will but a fortnight before. He was first buried in the city of Pavia, but was afterwards brought to England, and interred at Clare in Suffolk.

Dugd. Bar. II. 167. Weever 742. Sandford, p. 222. in which last see the ceremonial of the marriage, which probably cost the Duke his life by high living.

Dugdale has given partial abstracts of these two last wills.

## JOHN EARL OF PEMBROKE.

EN noun de Pier, de Fitz, et de feint Efpirit, Amen. Jeo John de Haftynges, Counte de Penbrok, de feine memoire, face mon teftament en manere qe fenfuit. Adeprimes je devife ma alme a Dieu et a n're Dame, et mon corps a fevelier[a] en l'eglife de Seint Paul de Loundres, ou une tombe a faire en la partie devers le north a travers del fouverain autre de mefmes le eglife, quele tombe jeo voel qe foit acordaunt come affiert[b] a tombe Elizabeth de Burugh qe gift a la menoreffe en Loundre hors de Algate. Et auffint je devife pur la fefur de mefme le tombe cxl li. fi meftre eft ou plus folon l'avis de mes executours. Item je devife pur couftages a ma fepulture et diftribucion a faire as poures ccc li. ou plus par l'avis mes executours avauntdit, et auxint jevife et fu de confentement qe Anne ma chere compaigne apres mes dettes perpaiez aiet de mes biens et chateux queconqe tut qe a luy purra appertenir refonablement folonc lei et ufage d'Engleterre fauns afcun contredit. Item je devife pur couftages a fundacioun des freres deins la ville de Co..eneb'[c] cccc li. a difpender illoeqe par mes executours fi

---

[a] *enfevelir*.   [b] as like as it can be made.
[c] Original MS. fcarce legible. It was probably fome foundation that never took place.

freres y vuillent enhabiter, et fi les ne voillent illeoqe
enhabiter, ou qe aucun autre arreſt a ſoit purquoi il ne poet
eſtre fait, adonq' je vuil qe les avant dites cccc li. et
autres cc li. ſoient diſpenduz par avis de mes avantditz executours, ceſtaſſavoir damortier[d], deux chapelleynes chauntantz
en l'egliſe de Seint Paul ſuſdite pur les almes de ceaux qe
j'ai nomes a une de mes executours, et qe le demoerant[e] du
dite ſomme ſoit fait a la egliſe de Chartehous en Loundres
hors de Newgate, pur les almes avantdites enſemblement en
alouance de deniers qe nous avons pitea[f] grante a dite meſon
en acomplicement del avowe par nous autre foitz fait en
Gyen. Et ſi deſtourbance iſoit[g] qe la dite perpetuite des
chapelleiñes ne puit eſtre fait come avant eſt dit, je voel qe
les avantditz vi c li. ſoient deſpenduz autrement en rele-
vacion de meſon de Chartehous ſuſdit, et des autres poures
meiſons de religion en Engleterre et en Gales ſolonc l'avis
de mes executours. Auxint je deviſe qe touz mez dettes
ſoient paies par meins de mes executours et par meins dez
feffez de mes manoirs. Auxint je deviſe qe touz les deniers
avant nomes et qe ſerent nomes en ceſt teſtament ſoient levez
et paies de les iſſues provenant des manoirs et ſeignouries qe
les feffez depar moi tenount de mon doun. Auxint je deviſe
a les freres de les quatre ordres a prier pur m'alme c li.
par diſpoſicion de mes executours. Item je deviſe a departir
entre les ſervants de mon hoſtel qe de lour travaile ne

[d] amortize.  [e] remainder.
[f] Quære *ptie*, i. e. *partie grante*, in part granted.  [g] ſhould be
ſount.

fount pas regardez a temps de ma mort c li. par mes executours fufdits, confidere la porcion du temps de checuny demoure vers nous et a bone fervice qu'il m'a fait. Auxint je devife a partier entre mes povres naifs[h] de mes manoirs cc li. par meins mes executours. Auxint je devife a defpendre pur m'alme et les almes avantnomes, en meffes et almoign a la mefons de Chartehous & autres povres mefons par avis mes auantditz executonrs c li. Auxint je voel qe chefcun de mes executours qe travaillera pur l'execucion de iceft teftament pregne ces coftages refonablement et eftre ce[i] pur fon travail x li. Le refidue de touz mes biens je devife a difpendre par avis de mes executours pur m'alme et l'almes avantnomes en melior manere come leur femblera qe foit a fere pur profit de les almes avantditz. De ceft teftament je face mes executours le Reverent Pier en Dieu [k] William evefqe de Wynceftre, Meff' Henr' Seign'r de Percy, S'r Waut' Amyas, S'r John de Barowe, clerk, Rauf' de Walfham et Thomelyn Crickelade. Efcrit en Loundres v jour de May l'an mil. ccc. lxxii. Item jeo devife qe la fomme en quoi je ou tenuz a ma tres puifante Dame et Mier[l] qe Dieu affoible, qe ce foit fait et diftribuyt pur l'alme a n're avandite miere en le melour manere qe fera avys a mes dits executours, et a plus profit de fa alme.

[h] fervants born on my eftates.
[i] *eftre ceo*, befides this. Kelham.     [k] William of Wykeham.
[l] Agnes, daughter of Roger Mortimer, earl of March, remarried to John de Hakelut, died 42 E. III. By her will 1367, fhe orders her burial in the church of the Minoreffes without Aldgate. Dugd. I. 577.

Probatio

Probatio dicti Testamenti xvi Kal. Augusti Anno D'ni 1376, infra cepta fratrum predicatorum conventus London. coram Archiep' Cantuar'.

Regist. Sudbury, fol. 91. b. 92. a. in the Archiepiscopal Registry at Lambeth.

---

Aliud Testamentum predicti JOHANNIS COMITIS PENBROK'.

IN Dei Nomine Amen. Ego Johannes de Hastynges, Comes Penbrok', sana mente propria voluntate, condo testamentum meum in hunc modum. In primis lego animam meam Deo, et beate Marie, et omnibus sanctis; et corpus meum ad sepeliendum in Anglia in monasterio fratrum predicatorum Hereford', in choro coram magno altari. Item volo et ordino quod de bonis meis hic et alibi existentibus servitores mei bene respiciantur, et remunerentur unusquisque secundum gradum suum, et specialius illi qui in regnis Castell' et Francie multos labores et angustias racione mei sustinuerunt, ad quod faciendum districcius quo potero consciencias executorum meorum onero per presentes. Item volo et ordino quod executores mei distribuant de bonis meis pro anima mea secundum facultatem eorundem, secundum quod viderent melius

expe-

expedire, et secundum quod bona caritas exigit et requirit, et hoc cicius quo bono modo fieri poterit, sicut volunt respondere coram summo judice. Executores meos constituo tales, videlicet, Dominum Walterum Amyas, Radulphum de Walsham et ceteros secundum quod continetur in testamento meo facto in Anglia ante recessum meum ultimum de eadem. Scriptum in presencia mea coram hiis testibus in Dominica in ramis palmis, videlicet, Domino Mauricio Wych, Fratre Alexandro Bache confessori meo, Thoma More, Waltero Atte Watere, Johanne Guybon, Stephano Hamme, et ceteris qui tunc adherant, Anno Domini millesimo ccc septuagesimo quarto, secundum computacionem ecclesie Anglicane. In quorum omnium testimonium sigillum meum manu mea propria presentibus duxi apponendum.

Probatio dicti Testamenti coram Simon Archiep', Cant' 16 Kal. Nov. 1376, apud Lambeth. Registr. Sudbury, fol. 92. b.

John Hastyngs, earl of Pembroke, was son of Laurence, born 21 E. III. and having obtained a divorce from Margaret, daughter of E. III. in 42 E. III. married Anne daughter and heir of Sir Walter Manney, founder of the Charterhouse, which occasions the earl's bequests to that house. He was an active commander in the French wars, being made lieutenant of Aquitaine; but in attempting

## JOHN EARL OF PEMBROKE.

attempting to relieve Rochelle by sea, his fleet was burnt by the Spaniards, and himself carried prisoner into Spain, where he suffered four years rigorous confinement. After his release he went to Paris, where he soon fell sick, as supposed, of poison, and died on the road to Calais, April 16, 50 E. III. He was buried first in the choir of the Friars Preachers at Hereford, but removed to the Grey-friars, near Newgate, London. Dugd. Bar. I. 576, 577.

## PHILIPPA COUNTESS OF MARCH.

EN noun de Dieu, Amen. Jeo Philipe de Mortemer, Counteſſe de la Marche, eſteant en bone et faine memorie le vynt primer jour de Novembre l'an du grace mil troiſcentz, ſeptant et octantiſme, face et ordeygne mon teſtament et ma derreine voluntee en ceſte manere. En primes jeo deviſe m'alme a Dieu et mon corps en enſevelir en l'egliſe conventuel de la Seint Trinitee en le priorie de Buſteleſham Mountagu[a]. It'm jeo deviſe pur les coſtages faire et pur doner en almoigne as poures pur m'alme et autres deſpenſez le jour de ma ſepulture, ove la veſture de cent homes de cheſcun manere degree, et a tenir le xxx jour de mon obit, et la demeore [b] de ma meigne [c] tanqe al temps qe mon corps ſoit enterre cent ſeſſant livres, le quel enterrement ſoit fait en manere deſouth eſcript. C'eſt aſſavoir qe v groſſes cierges qarrez et IIII mortiers de cire ſoient mys entour mon corps et .... en dite manere, et qe xxi torches ſoient au dirige, et xxviii torches lendemayn a la meſſe, les queux XLIX torches ſoient deviſez aſcuns a remeindre a la dite eſgliſe de Buſteleſham et les

---

[a] Biſham abbey, founded by William Montacute earl of Saliſbury, her father, 1338, for Auſtin canons. Dugd. Bar. I. 647. Tanner's Not. Mon. p. 16.
[b] *demorance, demoree, demoerge,* delay.
[c] houſhold. Kelham.

autres

autres as diverses esglises solom la discrecion de mes executours, et qe barrez ᵈ soient faitz entour mon corps covertz de drap bleu sanz autre herce, et les draps d'or qe j'ai solont mys sour mon corps, les queux apres l'enterement remeyndrount a la dite esglise de Busteleshame, et le drap bleu susdit soit donee entre poures.

It'm jeo devise pur ma toumbe faire quarrant livres.

It'm jeo devise al priour de Bustelesham a prier pur m'alme x marcs.

It'm al south priour ᵉ illeoq' lx s.

It'm a chescun chanoignon illeoq' xl s.

It'm al overaigne de mesme l'eglise deux centz livres a tiel entent qe les priour et covent de la dite maison tiegnront solempnement le jour de mon anniversarie as touz jours.

It'm jeo devise a la dite esglise de Bustelesham tote ma chapele entiere ove touz lours appurtenance c'est assavoir vestiments, livres, chalices, cruets, chaundeliers d'argent, tabletz depeyntz et enbroudez, a servir al altier de Seint Anne, devant le quel altier mon corps surra enterre en la secounde arche encountre mon treshonoure Seignur mon piere ᶠ qe Dieux assoille; hors pris mes meillours vestiments ove iii capes de suyte queux jeo devise a l'abbeye de Wyggemore ᵍ, et mes blanches vestimentz queux jeo devise a la maison de Lyngbrok' ʰ.

ᵈ barrs.   ᵉ sub-prior.
ᶠ William de Montacute, earl of Salisbury.
ᵍ Wigmore priory, founded by Ralph de Mortimer 1100, refounded by his son Hugh 1197.
ʰ A priory of Austin nuns on the river Lug, in Herefordshire, founded by some of the Mortimers, t. R. I.

It'm jeo devife a mefme l'autier de Seint Anne un tablet le meillour d'or qe j'ay achate de John Paulyn.

It'm jeo devife a fervir a mefme l'autier de Seint Anne deux bacyns d'argent ove les armes de Mortimer et Mountagu en lez fountz ennamaylez.

It'm jeo devife Efmon[i] mon fitz un lit de bleu taffata enbroudez des afnes merchez en l'efpaule ove une rofe, c'eft affavoir, une celure entiere, III curtyns de taffata, un quilt enbroudez de mefme la feute, IIII tapets de tapiterrie, VI tapets pendantz de worftede, un canvaffe, un matrafs, II fuftians, un quilt poynt blank, un paire de lyncheux[k] du drap de Reyns, un coverlet de worftede, pur mefme le lit, un covertour de bleu demy puree, un keverchief de menyver de drap de camaka plonket[l], un coupe et un ewer de berill garnicee d'or.

It'm un anel d'or ov un rubie la verge ennamaylez de ruffet.

It'm a dit Efmon mon fitz un anel d'or ove un piece de la vraie croyce ove le fcripture, *In nomine Patris et Filii et Spiritus Sancti*, Amen.

It'm a dit Efmon un firmayl[m] bleu ove deux mayns tenantz un dyamond.

It'm un pair des anees[n] les gaudes[o] des croices rouges enamaylez; le dit anel ove la vraye croice, firmail, et anees devoir garder four ma benifon.

---

[i] Edmund her younger fon, who fucceeded his father, and whofe will follows.

[k] fheets.  [m] chain.

[n] [o]

It'm a dit Esmon un hanap' d'argent ove l'escochon fait de deviz de armes de Mortimer ovesqe le coveracle. It'm a mesme Esmon un hanap' suforre ove le covercle countrefait d'une rosse [p]. Et pur oster toute manere matier de diffencons et debatz qe pourront suroere entre mon dit trescher fits Esmon et mes executours pur toutes maneres accions et demandes qe mon dit trescher fitz Esmon purroit per qeconqe voie demaunder, chalanger, ou clamer des mes biens apres mon decees, jeo lui devise cynk centz livres, a prender de la dette qe surra a moi due le jour qe jeo moi lerra morir [q], deinz mes seignouries, les queux D centz livres et toutes les autres choses desuisnomez sont a mon dit trescher fitz Esmon devisez sour tiel condicion q'il ne clayme ne demande d'avoir nulles maneres, principaltes, ne autres choses en lieu d'icell, ne nulle autre rien de mes biens ne dettes, ne nule manere destourbance face a mes executours, et q'il soit eident [r], et doigne pleyne poair a mes executours et a lour assignes du lever primerement tote le remenant de ma dit dette q'adonqes a moy surra due en toutes mes seignouries a perfourmir cest mon testament et ma darreyne voluntee. Qe yous resquier trescher, filz, pur la grande affiance qe j'ai en vous et doi de reson avoir, qe vous sur ma benison ne vull' de voz destourbez mes executours, de ceo q'ils dussent avoir de reson a perfournir cest mon testament et ma darreyne voluntee come desuis est dist. Et pur l'affiance qe

[p] rose.  [q] *lerra morir*, shall die. Kelham.  [r] aiding.

j'ay

j'ay de loyalte en Sir W. de Afton & Sir W. Wynter deux de mes executours, jeo voil qe mon veffel d'argent entierement nient ˢ par moi devifee, c'eft affavoir pottz, piecez, coillers ᵗ, hanapers, bacyns, ewiers, plates pur efpicerie, chargeours, efqueles, fauciers, qe furront les mefnez ᵘ le jour qe jeo moi lerra morir, auxi bien le veffel blank come d'or, et fuifonre ou ennamaylez, foient livre as ditz Sir William et Sir William a perfaire entout ma entente come ils font pleynement enfourmes de ma darreyne voluntee, fauns amenufer ˣ afcun parcel du dit veffel four peril de lour almes, et come ils voudront refpoundre de ceo al jour de juggement. Et comment qe j'ai devifez diverfez chofes de mes biens en mon teftament come defuis eft dit, as finguleres perfones, jeo voil et charge mes executours qe nulle parcell d'icelle foit dilivere a nully tanqe mon corps foit enfevelee et mes dettez parpaiez. Et le refidu de mes biens jeo voil q'il foit entierement al ordinance de mes executours, primerement mes dettes acquitez. Et a faire due execution de ceft mon teftament jeo face et ordeigne mes executours les perfones defouthefcript, c'eftaffavoir Sir William de Afton, Sir William Wynter, Ph' Holgot et Rob't Wyk, pur faire enfuit qe purra eftre pleifance a Dieu, et falvacion de m'alme. Et fur la graunde affiance qe j'ai en le Reverent Piere en Dieu evefq ʳ de Wyncefter, c'eft affavoir Sir William Wykham, et en mon trefcher et bien amee en Dieu Monf'r John de Bromwyeh, jeo les requer efpecialment

ˢ not.    ᵗ fpoons. K.    ᵘ q. remaining.    ˣ diminifhing.

en oevre de charite, q'ils foient eidants par toutes les bones voies q'ils purront a mes executours qe ceſt ma derreine voluntee purra eſtre accompliz. Donee a Plomeſtede[y] le jour et l'an fuifditz.

> Probatio dicti Teſtamenti coram Will' Courteney, Archiep' Cantuar', apud Lambeth, 9 die menſis Februar' A. D. 1381.

> Regiſter Courteney, fol. 189. b. 190. a. in the Archiepiſcopal Regiſtry at Lambeth.

Philippa, daughter of William de Montacute, was married to Roger de Mortimer, earl of March, who died 34 E. III. in Burgundy, where he commanded the Engliſh army, and was buried in Wigmore priory. She had by him two fons, Roger, who died in his father's life-time, and Edmund who fucceeded him. She died 5 R. II. 1381, and was buried at Biſham abbey, among her own relations, of whoſe tombs, nor of the place, no remains appear at prefent. Dugd. Bar. I. 148.

Probabl Plumſtead in Kent.

# EDMUND EARL OF MARCH.

EN le noun de Piere, de Filz et de Seint Efpirit, Amen. Nous Efmon de Mortimer, Counte de la Marche et d'Ulveftier, Seign'r de Wyggemore, en feine et bone memoire le primer jour de moys de May, l'an du grace mill troys cent octantifme, ordenons et faceons n're teftament en cefte manere. Primerement nous devifons n're alme a Dieu tout puiffant qi la crea, et mon corps a enfeveller et le corps de ma feme qe Dieu affoile enfemble en la efglife del abbeye de Wyggemore al feneftre del haut autier, et chargeons fermement nos executours de cefte n're teftament q'ils ne facent couftages groffes ne outrageoufes a n're entierement, et q'il n'y eit entour n're corps plus qe cynk cierges ardantz tan coms le fervice foit enfaifant; mais nos volons et devifons qe cent torches de cire covenables foient ordenez pur n're dit entierement, les queles nous volons q' apres le fervice fait foient diftribuez a les efglifes parochieles environ le dit abbeye pur l'ordenance de noz executours pur fervir a feint facrement.

Item nous volons qe de nos biens foient primerement paiez a Roger filz John de Mortemer D li. pur queux nous fumes obliges par eftatut merchant[a] en cas qe nous ou nos exe-

---

[a] A *ftatute merchant* is a bond of record, acknowledged before the clerk of the ftatutes merchant and lord mayor of the city of London, or two merchants affigned for that purpofe; and before the mayors of other cities.

executours ne lui faceons performir les covenantz comprifes en certeines endentures faites entre nous et lui fur mefme l'obligacion.

Item q' profcheinement [b] apres touz nous autres debtes dues par qeconq' voie foient duement paiez et acquitez de mefmes nos biens, et primerement ceux debtes pur queux nous ou afcun autre pur nous fumes obliges parfait.

Item nous devifons al ovraigne del efglife de l'abbeye de Wyggemore mill. livres a emploier en mefmes l'ovraigne pur l'ordenance de ma tres honourez dame et meere, et de mes executours, et par la fervewe [c] del evefq' de Hereford q'adonqe ferra, et de Sire John de Byfhopefton, Monf'r Piers de la Mars, Sire William Ford, Sire Waut' de Colmpton, et Hugh de Borafton.

Item nous devifons a mefme l'abbeye de Wyggemore n're meillour chapelle entiere, c'eft affavoir, un celure, deux curtyns batuz [d], trois aubes, trois amytes, deus eftoles, trois fanons, trois ceyntres, deux tonicles, trois chapes, deux frounteles, un towaille ov' un frontell' de drap d'or, un cas ove un corporas, un long towall pur l'autier et cordes pur le dit chapelle, un graunt croys d'or affize de perie [e] ove relique de la croys notre feignur et un piler d'or ove une piece

---

cities and towns, or the bailiff of any borough, &c. purfuant to the ftatute 13 E. I. *de mercatoribus*; the recognizance to be inrolled and kept by the clerk, and a counterpart by the mayor, as alfo an obligation figned and fealed by the debtor, and its counterpart. *Jacob's* Law Dictionary.

[b] *next*, from profchain. [c] fupervifaunce.
[d] [e] fet with ftones.

du piler n're feign'r ove ix perles et un faphir en le fommet, et l'os<sup>f</sup> Seint Richard Confeffour, evefq' de Ciceftr', & le doy<sup>g</sup> de Seint Thomas de Cantelowe<sup>h</sup>, evefq' de Hereford, et les reliqes de Seint Thomas ercevefq' de Cantirbirs, et tous nos autres meindres reliqes, forfqe ceux qe ferront devifes enapres<sup>i</sup>, et un miter d'or ov perrie<sup>k</sup> & l'anel<sup>l</sup> ove le faphir q'eft en la garde de n're treforie illeqe, un graunt croys d'argent fuforrez ove une large pie efteant fuz lions et les ymages de Marie & John, deux chandelers d'argent enamaillez, un groffe chalys d'argent fuforrez, le pie enamaillez, ove une patene et deux foiles et un feyn<sup>m</sup> d'argent fuforrez, un table pur pees d'argent et enamaillez, un cenfer d'argent fuforrez, un ftop'<sup>n</sup> ove un dafsher<sup>o</sup> d'argent fuforrez, et deux bacyns pur l'autier d'argent fuforrez; toutes les queles chofes avantdites nous ordenons et volons qeles y demorent a la dite efglife perpetuelment fanz eftre alloignez pur nulle caufe ficome plus pleinement eft contenuz en nos autres lettres eut a eux faites.

<sup>f</sup> A bone of St. Richard de la Wich, who was bifhop of Chichefter from 1245 to 1253, and was canonized. Godwin de præf. 505.
<sup>g</sup> *doigt*, finger.
<sup>h</sup> Cantelupe bifhop of Hereford, from 1275 to 1282, chancellor of Oxford, and lord chancellor, and canonized.
<sup>i</sup> hereafter.   <sup>k</sup> ftones.   <sup>l</sup> the ring.
<sup>m</sup> *feynt*, girt or band, or *ceint*, a bell. K.
<sup>n</sup> a holy water *ftoup* or veffel.
<sup>o</sup> with a fprinkler.

It'm

## EDMUND EARL OF MARCH.

It'm nous devisons al abbeye de Lysnes [p] un piece de piler n'r̃e Seign'r entitlez ove une bille AL ABBEYE DE LYSNES.

It'm nous devisons a la priorie de Walsyngham une chapelle blanche [q], cest assavoir, deuz curtynes, trois aubes, trois amytes, deux estoles, trois fanons, un chesible, deux tonicles, trois chapes, deux fronteles, un towaill ove un frountell, un longe towaill pur l'autier, un cas pur un corporas ove le corporas acordant a la chapele, toute d'une seute.

It'm nous devisons al abbeye de Tynterne une chapelle de rouge entier, c'est assavoir deux curtynes, trois aubes, trois amytes, deux estoles, trois fanons, trois ceyntres, un chesible, deux tonicles, trois chapes, deux fronteles, un towaill ove un frontell, un cas ove un corporas, tout d'une seute.

It'm nous devisons a la priorie de l'Anthoneny [r] (al l'Anthoney le premier en Gales) une chapelle entiere de drap d'or palorz [s] rouge et bleu, c'est assavoir deux curteyns de taffata rouge et bleu palee, trois aubes, trois amytes, deux estoles, trois fanons, trois ceyntres, un chesible, deux tonicles, trois chapes, deux fronteles, un

[p] Lesnes abbey, in Erith parish, Kent, founded 1178, by Richard Lucy, chief justice of England.

[q] The furniture of this chapel was all *white*, as the following were of other colours.

[r] Lantony, Llanhodeni, or Lantonia prima, in Monmouthshire, founded by Hugh de Lacy, about 1108, removed in part to Gloucester suburbs, 1136. Tanner's N. M. 328.

[s] paled.

towaille ove un frontell, un longe towaille et un cas ove un corporas, tout d'une feute.

It'm nous devifons a la priorie d'Ufqe[s] une chapelle entiere blanche poudres de rofes rouges, c'eft affavoir deux curtyns, trois amytes, deux eftoles, trois fanons, trois ceyntres, un chefible, deux tonicles, trois chapes, deux frounteles, un towaille ove un frontell, un cas ove le corporas ove la meyndre chalys d'argent fuforrez ove le patene, deux cruetes et un tablet pur pees et un feyne toutz d'argent fuforrez.

It'm nous devifons a la priorie de Chirbury[t] un coffre d'argent fuforrez et enamaillez ove quartre griffons en le pie pur fervir corps notre feigneur, a demurer perpetuelment en le dit priorie, et quarrant marcs d'argent pur eftre enploiez en veftimentz par la furvewe del evefq[r] de Hereford qi pur le temps ferra, a demureres perpetuelment en la dit efglife et priorie.

It'm nous devifons a notre chanterie en l'abbeye de Wyggemore notre meyndre croys d'argent fuforrez ove les ymages Marie et John, et l'ymage de Seint Efmon d'argent fuforrez, le porthors gemelez[u] et le greindre[x] miffal, et la chapele de bleu ove les rais d'or, c'eft affavoir, deux frountels, un towaille ove un frountell, deux curtyns, et un veftiment entiere pur un preftre de mefme la feute, un corporas

---

[s] Ufk, or Cairufk, a fmall priory in Monmouthfhire.

[t] A priory of Black canons firft founded at Snede, by Robert de Boulers, t. H. III. Tanner's Notitia, 453.

[u] double, or pair of.   [x] largeft.

ove la caas, et le chalys d'argent fuforrez ove deux fioles ove un table pur peés, et un feyne d'argent qe font toutdys[y] ove la dite chapell, et un veftiment noir tout entier pur un preftre, ove deux fronteles, un towaille ove un frontell, un cas pur un corporas ove le corporas; & toutes ceftes chofes avantdites volons q'eles demoergent perpetuelment a mefme notre chanterie fans eftre efloignez par nulle voie.

It'm nous devifons a les abbeyes & covents de chefcun des maifons de religioufes defouz efcritz quarrant livres; iffint qe l'abbeye & covent de chefcun des ditz maifons veullent[z] emprendre et faire feurtee a noz executours de faire chanter en lour efglifes chefcun jour durrant un an profchein apres qe paiement des avantditz XL li. lour ferra faite un meffe de requiem privee pur les almes de nous et de trefchiere compaigne et les almes de touz chriftenes par un chapellein feculer ou regulier, le quel dirra chefcun jour avant q'il chantera placebo & dirige pur nous et touz chriftenes fans note, et q'un jour en chefcun fymaigne durront le dit an ferra dit pur nous & tous chriftienes en lour queer de tout le covent qi ferront prefent placebo & dirige ove note folempne, ove une meffe de requiem a note lendemain, ceft affavoir a les abbeyes & covents de Wyggemore, Lyfnes, & Tynterne.

It'm nous devifons a les abbeys, priories, meftres, gardeins & covents de chefcune maifon de religioun de fouz efcriptz, quarrante marcs en mefme la fourme et

---

[y] *tous jours.* Mot Picard. Lacombe.   [z] borrow.

fouz

souz mesmes les condicions, cest assavoir a les abbeys & covent de Lanternan[a], Comhir[b], & Tilteye[c], et a les priories & covent de Walsyngham, l'Anthoneny le primer en Gales, Bustelesham, Chirbury, Goleclyve[d], Stokes[e], Anglefeye[f], et croys Roys[g], et a les maitres & covent de les hospitales de Seint John de Brugwater[h] & de Lodelowe[i], et a les gardeins & covents des freres menours de Walsyngham, Babbewell[k], Brugwatier, Glouceſtr' & Salop', et a les priories et covents des freres Auguſtyns de Clare, Lodelowe & Wodehous[l].

It'm nous devisons as priories & coventz de chescun des maisons desouz escritz, vynt marcs, issint qe chescun de eux veulle emprindre et faire surtes a noz executours a trover un chapelleyn de eux mesmes ou autre qi dirra chescun jour en lour esglise placebo & dirige sanz note, un

[a] Llantarnan in Monmouthshire, a Cistertian abbey. Tanner, p. 331.
[b] Cumhyre, a Cistertian abbey in Radnorshire, founded 113 Ib. p. 721.
[c] An abbey of White monks in Essex. Ib. 129.
[d] Goldcliff in Monmouthshire. Ib. p. 328.
[e] There were three religious houses of this name. Stoke Cursey c. Devon. Ib. 99. Another c. Somersetshire, p. 476, and the college in Suffolk, p. 114.
[f] Anglesey, c. Cambridge, a house of Black canons, founded by H. I. Ib. 42.
[g] The Austin priory at Royston, or *De cruce Roesiæ*, c. Herts.
[h] Bridgewater, founded by one William Bruce, before 15 John. Ib. 473.
[i] Of very antient foundation. Ib. 445.
[k] A house of Grey-friars, just without the N. gate of St. Edmund's Bury, founded 1263... Ib. p. 527.
[l] Near Clebury Mortimer, c. Salop, founded on the first coming of the order into England, about 1250.

collecte

collecte eſpecial pur noz almes et les almes de touz chriſtenes pur tout un an proſchein apres q'ils averont receux le dit paiement; ceſt aſſavoir a les priour et covent de Sandelford jouſte Neubury[m], Clifford[n] en Gales & Suelleſhales[o] jouſte Whaddon.

It'm nous deviſons a les religiouſes dames la prioreſſe & covent de Lyngbroke vynt livres en manere et condicion eſpécifiez preſcheinement devant.

It'm nous deviſons a les religiouſes dames l'abbeſſe et covent de Bruſyerd[p] quarrant marcs, iſſint qe les dites dames durrant un an proſchein apres q'eles averont receux le dit paiement diſent cheſcun jour en loure quere placebo et dirige pur nos almes et de touz chriſtenes, et q'un lour chapellein qi chantera en la dite maiſon die cheſcun un collecte eſpecial pur nous en ſa meſſe durrant le dit an et qe meſmes les dames dient un jour en cheſcune ſymaigne durrant le dit an placebo et dirige ove note en lour dit quere, ove meſſe ſolempne & requiem lendemain pur les almes de nous et de touz chriſtenes.

It'm nous deviſons a les religiouſes dames la prioreſſe & covent d'Ulture[q] quarrant marcs ſur meſmes condicon et forme.

[m] Sandleford *juxta* Newbury c. Berks, founded for Auſtin canons before 1205. Ib. p. 19.
[n] A Cluniac priory in Herefordſhire, founded t. H. I; Ib. p. 174.
[o] Snelleſhall in Whaddon pariſh, a ſmall priory of Black monks, founded t. H. III. Ib. p. 30.
[p] Bruſyard, c. Suffolk, granted to the nuns minoreſſes of St. Clare, 40 E. III. Ib. p. 531.
[q] Quære *Ulſter*.

It'm.

It'm nous volons et devisons qe si ascune des maisons susdites refuse notre devys susdite a cause de la charge monstre[r] come est dit, q'adonqe la some devisez a la maison ensi refusante, soit liveres par noz executours a autre maison, possession[s] ou mendinant qe le voedra acceptier ove le charge avantdite.

It'm nous devisons a treshonoure dame & meere un hanaper de berill garniz d'argent susorrez.

Item nous devisons a Roger notre fitz et heir le hanaper d'or ove le covercle nomes Benesonne et notre espeie[t] garnisez d'or qi fut a bon Roy Edward, le grand corn' d'or ove le bensoun de Dieu et le notre; issint q' apres le decees n're dit filz l'avantditz hanaper ove le covercle, dit espeye et le grand' corn d'or remeigne a son proschein heir, et issint de heir en heir perpetuelment; et auxi notre grante lit de noir satyn embroudez des blankes lions ove les rosers d'or ove les escuchons des armes de Mortimer et d'Ulvestrier, ove la chambre[u] toute entiere, et auxint une coupe d'argent susorrez et enamaillez ove joeux des enfantz[x] et un saler[y] d'argent susorrez en manere d'une cheon[z]. It'm des meillours bacyns d'argent deux susorrez, deux des meillours bacyns blanks d'argent, deux ewers d'argent, un poot d'argent dim' galon', deux pootz d'argent chescun de dim' galloun, vi peces d'argent plattes, deux douszeins des coellers[a]

---

[r] q. for monstree, set forth, or *montee*, amounting.
[s] q, *profession*.   [t] epee.
[u] the furniture of the chamber.   [x] *jeux des enfans*.
[y] saltseller.   [z] in the shape of a dog.   [a] spoons.

d'argent,

# EDMUND EARL OF MARCH.

d'argent, deux coellers d'or ove les testes de dames, un plate d'argent suforrez, quartre chargeours et deux douszeins des esquelles, et deux douszeins des saucers d'argent. It'm notre meindre corn' d'or ove le baudrik [b]. Et en cas qe notre dit fitz devie [c] avant q'il soit de pleine age sanz heire de son corps engendrez, volons qe toutes les choses avantdites demoergent a notre filz Esmon [d] sur mesme la forme.

Item nous devisons a notre dit filz Esmon trois cents marches [e] de terre come pluis pleinement surra declarrez en autr' escript a lui et ses heirs de son corps a engendres, la reversion a nous et a nos heirs, et auxi deux douszeins des esquelles et deux douszeins de saucers d'argent, deux bacyns, et deux ewers d'argent, un saler en la manere d'une lyoun ove le pee d'argent suforrez, deux coellers d'or, & deux douszeins des coellers d'argent, un de noz grantz plates pur espices d'argent suforrez, un grand coupe ove un ewer de mesme la seute d'argent suforrez en manere d'une rose, VI peces plattes d'argent, deux pootz d'argent chescun de dim' galoun & qartre cent marcs d'argent, et un lit blank de sandale poudres des roses rouges ove le chambre entiere.

[b] belt.     [c] die.
[d] Edmund, his younger son, born at Ludlow, 15 Id. Nov. 1374, suffered a defeat from Owen Glendwr, on a mountain called Brynglase, near Knighton in Melenith or Radnorshire, 4 H. IV. 1407. Dugd. Bar. I. 150. Hist. Wigmore in Monast. Ang. vol. II. 228. Pennant's Wales, I. 327. & aut. ibi cit. Some Historians pretend that he married a daughter of Owen Glendour, by whom he had divers children. Some say his nephew the E. of March and his brother were taken with him; but Dugd. Bar. I. 151. says they were taken the year before.
[e] *de terre* or *marche*, is land valued at one mark.

Item

## EDMUND EARL OF MARCH.

Item nous devisons a n're fille Elizabeth [f] un saler en manere d'un chien, & un hanaper d'or, ove un chaplet des roses de rouge cler tout entour & deux centz graunds perles.

Item nous devisons a n're fille Philippe [g] un coronal d'or ove perie [h] & deuz cents graunds perles, & auxi un sercle ove roses, emeraudes & rubies d'alisaundre [i] en les roses, et le rouge lit ove les parkes [k] ove les rouges tapites pur la chambre entiere, et un hanaper, et un ewer d'or ove deux saphirs en le sommet, & mill' livres d'argent en cas qe le ne soit pas notre heir.

Item nous devisons a Symond Suddebury, ercevesq' de Canterbirs, une coupe ove le covercle et ove une tripere [l] ovesqe deux lions d'argent susorrez et enamaillez.

Item nous devisons a William Courteney, evesq' de Loundres, une coupe de berill ove un long pie d'argent susorrez & ennamaillez pur le corps notre Seigneur.

Item nous devisons a friere John Gilbert, evesq' de Hereford, un plate d'argent pour espices & ennamaillez ove les armes de Mortimer en la founce [m], et un anel ove quatre rubies & un diamant en mylieu.

Item nous devisons a notre treschier friere Monf'r Henri Counte de Northumbr' [n] un hanaper de tortelez [o] ove une estelle [p] en le founce & un nouche ovesq' un ource.

[f] wife of Henry Hotspur.
[g] Wife of John Hastings, earl of Pembroke, Richard earl of Arundel, and John lord St. John.
[h] With stones. Dugdale, not understanding it, leaves a blank.
[i] of Alexandria.
[l] tripod. [m] bottom.
[n] Father of Henry Hotspur, who married this earl's daughter.
[o] Wreathed work. Dugdale translates it *of a tortois*. Bar. I. 150.
[p] *estoile*, star.

Item nous devisons a notre fitz Monſ'r Henry Percy un petite nouche en manere le corps de cerf & teſte d'egle.

Item nous devisons a Monſ'r Richard Leſcrop' un hanap' d'argent fuſoriez plat.

Item nous devisons a Monſ'r Joh' Lovell un coupe ove le covercle d'un piere d'ynde ⁱ.

Item nous devisons a Sire John de Biſhopeſton un anel d'or ove un rubie engravez q'eſt ſignet, & un bacyn & un ewer d'argent. Item nous devisons a Thomas notre friere cent livres.

Item nous devisons a Sire William Forde ſys eſquelles, & ſys ſaucers d'argent, et un tablet d'argent fuſorrez et ennamaillez de la geſnie ʳ n're dame.

Item nous devisons a Sire Waut' de Colmpton un bacyn et un ewer d'argent, et vynt marcs.

Nous devisons a Sire John de Briddlewode un hanap d'argent appellez Waſſaill ˢ.

Item nous devisons a Sire John de Kepſton vynt marcs.

Item nous devisons a Sire John Pers vynt marcs.

Item nous devisons a Monſ'r Pers de la Mare ſys eſquelles & ſys ſaucers d'argent.

Item nous devisons a Sire Hugh de Boraſton un tablet ove les ymages de Seint John et Seynt Kateryne par dehors, et dys livres.

ⁱ blue.

ʳ *geſine* is l'etat d'une femme en couche; *geſſine*, le ceremonie et le feſtin des relevailles; &*jhazen*, une nouvelle accouchée. Laccombe. Q. the labour or the purification of our Lady.

ˢ Waſſel or Grace-cup. A corrupt pronunciation of *wacs hael*, be of health. See the notes to Dodſley's Old Plays, 1779, vol. VI. p. 437. vol. X. p. 280.

Item nous volons qe nos ancienz servauntz miegnals[t] de notre hostell, les queux nous n'avons point reguerdonez [u], eient chescun d'eaux cent soulez [x], et chescun vadlet [y] cynk marcs, et chescun garceoun deux marcs.

It'm nous volons qe de touz nous autres biens qe remeindront apres nos dettez acquitez et ceste notre devys perfourmez, qe nos executours eut ordenent en autres oevres de charitee a faires deinz la terre d'Engleterre solonc ceo qe lour semblera meulz affaire. Et a ceste notre testament executier et perfourmer nous ordenons les tres reverendes piers en Dieu, William Courteney evesq' de Loundres, et friere John Gilbert evesq' de Hereford, Monsr Henry counte de Northumbr', Monsr Piers de la Mare, Sire Wautier de Colmpton, Sire John de Briddewode, Sire John de Kepston, et Sire John Piers nos executours. Presents notre filz Henry Percy, Meystr' John de Colton, dean D'evelyn [z], Monsr Hugh Chene chevalier, Thomas n're friere, Henry de Cornewaill esquires, et Sire William Stutevyle chapellein qi l'escript. Et volons qe cest notre devys soit survewe par notre tres reverend piere en Dieu Symond Sudbury ercevesq' de Cantirbirs, ma tres honourez Dame et Meere, et Monsr Richard Lescrop. Escript a Dynebegh les jour et an susditz.

Probatio dicti Testamenti coram Willielmo Courteney, Cant' Archiep'; 22 die Januar' 1382.

[t] menial.  [u] rewarded.  [x] *solz* or *souz*, pence.
[y] valet.   [z] Dublin.

Regist.

Regist. Courteney, fol. 188. a. b. fol. 189. a. b. in the Archiepiscopal Registry at Lambeth.

Edmund, son of the preceding lady by Roger de Mortimer, earl of March, was born at Langenith, 1351, 25 E. III. and succeeded on his father's death to his titles and estate. He was lord lieutenant of Ireland three years, and died [a] at Cork, 1381, in his 29th year, and was buried with his wife at Wigmore abbey, to which he had been a great benefactor, and had procured for it the privilege of the mitre. He married Philippa, daughter of Lionel duke of Clarence by Elizabeth, daughter and heir of William de Burgh, earl of Ulster, by whom he had two sons, Roger born at Usk, 1361, and Edmund born 1374 [b], and two daughters, Elizabeth born at Ludlow 1375, married to Henry Percy, surnamed Hotspur, and Philippa, born at Ludlow 1376, wife of John Hastings, earl of Pembroke [c]; Richard earl of Arundel, and John lord St. John. Dugd. I. 148. 150. Dugdale gives him only one brother Roger who died in his father's lifetime; but by this will, p. 115. he should seem to have had another, *Thomas*.

[a] *vertitur in non esse*, says the History of Wigmore abbey, in Mon. Ang. II. 227.
[b] See note *d*, in p. 113.
[c] This first marriage not mentioned in the History of Wigmore.

THOMAS

## THOMAS EARL OF KENT.

IN the name of God, Amen. In the day of the refurrection of our Lord J'hu Crift, the yer of hym a thoufand thre hondred four fcore and feventene. I Thomas of Holand, erl of Kent and lord Wake, beyng in hol memorie, ordeyne and make my teftament in this wife. Firft, I yeve and bytake my foule to our Lord J'hu Crift, and to hys mercy, and to the help and grace of our Lady, his blisfol moder, and the help of alle feyntes of hevene, and my body to be buried as fone as hit goodlich may, in the abbeye of Brune[a]. And I yeve and devyfe to [b] Alys my wif, and Thomas my fone, al my catayl and godes moebles, praying my wyf for al the love and truft that hath ben bytwyn us, and alfo praying and chargying my fone, upon my bleffying, that they by good love and on affent governe hem in fwych wyfe, that at hur power my dettes mowe be quyted, and my old fervantes iholpe yn defcharge of me. And to execute my will and devys aforefayd, I ordeyne and make my wyf and fone aforefayd myn executours.

[a] Brune or Bourn in Lincolnfhire.
[b] Alys his wife was daughter of Richard Fitz Alan earl of Arundel, whom he married 38 E. III. Sandford, p. 216. Dugdale, Bar. I. 75.

Probatio dicti Teſtamenti coram Thom' Arundell', Cantuar' archiep', 10 die Maij, Anno Domini 1397, apud Lambeth.

Regiſter Arundell, pars prima fol. 157. a. in the Archiepiſcopal Regiſtry at Lambeth.

Thomas, ſon of Thomas Holand earl of Kent and Lord Wake of Lydel, and Joan who afterwards married the Black Prince, was born 1350, being 10 years old at his father's death 1360. He was marſhal of England, 3 R. II. which office was taken from him ſix years after, and he was appointed Conſtable of the Tower of London, and governor of Cariſbrook-caſtle, 4 Julii, 20 R. II. He died in the year 1397, leaving Thomas his eldeſt ſon, Edmund, and five daughters. Sandford, p. 216. Dugdalé, Bar. I. 75.

RICHARD

## RICHARD EARL OF ARUNDEL.

EN noun du Piere, du Fitz, et de Seint Eſpirit, Amen. Jeo Richard counte d'Arundel et de Surr', le quart jour de Mars, l'an del incarnation noſtre Seignour J'hu Criſt mill. ccc quatre vintz et douſze, et l'an du regne le Roy Richard Seconde ſeſzime, en moun chaſtel Philipp en bone et ſeine memorie face mon teſtament en la manere q'enſuyt, ceſt aſſavoir.

Primerement jeo deviſe m'alme a lui tou puiſſant Trinite, moun corps d'eſtre enterres en la priorie de Lewes en un lieu derere haute autier, la quele j'ai monſtre a mes treſchiers en dieux Danz Johan Chierlieu[a] priour illoeqes et frere Thomas Aſſhebourne mon confeſſour. Et en cas qe ma treſchiere compaigne E [b], qe Dieux aſſoile, ne ſoit en ma[c] enterrez et ſevelez en le lieu par moy ency monſtrez jeo veule et charge mes executours qe toſt apres mon deces ma dite compaigne ſoit remoeve hors de la ſepulture ou q'ele eſt a preſent tanq' le dit lieu et ceo ſoit fait devant ma ſepulture en toutes maneres, et veule et charge mes executours qe ma herce ſoit fait maes[d] de cynk cierges bien grandes ove les mortiers en manere come fuiſt entour le corps de mon treſhonure Seignour et piere, qi Dieux aſſoile, auxi pres come home purra reſembler cel herce jeo vuile et ordeigne qe ce ſoit fait. Et auxi je charge mes execu-

[a] John de Cariloco who occurs prior, 1364 and 1377. Willis.
[b] Eleanor, daughter of Henry duke of Lancaſter, his ſecond wife.
[c] Sic Orig.
[d] *mais*, pas, excepté, plus, dès que. Lacombe. *but, only.*

tours

tours q'en quel lieu d'Engleterre qe je trefpace de ceft fecle, qe tantoft apres mon corps foit fi privement menez come home purra tanq' a la dite priorie: Et ne vuile en nulle manere qe nulles genz armez, chivalx, herce, n'autre qe je n'ay devife pardevant, ne nul autre bobaunce [b], foient faitz entour moy, forfq' foulement come avant eft dit. Et fi enfy foit qe je trefpace de ceft fiecle en terre eftrange hors d'Engletere, jeo vuile, fi mon corps ne purra refonablement eftre cariez au dit priorie, q'adonqes je foy enterres ou qe mes executours ou ceux qi font entour moy au jour de ma moriant en terre eftrange de jent [c] qe foit melx [d] al honour de Dieux et efportable [e] pur m'alme, en lieu covenable et a pluis pres qe home purra a la place qe jeo trefpafferay. Item jeo devife pur les defpenfes affaire entour mon enterrement atant [f] d'argent come mes executours verront qe foit pluis a l'onour de Dieux et profit pur moy et m'alme, fique qe nul voie ceo ne paffe mye mill marcs, ove la monoie qe ferra donez pur m'alme jour de mon dit enterrement, et ove le herce, et toutes autres defpenfes et coftages qe forrount faitz illoeqes pur moy au dit jour. Item je devife et ordeine touz mes laynes [g] et touz mes autres chateux et eftoor [h] vif et mort, et touz mes veffelements et apparailles d'or, d'argent, et ennorez [i], forfprifez les ornementz pur la chapel queux j'ai done et deliverez a la

[b] extravagance, fee before, p. 84.
[c] *de gent eftrange*, of ftrange people.   [d] *mieux*.
[e] q. *efploitable*, profitable, as p. 126.   [f] *autant*, fo much.
[g] q. wool.   [h] chattels and ftore.
[i] gilded; as *furzorrez* in preceding wills.

college

collegé d'Arundell en ma vie, et auxi devife come piert [k] par mon teftament a demorer en la dite college perpetuelment, d'eftre venduz par mes executours attantz [1] come ent befoigne pur acquiter tout le dette qe je doy a mon trefhonure feignur et piere qi Dieux affoille; primerement ceo qe ne foit mye parfournez de foun devys per le teftament en efpecial: et auxi de faire paiementz de mes propres dettes a tous yceux qe mes ditz executours purront avoir verray conufaunce qe je fuy par afcune voie en dette, et ceo fi toft come ils purront apres mon deces en defcharge de l'alme mon dit trefhonure feignour et piere et de la meen et de ma confcience e . . . . . celuy qe je fuy fi grandement tenuz. Item coment qe mon dit trefhonure feignour et piere en fa vie ordeina en la chapel deinz la chaftel d'Arundell un chaunterie de fiz chapelleyns et trois clercz a fupport certein charge, quele chaunterie devant fa moriant ne fuift mye par luy emplyz, perount [m] en fa vie il moy chargea efpecialment par foun dit teftament, a pluiftoft qe je purroi del parfaire perpetuelment a durer, du quele ordenaunce depuis vewe et avys par difcrecioun des fages pur diverfes objeccions et periles par l'ordinaunce du dite chaunterie en la dite chapelle qe purroient avenu en areriffement [n] d'icell, peront [m] il ne la purroit feurrement eftre eftablez, et furceo confiderez la defolacie de l'efglife parochiele d'Arundel de divine fervice qe par cynk moygnes

---

[k] appears.    [1] for as much.    [n] wherefore. K. whereby.
[a] backwarding, hinderance.

aliens

aliens foloit eftre ferviz, et retrettz° a caufe de le guerre, fiq' mefme l'efglife efteroit come defolacie et anyntiz ᵖ, et l'almoigne qe l'ay fuift de divine fervice relever, pur encres de devocioun de le people, honour a feinte efglife, et merit pur les almes pur queux ceo ferroit foundez, et nomement a l'alme de mon trefhonure feignur et piere, principal caufe de celle fundacion du college; Jeo ordeigna les avantditz fiz chapelleinz en la dite efglife, et addy a ycell autres cynk chappeleinz feculers en lieu de cynk moygnes qe la foloient eftre, et enoutre de devocioun deux autres chapelleins de perfourmer la noumbre de trefze, ou troiz deknes, troiz fubdeknes, deux accolitz, fept quorifters, et deux facriftes, ove troiz vadletz, et deux garceons pur eux fervir, enfy deftier illoqes fur la fondacioun et la volunte mon dit trefhonure feignur & piere un perpetuel college de trefze chapelleins, dount un nome eft meiftre, et quinze clercz come dit eft fundiz en l'onur del tout puiffant Trinite, et pur l'alme mon dit trefhonure feignour & piere, de fupport foun charge, et prier pur l'alme de ma trefhonure dame et miere, pur moy, ma trefchiere compaigue, qe Dieux affoile, noz enfantz, allies, fucceffours, et autres limitez en leur fundacioun et ordinaunces, pur touz jours; le quele college j'ay en partie endowe de poffeffiouns efpirituelx et temporelx. Et de le remanaunt de pleyne endowement du dit college fur mes ordennances et charges en ycelles doune ᑫ, le meiftre et chapelleins ne foient feurs jour de ma mo-

° *withdrawn.*   ᵖ *aneantie.*   ᑫ *donnez.*

riant,

riant, jeo vuile qe mefme le meiftre et chapelleins et lour fucceffours, preignent la fumme annuelment de mes manours de Angermyng[r], Wepham[s], Warnecamp[t], Soucftoke[u], Tottyngton[x], Upmerdon[y] & Pyperyng[z], del annuel rente qe je lour ay done en les ditz manoirs par licence noftre Seignur le Roy, tanq' per mes heirs ou executours terres ou efglifes nient charges foient donez et appropiez a eux et a lour fucceffours a touz jours, a plein et cler value de la quantite du dit endowement aderere[a]. Item coment qe mon dit trefhonure feignure et piere, qi Dieux affoille, devifa a moy par foun teftament certains veffelmentz, joialx, et livres a demurrer la greindre partie perpetuelment en la chapel deinz le chaftel d'Arundell, pur la chaunterie illeoqes par luy purpofe, la quele depuis qe ele eft chaunge en l'efglife parochiele, par certeins caufes avant declarez, pur le meulx perpetuelment adurer, pur greindre meryt a l'alme mon dit trefhonure feignur et piere, qi Dieux affoille; Jeo vuille et ordeigne qe mefmes les veffelmentz, joialx, livres, et autres ornamentz pur la chapel, queux j'ai deliverez au dit college en ma vie, foient appurtenantz et demurrantz au dit college pur tous jours, fi bien come ceux qe

[r] Angmeryng E. for which he obtained a weekly market and fair from R. II. Dugd. I. 318.
[s] Wepham in Arundel rape, as the foregoing.
[t] quære, *Warnham* in Bramber rape.
[u] q. Southwick in the fame rape.
[x] Tottington. There is a place of this name both in Arundel and Bramber rape.
[y] Upper Merden in Chichefter rape.
[z] Peppering in Arundel rape.
[a] *aderè*, tout du fuite, Lacombe; *in arrear*.

j'ai

## RICHARD EARL OF ARUNDEL.

J'ai ordeine et devife par ceft mon teftament et volunte, lefqueux je vuile q'ils foient deliverez bientoft apres ma moriant au dit college, illoeqes a demurrer perpetuelement. Et outre par efpecial je vuile qe le dit college eit deliverance des autres draps et veftimentz pur la chapel, de drap blanc, de foy embroudez et batuz ove [b] M. d'or, fi bien la meyndre veftement come le greindre, ove tout l'apparail d'icell', les queux j'avoie de doun ma miere de Norff[c]. Et auxi pur ceo qe ma trefamee compaigne moy dona a noftre marriage un veftiment de rouge drap d'or ove l'autier et tout l'apparail icell, laquele je vuile qe ma dite compaigne eit le dit veftiment quel ele moy enfi dona a terme de fa vie, fi

---

[b] Sic Orig.

[c] This expreffion (which at firft view feems irreconcileable with what Dugdale, I. 320. and Vincent, p. 26, fay, that this earl's mother was Eleanor daughter of Henry Plantagenet earl of Lancafter) is fatisfactorily cleared up by the following obfervations of a judicious friend:

"It is yet a cuftom in the North for parents, whofe children intermarry to call brothers and fifters; Richard earl of Arundel, upon this principle, calling Elizabeth lady Mowbray his fifter, of courfe Margaret dutchefs of Norfolk would be his mother, and he might have the vanity to call her fo, as being a woman of high rank and fortune. See the following pedigree.

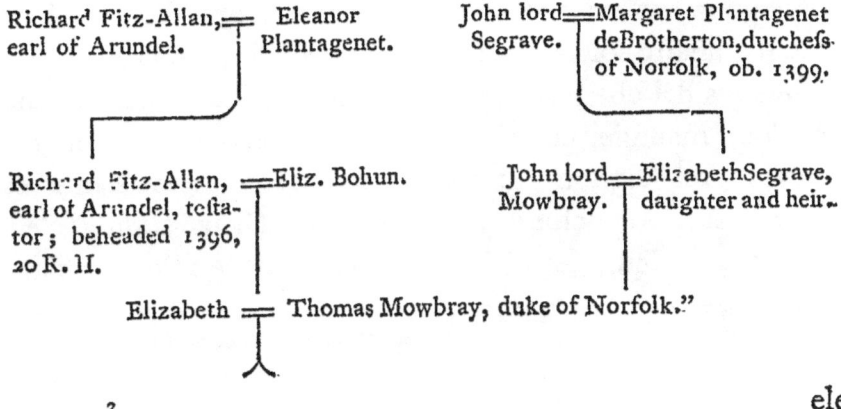

ele

ele defire grandement de l'avoir, ele empriaunt qe ele vorroit la leffer a dit college, en remembrance de ele, fi bien come de moy, quant ele verra temps, et ove l'eide noftre feignour tout puiffant, tout foit il jammes fait uncore ne ferra le dit college qe bien poy le pluis povre. Item je vuile et charge fermement mes ditz executours, q'en nulle manere ils ne ferrount livere a nully de la dette, en partie ne en tout, ne de nulle autre chofe qe je doy a mon dit trefhonure piere, qi Dieux affoile; maes qe mes ditz executours parfacent la volunte mon dit trefhonure Seignur et piere ovefq' fes executours, folonq le purport de fon teftament, de ceo qe ent ferra aderere jour de ma moriaunt nient parfourmez, come en un remembraunce qe j'ai leffe enclofe deinz ceft mon teftament appiert; et qe celles chofes foient mys en execucioun et parfaitz auxi en hafte come home purra et favera apres mon deces, et come temps refonable le dorra[d] apres qe je foy a Dieu comaundez. Item jeo devife et ordeine quatre centz marcs d'eftre par mes ditz executours emploiez en un parpetuelle memorial ordeignez en ma meafoun de Lewes, come ils verroient meulx affaire folom lour bone difcrecioun, come en eide et encres del chanfure[e] pur les moignes, et en amendament de lour maunger et boire jours d'anniverfairs de mon dit trefhonure feignour et piere, ma trefhonuree dame et miere, et ma trefchiere compaigne, qe Dieux affoill; c'eft affavoir, chefcun des ditz jours une quantite folom l'affair-

[c] praying or requefting her to leave the fame to the faid colleges.
[d] fhall give.     [e] q. fong-money, or allowance for finging maffes.

ment

ment ᶠ qe la dite fumme vorra a ces annuelment extendre, pur prier pur les almes avantditz, pur moy, et mes enfauntz. Et qe le priour illocqes qi ferra pur le temps, et fes fuccef-fours priours du dite meafoun, a lour primere entree paren-tre ᵍ lour autres charges, foient primement jurez a garder et faire cel charge folom mon dit devys, et pur difpofer la dite fume annuelment par tiele mannere come je l'ai avaunt devifez: fi mes ditz executours verount qe cefte ordi-nance ne purra eftre parfournez, adonqes je vuile bien qe la dite fomme foit difpofe folom l'ordinaunce de mes ditz executours, iffynt qe toutes maneres de la dite fome foit exploitez en encres et enefpecial a perpetuelment aprier pur les almes pur queux je fuy tenuz a prier, pur moy et touz criftienz. Item je donne et devife cent livres a l'efglife cathedral de Ciceftre, d'eftre difpofez apres mon deces par mes ditz executours folonc lour difcrecioun come ils verrount pluis honourable a Dieux, et efploitable ʰ a mefme l'efglife en remembraunce de moy; et a l'abbey de Hamound ⁱ, par mefme la manere cent marcs, iffint q'il foit veu par mes ditz executours qe les ditz fomes foient ex-ploitez ᵏ en afcune chofe come foit en l'onour de Dieux et amendement des ditz meifouns: fy ceo ne poet eftre par-petuel, qar ˡ je averoie meulx qe ceo ferroit parpetuelment adurer, qe autrement fy ceo purra bien eftre coment qe ceo ferroit bien poy ᵐ de tielx fommes. Item jeo charge mes

ᶠ proportion, or what it will make.  ᵍ q. among.
ʰ profitable, from *efploiter*, profiter. L.
ⁱ Haghmon abbey in Shropfhire, founded for Auftin canons, 1110, by William Fitz Alan of Clun, anceftor of the teftator.
ᵏ expended.   ˡ *car*, for. L.   ᵐ very near. K.

executours q'ils facent gree et satisfaccion as touz yceux qi soy veulent compleindre d'ascun grief ou mesprison q'a lour ay pluis ou meyns fait, dount ils purrount avoir evident prove ou verraie conusaunce, solom ceo qe mes biens vuillent a ceo extendre en descharge de m'alme, sitost come y purra estre fait apres mon deces. Et nomement al abbe et covent de Fyscamp pur le purchace del manoir de Bury[n], par ticle manere qe soit resonablement greable a eux, en descharge de l'alme mon treshonure seignour et piere, qi Deux assoile, et de la mien, si jeo ne le face en ma vie. Item je devise a ma treschiere compaigne Philippe le lit bleu de l'overaigne de tapiterye de mes armes, et de les armes ma dite compaigne departiz en ycelle. Item un lit rouge et bleu pale, q'estoit pur la nief. Item un lit noir de soy, ov tout l'apparaille de les trois lits avantditz, ensemblement ove touz les autres litz q'ele avoit de ses propres quant ele fuist mariez a moy. Item le grand sale[o] q'estoit darreynement[p] fait a Loundres del overaigne de tapeterye blew, ove roses rouges en ycell, et mes armes et les armes des mes fitz, le Counte Marschal, le Seignure de Charletoun, et Mons'r William Beauchamp[q]. Item jeo devise qe ma dite compaigne Philippe eit pur sa chapel tout l'apparail pur la chapel q'estoit trusse[r] ove moy, et la meindre petit autier

[n] Bury in Arundel rape, Sussex.
[o] furniture or hangings of the hall.       [p] lately.
[q] Thomas lord Moubray was the second husband of his eldest daughter Elizabeth. John Charleton lord Powis married Alice his youngest, and William Beauchamp lord Bergavenny, Joan his second daughter.
[r] found. K. sed q.

de

## RICHARD EARL OF ARUNDEL.

de drap de ſoy noir, ove l'apparail d'icel. Item je deviſe qe ma dite compaigne Philippe eit pur le botellerye et celer deux pottes d'argent, cheſcun contenaunt un potel, 11 hanappes d'argent enorrez, outre ſa propre hanap appelle Bealchier, un dozen de peces d'argent, un dozein de quilers d'argent, les deux ſalers d'argent enorrez, queux ma dite compaigne moy dona a moun aun doun[s] a chaſtel Philipp, et deux autrez meindres ſalers d'argent, l'un ove coverture et l'autre ſans coverer. Item deux chaundelers d'argent pur ſoper[t] en yverne[u], ove haut pees, et mees eſchochouns pendantz ove trois quartres ſur meſmes les chandelers et les ſuages[x] enbataillez et enorrez. Item pur l'ewerye un paire baſyns d'argent ennorrez de mes armes, deux baſſyns, deux ewers ſengles d'argent, et un paire baſſyns, deſquex ele eſt acuſtume a laver devant maunge et ſoper. Item pur la cuſyne trois dozeins des eſquelx, deux dozeins des ſaucers, et quatre chargeours tout d'argent. Item jeo deviſe qe l'apparail pur le teſte des dames, ſibien de perlees come d'autre attyre, quele j'ai liveree a ma treſame compaigne en ma vie, qele l'eit en ſa volunte durant ſi vie, et apres la deces de le, qe le dit attyre ſoit preſtement departiz entre mes fitz Richard et Thomas[y], a

---

[s] my new year's gift.
[t] for ſupper: this word is not in the gloſſaries.
[u] in winter.     [x] q. *ſervages*, ſervices. L.
[y] Richard died young in his father's life without iſſue: Thomas ſucceeded his father; and 6 Hen. IV. married Beatrix natural daughter of the king of Portugal. Dugd. Bar. I. 320. Richard ſeems to have been *eldeſt* ſon, though not noticed as ſuch by Dugdale or Vincent. He is always named firſt in this will, and in p. 131. is called his *heir*, by way of eminence.

cause q'ils fount femblables d'avoir femmes, fi Dieu lour graunte la vie, s'ils ne foient mariez devant mon deces; et auxi qe ma file de Charletoun en eit fa part owelment[z] departiz entre mes ditz deux fitz et ele, fans afcune autre departefoun affaire du dit attyre, fynoun en manere come avant eſt dit; affiauntz pleynement en ma dite compaigne, qi fi ele foy feute[a] d'avoir autre marry, q'ele vuille et ordeyn par tiel manere et fy feurement, qe la ditte attyre ne foit ouſtez[b] de mes avantditz enfantz. Item je vuile et ordeine qe fa ma dite compaigne eit tiel iffue par moy come avaunt eſt dit, et q'ele parfourne les condicions fibien de ele come dez ditz enfantz foit il mal ou femmel, q'adonques touz les devifez et ordinaunces faitz adevant fibien a ele come a lez ditz enfantz foient tenuz et parfournez. Et fi ma dite compaigne ait tiel confeil, ou ne voet parfournir les ditz condiciouns, qe touz les chofes a ele et au dit enfant foit il mal ou femall paramont devifez foient reſtreintz, et qe ele, ne le dit enfaunt, n'eit nulle chofe de moun dit devys, finoun la chapel qe je avoie ovefq' ele, enfemblement ove lez litz, excepte la chapel, lit, et fale que je avoie de doun ma honure miere de Norfolk al marriage de ma dite compaigne quele j'ai devife en autre lieu. Item je devife a mon fitz Richard moun chapel ove tout apparail de drap velwet rouge ove angeles et archanngeles de enbroudez fur ycell, et auxi un veſtment fengle de drap rouge de foy ove blancs rofes fur ycell. Item je devife a mon dit fitz

[z] equally.
[a] q. *feure*, fure; or perhaps *fente*, if ſhe ſhould be *inclined* to marry again.
[b] *oſtes*, taken from.

mon

mon grand lit ove l'entier apparaille pur la chambre blanc
et blew, et auxi un rouge lit eſtandard ᶜ appelle Clove, et
auxi le lit de ſoy ove demy ceel, enbroudez ove les armes
d'Aroundell et Garreine, ove touz les apparall des ditz litz.
Item a mon dit fitz la grand ſale des armes d'Arundell et
Garreine quartelez, et un dorcer de arras. Item dorcer
d'arras qu'eſt acuſtume d'eſtre pur la chambre pane a
Arondell. Item je deviſe a mon dit fitz Richard de veſ-
ſelment, ſibien en la chapel, except ceo qe j'ai ordeine pur
le college d'Arundell, en cheſcun office pur l'hoſtel ᵈ, come et
ſolom ceo qe mes executours verrount qe mes biens ſoy
extenderount en paiement de les dettes de mon treſhonure
ſeignur et piere qi Dieux aſſoill, ſibien come de ma dette
propre; et a cauſe qil eſt mon heir, je vuile q'il ait pluis de
dit veſſel qe acun de mes fitz ou files, les condicions avantdites exceptes. Item je vuile qe mon treſchier fitz Thomas
eit del jour de ma moriaunt enavant c li. annuelment de
mes ditz executours en eide de ſa ſuſtenaunce, tanque les
manoirs de Begenever ᵉ, Sullyngton ᶠ et Schapewyk ᵍ a luy
ſoient donez et eſcheiez ʰ par ceux qe les ount en demeſne,
et en reverſioun a luy et a ſes heirs malles de ſon corps
engendriez, et pur defaute de tiel iſſue malle la remeindre
d'icel a mes droitz heirs ſeignures d'Arundell as touz jours.
Purvew totefoitz quant aſcun des ditz manoirs luy ſoit donez

ᶜ q. a *ſtanding* bed, or one whoſe teſter reſted on pillars.
ᵈ houſe.   ᵉ q. *Bignor*, in Arundel rape.
ᶠ q. Sulton in Arundel rape.   ᵍ q. Shapwick, co. Somerſet.
ʰ *eſchus*, eſcheated.

ou efcheiez en manere avantdit, iffint qe mon dit fitz Thomas purra prendre les profitz qe a cel temps luy foit rebatuz[j] de fon dit paiement annuel de cent livres ataunt come le dit manoir ency a luy done foit refonablement de value. Et quant il eit en mains des ditz manoirs a la fomme de centz livres annuelz avantditz, q'adonqes l'entier paiement de mefme la fomme par mes executours foit outrement defcharge pur touz jours; et en defaute qe les ditz manoirs ne vaillent tanqe a la dite fomme, je vuile qe mes executours et feoffez le perfournent a la dite fomme de c liv' come avant eft dit. Et outre vuile qe fi mon chatell fon voet extendre outre les dettes mon feignure et piere, qi Dieux affoile, fibien come mes dettes, qe mon dit fitz Thomas ait deux centz livres de monoie d'eftre difpofe par mez ditz executours a fon meillour oeps. Item je devife a mon fitz Thomas un veftiment fengle de foy diaprez de blanc, qe feuft fait a mefme le temps qe le darrein autier de rofes eftoit fait. Item mon lit blew de foy eftandard enbroudez ove griffons, ove entier feele[k], et auxi le lit rouge et blew de fatyn de dymy feele ove touz les apparailles d'icell. Item a mon dit fitz un petit dofer de arras enbroudez dor en certeins lieux d'icell, quele Monfieur William Brian moy donna. Item un grande fale blanc et rouge enbroudez ove babewynes[l] ove mes armes en myelieu de les bordures et en les bittiz[m] qu'eftoit acuftume d'eftre a Reygate; et de veffel

---

[j] abated.  [k] whole tefter diftinguifhed from half tefter.
[l] Lacombe explains *babeines, levres* de certains animaux. q. faces or heads.  [m]

d'argent

## RICHARD EARL OF ARUNDEL. 133

d'argent de chefcun office pour l'ouftell[n] folom ceo qe femble a mes executours, toufdiz eiantz confideracioun a mes dettes et devifes fuifdits. Item je devife a ma trefchiere file de Charleton un petit tablet d'or enamaillez de deux foilles, ove un ymage de la incarnacioun[o] de notre dame dedeins. Item je devife a ma file Elizabeth un nouche ove de lyouns et corouns qe moy fuift done par mon trefchier fitz foun marry, et a ma file une nouche a foer[p] de rofe ove perlees. Item je devife qe ma file de Charleton ait mon lit de foy rouge ov entier feele, qu'eft acuftume d'eftre a Reigate, ove tout l'apparaill d'icell. Item je devife a ma file Marefchal[q] mon lit de arras, ove touts les tapits qe j'avoie a la fefaunce[r] d'iceftes fait en mefme la pais[s], except les trois doffers de arras qe j'ay devife en autre lieu. Item je devife a ma file Margarete moun lit blew qu'eftoit acuftume d'eftre a Loundres, ove tout l'apparaill d'icell. Item je vuille et devife qe ma trefchiere file Margarete eit annuelment de mes executours pur fa fuftenaunce centz marcs, tanq' ele foit refonablement mariee[t], en eide de fa quele marriage jeo luy donne et devife mille marcs en efpecial, d'eftre auxi paiez par mes executours en meilloure manere qils purrount ou faverount, fy ma dite file ne foit mariez en ma vie. Et vuile outre qe mes ditz executours en ceo q'ils averount de quoy

[n] Maifon. L. houfhold.
[o] A picture of the incarnation of the Virgin Mary. [p] *al foer*, like. K.
[q] Elizabeth, firft married to William earl of Salifbury; fecondly to Thomas lord Mowbray earl Marfhal. Dugdale I. 318.
[r] q. at the making of thefe.
[s] q. in Flanders where the arras was made.
[t] She was afterwards married to Sir Rowland Lenthall, knt.

outre

outre mes charges et dettes, encreſſent la dite ſomme pur ſa mariage a un reſonable quantite, s'ils le veient profitable a faire pur avauncement de l'eſtat de ma dite file, ſolom lour bone deſcretioun, ſiq' la ſomme entier ne paſſe mye en nulle mannere mille et cynk centz marcs a pluis haut. Item je deviſe a mon treſchiere et honure frere l'erceveſque d'Everwyk[u] mon coupe enorrez et enamaillez ove le cerf ſur le covercle, en remembraunce de moy & de m'alme. Item je deviſe a ma treſchiere ſoer de Hereford[x] mon coupe ove coers[y], et a ma treſchiere ſoer de Kent[z] mon coupe de troisfoilles, c'eſt aſſavoir, ſi mes dits ſoers ſoient naturelx[a] et tielx come ils deveroient de reaſon en eide et par-fourniſſement de ceſt mon teſtament, et autrement ils n'eient nient de moun devys avauntdit. Item je deviſe a ma miere de Norffolk un crois d'or en un cas rouge de quyre[b], et auxi a ma dite miere, un Agnus Dei d'or enamaille et en un coſte ſa coronacioun[c] et l'autre ſeint Fraunceys ove xvii perles, en remembraunce de moy et de m'alme. Item je deviſe et ordeine a ma honure dame et niece de Glouceſ-tre[d] en remembraunce de moy, et qe ele vuile eſtre bien-voillant a mes ditz executours, un petit tablet d'or de troisfoilles, ove un crucifix dedeins, et la coronacioun[c] en la

[u] Thomas Arundel, biſhop of Ely 1374, tranſlated to York 1388, to Canterbury 1396, Chancellor of England, died 1414. Godwin.
[x] Joan, wife of Humphrey de Bohun, earl of Hereford.
[y] hearts. K. Dugdale tranſlates it *cover*.
[z] Alice, eldeſt ſiſter, married to Thomas Holland earl of Kent.
[a] kind.   [b] *cuir*, leather. K.   [c]
[d] Eleanor daughter of his ſiſter Joan counteſs of Hereford, and married to Thomas of Woodſtock duke of Gloceſter.

ſummite,

summite, et enamaillez dehors. Item je devise a la measoun de Robertesbrugge [e] en eide de supportacioun de lour wallyng encountre le mer [f] xx li. Item je devise et ordeine qe les measouns des freres religeous, especialment Aroundell, et auxi Lewes, Cicestre, Wyncester, Canterbirs, Guldeford, et Loundres, soient regardez par l'avys de mes executours come ils soient tenuz de prier pur les almes mon tres honure seignure et piere, ma tres honure dame et miere, ma tres chiere compaigne qi Dieux pur sa grande mercie et passioun q'il suffrit pur eux et pur tous cristiens, eit mercy de eux trois, et de nous touz quant nous trespassoms hors de cest siecle; Amen. Item je devise les condicions susdites a plein parfourner a la measoun d'Ely [g] en eide de la fesure de la novelle haute autier illoeqes xvi li. xiii s. iiii d. Item, en mesme la condicioun, a la measoun de Westmonstre des moignes xl li. Item en semblable manere je vuille et ordeine qe chescun des measouns, de Cantirbirs [h] pur Seint Thomas, Seint Edmundesbury, Seint Johan de Beverley, ait xl li. Item je vuile et charge mes executors qe chescun servant qi m'a serviz soit regarde pur soun travaille solom le service qe m'a fait, et le temps q'il m'a serviz, toutditz considerez les grandes feez [i] q'ascuns ount de moy et autres avantages. Et je charge auxi mes

[e] Robertsbridge a Cistertian abbey in Sussex, founded 1176.
[f] Their sea walls.
[g] The Benedictine priory at Ely.
[h] This is to be read with a comma after *measouns*, meaning three several religious houses; at Canterbury, St. Edmundsbury, and Beverley. The first dedicated to St. Thomas, and the last to St. John.
[i] fees, wages.

executours ſi avaunt[k] come je puiſſe, et come ils vuillent re-
ſpoundre devaunt Dieux, q'ils ordeynent par tiel manere pur
mes ditz ſervantz qe tote manere bone conſcience ſoit garde,
eiauntz conſideracioun a les deviſes et voluntees de mon dit
tres honure ſeigneur et piere, qi Dieux aſſoile, nient parfour-
niz, leſqueux je charge fermement mes ditz executours
bien et duement garder et parfournir en touz pointz. Item
je deviſe et ordeigne pur mes ditz executours bien et duement garder et parfournir en touz pointz. Item je deviſe
et ordeyne pur mes ſervantz en manere come eſt ſpecifiez
pluis au plein en l'article prochein precedent. Item je vuile
et charge mes executours, come ils vuillent reſpounder devant
Dieu, qi s'ils veient qe mes biens ne vuillent extendre de
parfourner mes voluntees ſuiſditz, q'adonqes q'ils facent mon
enterrement auxi leger[1] come ils purrount reſonablement.
Item je vuille et ordeyne qe les meaſouns de religiouſes en
le counte de Salop[m] ſoient par tiele manere regardez q'ils
ſoient tenuz a prier pur les almes mon treshonure ſeignure
et piere, ma treshonure dame et miere, ma treſchiere compaigne, qe Dieux pur ſa grande pite eit mercy de lour almes,
et pur moy, mes heirs, et pur touz criſtiens. Item jeo
vuile et ordeyne qe les ordres queux j'ai de mon grande
conuſſaunce et autres meaſouns ſoient regardez ſolom la
bone et ſage diſcrecioun de mes executours; et qe mes
biens ſoy vuillent extendre, toutdiz eiaunts conſideracioun

[k] ſo far as.      [1] as ſlightly.
[m] The Fitz Alan family founded in Shropſhire Haghmon abbey and Wombridge priory. Tan. Nat. Mon. 448. 449.

a mes excepciouns fufdites. Item je donne et devife a frere Thomas Afshebourne mon confeffour, d'avoir m'alme en remembraunce ficome je m'offre en fa perfone, cent marcs. Item je vuille qe l'avowefoun de Yvele [m] foit venduz auxi toft come home purra apres mon deces refonablement, et les deniers d'icell loialment emploiez par mes ditz executours en meilloure mannere q'ils faveront en parfourniffement du teftament et voluntee mon feigneur et piere, qi Dieux affoille. Mes fi cas aveigne qe mefme l'efglife voide devaunt qe l'avowefoun enfy purra eftre venduz, et qe afcun de mes fitz vuille eftre home de feinte efglife foit able de l'accepter et occupier, q'adonques je vuille et prie mes feoffez de ycell de luy prefenter a ycell. Et autrement mon clerc Robert Pobelowe s'il foit en vie et la vorroie avoir. Et fi le dit Robert ne la vorroie avoir, ou ne foit en vie a temps de l'avoidaunce, q'adonqes je vuille qe mefme l'efglife foit done a monn chapellain fire Johan Gamil. Et fi le dit fire Johan ne la vorroie avoir, ou ne foit en vie a tiel temps come eft dit, q'adonques foit prefente a ycelle afcun fufficeaunt perfone de ma prochien linage qi pluis foit able a ycelle, par difcrecioun de mes executours. Et en cas qe nul de ma prochein linage ne voet accepter la dite efglife, ou qe ne foit able a ycelle, q'adonques je vuille qe mes ditz executours ordeynent qe

[m] q. *Ewell* vicarage, Surry, which Ecton fays was appropriated to Newark priory, or Chertfey abbey. Yeovil in Somerfetfhire (written *Yevil* and *Evill* in Ecton) was appropriated to Sion abbey. There is alfo an *Ewell* in Kent, which likewife belonged to a religious houfe.

soit presente a ycelle un sufficiaunt persone tiel come lour semble par lour bon avys et discrecioun pur le meulx, tout diz d'avoir pur recomender une tiele persone qe moy ad longement serviz. Item je vuille, en cas qe mes biens et chateux avantdiz ne vuillent suffire d'acquiter mes dettes, devisez, et charges de cest mon testament en nulle manere, ou q'ils ne porrount estre acquites pur nulle autre voie qe j'ay ordeyne, q'adonques mon haustel de Pulteney's[n] en soit venduz, et ove les deniers d'icell la duytee[o] de monn dit testament serviz. Et sy besoigne ne soit, ne cause necessaire la donne de la vent dycell, q'adonques je vuille et pre mes feoffez d'icell de doner mon dit houstel a mes droitz heirs seignures d'Arundell pur touz jours en la pluis seure manere q'ils le saveront ordeyner et deviser. Item sy ensi soit qe mes biens et chateux ne vuillent suffire pur faire satisfaccioun et restitution a mon dit treshonure seig-

[n] The capital messuage called the Cold harbor, in the parish of All Saints, *ad fœnum*, in Dowgate-ward, being purchased by Sir John Poulteney, who was four times mayor, and dwelt in it, took the name of *Poultney's Inn*. He gave the whole, with the wharf adjoining, to Humphrey de Bohun earl of Hereford and Essex, and died 1349. It is not improbable our earl of Arundel had this house in right of his wife, neice to this Humphrey. In 1397, 21 R. II. the year after his execution, John Holland earl of Huntingdon was lodged there, and Richard his brother dined with him. It was then counted a right fair and stately house. In the next year Edmund earl of Cambridge was there lodged; and it retained the name of Poultney's Inn, 26 H. VI. It belonged, 1472, to Henry Holland duke of Exeter. Richard III. granted it to the Heralds 1485, and in the reign of Henry VIII. the bishop of Durham's house being taken into the king's hands, bp. Tonstal lodged here, since which it came to the earls of Shrewsbury, of whom the last in Stowe's time took it down, and built on the scite a number of small tenements let out for great rents. Stowe's Survey, p. 252. fol.

[o] *duitz*. K. duty, obligation.

## RICHARD EARL OF ARUNDEL.

nur et peire, qi Dieux affoile, fibien come pur parfourniffement de ceft mon teftament et ma entente; adonques je vuile et charge mes ditz executours q'ils parfacent bien et duement fi en hafte come ils le bonement purrount, et q'ils eient de quoy apres moun decees en manere come j'ay ordeyne et declare ma entention defouz mon feal a mes executours et autres perfones de m'affiaunce [p], queux je prie et charge fur peril de lour almes q'ils le mettent et fuffrent eftre mys en bon et loialle execucioun, pur acompliffement de ceft mon teftament, et ma entiere voluntee, attaunt come y befoigne, et en null autre oeps, et outre ent ordeynent folonc ma voluntee et limitatioun fanz tariaunce, delay, ou contrariouftetee [q] qeconqe, coment ils vuillent refpoundre devaunt lui tout puiffaunt Seignur al jour de juggement: purvew totfoitz en execucion de cefte ma voluntee, qe les devifees et ordinaunces pur mon dit trefhonure feignur et piere, qe Dieux affoile, foient primerement ferviz, et depuiz mes devifees propres, folom ceo qe femble a mes ditz executours qe pluis foit honurable a Dieux, et profitable a ma alme. Item je ordeine et devife qe les coroune [r], bible en deux volumes, et un paire decretalx en fraunceis, et un grand paire de pater noftres d'or, ove un grand fermaille d'or, ovefq' certeines autres joalx et reliqes, contenuz deinz un petit forcell [s] de blanc liez d'argent, ove des liouns maffez [t] enorrez, queux mon dit trefhonure feig-

[p] my confidence.     [q] contradiction.     [r] coronet.
[s] q. ftrong box. *Forceret*, or *forchiere*, is explained by Lacombe *petit coffre*.
[t] q. *mafles*, male; or rather maffive.

nur et piere, qi Dieux affoile, devifa a moy et a mes heirs apres mon deces, a demorer perpetuelment de heir en heir feignures d'Arundell en remembraunce de luy et de s'alme; et en cas qe mon dit heir foit deins age, qe mefmes les coroune, bible, decretalx, et touz les ditz joialx et reliqes, toftpres mon deces foient falvement par mes ditz executours menetz et mifez en feure lieu a garder tanq' au plein age de moun dit heir, et adonqes de luy eftre deliverez par charge come il vorra refpoundre devaunt Dieu, mon dit trefhonure feignure et piere, qi Dieux affoille, et moy, au jour del juggement; Et purceo qe jeo entendy bien qe mon dit fitz et heir n'eftoit mye a la fefaunce d'iceftes d'age defy plenerement entendre fi grand charge, fi ne leffay jeo en parole ne en grand dit a luy, maes en fait et en cefte moun teftament je luy charge fi avant come je purra, et come il vorra refpoundre al jour de juggement, come defuis eft dit, quant il viendra a refonable age de entendre ceo qe a homme appertiendra, et fanz afcune fubtilite fefaunt en ycelle, eiaunt confideracioun qe coment je m'ay grandement doubtez de n'en offendre encountre le charge qe j'avoie en cefte article de moun dit trefhonure feignure et piere, qi Dieux affoile, par refoun moun dit fitz foy deveroit doubtier d'affez pluis qe je n'avoie caufe, car meindre caufe avoy jeo de moy doubter qe n'avoie qe le foule charge mon dit feignur q'il n'ad s'il ne face les voluntees fibien de mon dit feignur come de moy, par quoy foit moun dit fitz bien avys fi bien de fa alme, come pur la boune governaille

naille de fa perfone, come en temps q'il ferra en le mounde a plefaunce de Dieu, q'en la parfourniffement fi bien de ceft article come d'autres qe j'ay devifez en ceft mon teftament, et de mes autres darreins voluntees qe a luy apperteignount d'acompler, qu'il foit preft et toutdiz de bone voluntee et fans feintyfe, ou en afcune manere double, en afforfaunt [u] et aidant mes executours, et nomement ceux qi prendront l'adminiftracioun de mon teftament et voluntee fufditz, en acompliffement et parfourniffement de mes voluntees avant declarez. Item en cas qe par chaungeabletee du fiecle, fortunes, ou autres empefchementz qe purrount avenir en apres, afcuns de ceftes devifes ne purrount eftre executez en manere come il eft fpecifiez en yceftes, ou autrement, qe mes executours verrount per autre voie et par bone et fage difcrecioun qe mes devifees propres purrount eftre faitz en meilloure manere qe je n'ay devifez, Jeo vuille et donne poar a mes ditz executours q'en les materes [x] fur queles afcun tiel cas aviendra en enpefchement fur moun teftament et voluntee, q'ils le ferrount par bon avifement redreffer en mannere come il ferra pluis profitable, meritorie, et expedient a m'alme; mes per nulle voie qe afcune chofe foit chaunges du teftament mon trefhonure feignure et piere, qi Dieux affoile, eins q'il foit parfourny fi pres come refonablement ceo purra faire per afcune voie, folom le purport et effect d'icell, fi noun qi je vuille qe l'ordynaunce del college foit fait en manere come eft fpecifie en ceft mon teftament. Et furceo je charge mes heirs fur ma beniceoun, et come ils vuillent autrefoitz refpoundre devaunt

[u] ftrengthening. K.     [x] matters.

le

le tout puiffant trinite, et moy, prie et charge touz mes autres fucceffours fi avant come je puiffe, fur peril de lour almes, et come ils vuillent refpoundre de la charge al jour de juggement, q'ils ne nul de eux mettent ne mette impediment, deftourbaunce, objeccioun, n'autre contrarioufetee qeconqe, de cefte jour en avant encountré cefte ma entente, ne encountre nulle ordinaunce qe j'ay fait et ferra, pur affeuretee d'icell, en arreriffement de monn purpos, et qu'ils y foient bones feignures et patrons, aidaunts pur fuftenaunce de la dite college come ils fount et toutdiz ferrount, attaunt come il dure en perpetuelle memorie et priere illoeques pur merit de lour almes. Item je donne et devife a mon trefchier fitz de Charletoun un coupe ove une ewer covenable, Monf. Johan Cobham un coupe ove un ewer, Monf. Richard le Scrop un coupe ove un ewer, Frere Thomas Afshebourn un mafer[y] covere et frettez d'or, Monf. Payn Tiptot un hanap d'argent enorrez, et deux de les meilloures chivalx, Monf. William Percy un hanap d'argent coverez, et a Johan Cokkyng, Thomas Younge, et Thomas Harlyng, a chefcun de eux un hanap d'argent en remembraunce de moy. Et a parfournir et mettre en executioun ceft ma voluntee et touz mes

[y] Lacombe explains *mazer*, the material of which were made drinking veffels, thence called *mazelins, mazefins,* or *mazetins:* and Kelham explains *mazer (hanap de)* a bowl made of mazer. Du Cange fays, *mazer, mazerinus, mazarum, mazdrinum,* are the name of *pretious cups;* of what material he does not determine, but inclines to think them the *pocula murrhina* of the antients, called in later writers *hanaps de madre:* and then they will be made of precious ftones, which, from the many inftances of them being mounted in filver, recited by Dugdale, is much more probable than that they were of *maple wood* as Somner thought. Here, and in fome other inftances, the material is put for the veffel.

divifees

divisees avantditz; Jeo face et ordeine mes executours le tres reverent piere en Dieu mon treschier et honure frere d'Everwyk, mon treschier fitz de Charltoun, mes treschiers amys Monſ. Johan de Cobham, Monſ. Richard Lescrop, Monſ. Payn Tiptot, Frere Thomas Afshebourne, Sire Robert Pobelowe, Sir Johan Gamul appelle Ruffell, John Cockyng, Thomas Yonge, et Thomas Harlyng, les queux je pri d'entier coer, fur le graund affiaunce qe j'ay en eux, et en chefcun de eux, qu'ils vuillent prendre l'adminiſtracioun de mes biens, et les mettre en loial executioun, fytoſt come ils purrount apres moun deces, folom ceſte ma voluntee come y poet pluis eſtre pur l'onour de Dieu, et profit a ma alme. En teſtmoignaunce du quele chofe a yceſtes mes darreines voluntees j'ay mys moun feal; done jour, lieu et an fuifditz.

[N. B. A blank is left in the Regiſter Book for the Probat.]

> Regiſter Arundell pars prima, fol. 183. b. 184. a. b. 185. a. b. 186. a. b. in the archiepifcopal regiſtry at Lambeth.

Richard Fitz Alan, fourth earl of Arundel, fon of Richard the third earl, and Eleanor his fecond wife, daughter of Henry earl of Lancaſter, ferved king Richard II. in his different wars, and as admiral of his fleet: He was in the commiſſion that fentenced Michael de la Pole the king's favourite, and joined the lords againſt the duke of Ireland. The king attempted to furprize him in his caſtle at Ryegate,
but

## RICHARD EARL OF ARUNDEL.

but soon after restored him to his commands by sea and land. 12 R. II. he purchased a licence to marry for his second wife Philippa daughter of Edmund Mortimer earl of March, and widow of John Hastings earl of Pembroke. The same year he was in parliament divested of all his employments, and eight years after received sentence of death, and was beheaded in Cheapside, the king himself being a spectator; Thomas Mowbray earl Marshal, who had married his daughter, being the executioner that bound up his eyes, and the earl of Kent his nephew guarding him. He was buried in the Austin Friars church in London. By his first wife Elizabeth[z], daughter of William de Bohun earl of Northampton, he had three sons[a]; Thomas his successor, Richard and William who died young: and four daughters; Elizabeth first married to William de Montacute eldest son to William earl of Salisbury; secondly, to Thomas lord Mowbray earl Marshal and of Nottingham; thirdly, to Sir Gerard Uflete knt. and fourthly to Sir Robert Goushill knt[b]. Joane wife of William de Beauchamp lord Bergavenny. Margaret wife of Sir Rowland Lenthal, knt. and Alice married to John Charleton Lord Powis. Dugd. Bar. I. 320.

[z] Her portrait and her husband's were formerly in the windows of Arundel church. He kneeling in armour with a coronet, and on his tabard *Albeny* quartering *Warren*. She had the same arms on her mantle, and on her kirtle *Bohun*.

[a] See Note in p. 129.

[b] With whom she was buried at Hoveringham, co. Nottingham, where in the S. aile is a fine monument with their effigies, she on the right hand in robes, her coronet on her head, her right hand in his; he in armour, his left hand on his sword.

## JOHN OF GAUNT.

EN noun de Dieu le pier, du filtz, & de feint efpirit, Amen. Jeo Johan fitz du Roy d'Engleterre, Duc de Lancaftr', en bone memoire le tierz jour de feverer, l'an du grace mil trois centz quatre vingtz dis & fept, ay fait mon teftament par maner qu'enfuyt. En primes jeo devife m'alme a Dieu & fa trefdouce miere Seinte Marie & a le joy du ciel, & mon corps a eftre enfevelez en l'efglife cathedrale de Seint Poule de Londres, pres de l'autier principale de mefme l'efglife, juxte ma trefchere jadys compaigne Blanch illeoq's enterre. It'm je devife parochiell [a] ou qe jeo moerge tout ceo q' mes executours y voillent donner en noun de mon principall, quelle par le ley y doit eftre donnez pur mortuair; et ce cas que jeo moerge hors de Loundres jeo voille & devife qe la prim' nuyt qe mon dit corps ferra apportez a Londres qe foit portez tut droit as frers Carmes en Fletftrete pur ycelle nuyt, y avoir les exequies, & lendemain la haut meffe de requiem, apres quelle meffe jeo voille foit mon corps removez & portez tut droit a la fuifdit efglife de Seint Poule, pur y avoir ycelle nuyt les exequies, & lendemain la haute meffe de requiem & la fepultur'; & en quelle lieu qe jeo moerg

[a] to the parifh.

jeo voille & devise que apres mon trespassement mon corps demoerge desur la terre nemy enterez qe quarant jours, & doune en charge [b] a mes executours qe dedeinz yceulx quarant jours nulle encerement [c] de mon corps ne soit fait, ne faynez privement n'en appert. Item jeo voille & devise qe chescun jour des suisditz quarant jours soient pur m'alme donnez ad pov's gentz de pays cynquant marcs d'argent, & la veille de ma sepulture trois centz marcs d'argent, et la jour de ma sepulture cynk centz marcs d'argent, s'il semble a mes executours qe ceo purra estre fait, considere la quantite de mes biens & austres mes ordinaunces & devys; les ditz somes ne purront de tout estre donnez as pov's com desuis, adonques mes executours a leur discrecion facent donner as pov's chescune des ditz quarant jours autielles sommes com faire purront, le quantite de mes biens & mes aultres ordinaunces & devys considere. Item jeo devise entier pur ardre entour mon corps le jour de ma sepulture primerement dis grossez ciergez en noun des dis comandementz de n're seignour Dieu, countre les queux j'ay trop malement trespassez, suppliant a mesme n're seignour Dieux que ceste ma devocion me p'miss' remedier de tuit cella q' encontre les ditz comandements ay multz sovent & trop malement fait, & ferfait, et qe desuis yceulx dis soient mys sept cierges grosses en memoir des septz oevres [d] de charite es queux j'ay este negligent, et pur les septz mortielx pecches,

[b] I give in charge.
[c] no *cering* (or embalming) of my body be made or pretended, within the forty days, privately or publicly.
[d] *oeuvres*.

## JOHN OF GAUNT.

& defuis yceulx fept jeo voille qe foient mys cink cierges groffes en l'onur des cink plaies principalx n're feignour Jefu, et pur mes cynk fcens ᵉ lefquelx j'ay multz negligentment defpendie, dounte je prie a Dieu de mercy; et tout amont yceulx cierges jeo voille qe foient trois cierges en l'onur de la benoit trinite a la quele jeo me rende de touts les malx qe fait ay, enfuppliant de pardon & de mercy pur la mercy & pite q' de fa benigne grace il a fait pur la falvacion de moy & d'autres peccheours. Et voille bien qe de parentre les fuifditz cierges foient mys entour mon corps morters de cier, tieulx & atantz come a mes ditz executours plerra de y mettre. Item jeo voille qe mes executours facent prier mes cofyns & amys d'eftre a ma fepulture pur prier pur m'alme, fan ce faire de mon devys autre folempnitie ne fefte, fi ceo ne foit as pov's gentz a prier Dieux pur m'alme. Item jeo voille, ordeigne, & devife qe de leftoutes mes biens & chateulx mes executors apres ma mort devant leftoutes mes aultres ordinances & devys facent paier leftoutes mes dettes qe le jour de mon trefpaffement ferront duz, favant qe fi nulle dettes lors ferra demande la quelle pur negligence, nounchalure ᶠ, poverte au temps, male talent ᵍ, ou autre defaut foit aderier noun paie come reafon demaunde, & purra par evidence ou par bon' confcience eftre trovee qe foit due, a demandant, qe mes executours la facent paier fi avant s'ils averont de quoi de mes biens & chateulx, except toutz voiez qe jeo ne voille par nulle voie q'ils paient afcune

ᵉ *fens*, fenfes.   ᶠ indifference.   ᵍ refentment.

dettes

dettes pur l'arme $^h$ en voiage qe mon tresame frere le Duc de Everwyk $^i$ devant ore fist en Portugole, dount jeo me teigne de tut quites devant Dieu & tout la mounde, mes des toutes autres dettes jeo voille que resonable gree soit fait, et auſſi voille & ordenne & devise q' ſi a ascune temps de ma vie j'ay ehu $^k$ aucuns terres, ten'tz $^l$, rentz, ſervices, ou or ou argent, ou autres biens moebles d'acune autre persone ſanz juste & due title, ou a autre ay fait tort ou injurie, combien qe de present ne cognoiſſe nulle en eſpeciale meintenaines $^m$, ſi en temps avenir il puiſſe eſtre duement preuvez, mes executors facent plain reſtitucion & amends, ſi avant ils averont de quoy de mes biens & chateulx, des quelx facent ils auſſi couſtage convenables pur ma ſepultur & entour mon corps del jour de mon treſpaſſement, juſques au temps qe mon enterment ſerra acompliz, & auxi paient a mes ſervitours lours regardes per mon ordenns $^n$, & outre ceo q' mes executours pregnent de mes biens en leurs mains un tiel ſome convenable, de quelle ils purront faire & acompler toutz les chanteries & obitz en ceſte mon teſtament ordennes pur m'alme et pur les almes de mes treſcheris jadis compaignes Blanche & Conſtance qe Dieux aſſoille. Et

$^h$ the army.

$^i$ Edmund Plantagenet Duke of York, fifth ſon of Edward III. was ſent, 1381, with an army into Portugal, to ſupport his brother John of Gaunt in his claim of the crowns of Caſtile and Leon, in right of his wife Conſtance daughter of Peter the Cruel. They defeated his antagoniſt John. King of Caſtile with great ſlaughter; but the king of Portugal granting him peace, the Engliſh were conducted home with no ſmall mortification. Sandford, 375. Rapin, IV. 383. 398.

$^k$ eu, had. $^l$ tenements.

$^m$ though at preſent I know of none in ſpecial maintenance.

$^n$ their rewards, fees, ſalaries, according to my commands.

depuis

depuis facent mes ditz executours acomplir mes devys desoubz expresses si averount com de mes biens & chateulx ils averont, de quoy issuit toutz voies q[r] si apres les coustages affaire entour mon corps apres ma mort & ma sepulture & enterement plainement acompliz, & apres qe trestouts[o] mes dettes serront paiez & restitucion faitz des torts & injuries com desous, & les regardes par moy ordennez de tout paies a mes serviteurs, & pris & reservez es mains des executours la somme pur les chanteries & obits suisditz, mes biens & chateux lors remainantz es mains de mes executours ne suffisent my pur en acomplir mes devises desoubz expressez, qe de mes dites devys & de chescune de yceulx soit rebatement[p] fait solom la descrecion de mes executours, exceptz toutz voiez les choses desobz limitez a mon tres sovereigne seignour le roy, les queulx jeo voille qe luy soient livrez come chose a luy donne en ma vie. Item jeo devise a la suisdit aultier du Seynt Poule mon graunt lyt de drap d'ore, le champ piers[q] poudres des roses d'or myses sur pipes[r] d'or, et en chescun pipe deux plums d'ostrich blankes[s], les curteines de taffeta piers batuz de sembleable ovrage, XIII capits de tapiterie texes[t] de la suite, & a mesme l'autier mon vestement[u] de satyn blank enbroudez d'ore, donc l'ovrage est un raille[x] passant parmy

<sup></sup>

° all; in the fullest sense of the word; all and every.     p abatement.
q q. partly, parcel.
r q. pipes or tuns, or staves: for Lacombe gives both senses.
s Over against the duke's tomb at St. Paul's, in the border of a south window, was painted, among many other arms of the first house of Lancaster, his device, being in a field S. 3 ostrich feathers Ermine, the quills and scrolls Or, to distinguish them from his elder brother prince Edward. Sandford, p. 249. n.
woven. K.             here it means furniture.             x corons

corons d'or le quelle jeo achatay de Courtenay, broudier de Londres[y], & contient le veftement deux frontiers per l'autier, & un chefcun frontiers trois groffes tabernacles d'ore & groffes ymages d'or enbroudez en ycelle, un chefible, deux tunicles, III aubes, II eftoles, III fanons, III copes, & un covertur pur le letton[z], un corpora, II courtins, II touailles pur l'autier l'une aieant petit front enfemble, & mon entiere veftment de camaca[a] noir fait a deferver pur meffes de requiem enbroudez d'une crucifix d'or ovefq' les trois corporax & autres pieces a ycelle veftiment appurtenantz. Et voille toutz voiz qe treftouts ceftes chofes a le fuifdit autier principall de Seint Pouls devifez ovecq' treftouts leurs appurtenances demoergent a mefme l'autier a toutz jours pur ycelle autier a honuer, & entoure ma fepultur' fauz eftre a nule autre oeps convertez, ne d'illoefques efloignez par nule voie. Et voille qe mes executours de mes biens facent purchacer en Londres, ou dehors la ou pluis profitablement ceo faire purront, atant de terre, ou de rent, appropriacion des efglifes, ou aultres poffeffions donc ils me purront faire avoire pur m'alme & l'alme de ma dit nadgairs compaigne Blanch pur toutz jours en la fuifdit efglife de Saint Poule deux obitz, ceft affavoir, pur m'alme un obit folempnement a celebrer chefcune an le jour de mon trefpaffement, & pur l'alme de ma dite nadgaires compaigne Blanch un obit folempnement a celebrer chefcun an le XII jour de fep-

[y] of Courtenay, embroiderer at London.
[z] q. lettron, as hereafter, p. 152.
[a] *Camoca, camuca, camucum, camaca, pannus de camoca, velvel camocas,* fo often mentioned in antient wills, is explained by Du Cange as a kind of rich ftuff or filk.

temb'

# JOHN OF GAUNT.

temb' a toutz jours, & auſſi voille jeo, ordenne, & deviſe que de mes biens & chateux mes executoures facent ordeignier & eſtabler en l'avant dite eſgliſe de Seint Poule, un chanterie des deux chapelleins a celebrer divines ſervices en ycells a toutz jours pur m'alme & l'alme de ma dite nadgairs compaigne Blanch, et que a ce ſuſtenir perpetuelement ſoient donnez & amortizez certeinz terres & tenementz en Londres des queux la reverſion eſt purchacez a mon oeps, reddant ent par an vint marcs a dame Katerine del Staple a terme de ſa vie. Et voille que durant ſa vie el en ſoit paie del iſſues de manoir de Bernolſwyk en counte d'Everwyk, des queux iſſues ſoit auxi ſuſtenuz la dit chanterie durant la vie de dit Katerine. Item pur eſtrem devocion q' j'ay a la monſtier de ſeint Eſmon de Bury en counte Suff' jeo deviſe au dit monſtier mon rych veſtment de perill [c] ceſt aſſavoir, un cheſible ovecq' les parures d'une aube & d'un amitte, un eſtole, & un fanon de rouge velvet enbroudez d'un frett d'or & en cheſcune un maſcle de la frette un augnell de perill [d], & en cheſcune autre maſcle un eſcochon de perill faite des armes de Seint George, & a cella un touaill ovecq' un petit frontier pur l'autier de velvet vert enbroude de perill, l'ovrage [e] teſtes des xii apoſtres enſemble, & l'une des deux pieces de drap pur un autier enbroudez d'or, queulx j'a achatey a Dameux [f] faiz [g]

---

[b] Barnoldſweek in Stancliffe hundred, in the Weſt Riding of Yorkſhire.
[c] q. *perle*.   [d] ring, or perhaps angel, of pearl.
[e] the work or pattern.
[f] q. ad Amieux, as hereafter.   [g] made, i. e. workt, with

de

de n're feignour Dieu & de fa trefdouce miere Seint Marie[h] & des dufz apoftres, & treftoutes mes draps d'armes texes d'or pur parcelles q' font faiz de Dieu & de n're dame, except ceulx qui fount ailliours en mon teftament devifez, & mon veftment rouge de drap d'or donc la champ fatyn & l'ovrage angils d'or, ovecq' treftoutz parcelles & pieces qe a cele veftment appartiegnent enparavant a l'abbe & covent de ycelle monftier, q'ils pur ceftes chofes me facent avoir en ycelle monftier de Seint Efmond un obit perpetuele a tenir chefcune an le jour de mon trefpaffement. Item jeo devife al monftier de n're dame de Nicol[i] ma tierce chalice d'or fait a Burdeus q'ad un crucifix grave defuis la pie & en la patens[k] un vernicle[l] grave, ma table d'or en ma chapell, la quell table jeo appelle Domefday achatez a Amien[m] & mes plus grantez chandeleurs d'or faitz pur ma chapell, & mon novell veftment de drap d'or la champe rouge ovez des faucons d'or contenant dieux frontiers, & II touailles pur l'autier, un chefible, deux tunicles, trois aubes, trois amyttes, II eftoiles, III fanons, III copes, & un drap pur le lettron[n] & II curteins pur l'autier raiez de foi, & l'un piece pur un autier enbroudez d'or lequel ie achatay a Amienx[m] faitz de n're feignour Dieu & de fa trefdouce miere Marie & des XII apoftres. Item jeo devife a le

[h] Lincoln minfter, or cathedral, dedicated to the Virgin Mary.
[i] See a chalice, with a crucifix engraved on the foot, taken out of the graves of one of the archbifhops, and kept in the veftry at York. Drake's Ebor. 479, 480.
[k] the paten.
[l] q. a Veronica.
[m] q. Amiens as before.
[n] q. *lettrin*, catafalque. L.

novell

novell ° eſgliſe collegialle de n're dame de Leyceſtre mon rouge veſtment de velvet enbroudez de ſolailes d'or oveſq' treſtout l'appareille a ycelle veſtment appurtenante & a celle treſtouts mes meſſalx ᵖ & autres livres de ma chapell qe ſont del uſe & ordinale de la eſgliſe cathedrale de Sarum, & qe ſont ne ferront aillours en ma vie deviſez. Item jeo deviſe a l'autier principale des frers Carmes en Londre mon veille veſtment blank de drap d'ore apelle Rakamas, ovecq' tout ceo qe a ycelle veſtment appurtient; a celle xv marcs d'argent en l'onur des xv joyes de n're dame. Item jeo deviſe as trois autres ordres des frers en Londres, com as Precheours, Minours & Auguſtins, a cheſcun ordre x marcs, dont les v marcs en l'onur des v plaiez principalx de n're ſeignour J'hu, et les autres v marcs en l'onur des v joyes de n're dame. Item jeo deviſe a covent de Minoreſſes pres la tour de Londres cent livres d'argent d'eſtre paie entre eux. Item jeo deviſe a cheſcun pov'e heremite & recluſe aiant maiſon en Londres ou dedeins v lieues environ, en quel il demoert, trois nobles, en l'onur de la benoit trinite. Item jeo deviſe a cheſcun des noneignes ᑐ deins Londres & en les ſuburbs v marcs, en l'onur des v joies de n're dame & a les noneignes de Clerkenwell vint livres d'argent. Item jeo deviſe a cheſcun maiſon de lepres deins v leues entour Loun-

---

° Then newly founded by his wife Blanch's father Henry duke of Lancaſter, whoſe will ſee before.
ᵖ miſſals.   ᑐ nuns.

dres charges de v malades, v nobles, en l'onur de v plaiz principalx de n're feignor J'hu, & a ceulx qe font meniz charges troice nobles, en l'onur de la benoit trinite. Item jeo devife a chefcun maifon de Charthous en Engletere vint li'. Item jeo devife as prifones de Newgate & Ludgate en Loundres cent marcs, pur eftre departe par entre eulx par mialty[r] manire come multz[r] leur purra profiter folom la defcrecion de mes executours. Item jeo devife a ma trefcheer compaigne Katerin deux meillor nouches qe j'ay apres le nouch qe j'ay devife a mon trefredoute feignour & nevu le Roy, & mon pluis grant hanap d'or lequelle le counte de Wyltes donna a Roy mon feignour, & il le donna a moy a mon alee en Guyen darreinement devant la date du ceftes, enfemble ove toutz les hanaps d'or q'ele mefme m'a donne devant ore, lefqueulx ferront les meins le jour de mon trefpaffement, & enfemble ovecq' treftoutz les ferniculs[s], anelx[t], diamandes, rubies, & autres chofes qe ferront trovez en un petit cofre de cypres[u] qe j'ay, donc jeo porte le clief mon mefmes; & auffi q' apres ma mort ferront trovez en ma bource, le quel port mon mefmes defuz moy enfemble[x], & mon veftment entier de drap d'or, la lite[y] & la fale de fa fuyt, ovefq' treftoutz les copes, tapites pur le chambre, cuiffins, clofet oreillers, drap enbroudes pur

---

[r] *mialtz, mieultz, multz,* beft.    [s] *fermilet,* clafp, buckle.    [t] rings.
[u] Cyprefs wood.    [x] which I wear myfelf about me.
[y] *lit.*

la sepulcre[z] & toutes autres pieces de la suyt, de qel condicion en entaille qe soient, quels je achatay de ma treschere cousyn la Duchesse de Northfolk[a] aussi entierement sang riens ent enbeseiller[b] com jeo les avoy de ele, dont le champ rouge frette d'un noir traille[c] & en chescun place ou qe le frette se joynte un rose d'or, en chescun un mascle de la frette un tielle letre ℳ noir, en chescun aultre mascle un leopard noir, & a cella jeo devise mon grant lit de noir velvet enbroude d'un compasse[d] de ferures[e], & gartiers, & un turturell en mylieu de les compasses avecq' trestout les tapites & tapicerie & cuissins a ycelle lit ov chambres appurtenantes & a cella jeo le devise trestouts mes autres lits faitz pur mon corps, appelles en Engleterre trussyng beddes, ove les tapites & autres appurtenances, & mon meillour cerf ov le bonne rubie, & mon meillour coler[f] ovecq' touts les diamandes ensemble, & mon second covertur d'ermyn, & deux mes meillors mantils d'ermyn ovecq' les robes de la suyt; et a cella jeo devise a ma dit compaigne trestoutes les biens & chateulx de quelconq' natur ou condicion qe soient, les queles ele avoit devant les espousailles entre moy & ele celebrees, ovecq' trestoutz les aultres biens & joialx le queulx jeo luy ay donne depuis les

[z] The sepulchre of our Lord, which was on the N. side of the altar in many churches. See a curious description of it at Northwold in Norfolk. Blomef. I. 517, who refers to others in the churches of Hurstmonceaux, c. Sussex, and Stepney. See also Ib. p. 487.
[a] Margaret Bretherton, created Dutchess of Norfolk for her life. 21 R. II. Dugdale I. p. 399. Vincent, p. 344.
[b] q. embezzle. Not in any Dictionary.
[c] q. black lattice work. [d] circle.
[e] fetter-locks, the badge of this house. [f] collar.

espousailles suisditz, & le quelx biens & joialx sont en la garde de ma dit compaigne nient expressez en l'inventaire de mes biens. Item jeo devise a ma tresredoute seigneur & neveu le roy le meilliour nouche qe j'avois le jour de mon trespassement, & le mein meillour hanap d'or coverez, le quel moy donna ma treschere compaigne Katerin le jour de l'an renoef darrein passez [g], & mon saler d'or ovecq' le gartir, le coler overez, entour le saler un turturell assis desuis le covercle, & a cella xii draps d'or donc la champ rouge satyn raye d'or, les quelx draps j'avoye ordenuz d'en faire un lit, lequel n'est uncore comencez, & un covertur d'ermyn le meillour qe j'ay ovecq' la coverchiefs de la suyte ensembler, & la piece d'arras, la quelle le Duc de Burgoyn me donna a darrein qe jeo estoie a Calays devant la date du cestes. Item, jeo devise a ma trescher frere Duc d'Everwyk un hanap' d'or coverez. Item, jeo devise a mon treschere filtz Henry Duc de Herford, Counte de Derby [h], deux les meillours peces drap d'arras que j'ay outre ceulx q'en especial j'ay en cest mon testament, dount l'un me donna mon tresredoute seigneur & neveu le Roy & mon tresame frere le Duc de Gloucest' qui Dieux assoille, l'autre au temps qe je retourna darreinement d'Espaine devant la date du cestes, & mon grant lit de camaca eschette [i] blank & rouge, enbroude d'un arbre d'or & un turturell assis desuis l'arbre, ovecq' xiiii tapitz de tapiterie, & a cella mon grant lit

[g] renuef, renouef, renouvelle. L. The last past, or the last new year.
[h] afterwards king Henry IV.
[i] q. *escheque*, chequered.

de drap d'or, le champ piers overez<sup>k</sup> des arbres d'or, & juxte chefcun arbre un alant<sup>l</sup> blank liez a mefme l'arbre, ovecq' la veftment de la fuyt & toutes les tapitez de tapiterie faitz a ycell, & en outre jeo lui devife toutz les armures, efpies, & dages, qe ferront miens le jour de mon trefpaffement except ceulx q' aillos<sup>m</sup> fount devifez ou donnez; & plus outre jeo lui devife IIII chargeors, deux duzein de efcuilles, & fis faucers d'argent, & a cela jeo lui devife un fermaile d'or del veile manere, & efcriptz les nons de Dieu en chefcun part d'ycelle fermaile, la quele ma trefhonour dame & mier la reigne qe Dieu affoille me donna, en comandant qe jeo le gardaffe ovecq' fa benifon, & voille q'il la garde ovecq' la benifon de Dieu & la mien. Item, jeo devife a ma trefchere fille Phylypp' Roigne du Portugale mon fecond meillour cerf d'or & un hanap d'or coverez. Item, jeo devife a ma trefchere fille Katerine Roigne de Chaftill & de Lyon un hanap d'or coverez. Item, jeo devife a ma tres chere fille Elizabeth Ducheffe d'Exceftre mon blank lit de foi overez des egles bloyes difplaies, les curteins de taffeta blank batuz de la fuyte, XIIII tapitz de tapiterie, & mon meillour nouch qe j'ay apres ceulx qe font devifez. Item, jeo devife a mon trefcher filtz John Beaufort Marquis de Dorfet deux douzein de efcuilles, & un douzein faucers, deux pottes demy galons d'argent, pur le vin, un hanap d'argent endorrez, II bacins, & II eauers d'argent. Item, jeo devife a reverent pier en

<sup>k</sup> the field partly wrought.
<sup>l</sup> *alan*, a dog. L.
<sup>m</sup> *ailleurs*, otherwife.

Dieu & mon tresame fitz l'evesq' de Nicol [n] un douzein des escuilles, & douzein saucers deux pottes d'argent de galons pur le vin, un hanap d'argent endorrez, ovecq' un bacyn, & 1 eauer d'argent, & mon entier vestment de velvet jane ovesq' les choses appurtenante au cell vestment, & a cella mon messale & mon portheus qe furent a mon seignour mon frere Prince de Gales qe Dieux assoille. Item, jeo devise a mon tres chere filtz Thomas Beaufort leur frere [o] un douzein des escuilles, & un douzein saucers, deux pottes d'argent demy galons pur le vin, & sis tasses d'argent. Item, jeo devise a ma tres chere fille leur seure Countesse de Westmorland & dame de Nevyll un lit de soy & un hanap d'or decovrez [p] ovecq' un eauer. Item, jeo devise a mon tres chere Henry, fitz ayzn [q] de mon tres chere filtz le Duc de Herford, un hanap d'or. Et a mon tresame filtz John [r], frere du dit Henry, filtz de mon dit filtz, un hanap d'or. Item, jeo voille & devise qe si apres costages affairs entour mon corps apres ma mort & entour ma sepultur, & entierement plainement accomplez, & apres qe trestoutes mes dettes serront paiez & pleinere restitucion fait des tortes & injuries par moy & mes ministres a mon oeps faitz, & lez coustages de mes executours en faisant execution du cest mon testament, & auxi mez servitors regardes & liveretz

---

[n] Cardinal Beaufort. He held the See of Lincoln but six years, being translated to Winchester 1404, where he sat 43 years, and died 1447, having been a bishop 50 years, the longest instance in England, says Godwin, except abp. Bourchier in Henry VIth's time.

[o] his youngest son by Catharine Swinford.   [p] uncovered with an ewer.

[q] *aisne*, eldest, afterwards king Henry V.

[r] Afterwards Duke of Bedford and Regent of France.

regardes

regardes a eaulx paiez, & la fome gardee es mains des executours pur la fundacion des dites chanteries & obitz com defuis, adonques de les dettes qe lore[s] me ferront duz quant ils purront eftre levez, foient par mes executurs paiez a la fuifdit monftier de Bury mil livres, et a ma fuifdit compaigne Katerine deux mil livres, a mon dit filtz le Duc de Hereford mil livres, a mon dit filtz le Marquis[t] mil livres, a mon dit filtz Thomas Beaufort mil marcs, a mon tres chere bachelier Monf'r Thomas Swynneford cent marcs, a Monf'r Waut' Blount, Monf'r Chamblayn cent marcs, a Monf'r Hugh Shireley cent marcs, a Monf'r Ric' Aburbury le fils cynquant marcs, a Monf'r Wyllyam Par cynquant marcs de mon devys, iffint touz voiez que fe atant ne puiffe lors eftre leues des dictes dettes refidues, adonques de ceft mon devys foit rebatement a chefcun perfon de l'afferant[u] par ordinances & defcrecion de mes executours. Item, jeo voille, ordenne, & devife qe de mes biens & chateulx mes executours facent ordenner & eftabler en la novel efglife de n're Dame de Leyceftre un chanterie de deux chapelleins a celebrer divines fervices en ycell a toutz jours pur moy & m'alme & l'alme de ma nadgaires trefame compaigne Dame Conftances illeouques

[s] *lors*, then.
[t] John Beaufort, earl of Somerfet, his eldeft fon by Cath. Swinford, before-mentioned, created Marquis Dorfet, 21 R. II. But as this creation was by that king, who had alfo firft granted the title of Marquis to his favourite Robert de Vere; Henry IV. abolifhed it; and notwithftanding the petition of the commons in parliament, the earl himfelf gave it up. Sandford, p. 324.
[u] every one according to what he can afford.

enterres,

enterres, & pur tenir & faire tenir en la difte efglife un obit pur l'alme de ma dite nadgairs compaigne le xxiiii jour de Mars annuelement as toutz jours. Et qe a ceo fair & fuftenir perpetuelement mes ditz executours par l'avys de gents de loy de mes biens facent fufficeantment endower la fufdite efglife pur le fuftentacion de les chanterries & obitz fuifditz. Item, com einfi foit qe de l'annuite ou penfion annuel de quarant mil frankes en la quell m'efte tenuz mon trefame filtz le Roy de Chaftiell & de Lion certens fummes font oncore a derier nient paiez, non efpecial ordenuz d'eftre paiez a moy, ne a mes procures a mon oeps, fi voille & devife qe de toutz ces tiells fommes par mon dit filtz enfi a moy duez nient paiez, ne uncore ordenuz par efpeciale d'eftre paiez a mon oeps, mon tres fovereigne le Roy au le tierce denier de ceo qe per fon fovereigne aide en ferra recoverez par mes executours, & clerement reftez ouftre les couftages & expenfez. Item, jeo devife, voille, & ordeigne Imprimerement & principalement de treftouts mes biens & chateulx foient treftoutz mes dettes pleinement acquites, & les extorcions, tortz, & injuriez par moy & mes miniftres a mon oeps faitz reftorez & amendez folom la defcretion de mes executours, & les couftages refonables entour mon corps del jour de mon trefpaffement jufques au temps que ma fepulture & les couftages de mon entierement ferront acomplez, depuis de la refidue de mes biens foient mes fervitours regardez folom le difcretion de mes executours, et les

fuifdits

suifdits mes legats acomplez & parformez par les dits mes executours, fi avant com ils averont de quoy de mes biens & chateux, & la refidue de mes biens & chateulx fi nulle y ferra demorez, Jeo voille que par mes executours foit difpofe pur m'alme le plus profitablement q'ils en faveront devifer. Item, com de la fomme des francqs del annuele penfion des quarant mille francqs[x] a moy & de clere[y] memoir la fuifdite Conftance quant il viveit ma compaigne, fille & heir de clere[y] memoir Petre jadys Roy de Caftill & de Leon, a terme de vie & de la vie de la dicte Conftance lors ma compagne, & de l'autre de nous furvivant, grantes, conftitue, & folempnement promys par le

[x] The duke gave up his claim to the crown of Caftile in confideration of ten thoufand pounds (*libre*) yearly penfion to him, and the fame to his dutchefs Conftance (Walfingham, p. 342) and 200,000 *nobles* in hand. Sandford, p. 252. Rapin (IV. 420) fays, the king of Caftile bound himfelf to pay down 600,000 *livres*, with a yearly penfion of 40,000 during the lives of the duke and dutchefs. Carte (II. 575) fays, the duke of Lancafter was to be paid 200,000 *crowns* towards the charges of his expedition, and to receive 100,000 *florens* annually, and his wife Conftance as much, for their refpective lives. Of the contemporary hiftorians quoted by the latter, Walfingham fays nothing of the money in hand, but that the duke had from the king *fummam multam minis*. The life of Richard II. printed by Hearne leaves a blank for the fum. Froiffart III. c. 138. p. 328. fays, that on the marriage of the duke's eldeft daughter with the king's fon, the king gave him much land and territory in Caftile, and a great number of florins, about 200,000 nobles. One of the duke's followers told Knighton that the *fecond payment* was fent by the king of Spain in chefts of gold, on forty-feven mules. He did not enquire about the firft; but adds, that hoftages were given for an annual payment of 16000 marks for the duke's life, and 2000 *per annum* to the dutchefs if fhe furvived. p. 2677. The Abrégé Chron. de l'Hift. d'Efpagne, p. 548. fays, the king paid the expences of the war, and a confiderable penfion to the dutchefs. Such is the variation of hiftorians, or the value of money in different nations. The inftrument in Rymer, VII. 603. is only an order from the king to receive the fixty hoftages for the payment. Dated Weftminfter, 26 Aug. 1388.

[y] of famous memory.

puiſſant Prince Johan jadys Roy de Caſtill & de Lyon
& de Portugale par occaſion danemys[z] accordez, tranſac-
cion & amicable compoſicion ſur les drois de roialmes
de Caſtill & de Leon, Tolete, Galicie, Sicilie, Cordube,
Murcy, Gienn, d'Algarve, & Algiozire, & de les ſeignouriez
de Lace, Biſcay & Molyne faitz parentre le dit Johan jadys
Roy de Caſtill & de Leon & du Portugale & moy &
Conſtance lors ma compaigne ſuiſdite, ſi com pluis au
plaine eſt contenuz en lettres & inſtrumentz obligatorys
ſur les traicties, compoſicions, & tranſaccions ent[a] faitez,
les queulx letres & inſtruments jeo voille icy avoir pur
inſerteez, pluſours ſommes des franqs a moy nottairement
ſoient duz & remaignent nient paiez, Jeo voille, ordenne,
& deviſe qe mes executours deſoubz eſcriptz que les conq'z
ſommes des francs pur quelſconqz ans, termes & temps aderier eſtieantz, en toutz lieus & en quelconcq'z lieu qe ce
ſoit, demandent, exigent, & levent de quelconq'z perſones
& perſon de les queles les ditz ſommes des francqs doient
eſtre demandez, exiges ou leves, par toutes voies, manere
& forme meilliours qe purront yceulx mes executours, &
leur ſerra avys qe ſerra pluis expedient de faire, ſolom tout
force, fourme, & effect de les letres & inſtrumentz obligacions des quelx mencion eſt fait deſuis; & de ceſt mon
teſtament & darrein volunte, a l'execucion d'ycelles bien
& loialement faire jeo face, ordeine & conſtitue les reverents piers en Dieu Richard [b] Eveſq' de Saresbure, Johan

[z] ç. *d'amitiez.*  [a] thereon.  [b] Richard Metford, 1395—1407.

Eveſq'

## JOHN OF GAUNT.

Evesq' de <sup>c</sup> Wyrcestr', mes tres chere & tresames cousyn & compaignons Thomas Count de Wyrcestre, seneschale del houstell de mon tresredoute Seigneur le Roy, & Wyllyam Count de Wyltes tresorer d' Engleterre, mon tresame filtz <sup>d</sup> Rauf Count de Westmerland, Monf'r Waltier Blownt, Monf'r Johan Dabruggecourt, Monf'r Wyllyam Par, Monf'r Hugh War'ton, Monf'r Thomas Skelton, & Johan Cokeyn, chief feneschall de mes terres & poffeffions, Sir Rob't Qwytby mon attornee generall, Piers Melburn, Willyam Keteryng, Robert Haytfield, countrerollour de mon hostiell, Sir Johan Legburn mon receviour generall, & Thomas Longley clerk, mes executours, donant a eux & a chefcun d'eulx plein pouar & auctorite de trestoutz mes biens & chateulx adminiftrer & de toute ceo faire executier qe as bons executours par quelconqe voie refonable & juftifiable il appartient, premierement & en efpeciale par maniere com jeo lour a devyfe defuis, & en autre com lour tres fage defcrecion & bone confcience leyr purra fembler qe mieultz foit pur moy affaire & pur la fervice de Dieu & de fa trefdouce miere Marie, ayantz mes ditz execu-

<sup>c</sup> This was John Green whom the monks chofe bishop 1394, on the death of Wakefield, and whom Walfingham (p. 389.) mifcalls *Robert Tideman*, confounding him with Tideman de Winchcomb, whom the Pope, at the defire of R. II. to whom he was phyfician, obliged the convent to accept. This will therefore fettle the lift of Worcefter bifhops, among whom John does not appear, though the king confirmed his election 4 Maii, 2 Pat. 18 R. II. m. 18. and he actually fat till the Pope tranflated Tideman, who had not the temporalities till July 21. 1 Pat. 19 R. II. m. 20. Godwin, ed. Richardfon, p. 465.

<sup>d</sup> fon-in-law, as p. 171.

tours

tours de mes biens lour couftages refonables droit come par loure fait ils voillent refpondre devant Dieu le haut jour de juftice. Item, pur ceo qe afcun foiz un des executours deputez al teftatour qi mort eft nient fachant, les autres executours, mes de tout ignorantz, pur fon finguler profit recevant des grantez fommes dues a fon teftatour certein pur certie, & afcun foiz la meindre partie apliant & convertant a fon propre oeps, ad remys la refidue d'icelles fommes fraudeloufment & contre bone confcience & graunt prejudice del teftatour & de fes executours & en graunt peril d'alme de tiel fraudelens, & de mal enfample des plufours, pur ceo pur efchuir tiel fraude, voille jeo ordenne & defpone, & auffi charge mes dits executours, qe nulle d'eux fans confaile, voulente, confent auxi & aflent expreffe del greindre partie des ditz executours de & fur grandes & groffes fommes de monnoys, ne face acquitances generalles ne particulers a nuly, ne aucun acquite de l'une ou abfolve: mes qe mes ditz executours ne facent le contraire; je a doune & referve toutes & quelconq' povoir en celle partie. Et pur furvoier & faire veir q'ils enfi ferront jufques al complifement de ces mes darrens voulontes jeo prie & a mon tres redoute feignour tres humblement jeo fupplie come a mon Roy & fovereigne feignour terrien[e] en qui devant touts autres jeo me pluis affiee[f], qu'il de fa incomparable bontes & en acompliffement de fes gracioufez promeffes les qels de fa noble feignorie il m'a fait, en ceo cafe luy

---

[e] earthly.      [f] confide.

pleafe

## JOHN OF GAUNT.

pleafe me eftre bon feigneur, & du ceft mon teftament foverein furveoire & comandoir, que foit leffe ne changee ceo que jeo paramont ay devife; & apres luy, fon trefhonourable eftat & honoure tout jour fauvez, jeo face furveoirs [g] de mefme le fait mon trefcher & trefentierement bien afme frere Efmon Duc d'Everwyk, mon trefcher & trefentierement bien ame neveu Edward Duc d'Aumarle [h], les tres reverentz piers en Dieu Rog' erchevefque de Cantirbure, Ric' [k] erchevefque d'Everwyk, & le reverent pier en Dieu l'evefq' de Nicole mon trefame filtz; en priant a mes fuifditz frere naturel & neveu, qui de reafon & de nature me deuffient eftre pluis procheins amys, & as ditz tres reverents piers en Dieu & mon trefame filtz, com a mes peres efpirituels qi de refon & d'efpiritue te me deuffent eftre efpirituelx amys, q'ils, ovefq' mon tres redoute feignur le Roy fufdit, fon honur toutzdis fauvez, me voillent eftre bons furveoirs de mon dit teftament, &, s'il enbufoigne pur le meilliour de moy en comfort de mes executours fuifdits, comandent & ordenent coadjutors, que pur necgligence,

---

[g] fupervifor.

[h] Edward Plantagenet duke of York, eldeft fon of Edmund de Langley, the teftator's fifth brother. He was created duke of Albemarle 21 R. II. of which title he was deprived 1 H. IV. He was flain at Agincourt, and buried at Fotheringay. Sandford, 380.

[i] This muft be a miftake, for *Thomas* Arundel was archbifhop of Canterbury from 1396 to 1414.

[k] Richard Scrope from 1397 to 1404, when he was beheaded for attempting to reftore R. II. He had the temporalities of this fee, Jan. 21, 1397. Godwin.

[l] Hen. Beaufort. [m] be neceffary.

nonchalur

nonchalur, male talent, n'autre defaute, cestes mes dits volentes, ordennances, & darreins devys ne soient par voie de monde lessez [n], ne en autre manere que par desous est escript changies, ne tournes, come ils voillent respondre devant luy qu'est Roy des toutz roys, & ad le seurveue de toutz terriens faits & pensez [o] pur quelx il rendra guerdon a chescun solom son desert. En foy & tesmoignance de trestouts cestes choses pur dessus escripts com a ceste mon testament j'ay fait mettre mon seale de mes armes, de quelle cele pur greindre conissanz & affirmance de mon propre fait j'ay mesme mys en le dorce mon signett quele je porte toutes jours mon mesmes, le jour & an suisditz, & les gents desoub escripts en ay requis de les tesmoigner; c'est assavoir, meistre Johan Kynyngham, doctour en theologie, Sire Johan Neuton, parson de l'esglise de Burbach, Sire Wautier Piers, person de l'esglise de Wymondham, Wyllyam Harpeden, & Robert Symeon, escuiers.

Subscripcio. Et ego Johannes de Bynbrok, presbyter, Lincoln' dioc' publicus apostolica & imperiale auctoritate notarius, una cum reverendis & discretis viris fratre Johanne Kynyngham in theologia professore, D'no Johanne Newton rectore ecclesie paroch' de Burbach, & Waltero Piers rectore ecclesie paroch' de Wymondham, ac Willo Harpeden, & Roberto Simeon armigeris, Norwyc', Lincoln' & Exon' dioc', Anno Do-

---

[n] omitted.

[o] and has the oversight of all earthly deeds and thoughts, for which he will render a reward to every one according to his deserts.

mini, menſe, & die ſupradict', indiccione ſeptima pontificis ſanctiſſimi in X'po patris & domini noſtri domini Bonifacii divina providencia pape noni anno decimo, preſens interfui ubi & quando illuſtriſſimus princeps & dominus Johannes filius Regis Anglie, Lancaſtr' Dux ſupradict. in camera infra caſtrum ſuum Leyceſtr' ſituat' dict. Lincoln' dioc' perſonaliter exiſtens in manibus ſuis tenuit preſentem ſcripturam ſuperſcriptam, & ipſam in teſtim' ſuperius deſcriptos ad hec ſpecialiter vocatos & rogatos, ac mei preſencia palam & publice fatebatur & expreſſe dixit ſuum eſſe teſtamentum, ac ſuum protunc ultimam continere voluntatem, quam quidem ſcripturam ſive teſtamentum una cum quodam codicello eidem ſcripture tunc inferius annexo voluit & vult juxta ipſorum tenorem & effectum fieri & compleri, eaque ſicut premittitur fieri vidi & audivi, ac de mandato ejuſdem principis ac ducis hic me ſubſcribendo ac ſignum meum hic apponendo conſuetum, in hanc publicam formam redegi rogatus & requiſitus in fidem & teſtimonium omnium premiſſorum interlinear' illius diccionis *autres* ſuper undecimam lineam, ac raſuras illius dictionis *ordre* in triceſima quarta linea & illarum dictionum (*et les couſtages reſonables entour mon corps del jour de mon treſpaſſement juſques au temps qe ma ſepulture*) in ſexageſima quarta linea, preſentis teſtamenti approbo, ego Johannes notarius antedictus.

CODICIL-

## CODICILLUS.

IT'M, la ou jeo Johan filtz du roy d'Engleterre, Duc de Lancaftre, ay purchacez & fait purchacer a mon oeps diverfez feignouries, manoirs, terrez, tenemens, rentes, fervices, poffeffions, & advoefons des benefices de feint efglife, ove lours appurtenances, des quelx devant les efpofailles d'entre moy & ma trefame compaigne Katerine celebrees, jeo luy a fait doner aucunes parcelles a avoir a terme de fa vie, & d'aucunes parcelles j'ay fait enfeffer mon trefame filtz Johan Beaufort Marquis de Dorfet a avoir a lui & a fes heirs de fon corps iffantz, folom la contenue des feffements fur ceo faitz, & d'aucunes autres parcelles font de ma ordinance diverfez perfonez enfeffez, au fyneq'ilz doient as autres feoffement ou feoffements faire a ma volente, ordinance, & devys, quant ils ferront achetez, & a ceo de part moy requis, fi ay jeo fait faire cefte cedule annexe a ycefte mon teftament contenante ma darreine & entier volente toucheant les fuifditz feignouries, manoirs, terres, tenementz, rentes, fervices, poffeffions, reverfions, & advoefons, ove lours appurtenances, laquele ma volunte jeo voille que foit a toutz convee & effectuelement acomplee en toutes pointz, des quelx jeo ne ferra autre ordenance en ma vie. Et eft tiel ma ordenance & devys: Primierement jeo voille que toutz les feignoires, manoirs, terres, tenementz, rentes, fervices, poffeffions, reverfions, & advoefons, ove lours appurtenances, per manere que defuis purchafes & com defus

donnes

donnes & grantez a ma dite compaigne a avoir a terme de sa vie, remaignent a ele tuit entierement solonque l'effecte & purpous des douns & graunts a ele faitz, la reversion d'ycelles que de ma ordenance sunt taillez per fyn ou autrement, toutz foiz remaignent a celuy ou a ceulx a qui ou as quelx ils sont taillez. Et que la reversion de toutes autres seignouries, manoirs, terres, tenementz, rentz, services, possessions, reversions, & avoesons, ove lours appurtenances, es quelx ma dite compaigne a estate a terme de sa vie, & lesquells ne sont de ma ordeignance taillez, soit donnez a mon trecher filtz Thomas Beaufort frere du devant dit Johan, ensemble & avecque la reversion de toutz les seignouries, manoirs, terres, tenementz, rentz, services, possessions, reversions, & avoesons, ove leurs appurtenances, que furent a Edward de Kendale, laquele reversion j'ay fait purchacer de Dame Elizabeth Croiser, & les seignoires, manoirs, terres, tenementz, rentz, services, possessions, reversions, & avoesons, ove lours appurtenances qe, Dame Elizabeth Barry tient a terme de sa vie, a avoir au dit Thomas & a ses heirs de son corps issants; & pur defaut d'issue du dit Thomas, la remeindre au dit Johan & a ses heirs de son corps issants; & pur defaut d'issue de dit Johan la remeinder a ma tresame fille Johane leur seur contesse de Westm'land & a ses heirs de son corps issant; et pur defaut d'issue de dit Johane la remeindre a mes drois heirs q'ils serront heirs de heritage de Lancastre. Item, jeo voille que l'avant dit Johan Beaufort mon filtz ait

ait a luy & a ſes heirs de ſon corps iſſants toutes les ſeignouries, manoirs, terres, tenementz, rentz, ſervices, poſſeſſions, reverſions, & avoeſons, ove lours appurtenances, que de ma purchace & de ma ordinance luy ſount donnez ſolom l'effect & purpoys de doun & grant a luy ent faiz. Item, jeo voille que les certeines terres & tenementz en la cyte de Londres a mon oeps nadgairs purchacez d'une Dame Katerine del Staple en rendant a ele vint marcs per an a terme de ſa vie ſoient per le coungie[p] de n're treſſovereigne ſeignour le Roy donnez a un chanterie a eſtre fundie des deux chapelleins, a celebrer devines ſervices en l'eſgliſe cathedrale de Seint Poule du Londres, pur les almes de moy & de ma treſcheer nadgairs compaigne Blaunch, que Dieux aſſoille, quelle chanterie jeo voille que mes executours facent founder en meilliour manere des biens que ſerront les miens le jour de mon treſpaſſement ſi jeo ne face fonder & ordenier en ma vie. Item jeo voille que mon treſcher bachelier Monſ'r Robert Nevill, Wyllyam Gaſcoigne, mes treſchers eſquiers Thomas de Radclyf and Wyllyam Kat'yng, & mon treſcher clerk Thomas de Langley, qui de ma ordenance ſunt enfeffez en manoir de Bernolſwyk en counte d'Ewerwyk, facent annuelement paier a mes executours pur outre a l'avant dit Dame Katerine del Staple les ſuiſdites vint marcs per an a terme de ſa vie; & outre ce facent les ditz enfeffez paier des iſſues ſuiſditz a mes ditz executours autres vint marcs

[p] *conge*, leave.

per

per an a eftre per eulx outre paiez as deux chapelleins celebrantz divines fervices en la dit efglife cathedrale de Seint Poule pur m'alme & l'alme de ma dite jadis compaigne Blanch a un aultre jouft [a] le leu de n're fepulture, tanq' a temps que ferra illeoucq' fondue & endowe un chanterie perpetuele de deux chapelleins a celebrer divines fervices pur les almes de moy & de ma dite nadgairs compaigne Blanch. Et outre ceo paient les dits enfeffez as dits executours autielle fomme per an de laquele fomme ils purront faire annuelement eftre celebrees deux obitz en la dit efglife de Seint Poule, c'eft affavoir un obit pur moy le jour de mon trefpaffement & un autre obit pur ma dit nadgairs compaigne Blaunch le douzifme jour de Septembre d'an en an, tanque au temps que terres, tenementz, rentz, ou autre fuffifant poffeffions, foit donne & amortize pur la perpetuelement fuftentacion des ditz obitz. Et voille que la refidue des ditz iffues foit paie a mes ditz executours pur outre paies en partie de paiement de la fuftenance de deux chapelleins celebrantz fervices divines en la novell efglife collegiate de n're Dame de Leyceftre, pur m'alme & l'alme de ma trefchiere nadgairs compaigne Dame Conftance illeouques entierree, & pur un obit a celebrier illeouques pur l'alme de ma dite nadgairs compaigne Conftance le vint & quart jour de Mars d'an en an, tanque au temps que en la fuifdit novell efglife collegialle ferront fufficientement fonduz un chanterie perpetuele de deux chapelleins a celebreer

[a] *juxta*, near.

divines services pur l'alme de moy & de ma dit nadgairs compaigne Conſtance illeouques enterree, & auſi un obit pur l'alme de le [r] a celebrer perpetuelement le jour de Mars ſuiſdit. Adonques ſoit eſtate faite du dit manoir a mon treſame filtz aizne Henry Duc de Herford, & a ſes heirs de ſon corps, & pur defaute d'iſſue de dite Henry la remeindre a mes droiz heirs. Item, touchant les Wapentakes de Hangeſt, Hangweſt & Halykeld en Rychmondſchir, les queulx j'ay devaunt ore faite grantier a mon treſame filtz en ley Raufe Counte de Weſtmerlande & a ma treſame fille Johane ſa compaigne, a avoir a terme de leurs vies, jeo voille q'ils les aient a eulx & a leurs heirs malz de lour corps iſſantz, & pur defaut d'iſſue de heir male de lour corps la remeindre à l'avant dite Johan mon filz & a ſes heirs de ſon corps iſſants, & pur defaut d'iſſue de dite Johan la remeindre a dit Thomas & a ſes heirs de ſon corps iſſants, & pur defaut d'iſſue de dit Thomas la remeindre au dit Johane & a ſes heirs de ſon corps iſſants, & pur defaut d'iſſu de dit Johane la remaindre a mes droiz heirs de Lancaſtre. Item, jeo voille que toutz aultres ſeignories, manoirs, terres, tenementz, rentz, ſervices, poſſeſſions, reverſions, & avoeſons, ove leurs appurtenances, a mon oeps purchaces & remaignants uncore es mains des effeffez [s] pur moy a ceo ordennes, ſoient apres ma mort, ſi jeo ne face autre ordenance en ma vie, donnez a l'avant dit Thomas mon filtz, a avoire a luy & a ſes heirs de ſon corps iſſants, & pur

[r] ſoul of him.    [s] feoffees.

defaute d'iſſue de ſon corps iſſants la remaindre a l'avant dit Johan ſon frere & a ſes heirs de ſon corps iſſants, & pur defaute d'iſſue de dit Johan la remaindre a la ſuiſdite Johane leur ſeur & a ſes heirs de ſon corps iſſants, & pur defaute d'iſſue de la dite Johane la remaindre a mes droits heirs que ſerront heirs del heretage de Lancaſtre; voillantz toutz voies que toutes yceſtes mes voluntees, ordinaunces & devys en ceſte cedule comprys ſoient toutz accompliez per ceulx que averont l' eſtate & povor, et per l'avys, ordenances, & conſeille de gentz de ley en le pluis ſur manere que en ceo purra ordenner.

Regiſt. Hen. Beaufort. fol. 13. b. to fol. 18. a. incluſ'. In the epiſcopal regiſtry at Lincoln.

Edward III. by his wife Philippa, had iſſue this JOHN their fourth ſon, born at Gaunt [Ghent] 1340. In two years after his birth he was created earl of Richmond, and in 1361 duke of Lancaſter. In 1359 he married Blanch younger daughter and coheir of Henry duke of Lancaſter, who dying ten years after [1369] dutcheſs of Lancaſter, was buried in St. Paul's cathedral; and in her right her huſband obtained the three earldoms of Derby, Lincoln, and Leiceſter. Peter the Cruel, King of Caſtile and Leon (whom Edward Prince of Wales had inveſted in his kingdoms) left at his death, 1367, two daughters, who, to avoid the uſurper their uncle, had taken refuge in Gaſcoigne. The duke cauſed them to be brought to Bourdeaux,

deaux, and there married Constance the elder 1372[t], assumed the title of King of Castile and Leon, and supported his claim by force of arms, but without success. On the death of the Prince of Wales, he was appointed Regent of the kingdom, in the declining age of his father, and during the minority of his nephew Richard II. by whom he was created duke of Aquitaine in 1389; and six years after he set up in parliament his claim to the succession of the crown of England[u], which his son (afterwards Henry IV.) obtained, and so brought the great duchy of Lancaster to the crown. He took to his third wife Catharine daughter of Sir Payne Roet, and widow of Sir Otes Swynford, who had been his mistress in the life of Constance, and who survived him four years, and dying 1403, was buried in Lincoln Minster, where her monument, robbed of its brasses, remains on the West side of the altar, while those of his former wives were destroyed at the dissolution and by the fire of London. The duke departed this life at the bishop of Ely's palace in Holborn, about the Feast of the Purification of our Lady, A. D. 1399, and was buried with his first wife in St. Paul's cathedral. See their monument in Sandford, p. 256.

[t] She died 1394, and was buried in the collegiate church at Leicester, where Leland saw her monument of marble before the high altar, with her image of brass like a queen on it. It. I. 17.
[u] Sandford, p. 252.

By

# JOHN OF GAUNT.

By his first wife Blanch he had issue,

1. Henry, duke of Hereford and Lancaster, and earl of Derby, afterwards king of England.

2. Philippa, married to John I. king of Portugal 1386, died 1415; buried with her husband at the abbey of Batalha, where Mr. Twisse (Travels, p. 43.) describes the monument with their effigies cumbent [x].

3. Elizabeth, married first to John Holland earl of Exeter, beheaded at Cirencester 1 H. IV. and secondly, to Sir John Cornwall lord Fanhop: she died $142\frac{5}{6}$, and was buried at Burford in Shropshire. Her portrait, and that of her second husband were in a window at Ampthill church, engraved by Sandford, p. 259.

By Constance he had one only daughter Catherine, married to Henry prince of Asturias, son and heir to Henry count of Trastamare, base brother and successor to Peter king of Castile and Leon, to whose kingdom her husband succeeded by the name of Henry III. 1390, and their descendants were kings of Spain till Charles II. who died 1700.

By Catharine Swynford he had, 1. John Beaufort, created earl of Somerset 20 R. II. and next year marquis of Dorset; he married Margaret Holland daughter of Thomas earl of Kent; and dying 1410, was buried at Canterbury, where in St. Michael's chapel in the South transept is a most beautiful monument for him, his lady, and her second husband

---

[x] After seven kings of their issue had governed Portugal, it was invaded by Philip King of Spain 1580, and united to that crown till 1640.

Thomas duke of Clarence. 2. Henry, cardinal of St. Eufebius, bifhop of Lincoln 1398, and of Winchefter from 1404 to 1447, where he was buried behind the high altar, having been twice chancellor of England, and once at Jerufalem. 3. Thomas Beaufort duke of Exeter, admiral of England, earl of Dorfet; he married Mary daughter of Sir Thomas Nevil, died at Eaft Greenwich 1426, and was buried at St Edmundfbury, where his corps was difcovered 1772. (See Phil. Tranf. Vol. LXII. art. 33. and Archaeol. vol. III. p. 311.) 4. Joan Beaufort married firft to Robert Ferrers, fecondly to Ralph Nevill firft earl of Weftmorland, by whom fhe was grandmother to the famous Earl of Warwick the kingmaker, and dying 1440, was buried at Lincoln by her mother, where her brafslefs monument ftill remains.

ELEANOR

# ELEANOR BOHUN, DUCHESS OF GLOUCESTER.

IN dei nomine Amen. Jeo Alianore Ducheſſe de Glouceſtre, Counteſſe d'Eſſex, &c. eſteant en bon & ſain memorie, en moun chaſtell de Pleſſy, le ix jour d'Augſt l'an de noſtre ſeignour mil trois centz nonance & neof ſelonc le cours de l'egliſe d'Engleterre, entendant & conſiderant les mauveizcees & nouncertaineteez de ceſt variable & tranſitore monde, ordeigne & deviſe ma darrein voluntee & teſtament com enſuit. Enprimes je comande m'alme entirement a la graunt & innumerable mercy de noſtre tout puiſſant & tres merciable ſeignour J'hu Criſt, requerant l'aide de ſa benoite miere la tres humble virgine noſtre tres douce dame Seint Marie, de mon Seignour John le Baptiſt, et de tout la celeſtiel compaigne. Item, jeo deviſe pur ma ſepultur mon cors d'eſtre enſevelees en l'eſgliſe de l'Abbeie de Weſtmonſtre, eins la chapell de Seint Edmond le Roy & de Seint Thomas de Cantirbirs, juxte le corps de mon ſeignour & mari Thomas Duc de Glouceſtr, & cet'[a] fitz au Roy Edward la tierce, & tout ſoit qe le corps de mon dit ſeignour & mari ſoit en temps avenir remue, ſi veule qe mon corps repoſe & demure en l'avant dit

[a] f. Sept. for *ſeptieſme*, he being 7th ſon of Edward III.

chapelle & lieu. Et fi devife & ordeigne qe la jour de ma fepulture qe mes executours facent ordeigner qe mon corps foit covere de un tapite noir, ove un crois blank & un efcuchon de mes armes en mylieu du dicte crois, & IIII cierges toutes roundez, & VIII plain mortiers efteantz a les IIII covere[b]. Et xv homes & en efpecial choiftre[c] pur loiaux & doutant[d] dieux coment qe foit de lour age ou autre poveretie felonc le difcreffion de mes executours, tenant chefcun des dites povres homes un torch, ceft affavoir, cynk au tefte & cynk au checun coftee, & foit checun des ditz povres homes veftuz en un gowne, un large chaperon, un pares des chaufes de bon fort drap blu de profound colour, & foient les dites gounes & chaperons doubles ove blanket; auffi foit done a checun de eux un pare de folers[e], & un pare des drapes linges & xx d. d'efterlinges[f], a prier pur m'alme & pur l'alme de mon feignour & mary avantdite, & pur touz les vifs & morts en efpecial a queux jay efte tenus & pur touz criftiens. Item touchant les avantdites cierges, mortiers ne torches ne foient en nul maner enlumynes entour mon dite cheitif corps, fi non foulement en le temps de la fervice dyvine, & ceo fait le meindre du dites cierges, mortiers, & torches foient leffes a la fervice du dite chapelle qe je fui eins enterres. Item, jeo devife a le covent des moignes du dite

---

[b] q. corners. See before.
[c] q. of efpecial choice or fucceffion from *choite* or *efchoite*.
[d] q. *redoutanz*, fearing.
[e] *fouliers*, fhoes.
[f] Dugdale (Bar. II. 172) tranflates this *a fhirt* and 20 pounds.

abbeye

abbeye de Westm' le jour de ma sepultur x li. de monoye
pur lour pitance. Item, jeo devise d'estre distribuit entre
les povres per l'avys de mes executours mesme le jour c s.
Item, jeo devise a l'abbesse & covent des soers menuresses
juxte Londres dehors la porte de Algate mesme le jour
pur lour pitance VI li. XIIII s. IIII d. & un tonell de bon
vine. Item, jeo devise a le priour & covent de Lanthone
juxta Glouceftr' XIII li. VIII s. VI d. Et a Sire William
Shuldon, chanoign de dit lieu, c s. Item je devise a l'esglise
& abbeye de Walden ou mon seignour & piere est enterre
Hunfrey de Bohun, darreine Counte de Herford d'Essex &
de Northampton, Conestable d'Engleterre, un vestement,
le champ de baukyn [g] blue diapres des autres colours, ove
cerfs d'or de Cipre [h], cestassavoir deux tablementz, un
frountell, un chesible, II tunicles, un cape, III aubes, III
amyts ove les parurs qe a eux apertient, & si est l'orfreis
du dit vestiment tout de fyn drap d'ore de Cipre [h] le champ
rouge. Item, jeo ordigne & devise qe mes executours
facent celebrer, deinz aussi brief temps apres ma mort
come ils puissent, mille misses pur m'alme; xx de l'assump-
cion nostre dame, cl de requiem, l. de mon seignour Seint
John le Baptistre, l. de Seint John l'Evangelistre, xxx. de
Seint Leonard, xxx. de touz Seints, l. for the soule of Thomas sum tyme Duc of Glouceftre, xx. de nativite nostre
seignour, xx. de resurrection, xx. de l'assencion, l. de Seint

[g] *Baldckyrus*, pannus omnium ditissimus, of silk and gold thread. Du C.
[h] gold of Cyprus means of Cyprus work. So Du Cange; *Aurifrygia opere Cyprensi nobilissimo.*

Michell archangle, xx; et qe a tous ceuz dites messes, devant qe le prestre comence *Et ne nos,* qe le dit prestre die en haut tournant vers le poeple, "For the soule of *Thomas* sum tyme Duc of *Gloucestre* and *Alianore his wyf,* and all cristeyn soles, for charitee *pater noster;*" & turnier vers l'autier & dire un pater noster en secree, & comencier la messe, & en toutes les ditz messes soit dit le oreison de " Deus " qui es summa nostre redemptionis spes, qui in terra " promissionis, &c." ove le secretum & post com.[j] & les nouns de mon dit seignour & moy nomes la eins Thomas & Alianore. Item, jeo devise a madame & mere la Countesse d'Erford, un paire de pater nostres de corall de cynqaunt graunts[k] ove v gaudes[l] d'or en manere des longets, swages[m] & ponsonez[n], requerant a ele checun jour de sa benoison entirement a ma poverouse alme. Et en cas qe ma dite dame desvye[o] devant moy dounc devise jeo les dites pater nostres a l'abbesse de l'esglise des soers menuresses avantdit quele soit a y demurrer eins le dit abbey de lors enavant pur un memorial de moy. Item, jeo devise a mon fitz Humfrey, un lit de noir drap de damask. Item

[j] post communionem. [k] q. large beads.
[l] trinkets, gawdies.
[m] q. wild vine-branches. *Langos* les coursons de la vigue L.
[n] pinkt. [o] decease.
[p] Her only son by the duke of Gloucester, earl of Buckingham, whom, after the murder of his father (the kingdom being then in distraction) Richard II. took with him into Ireland; and when he heard that Henry duke of Lancaster was landed at Ravenspur, caused him, with the said Duke's son, to be imprisoned in Trim castle, where he continued till the duke obtained the crown, and then being sent for over to England, was shipwreckt, or as Walsingham, p. 401. died there, or at Chester, of the plague. Weever says he was buried with his ancestors at Walden. Dugd. Bar. I. 173.

un

un lit de foy de baudekyn le champ blu, ove overaignes de blanc ove entier celures, tefters, coverlitz, curtyns, & tapitz, qe a eux appertient. Item, deux pare lincheauz de Reyns, l'un pare de III foill [q], & l'autre pare de IIII. Item III pare des lincheaux de autre drap lienge des meillour. Item, un pare des fuftiens, II pare blankett, II materas des meillours, outre tout fon array & eftuf qe feuft deliveres a fes fervants a fon departir de Londres vers Ireland. Item un hanappe de beril gravez de long taille, & affis en un pee d'or, ove un large bordur paramont, & un covercle tout d'or ove I longe faphir fur le pomel du dit covercle. Item un Cronike de Fraunce en Frauncois, ove deux clafpes d'argent, enamayles ove les armes de Duc de Burgoign. Item I livre de Giles " de regimine principum" [r]. Item un livre de vices & vertues, & un autre rimeie [s] del " hiftorie de chivaler a cigne" [t] tous en Francois. Item un pfauter bien & richement enlumines ove les clafpes d'or enamailes, ove cignes [t] blank & les armes de mon feignour & piere enamailes fur les clafpes, & autres barres d'or fur les tiffues en maner des molets [u], quel pfautier me fuift leffes de remeindre a mes heirs & ainfy de heir en heir avauntdit. Item un habergeon [x] ove un crois de laton merchie fur le pis encontre le cuer, quele feuft a mon feignour fon piere. Item un crois d'or pendant par un cheyne ove une ymage

---

[q] q. breadth, from *feuille*.   [r]   [s] Poem.
[t] The fwan was the cognizance of Bohun.   [u] mullets.
[x] A coat of mail with a crofs of laten markt or wrought on the fpot oppofite to the heart (of the wearer).

du crucifix & IIII perles entour, ove ma benoifon, cǫme chofe du myen qe jay mieux amee. Item jeo devife a ma file Anne un efpiner[y] de linge drap, bordures les coftees de Accuby[z] vermaill & enbroudes & tout entour par anal fans enbrodure. Item un livre beal[b] & bien enluminee de legenda aurea, en Frauncois. Item le meilour palfrey qe jay a ....... Item un pare de pater noftres d'ore cont' xxx ariez[c], & IIII gaudes de get[d] qe fuerent a mon feignour & mari fon piere ove ma beneifon. Item je devife a ma fille Johanne un lit de foye de baudekyn noir le meilour. Item un lit de drap d'or de Cipre ove cignes, & letres de Y ove entiere celour. Item un lit petit pur un clofet de blanc tertaryn[e] batus ove lyouns & cignes ove entire celour, & de ceux ditz litz qe failent courtyn ove tapittis veule qe foit achatez covenablement a eux par l'avys de mes executours. Item II pare lincheux de reyn, l'un paire de III foiall, & l'autre de IIII. Item IIII pare de lincheaux d'autre drap linge de les meillours. Item deux materas, un pare fuftiens, III pare blanketts, outre touz les joialx ove apparaille ad eftre a fa propre oeps, devant lefcriv ... de ceftes. Item XII efquéles & XII faufers d'argent, merchez[f] ove mes armes. Item un hanap d'argent enorres coveres ponfonez ove refones de averill[g] & efteant fur un pee. Item un bacyn flat & un eawer d'argent ove mes armes en la flounce[h] du dite bacyn enamaillez & les fwages enorrez. Item VI peces d'argent novels & II potts quartes d'argent, et XII

[y] [z] [a] [b] [c]
[d] trinkets of jet. [e] Tartarian. Du Cange in voc.
[f] *marques*, marked. [g] [h] rim.

quillers

quillers d'argent. Item un livre ove le pfautier, primer, & autres devocions, ove deux clafpes d'or, enamaillez ove mes armes, quele libre jay pluis ufee, ove ma benoifon. Item jeo devife a ma fille Ifabella foer de les avantditz menureffes un lit de drap d'or de Cipre palez noir & rouge, ove entier celure, teftre, coverlit, courtins & tapittys. Item un bible de Frauncois en deux volumes, ove deux clafpes d'or enamaillez ove les armes de Fraunce. Item un livre de decretales en Francois. Item un livre de meiftre hiftoires. Item un livre " de vitis patrum," & les paftorelx Seint Gregoire. Item pfautier veil tanqe a la nocturn de " Exultate" glofez, autre livre novel du pfautier glofes de la primer, " Domine exaudi" tanqe a " omnis fpiritus laudet dominum," & fount les dites livres de Francois. Item xl li. de monoie. Item un feinture de quire noir ove un bocle & pendant & xii roundes & plaines barres d'or quel feuft a mon feignour & mari fon piere le quele il ufa mefmes meint avis[i] & apres q'il feuft on fon darrein defaife[k], ove ma beneifon. Item je ordeigne & devife mes dettes bien & loialment paies & ma voluntee perfourme, qe tout la refidue de mes biens moebles & nient moebles remeignont a mes executours & executrice de aucun difpofer entre mes povres fervants, & de faire & ordeigner pur l'alme de mon dit feignour & mari & du mien & pur toutz les vifs & mortz, as queux nous avions efte tenuz felonc la difcrecion & difpoficion de mes executours &

[k] quære, difeafe, illnefs. Or is this a cautious way of expreffing his tragical death?

executrice

executrice par l'affent de mes furveours. Item jeo defende a touz mez enfantz & a checun de eux, entant come je puiffe, q'ils en nul manere foient difturbant a mes executours de diftributier aucun manere de mes dites biens apres ma defir & voluntie & lour difcrecion. Item je ordeigne & devife qe fi en enfi foit qe aucun de mes dites enfantz defviont devant moy, ou devant q'ils foient de la age an apres ma trefpaffement, qe touz lez biens qe les ay devifez demure a l'ordenance de mes executours come mes autres biens propres, de faire pur eux & pur moy apres lour bon avys & difcrecion, fi noun lez xl lib. et feinture qe jay devife a ma file Ifabelle, veule qe remeigne a l'abbeffe & efglife de foers menureffes devant dites, coment qe aviegne a ma dite fille Ifabelle. A ceft ma darrein voluntee, ordeignance, & teftament, je ordeigne, face, & eftabliffe cefts mes executours & executrice Monf'r Jerard Braybrok le fitz, Sibille Beauchamp, John de Boys, feneschall de mon hoftell, Sir Nicoll Milx, parfon de Depden [l], Sir Hugh Peintour, chapeliein de ma franc chapell deinx le chaftell de Pleffy, Sire William Underwoode, parfon de Dedifham [m], William Newbole; & mes furveours, Sire Robert Exceftre, priour de Crichurch en Loundres, mon treschier coufin Monf'r Thomas Percy, Counte de Wirceftre, mon fiable amy Sir Thomas Stanley, clerc de Rolles. En teftmoignance de quele ceft ma darrein voluntee, ordeig-

---

[l] Nicholas Miles, rector of Debden, to which he was prefented 18 July, 1387, by the Duke of Gloucefter, in right of his wife, Newcourt II. 208.

[m] q. *Dedham*, in Effex.

nance,

nance, devys, & teftament, ay efcripts mefmes ceftes prefents & mis mon feal l'an, jour, & lieu fufdits.

Alianore, &c. ✠

N. B. A blank left for the probat.

Regifter Arundell pars prima, fol. 163. a. b. 164. a. in the archiepifcopal regiftry at Lambeth.

Eleanor was the eldeft daughter of Humphrey de Bohun earl of Hereford, Effex, and Northampton, and conftable of England. She was married to Thomas of Woodftock, feventh fon of Edward III. and duke of Gloucefter. After his unfortunate exit, fhe lived retired in his caftle of Pleffy in Effex; Richard II. having given her all her own wearing apparel, and two chariots, with fome other fmall articles, which had been feized by the mayor of London, and valued at 19 l. 4 s. 4 d. (Pat. 21 R. II. p. 2. m. 10.) Having lived to fee that king depofed, fhe died October 3, 1399, and was buried agreeable to her will in St. Edward's chapel at Weftminfter, where her portrait in brafs in a clofe gown and mantle remains entire, by the fide of her hufband's flab long fince robbed of its brafs. See it engraved in Sandford, p. 232. By the duke of Gloucefter fhe had one fon Humphrey, of whom fee p. 180, and four daughters; 1. Anne, married to Thomas earl of Stafford, and after his death, 14 R. II. the marriage not having been confummated, to his brother Edmund, flain at the battle of Shrewfbury, 4 H. IV.

4 H. IV. (Vincent on Brooke, p. 490. Dugd. Bar. I. 163. II. 172.) and again to William Bourchier earl of Effex, buried 8 Hen. V. at Lantoni, c. Gloucefter.   2. Joan, married to Gilbert fon of Richard Talbot of Irchenfield, but died unmarried 4 H. IV.   3. Ifabel, 16 years old, 1 H. IV. and a nun among the minoreffes at London. (Dugd. I. 172). 4. Philippa died young and unmarried. Sandford, p. 242.

EDMUND

## EDMUND DUKE OF YORK.

EN noun du pier, du fitz & du feint efpirit, Amen. Sachient touz gentz prefentz & a venir qe je Efmon Duc d'Everwyk, Counte de Cantebrugge, & Seignur de Tyndale, le xxv jour de Novembr' l'an du grace mill & cccc, et du regne n're tres redotes S<sup>r</sup>. le Roy Henry quart appres le conqueft fecounde, efteant en mon bon fens & pleine memorie, eyant regard q'il n'eft in ceft mounde chofe fi certeine come la mort moundeyne quant Dieu plerra, jeo face & ordeyne moun teftament & ma darreine volunte en la fourme q'enfuit. Primerement qe eftre<sup>a</sup> & devife m'alme a Dieu qi la fourma, & a la benoite vierge Marie & a touz les feints & feintes de paradis. Et moun corps a gifer a Langelee pres de ma trefame Ifabele jadys ma compaigne, qe Dieux affoille. Item, je vueil & devife qe touz les debtees qe pourront eftre trovez & coneux qe jeo doie de tout le temps de ma vie foient primerement paiez & agreez. Item je veill & devife qe deux preftres foient ordeignez par mes executours foubz efcriptz pur faire le divine fervice pur m'alme & pur les almes de toute moun linage perpetuelment. Item je vueill & devife qe pur les couftages de moun enterrement, & pur touz mes ditz debtes paier & agreer, tout ma veffell

<sup>a</sup> f. *jeo eftre*, I will.

d'argent

d'argent enfemblement ove touz mes joeaux, biens, &
chateux qe unqes ferrount trovez & contenuz en le inventary de toutz mes ditz biens & hors du dit inventary a
moun paffement du fiecle foient venduz & ordeynez par
mes ditz executours. Item, je vueill & devife qe toutz
mes debtes & les coftages de moun enterrement paiez &
agreez, & deux preftres ordeignez pur m'alme com dit eft,
fi afcune chofe des mes ditz biens y demourre qe de
celuy refidue foit fait regard a mes fervantz & officers qi
me de long temps bien & loialment avront fervi, come a
mes executours ferra advis de faire en difcharge de m'alme.
Et fi de celuy refidu aucune chofe remaint, je vueill q'il foit
ordeyne pur m'alme par mes ditz executours, & pur perfourmir cefte ma darreine volunte come deffus eft dit et declare.
Jeo fupplie a mon tres redotes feigneur le roy q'il luy pleafe
de fa gracioufe feignurie fourveour mes ditz executours.
Et pri & requier a trefreverent piere en dieu l'ercevefque de
Cantirbirs[b], l'evefque de Wynceftr.[c], l'evefque de Durham[d],
q'il lour pleafe de lour bonne volunte tant travailler qe
cefte ma darreine volunte puiffe eftre duement accomplie.
Et pur accomplier cefte ma dite darreine volunte je face
& ordeyne mes executours de ceft moun darrein teftament
ceft affavoir moun trefame fitz de Rotteland & mes
trefamez Piers de Mawan, fenefchal de moun hoftell, Sire
Thomas Gerberge, fenefchal de mes terres, Meiftre Thomas Wrofton moun chanceller, Henry Bracy moun treforer, Sire William Galandre & Richard Alcham mon

[b] Thomas Arundell.    [c] William Wykeham.    [d] Walter Skirlawe.

reycevour;

## EDMUND DUKE OF YORK.

reycevour; et outre ceo jeo veuil & ordeyne, qe toutes billes qe ferrount trovez & comiz al jour de moun dit paffement touchant acun doun ou devis come parcelle de moun dit teftament enfeellez de moun fignet foient pleynement acompliez per mes ditz executours come ma darreine volunte.

Probatio dicti teftamenti coram Thoma Cantuar' archiep' apud Lambeth, 6$^{to}$ die menfis Octob' anno Domini 1402, et tranflacionis noftre anno 7°.

Regifter Arundell pars prima, fol. 194. b. in the archiepifcopal regiftry at Lambeth.

Edmund, Duke of York, was the fifth fon of King Edward the Third, born at Langley in Hertfordfhire, 1341, 15 E. III. created earl of Cambridge 36 E. III. diftinguifhed himfelf with his brother John of Gaunt againft the Caftilians, after which he was created the firft duke of York fince the time of R. I. Having in vain oppofed the defigns of his nephew Henry on the crown, and feen England's fcepter in three different hands, he died at Langley Auguft 1, 1402. His monument (in the chancel of the Friars Preachers there, now the parifh church) is engraved by Gaywood in Sandford's Genealogical Hift. p. 359. He married firft, 1372, Ifabel daughter of Pedro king of Caftile (his brother John of Gaunt having married her fifter Conftance), and by her left iffue Edward earl of Rutland, afterwards duke of York, killed at the battle of Agincourt;

Agincourt; 2. Richard de Coningſburgh duke of York, father of Edward, ſlain at the battle of Wakefield, 1460. 3. Conſtance married to Thomas Deſpenſer earl of Gloucefter, and Richard Beauchamp earl of Warwick; ſhe died 1394, and was buried at Langley; ſecondly, Joan, daughter of Thomas earl of Kent, who ſurviving him was remarried to William lord Willoughby of Ereſby, but died without iſſue 12 H. VI. Dugd. Bar. II. 154 & ſeq. Sandford, 375 & ſeq.

RICHARD

# RICHARD II.

IN nomine fumme & individue trinitatis, patris & filii & fpiritus fancti, beatiffime Dei genitricis & virginis Marie, fanctorum Johannis Baptifte & Edwardi gloriofiffimi Confefforis, necnon & tocius celeftis curie, Amen. Inevitabilis mortis fentencia nulli omnino deferens, ymo[1], nobilitatem, potenciam, ftrenuitatem, genus, etatem, & fexum equali lance concludens, creature racionali nimis redderetur amara nifi poft curfum hujus vite fluctuantis continue vita beacior in patria fperaretur: Et proinde humane providencie fagacitas, fciens nature legibus diffinitum quod cercius nil morte incercius nil hora mortis, folebat horam diffolucionis hujufmodi nedum[2] operibus virtuofis, & meritoriis; fed eciam bonorum fuorum difpenfacione provida prevenire; ut fic hora ipfa inopinata fagaci ordinacione preventa queat fecurius expectari; quod nos Ricardus, Dei gratia qui farcine regiminis regni Anglorum jam ab etate[3] tenera per nonnulla tempora ex regis fupremi clemencia colla fubmifimus in regalis difcrecionis examine revolventes[4] ad teftamentum noftrum[5] condendum & voluntatem noftram ultimam regaliter[6] declarandam dum adhuc recenti & fana gaudemus memoria,

VARIOUS READINGS in the Copy printed in RYMER's FOED. vol. VIII. p. 75.
[1] *fummo ymo parcens [2] nondum. [3] etate ab [4] ponderantes
[5] *deeft. [6] regalem.

memoria, procedere decrevimus in hunc modum. In primis fiquidem, in puritate & finceritate fidei catholice exiftentes, omnipotenti Deo creatori noftro animam noftram⁷ quam fuo⁸ preciofo cruore redemit legamus, & eam fibi intenfiori devocione qua poffumus cum omni mentis defiderio commendamus. Pro corpore vero noftro, quocunque locorum nos ab hac luce migrare contingat, in ecclefia fancti Petri Weftmonafterii inter clare memorie progenitores noftros reges Anglie regalem eligimus fepulturam; illudque in monumento quod ad noftram & inclite recordacionis Anne dudum regine Anglie confortis noftre, cujus anime propicietur altiffimus, erigi fecimus memoriam, volumus tumulari, cujus quidem fepulture feu funeris noftri exequias more regio volumus celebrari, ita videlicet ut pro dictis⁹ exequiis quatuor herfie excellencie convenientes regali pro eodem funere noftro honeftius exequendo in locis fubfcriptis per executores noftros congrue preparentur. Quarum¹⁰ fiquidem due quinque luminaribus eximiis¹¹ & venuftis, regalibus exequiis condecentibus, in duabus ecclefiis principalioribus per quas corpus noftrum vehi contigerit¹², tercia vero cum totidem luminaribus pari forma in ecclefia Sancti Pauli London' honefte ftatuetur; quarta major¹³, principalior, & honorificencior, luminaribus infignibus & regali celfitudini congruentibus copiofe referta¹⁴ & magnifice¹⁵ ornata apud Weftm' ad difpoficionem & difcrecionem eorundem executorum noftrorum debite colloce-

---

⁷ meam   ⁸ fuam   ⁹ quod pro predictis   ¹⁰ quorum   ¹¹ *deeft.*
¹² .contingit,   ¹³ major.et   ¹⁴ refecta   ¹⁵ honorifice

tur.

tur. Item volumus & ordinamus quod corpus noftrum cum de loco ubi nos ab hac luce migrare contigerit verfus Weftm' deferri debeat per quatuordecim, quindecim, vel fexdecim miliaria in die fecundum [16] quod hofpicia congrue inveniri poterunt deferatur. Et [17] per totum iter viginti quatuor torchie [18] circa funus noftrum continue deferantur ardentes ufque ad locum quo funus noftrum hujufmodi fecundum difpoficionem executorum noftrorum quiefcere de nocte contigerit, ubi fingulis occurrentibus vefperis, ftatim poft funus illatum, exequias mortuorum folemniter decantari volumus cum miffa in craftino antequam funus ab illo loco transferatur viginti quatuor torchiis tam in exequiis quam miffa hujufmodi [19] circa funus femper & continue ardentibus; et quod ad viginti quatuor torchias hujufmodi addantur centum torchie ardentes [20], cum dictum funus noftrum per civitatem London' debeat deportari. Sic tamen quod fi infra fexdecim, quindecim, decem, vel quinque miliaria imo ubicunque eciam extra palacium noftrum Weftm' nos decedere contigerit, volumus quod in [21] quatuor locis infignioribus intermediis, & fi nulli fint hujufmodi loci [22] intermedii, in aliis locis competentibus, juxta executorum noftrorum difcrecionem, hujufmodi herfie per quatuor dies continuos cum premiffis folemnitatibus ordinentur. Quod fi infra palacium noftrum Weftm' nos decedere contigerit, volumus quod per quatuor dies fiant

[16] in die eodem  [17] *deeft.*  [18] torgie, *and fo throughout.*
[19] *deeft.*  [20] *deeft.*  [21] *deeft.*  [22] loca

folemnitates,

solemnitates, una existente hersia solemnissima, sed [23] ultima die fiant honorificenciores exequie. [24] Volumus insuper quod si adversante fortuna, quod Deus ex sua misericordia avertat, per maris turbines aut tempestates seu quovis alio modo corpus nostrum ab hominum aspectibus rapiatur, nec poterit reperiri, seu in talibus partibus et regionibus nature solvamus debitum, quod corpus nostrum ad regnum nostrum Anglie propter evidencia obstacula deferri non valeat, quod omnes solemnitates premisse que circa nostrum corpus in presenti testamento fieri sunt disposite, & presertim in monumento, ymaginibus, & omni alio apparatu pro nobis & bone memorie Anna jamdudum regina Anglie & Francie consorte nostra per suos ordinaturis, ac eciam cum ceteris obsequiis funeralibus & omnibus aliis plenarie observandis nullatinus immutentur. Item volumus & ordinamus quod corpus nostrum in velveto vel sathino blanco [25], more regio, vestiatur, & eciam interretur, una cum corona & sceptro regiis deauratis<sup>a</sup> absque tamen quibuscunque lapidibus, quodque super digitum nostrum, more regio, anulus cum lapide precioso [26] valoris viginti marcarum monete nostre Anglie ponatur. Item volumus & ordinamus quod quilibet rex catholicus unam habeat cupam sive ciphum aureum precii sive valoris quadraginta quinque librarum monete nostre Anglicane. Et quod omnia corone [27],

---

[23] scilicet      [24] *Rymer omits the 13 lines following to* Item.
[25] sathane blanio,      [26] precii sive.      [27] corone auree, ciphi;
<sup>a</sup> those in Edward the First's tomb were *silvered*.

cupe, ciphi, adaquaria [b] & vasa aurea, & alia jocalia de auro quecumque, ac eciam omnia vestimenta cum toto apparatu ad capellam hospicii nostri pertinencia, necnon lecti quicumque, & omnes vestes de aras [c], nostro remaneant successori, dumtamen idem successor noster ultimam nostram voluntatem plenarie confirmet, & executores nostros & [28] hujusmodi nostram voluntatem in qualibet sui parte integre ac libere exequi permittat. Quodque omnes annuitates & feoda familiaribus qui circa nos & nostram personam jugiter laborarunt, qui ex nostra licencia propter causas necessarias, utpote infirmitatem vel senectutem a presencia nostra recesserunt, & hiis eciam qui postmodum nobis, presertim circa personam nostram, servierunt & serviunt per nos concessas, juxta tamen dicti successoris nostri [29] & executorum nostrorum liberam discrecionem ratificet & confirmet. Item volumus & ordinamus quod de omnibus jocalibus nostris residuis, videlicet cercliis [30], nowchis [31], & aliis jocalibus quibuscunque, perficiatur nova fabrica navis ecclesie Sancti Petri Westm' per nos incepta [d] & residuum, si quod fuerit, remaneat executoribus nostris juxta nostram hanc voluntatem ultimam disponendum. Infuper volumus & ordinamus quod sex milia

[28] *deest.*    [29] *deest.*    [30] circulis,    [31] nochiis,

[b] ewers.    [c] Sic Orig. Q. garments of arras.

[d] Richard II. built the North porch of Westminster abbey, where are his arms supported by two angels, and under them this device, a white hart couchant under a tree gorged with a gold chain and coronet, borrowed from his mother Joan, and painted on the wall of the South cross. Sandford, p. 191.

marcarum

marcarum auri pro sumptibus sepulture nostre & corporis nostri delacione a loco ubi ab hac luce nos migrare contigerit usque ³² Westm' specialiter reserventur. Item volumus quod terre, redditus, & tenementa tot & tanta que ad quindecim leproforum & unius capellani pro nobis in ecclesia Sancti Petri Westm' celebraturi sustentacionem congruam sufficere poterunt impetrentur ᵉ ; ad que facienda ordinamus & legamus summam mille marcarum. Volumus eciam quod servitores nostri qui hactenus per nos remunerati non extiterant ³³ nec promoti, si qui tales fuerint, de bonis nostris usque ad summam decem milium marcarum secundum executorum nostrorum ³⁴ discrecionem inter eosdem distribuendarum precipue remunerentur. Item legamus dilecto nepoti nostro Thome duci Surr ᶠ decem milia marcar' ³⁵, & dilecto fratri nostro ³⁶ Edwardo duci Albimarlie ³⁷ duo milia marcarum ; & dilecto fratri nostro Johanni ³⁸ duci Exonie tria milia marcarum ; & dilecto ³⁹

---

³² versus     ³³ existerant     ³⁴ meorum     ³⁵ librarum,
³⁶ dilecto nostro consanguineo     ³⁷ d'Aumerlie     ³⁸ ³⁹ *desunt*.

ᵉ The succeeding revolutions prevented this bequest from taking place.

ᶠ Thomas Holland earl of Kent and lord Wake, son of Thomas Holland earl of Kent, and half brother to Richard II. was, after the attainder of Richard Fitz Alan earl of Arundel and Surrey, created duke of Surrey, and marshal of England, 21 R. II. of which honors he was deprived 1 H. IV. and conspiring against H. IV. was betrayed; and flying to Cirencester, taken and beheaded by the town's people, who rose upon him and the rest of the conspirators 1400. Vincent on Brooke, 528. He left no issue by his wife Joan daughter of Hugh earl of Stafford, who survived him, and died 21 H. VI. Vincent on Brooke, 528. He was appointed lieutenant of Ireland 22 R. II. and founded the Carthusian priory of Mountgrace in Yorkshire, to which his corps was removed from Cirencester. Dugd. Bar. II. 76, 77.

fideli

RICHARD II.

fideli noftro Will'mo Scrope<sup>g</sup> comiti Wyltfchir' duo milia marcar'. Ac refervatis executoribus noftris quinque vel fex milibus marcarum, quas pro liberiori fuftentacione leproforum ac capellanor' coram eis celebrator' per nos apud Weftm' & Bermudefey ordinator', volumus per dictos executores noftros expendi [40]. Item volumus & ordinamus [41] quod auri noftri [42] refiduum, folutis tamen noftrorum hofpicii, camere, & garderobe veris debitis, ad que perfolvenda legamus viginti milia librarum [43], noftro remaneat fucceffori, dumtamen omnia & fingula ftatuta, ordinaciones, ftabilimenta, & judicia in parliamento noftro decimo feptimo [44] die menfis Septembr', anno regni noftri vicefimo primo apud Weftm' inchoato, & in eodem parliamento ufque Salopiam continuato, & ibidem tento, facta, lata, & reddita, necnon omnia [45] ordinaciones & judicia [46] ac ftabilimenta decimo fexto die menfis Septembr' anno regni noftri vicefimo fecundo apud Coventr', ac poftmodum apud Weftm' decimo octavo die Marcii anno predicto, auctoritate ejufdem parliamenti facta, habita, & reddita<sup>h</sup>, ac eciam omnia alia ordinaciones & ju-

[40] *This whole fentence comes in at 43.*    [41] [42] *defunt.*    [43] See [40]
[44] 17.    [45] omnes    [46] *Rymer omits the 5 lines following to* que auctoritate.

<sup>g</sup> William Scrope was created earl of Wiltfhire 21 R. II. and the next year made lord high treafurer and knight of the garter, but H. IV. beheaded him at Briftol 1399. Vincent on Brooke, 594. Dugd. Bar. I. 661.

<sup>h</sup> The proceedings of all thefe feffions were of the moft extraordinary kind. The parliament ftrove to carry the prerogative royal to a higher pitch than any king of England had ever pretended to ftretch it, and eftablifhed fuch laws and cuftoms, as were deftructive of the Conftitution and Liberties of the people. Rapin IV. 433. The anonymous writer of Richard the Second's Life, publifhed by Hearne, p. 145. calls it *that great parliament.* The writer before cited and Dugdale (Warw. I. 142.) mention the preparations for the duel at Coventry between the dukes of Hereford and Norfolk at this time, but fay nothing of the feffion there.

dicia

dicia que auctoritate ejufdem parliamenti in futurum contigerit fieri, approbet, ratificet, & confirmet, teneat, & teneri faciat, ac firmiter obfervari: alioquin fi predictus fucceffor nofter premiffa facere noluerit vel recufaverit, quod non credimus, volumus quod Thomas, Edwardus, Johannes, & Willielmus, duces & comes [47] fupradicti, folutis prius debitis noftrorum hofpicii, camere, & garderobe, ac refervatis quinque vel fex milibus marcar' ut fupra pro hujufmodi ftatutorum, ftabilimentorum, ordinacionum, & judiciorum fuftentacione & defenfione, fecundum eorum poffe, eciam ufque ad mortem fi oporteat, refiduum habeant & teneant memoratum, fuper quibus [48] & fingulis eorum confciencias prout in die judicii refpondere voluerint, oneramus; pro premiffis vero omnibus & fingulis adimplendis fummam nonaginta unius milium marcar' ordinamus & deputamus, de quibus fexaginta quinque milia marcar' funt in cuftodia domini Johannis Ikelyngton, et viginti quatuor milia marcarum in manibus & cuftodia dilecti nepotis noftri Thome ducis Surr', de qua fumma volumus quod idem nepos nofter de decem milibus marcar' fibi fuperius per nos legatis folvatur. Et duo milia marcar' de preftito pro expenfis hofpicii noftri tempore quo reverendus pater Rogerus[i] archiepifcopus Cantuar' nofter extiterat thefaurarius per nos factus nobis ad prefens debent'. Item volumus quod omnia jocalia que nobis pervenerunt cum cariffima con-

[47] & comes *defunt. omitting above two lines.*  [48] quibus omnibus & fingulis fummam nonaginta, &c.

[i] Quære, if right, there was no fuch bifhop.

forte

# RICHARD II.

forte nostra Isabella regina Anglie & Francie[49], eidem, si nobis supervixerit, integre remaneant; quod si ei supervixerimus, tunc volumus quod dicta jocalia nobis & executoribus[50] nostris integre remaneant pro execucione hujusmodi nostre ultime voluntatis. Item volumus quod omnia indumenta ac robe corporis nostri, exceptis perlis & lapidibus preciosis, remaneant clericis, valettis, & gromis qui circa nostram personam jugiter laborarunt & laborant, juxta discrecionem executorum nostrorum inter eos distribuenda. Hujus siquidem testamenti nostri regii executores nominamus, facimus, & deputamus venerabiles in Christo patres Ricardum[k] Sarr', Edmundum[l] Exon', Tidomannum[m] Wygorn', Thomam Karliolen'[n], & Guidonem[o] Meneven' episcopos; dilectum fratrem[51] nostrum Edwardum[p] ducem Albimarlie, Thomam ducem Surr' nepotem nostrum, Johannem ducem Exonie[q] fratrem nostrum, & Will'm comitem Wyltschir', quorum cuilibet unum ciphum aureum valoris viginti librarum legamus, ac dilectos

[49] & Francie *desunt*.  [50] successoribus  [51] consanguineum

[k] Richard Metford was bishop of Salisbury from 1395 to 1407.
[l] Edmund Stafford lord chancellor, 1395—1419.
[m] Tideman de Winchcomb, 1395—1401. *Tadmanum*, Rymer.
[n] Thomas Merks 1397, deprived 1399, for his fidelity to his deposed master, H. IV. presented him to the vicarage of Thurminster Marshall, Dorset, 1403; he was also rector of Todenham, c. Glouc. 1404, and died 1409. Hutchins' Hist. of Dorset, II. 133.
[o] Guy de Mona, lord chancellor, 1398—1409.
[p] He was *first cousin* to R. II. being son of his uncle Edmund de Langley, and Rymer has *consanguineum* here and before, p. 196.
[q] John Holand duke of Exeter, second son of Joan by Thomas Holand earl of Kent, brother of Thomas Holand, created by R. II. chamberlain of England 17 a. r. earl of Huntingdon 11. a. r. duke of Exeter 21 a. r. beheaded and buried at Plestry 1400. Dugd. Bar. II. 79.

clericos

clericos & fideles noftros magiftros [52] Ricardum Clifford noftri privati figilli cuftodem, Ricardum Maudeleyn, Will'm Fereby, & Johannem Ikelyngton, clericos [53], ac Johannem Lufwyk, & Will'm Serle, laicos, quorum cuilibet expenfas & fumptus neceffarios dum circa execucionem prefentis noftre ultime voluntatis eos aut eorum aliquem vacare contigerit, juxta tamen [54] difcrecionem dictorum fuorum coexecutorum volumus perfolvi. Quos omnes & fingulos oneravimus & oneramus ut hanc voluntatem noftram ultimam debite exequi & quantum in eis eft adimpleri faciant, ficuti coram Deo voluerint refpondere [55]. Supervifores autem hujus noftri teftamenti creamus, ordinamus, deputamus & facimus reverendos in Chrifto patres Rogerum[r] Cant', & Ricardum[s] Ebor', archiepifcopos, Will'm [t] Wynton' epifcopum ac Will'm [u] abbatem mon' Weftm', Edmundum [x] ducem Ebor' avunculum noftrum, & Henricum [y] comitem Northumbr' confanguineum noftrum. Quos omnes & fingulos quantum ad nos attinet in Domino requirimus & rogamus, quatenus in hanc ultimam voluntatem & difpoficionem noftram debite & folicite quatenus opus fuerit fupervideant, ipfamque execucionem debite demandari faciant; refiftentes

[52] clericos noftros magiftros    [53, 54] *defunt.*    [55] Rymer's copy ends here.

[s] Richard Scrope, 1396, 1397, beheaded for attempting to reftore Richard. He was brother to the earl of Wiltfhire, mentioned in note [g].

[t] William of Wickham, 1366—1405.

[u] William de Colchefter elected abbot of Weftminfter 1386, died the year before the depofition of Richard. Dart II. xxxii.

[x] Edmund de Langley duke of York before-mentioned.

[y] Father of Hotfpur. He joined H. IV, on his landing, and afterwards rifing againft him, was defeated and beheaded at Bramham Moor. Dugd. Bar. I. 278.

vero

vero feu contradicentes prelati ecclefiaftica cenfura percellant & prout eorum officium exigit debite coherceant & compefcant, ficuti eorum Deo red dere voluerint racionem; cuilibet vero fupervisorum noftrorum hujufmodi unum ciphum aureum & unum adaquarium valoris quadraginta marcarum legamus ac eciam affignamus. In quorum omnium & fingulorum teftimonium atque fidem prefentem paginam five prefens teftamentum voluntatem noftram ultimam continens fuprafcriptam in fcripto redigi ac figillo noftro privato & figneto fignari, noftrique figilli magni appenfione, & proprie manus noftre fubfcripcione fecimus roborari. Datum, fcriptum, & ordinatum fuit prefens tefamentum in palacio noftro apud Weftm' fub anno domini mill'mo ccc$^{m^o}$ nonageffimo nono, indiccione feptima, menf' Aprilis die fexta decima, anno regni noftri vicefimo fecundo; prefentibus reverendo patre Roberto[z] ep'o London', ac nobilibus & ftrenuis viris Johanne Dorf' marchione[a] Thome[b] comite Wygorn', & aliis.

For an exact copy of this will (from the original in the Chapter-houfe, Weftminfter) the editor is happy thus publicly to return thanks to George Rofe, efq. It is printed very incorrectly in Rymer, vol. VIII. p. 75.

[z] Robert Braybrook, 1381—1404.
[a] John Beaufort, created marquis of Dorfet 21 R. II. See before, p. 175.
[b] Thomas Percy, brother to Henry Percy earl of Northumberland, note [x], created earl of Worcefter, and lord high admiral of England 1397, taken at the battle of Shrewsbury, and beheaded 1403. Vincent on Brook, p. 609.

D d

Richard

# RICHARD II.

Richard II. was the youngest son of the Black Prince, born at Bourdeaux 1366; succeeded his grandfather Edward III. 1377, when he was only eleven years old; and, after an inglorious reign of twenty-two years, in which some few traits of a good disposition shewed themselves through the dissipation, effeminacy, and favoritism of the age, was deposed and succeeded by his cousin Henry duke of Lancaster, Sept. 29, 1399, and on the February following made away. He was first buried in the church of the Friars preachers at Abbots Langley in Hertfordshire, but removed thence by Henry V. to Westminster, where a splendid monument of brass, with the figures of him and his first wife is still remaining. Engraven in Sandford, p. 203. and Dart.

He married first, 1382, Anne daughter of the emperor Charles, and sister to Wenceslaus king of Bohemia; she died without issue at Shene, 1394, to the great grief of her husband, and was buried in Westminster abbey. 2dly; 1396, Isabel eldest daughter of Charles VII. of France who was only seven or eight years old, and, surviving him, was sent home with all the wealth she had brought to Richard, but no dower[c], and married to Charles duke of Orleans. She died 1409[d].

[c] Montf. Mon. de la Mon. Franc. III. 126.
[d] Hen ult.

## HENRY THE FOURTH.

IN the name of God, Fadir, and Son, and Holy Goſt, thre perſons and on God. 1 Henry, ſinful wretch, be the grace of God Kyng of England, and of Fraunce, and Lord of Irland, being in myne hole mynd, mak my teſtament in manere and forme that ſuyth: Firſt, I bequeth to Almyghty God my ſinful ſoul, the whiche had never be worthy to be man but through hys mercy and hys graſe; whiche lyffe I have miſpendyd, whereof I put me whollily in his graſe and his mercy, with all myn herte. And what tym hit liketh him of hys mercy for to tak me to hym, the body for to be beryed in the chirch at Caunterbury, aftyr the deſcrecion of my couſin the Archbyſhcopp of Caunterbury[a]. And alſo I thank all my lordis and trew peple for the trewe ſerviſe that they have done to me, and y aſk hem forgivenes if I have miſſentreted hem in any wyſe. And als far as they have offendyd me in wordis, or in dedis in any wyſe, I prey God forgeve hem hit, and y do. Alſo y devys and ordeyn that ther be a chauntre perpetuall of twey preeſtis, for to ſing and prey for my ſoul in the aforſeyd chirch of Caunterbury, in ſoch a plaſe and aftyr ſoch ordinaunce as it ſeemeth beſt to my aforſeyd couſin of Canterbury. Alſo y ordeyne and

---

[a] Thomas Arundel, who crowned him.

devise that of my gooddis restitution be made to all hem that y have wrongfully grevyd, or any good had of theirs without just tytle. Also I will and ordeyne that of my goodis all my debtes be paied in all hast possible, and that my servants be rewardyd aftyr their nede and desert of service, and in especyal Wilkin, John Warren, and William Thorpe, gromes of my chambre. Also y will that all those that in eny wyse be bond in any debt that y owe in eny wyse, or have undertake to any man for eny debt that y owe, or that they can dewlye shewe hit, that all soche persons be kept harmlysse. Also I will that all fees and wages that ar not paied be paied, and in especiall to my servaunts of my houshold, befor eny oder. And also, that all myn annuityes, fees, and donacions, granted by me befor this tym be my lettres patents, be kept and paid aftyr the effect of the forseyd letters patents; and yn especiall to all hem that have bene trewe servaunts to me and toward me alway. Also y will and preym y son that he have recomendyd Thomas de la Crois, that hath well and trewly servyd me, and also in the same wyse Jacob Raysh and Halley. Also I will that the Quene be endowyd of the Duche of Lancastre. Also I will that all my officers both of houshold and other, the which nedeth to have pardon of eny thing that touch here offices both of losse and oder thing, they have pardon therof in sembable manere as I of my grase have be wont to do befor this tym. And for to execut this testament well and

and trulich, for grete tryſt that I have on my ſon the Prince, y ordeyne and mak him my executor of my teſtament foreſeyd, kalling to him ſoche as him thinkyth in his diſcrecion that can and will labor to the ſonneſt ſpede of my will, comprehended in this myn teſtament. And to fufill trewly all things foreſaid, y charge my foreſaid ſon upon my bleſſyng. Wetneſſyng my wel-belovyd couſins Thomas erchbyſhop of Caunterbury foreſeyde, and Edward duke of Yorke[b], Thomas biſhchop of Dureſme[c], Richard the Lord Grey[d] my chamberlayne, John Tiptoft[e] myn treaſuror of Englond, John Prophete wardeine of my privie ſeale; Thomas Erpingham, John Norbery, Robert Waterton, and many oder being preſent. In witneſſyng whereof, my privy ſeele be my commandement is ſet to this my teſtament. Iyeve at my manere of Grenwich, the xxi dey of the moneth of Janver, in the yere of our Lord MCCCCVIII and of our reigne the tenth.

[b] Son of Edmund de Langley before-mentioned. He was reſtored to his hereditary dignity of Duke of York, in parliament, 7 H. IV. 1405, and ſmothered to death in the crowd at the battle of Agincourt. (Dugd. II. 156, 157).

[c] Thomas Langley, who had been dean of York and lord chancellor, advanced to the ſee of Durham 1406, and cardinal 1411; died 1437, buried in his cathedral. Godwin.

[d] Richard lord Grey of Codnor, was much employed by H. IV. and died 5 H. V. buried at Ayleſford in Kent. Dugd. Bar. I. 711.

[e] Sir John Tiptoft was treaſurer of the houſhold, 9 H. IV. preſident of the exchequer, and treaſurer of Normandy, and chief ſteward of the king's lordſhips and caſtles in Wales, and the marches; lord Tiptoft and Powis; died 21 H. VI. (Dugd. II. 40). Where buried does not appear, but his wife Joyce, daughter and coheir to Edward Charlton lord Powis, has a monument in Enfield church.

Printed

This will is printed by Weever in his Funeral Monuments, p. 208. from a copy given him by Sir Simon d'Ewes, examined with the original under the privy seal.

Henry IV, only son of John of Gaunt, was born at Bolingbroke in Lincolnshire, 1366, created earl of Derby 9 R. II. earl of Hereford and Northampton in right of his first wife, created duke of Hereford 1397, 21 R. II. landed July 1399, at Ravenspur to claim the crown of England, which was set on his head at Westminster October that year by Thomas Arundel archbishop of Canterbury. The greatest part of his reign was a series of rebellion, war, and bloodshed, which he weakly hoped to expiate by a crusade, but died of an apoplexy in the midst of his preparations in the Jerusalem Chamber, in the abbot's house at Westminster, March 20, 1412, having reigned thirteen years and a half. He was buried at Canterbury, where his monument, with the figures of himself and second wife, in alabaster, remains opposite to that of the Black Prince. (See it in Sandford, p. 274. and Dart's Ant. of Canterbury, p. 85.).

Henry married Mary, younger daughter and coheir to Humphrey de Bohun, earl of Hereford, Essex, and Northampton, and sister to Eleanor duchess of Gloucester before-mentioned; she died 1394, five years before her husband came to the crown, and was buried in the new college at Leicester [f], where Leland thus describes

[f] Itin. I. 17. Knighton, vol. II. p. 2741.

scribes her tomb: "There is a tumbe of marble in the
"body of the quire. They told me that a countefs of
"Darby lay biried in it, and they make her, I wot not
how, wife of John of Gaunt, or Henry IV. Indeed
Henry IV. wile John of Gaunt lived, was called erle of
Darby." By her he had 1. Henry, afterwards king of
England; 2. Thomas duke of Clarence, flain in battle at
Bauge in France 1412, buried in St. Michael's chapel in
the S. tranfcept at Canterbury, as before obferved, p. 175.
3. John duke of Bedford regent of France under H. VI.
died 1435, buried in the cathedral at Rouen. 4 Humphrey duke of Gloucefter died fuddenly at St. Edmund's
Bury, not without fufpicion of being ftrangled, 1446;
buried at St. Alban's, where his monument ftill remains,
and his corps was found entire about fifty years ago.
5. Blanch, married 1402 to Lewis, afterwards duke of
Bavaria. 2dly, to       king of Arragon. 3dly, to the duke
of Bar. 6. Philippa, married to John king of Denmark.

Henry's fecond wife was Joan de Navarre, daughter of Charles II. king of Navarre, grandfon of John king
of France, widow of John earl of Montfort duke of Bretagne, whom he married 1403, at Winchefter; fhe furvived him many years; and dying July 10, 1437, at
Havering Bower, was buried with him at Canterbury.
Sandford, p. 270. Dart, p. 85.

JOHN

## JOHN BEAUFORT EARL OF SOMERSET.

IN Dei nomine, Amen. Anno ab incarnacione Domini fecundum curfum & computacionem eccl'ie Anglicane mill'mo cccc nono, menfis Marcii die decimo fexto, quafi videlicet hora prima, infra hofpitale beate Katerine virginis juxta turrim London. languens in extremis & prope mortem, fanus tamen mente & compos fenfuum, clare memorie Johannes nuper comes Somerfetie, cammerarius Anglie & capitaneus Calefie, teftamentum fuum nuncupativum fecit in hunc modum. In primis, legavit animam fuam Deo, beate Marie, & omnibus fanctis ejus. Item, legavit, voluit, & mandavit, quod debita fua quecumque fideliter folverentur, & quod fervientes fui remunerati forent de bonis fuis, quilibet juxta propria merita & congruenciam ftatus fui. Refiduum vero omnium bonorum fuorum ac execucionis premifforum pofuit folum & in folidum in difpoficione reverendi in Chrifto patris & domini domini Henrici Dei gracia Wynton' epifcopi, fratris fui, quem conftituit ipfius ultime voluntatis fue executorem unicum, ac dominam Magaretam uxorem fuam fupervidentem; teftibus Ric'o Gardinew hoftiario camere teftatoris predicti, Johanne Boys domicello, Thoma Herdi, Johanne Foreft, Johanne Firay, & aliis multis.

Quinto

## JOHN BEAUFORT EARL OF SOMERSET.

Quinto die Aprilis, A. D. 1410, in eccl' London' examinati fuerunt Ric'us Gardinew hoftiarius camere fuprafcripti teftatoris, ac Thomas Hille cuftos garderob' ejufdem, & dictus Walterus Baxceter capellanus, confrater domus fancte Katerine juxta turrim London', in forma juris, & predicti ex parte executoris fuprafcripti, & probacione teftamenti nuncupativi fuprafcripti; qui de dicto teftamento nuncupativo an fuit verum teftamentum ejufdem, fingillatim examinati, dixerunt quod fit, & quod prefentes fuerunt, & alii plures, quando teftator fecit hujufmodi teftamentum, ubi & quando audiverunt eum dicere quod voluit quod fuprafcriptus Dominus Wynton' frater fuus, ac hujufmodi teftamenti fui & ultime voluntatis principalis & plenus executor, & uxor fua fuprafcripta fupervidens; & quod voluntas fua fuit quod debita ftipendarior' Calef' de tempore fuo, & eciam alia debita fua ubique integre abfque defalcacione folverentur, & deinde familiares fui quidam ad fummam centum librar', quidam c marc', quidam XL li. quidam XL marc. quidam XX li. quidam viginti li. quidam xx marc. juxta eorum gradus, merita, & obfequia, remunerentur, & de refiduo faceret dictus executor fuus ficut cuperet quod idem teftator faceret pro eo in confimili cafu. Requifiti ulterius dicti teftes fi audiverunt tunc dictum teftatorem revocare aliquod teftamentum prius conditum, vel executores prius ordinatos, dixerunt fingillatim, ut prius examinati, quod idem teftator nec hujufmodi teftamentum prius conditum, nec executores tunc revocavit, nec aliquid pro tunc locutum fuit de teftamenti materia.

Probatio dicti teftamenti nuncupativi 5 die April' A. D. 1410, in eccl' cathedral' Sti Pauli, London', auctoritate Thome (Arundel) Cant' Archiep'i, coram Mag' Philippo Morgan utriufque juris doctore & curie audientie Archiep'i auditore.

Regiftr. Arundel pars 2, fol. 48, a. b. in the archiepifcopal regiftry at Lambeth.

John Beaufort, eldeft fon of John of Gaunt by his laft wife Catherine Swinford, was legitimated and created earl of Somerfet 20 R. II. and next year marquis of Somerfet and Dorfet; but the title of marquis being obnoxious, as before obferved, he gave it up 1 H. IV. and was appointed chamberlain of England, and captain of Calais. The earl died April 21, 1410, and was buried in St. Michael's chapel in the S. tranfept of Canterbury cathedral, where his countefs erected to him, her fecond hufband, and herfelf, a beautiful monument, with their three effigies in alabafter engraved in Sandford, p. 310; Dart, p. 68. He married Margaret third daughter of Thomas earl of Kent, who was remarried to Thomas duke of Clarence, fecond fon of Henry IV. and died December 30, 1440. Her figure on the tomb between thofe of her two hufbands, her firft on her left hand, and her fecond on her right. Her iffue were, 1. Henry born 1401, died

## JOHN BEAUFORT EARL OF SOMERSET.

died 1418, unmarried. 2. John created duke of Somerset 21 H. VI. buried at Winborn Minster with his wife Margaret under a beautiful monument with their effigies, miserably engraved in Sandford, p. 328. Their grandson was Henry VII. 3. Edmund earl of Morton, who, on his brother's death without issue male, was created duke of Somerset, marquis of Dorset, slain in the first battle at St. Alban's 1455, and buried in the abbey there. 4. Thomas, not noticed by Dugdale nor Sandford. 5 Joan married to James I. king of Scotland, and after his death to James Stuart son to lord Lorn. She died 1446, and was buried at Perth near the king. 6. Margaret married to Thomas Courtney earl of Devon, beheaded 1461. Sandford, 322—326. Dugd. Bar. I. 121—124. Vincent on Brooke 476—478.

ELIZABETH

# ELIZAPETH DE JULIERS, COUNTESS OF KENT.

IN Dei nomine, Amen. Cum hùmane condicionis fit ut cinis in cinerem revertatur, & ubi fumpfit originem ibi finem forciatur, hinc eft quod ego Elizabeth Julers comitiff' Kanc' bone memorie, fane mentis, car ... traditur autem non abfque infirmitate, videns et confiderans mortis periculum & hujus vite finem approprinquare, condo teftamentum meum in hunc modum. In primis lego animam meam fumme & individue Trinitati, fanctiffime Marie ac omnium celeftium fuperiorum[a] confortio. Item lego corpus meum ad fepeliendum in ecclefia fratrum minor' in civitate Wynton', in tumulo Johannis nuper comitis Kancie nuper mariti mei, ibidem abfque quacunque folemnitate feculari faciend'. Item lego & ordino quod fiant v ceree quarum quelibet fiat pond' v libr. ad comburend' circa corpus meum in obfequiis meis. Item lego, ordino, ac conftituo, ad diftribuend' inter pauperes per difcrecionem executorum meorum fubfcriptorum in diverfis locis xx li. monete. Item ad fabricam ecclefie fancti Swythini Wynton', VI s. VIII d. Item lego fabrice ecclefie de Ledhampton fuftentand' per difcrecionem paroch' difponend' XL s. Item lego conventui fancti Swythini

[a] Quære fpirituum.

thyni pro eorum pitantia die sepulture mee, XL s. Item conventui de Hyde pro consimili XL s. Item conventui monialium beate Marie Wynton' XL s. Item cuilibet collegio juxta Wynton', videlicet novo collegio beate Marie, collegio sancte Crucis, & collegio sancte Elizabethe XX s. Item lego cuilibet domui fratrum mendicant' de civitate Wynton', Cicestr' & Southampton' XL s. Item lego XIII fratribus Sancte Crucis XIII s. Item lego fratribus & sororibus hospitalis sancte Marie Magdalen' Wynton' XIII s. IIII d. Item lego cuilibet capellano seculari in eadem civitate Wynton' & cuilibet sorori in hospitali sancti Swythyni de Hyda XII d. Item lego conventui beate Marie de Buchefeld XL s. Item lego conventui beate Marie de Southwyk XL s. Item lego conventui de Notley XL s. Item conventui de Waverley XL s. Item lego vicar' coll' sancti Ricardi Cicestr' XL s. Item lego anachorit' in dicto collegio VI s. VIII d. Item lego cuilibet capellano in eadem civitate XII d. Item lego cuilibet capellano de vill. de Hanoute [a], Warblyngton [b], Bourne, Charlton [c], Blendeworth [d], Clanfeld [d], Katryngton [e], Wynnyng [f], & Farlyngton [g], XII d. Item lego fratribus minoribus Wynton' unum vestimentum nigrum, videlicet, chesible, III awbes, & II tunicles, cum I cap' nigr' de pann' aur'. Item lego eisdem

[a]
[b] Warbleton.
[c] There are two places of this name in Sussex, in the rapes of Bramber and Chichester.
[d] in Hampshire.
[e] Katherington. Ibid.
[g] q. Farringdon, c. Hants.

fratribus

fratribus xviii li. monete, ut orent & celebrent pro animabus Johannis mariti mei & omnium fidelium defunctorum. Item lego duobus capellanis honestis ad celebrand' in villa Oxon' pro anima mea per unum annum integrum x li. Item lego carissime sorori mee Alicie comitisse Kanc'[h] unum magnum portiforium notat' ut ipsa dictum librum post decessum suum disponat in usus pios tam pro anima sua quam pro anima mea. Item lego Johanne comitisse Kanc'[i] unum parvum missale & unum magnum legend'. Item lego priorisse de Noretoñ[k] cartam meam cum toto apparatu ad eadem pertinent'. Item lego inter tenentes meos de Bedhampton[l] decem quarteria frumenti & x quarteria ordei, & hoc cuilibet eorum marit'[m] necessitatem pacientem. Item lego inter famulos hosbandre[n] manerii de Bedhampton quinque quarteria ordei & mixt'. Residuum vero omnium bonorum meorum que habeo vel habere potero do & lego pure, spontanee, executor' meor' subscript' ut ipsi habeant & disponant prout eis viderint melius expedire. Hujus autem testamenti mei ordino, facio, & constituo executores meos

---

[h] Alice, daughter of Richard Fitz Alan earl of Arundel, aunt to the earl of Arundel, whose will is given p. 120. wife of Thomas Holland half brother to R. II. who succeeded his father as earl of Kent, 1360. Vincent on Brooke, p. 283.

[i] Joan, widow of the Black Prince, and mother of Richard II. was first married to Thomas Holland earl of Kent, who died 1360. Vincent on Brooke, p. 282.

[l] in Hants, of which she had an assignment in dower, 37 E. III. Claus. 379. 3. m. 25. & 14.

[m] q. *maritimam*; sufferers by the breaking-in of the sea.

[n] of husbandry.

Henricum

Henricum Beche, Johannem Merfedon capellanum, Gilbertum Bammebury, & Johannem Gyles. In cujus rei teftimonium prefentibus figillum meum in manibus meis prefentibus appofui. Hiis prefentibus, priore de Southwyke, Johanne Uvedale, Bernardo Lucas, Thoma Coke rectore ecclefie de Bedhampton, Thoma Pulter rectore eccl' de Wykeham, ac multis aliis. Dat' apud Bedhampton die Lun' xx$^{mo}$ die menfis Aprilis, Anno Domini mill'mo cccc$^{mo}$ undecimo, et anno regni regis Henrici quarti poft conqueftum duodecimo.

Probatio dicti teftamenti penultimo die menfis Junii, A. D. 1411. in eccl' Lincoln' coram domino Cant. archiep'o. Reg. Arundel pars 2. fol. 154. b. 155. a. In the archiepifcopal regiftry at Lambeth.

Elizabeth daughter of the Marquis of Juliers was married to John earl of Kent, fecond fon of Edmund of Woodftock earl of Kent, and fon of King Edward I. Her hufband dying 26 E. III. fhe was folemnly veiled a nun at Waverley abbey by William Edendon bifhop of Winchefter; but afterwards, quitting her profeffion, was privately married without licence to Sir Euftace Dabricefcourt knt. in a certain chapel of the manfion houfe of Robert de Brome, canon of the collegiate church of Wingham in Kent, by Sir John Ireland prieft, on Michaelmas day 1360, 34 E. III. For this the archbifhop of Canterbury enjoined them the following penance, that they fhould

find

find a prieſt to celebrate daily ſervice in our Lady's chapel in Wingham church, and another prieſt to do the ſame in their own houſe; that ſhe ſhould repeat certain pſalms, &c. daily; and that the ſaid Sir Euſtace, the next day after any carnal copulation had between them, ſhould abſtain from whatever diſh of fleſh or fiſh whereof they moſt deſired to eat, and relieve competently ſix poor people; and that ſhe ſhould go once a year to viſit Becket's ſhrine, and one a week eat only bread and a meſs of pottage, wearing no ſmock, and eſpecially in the abſence of her huſband. She died June 6, 1411, 12 H. IV. Dugd. Bar. II. 94, 95. ex Reg. Iſlip. Sandford 216.

EDWARD

# EDWARD DUKE OF YORK.

EN noun de Dieu tout puissant & filz & saint espirit & la benoite Trinitie & la glorieuse Vierge nostre dame sainte Marie & de saint Thomas le glorieux martir & de saint Edward le benoite confessour & de touz saints & saintes de Paradys: Je Edward Duc de York, de touz pecheurs le plus meschant & coupable, esteant en saine memorie, le XXII jour d'Auft, l'an de grace mill CCCC & quinsze & du reigne Monseig'r le Roy Henry quint puis le conquest tierz, face & devise mon testament & darreine voluntee en la manere qi ensuyt. En primes je devise mon alme a la grace & la mercy nostre seignour Jeshu Crist qui la crea, & fourma de nient, come celuy qui soyet le plus coupable, & disnaturele creature que unques il fourma, considerere es les grante courtoises & sufferance lesqueux de sa haute mercy il m'a de jour en autre monstres, non obstant ma fole vie, & la vilte de mes peches. Item, je devise mon corps estre ensevele en l'esglise parochiele deins mon collegge de Fodrynghay, en mye le quer[a] soubz une plat pere[b] de marble, c'est assavoir ad gradum chori. Item je devise & ordeigne qe mes dettes & restitucions si aucuns y soient dehuement premiez[c] soient paiez a plustost qe fair ce poura apres ma mort, devant toutes autres choses, en devant qe aucuns solempnites

[a] In the middle of the choir.
[b] *piere.*
[c] q. *proviez.*

soient

foient faitez entour mon enterrement, les queux folémpnites apres qe mes dettes foient paiez je veuille qe ils ne extendent outre cent livres en l'ordenance de mes executoures defqueux je veuille que cynqante marcs foient diftributz par démy gros [d] entre les plus povres qe y viendront les jours de mes exequies. Item qe mill meffes des plus povres religieufes qe on pourra trouverer foient a pluftoft qe faire ce pourra apres ma mort celebrez pour m'âlme, defqueux je veuille qe le prior & convent de Wytham en Selwode,[e] foient paiez pour cent meffes, pour chefcun meffe 11d. & femblalement le priour & convent de Beauvale en Shirwode,[f] pour L. meffes, chefcun des orderes des mendinantz en Londres & en ma vylé de Stamford pour L. meffes, en mefme la manere come deffuis, & le furplus de mill meffes fufditz es povres religieux come defuis, & en fpecial as convents de Charthous[g] de Londres, Coventre, & Heenton[h] jouft Bathe, folonc la difcrecioun de mes executours. Item s'il aviëgne qe par la voluntee de Dieu je trepaffe hors de ceft ficle in quel lieu qu'il foit forfpris a Fodrynghay pour y eftre enfevely, & en ce cariant illoeques[i], qe nulles folempnitees foient faites par la chemyn a mes coftages, except qe je veuille qe les chepelleins & clercs efteant a mon dirige & meffes chefcun jour

[d] half groats.
[e] A Carthufian monaftery in Somerfetfhire, the firft of the order in England, founded by Henry II. Tan. N. M. 476.
[f] Another houfe of Carthufians founded by Nich. de Cantilupe, 17 E. III. Ib. 411.
[g] Charter-houfe, or Carthufians.
[h] Henton; a foundation for Carthufians by Ela countefs of Salifbury, 1232. Ib. 474.
[i] carrying thither.

entre

entre eux departez XIII s. IIII d. la ou mon corps reposera chescun noet, & XX s. chescun jour & nuyt departiez entre les povres par denirs, & je vuille avoir sys torches ardantz entour mon corps chescun jour a messe & dirige, & chescun nuyt cynk tapiers, le quel cost je veuille qe soit ensy gouverne qe ne passe VI s. VIII d. le jour & nuyt, issint qe le cost chescun jour ne passe XL s. et je veuille qe sis de mes escuiers, & sys de mes vadlets, & deux chapellens m'accompaignent tout le chymyn, donc avera chescun esquier & chescun chapellein II s. jour, & chescun vadlet XII d. le jour pour costages par XV jours sans autres despenses faire. Item, je devise a mon seignour le Roy le meillour espee & le meillour dager qe j'ay. Item, je devise a ma tresamee compaignee Philippe mon lit de plumes & leopars ove l'apparaill, mes tapitz blanks & rouges au gartiers, lokers & faucons[k], mon lit de vert embroude ove une compas[l], mes deux grands pots d'argent endorrez, les basains couverts queux ele ad au present, ove les lokers & faucons[k] en mye lieu sur bloy[m] champ. Item je veuille qe touz mes servants meignalx[n] queux feurent demorrantz en mon hostel par un an entier devant mon aler vers Harflowe en la compaigne mon souverain seignour le Roy soient paiez par mes executours lour stipendies pour le terme prochein ensuant apres mon trepassement d'icest sicle, cest assavoir a un escuier L s. a un vadlet XX s. a un

---

[k] garters, fetterlocks and falcons; the badges of the house of York.
[l]         [m] blue.       [n] menial.

garceon

garceon º s. & a un page vɪ s. vɪɪɪ d. Item je veuile qe touz mes hopolandrs ᴾ huykes ᑫ nient furrez ʳ foient partiz entour ˢ mes ferviteurs de ma chambre & garderobe par la difcrecion de mes executours. Item qe mes felles & hernoys foient egalment partiz entre mes henxmen ᵗ, except qe je veuille qe Rokell ait le meillour. Item je veuille qe en touz meffes & autres priers qe on ferra dire pour moy qe Monfʳ Seignour le Roy Richard, Monfʳ Seignour le Roy Henry quart, Monfʳ Seignour mon piere Edmund Duc de York, madame ma miere Ifabelle fa compaigne, & touz autres trefpaffez de ceft ficle as queux Dieux pardoint, pour queux je fuy tenuz en ma confcience a faire prier, foient compris auffi avant come moy mefmes, qe Dieux de fa haute mercy eit mercy de eux & de moy le meyns digne de touz. Item, je veuille qe touz mes veftiments, crucifixes, ymages, tabernacles, baffins, ewers, fenfures ᵘ, fconfes, & autres joialx, & apparaillements unqore efteantz en mon chapelle, exceptes les biens & joialx queux j'ay mys en gage pour mon aler en ceft veiage vers France en la compaigne de mon tres foverain feignour le Roy foient apres mon deces deliverez a le maiftre, & fes compaignes de mon dit collegge pour eftre perpetuelment gardez en ycell par eux & lour fucceffours illoeqes a l'onneure de Dieu & fa glorieufe miere, de faint Thomas

---

ᵒ Sic Orig. Quære x s.
ᵖ *hopulandes, houpelands*, long cloaks. L.
ᑫ q. if not *huque*, a huke, or Dutch mantle. Cotgrave.   ʳ not furred.
ˢ *entre*, among.   ᵗ henchmen.   ᵘ cenfers.

le

le glorieux martir, saint Edward le Confeſſour & touz faintz. Item, je deviſe a Thomas Pleiſtede xxl. en memoire pour la natureſſe ˣ qu'il me monſtra quant je fuy a Pevenſey en garde. Item je deviſe a Philipp Beauchamp le haberjon ʸ qu'il ſoloit porter qui le Count Huntyngdon qui Dieux pardoint me donna, & outre ce l'eſpee qu'il port des miens, & dys livers en monoye. Item, je deviſe a Thomas Beauchamp mes brigaudiers ᶻ coverrez de rouge velvet chequete noire & blank, & dys livres en monoye. Item, je deviſe a Johan Popham mes nouvelles brigandiers ᶻ de rouge velvet queux Grove me fiſt, mon baſſinet ᵃ qe je port, & mon meillour chival except ce deſſûis. Item je deviſe a Diprant ma petite cote de maille, le piece de plate qe Monſ. ſeignour le prince ma donna apelle Breſt-plate, le pance ᵇ, qe fuiſt a mon ſeignour mon piere, qe Dieu aſſoill, mon houſell ᶜ, & mon chaperon de fere ᵈ. Item, je veuille qe la reſidue de mes biens & chateux, par ceſt mon teſtament nient deviſez, ſoient emploiez, diſpoſez, & diſtributz, pour l'alme de moy, mes parentes, bein faiſours & touz criſtiens par diſcrecion de mes executours. Et de ceſt mon teſtament accomplir je face & ordeigne mes executours mes chiers ſervants, approvez de loialte envers moy, Robert Wyntryngham clerc, Piers Manan eſcuier,

---

ˣ kindneſs.  ʸ *habergeon*, coat of mail.

ᶻ *Brigandine*, a faſhion of ancient armor, conſiſting of many jointed and ſcale-like plates, pliant unto and eaſy for the body. Cotgrave.

ᵃ baſnet, helmet.

ᵇ q. belly-piece, from *pance*, gros ventre. L. *pance*, a great-bellied doublet. Cotgrave.

ᶜ *houces*, houſings.

ᵈ my iron ſcull cap or morion.

Johan

Johan Muſton vicaer de Careſbrok, & Johan London chapellein, pour ent fair execution ſolonc le pourport d'ycell de quelle execution je veuille & ordeigne qe. Thomas l'eveſque de Durham, Roger Flore, Johan Ruſſell, & Laurence, eient la ſurvieu.

Probatio dicti teſtamenti coram Hen' Chichele Cant. archiep' ultimo die menſis Novemb' Anno Domini 1415, apud Lambeth.

Regiſter Chichele pars prima, fol. 284. b. 285. a. b. in the archiepiſcopal regiſtry at Lambeth.

Edward Plantagenet, ſon and heir of Edmund de Langley before-mentioned, p. 189, was created earl of Rutland and Cork 13 R. II. Of this dukedom he was deprived by Henry IV. and in revenge conſpired againſt him, but the conſpiracy being diſcovered by his father, he made his peace. He ſucceeded his father as duke of York and lord of Tyndale. He founded at Fotheringay a magnificent college [f], for which he was obliged to mortgage great part of his eſtate. He left England Aug. 13, 1414; was at the ſiege of Harfleur Aug. 16, and next day made his will. Having deſired to have the lead at the battle of Agincourt, October 25, he loſt his life in the heat and crowd, being a very fat man, and ſmothered to death. His body was brought to England, and buried

[e] Thomas Langley.
[f] See the contract for building it, Mon. Ang. III. pt. II. p. 162.

in the choir of his collegiate church under a marble flab, with his figure in brafs. After the diffolution, the choir being pulled down by the duke of Northumberland, to whom Edward VI. had granted it, the ftone was taken up; and the corps expofed to view. Queen Elizabeth ordered it to be re-interred in the church, with the grave-ftone over it, and a monument of free-ftone ftill remaining was erected for him on the South fide of the altar, with his arms, name, and date of his death. Dugd. Bar. II. 15. Vincent on Brooke, p. 620. Peck's Annals of Stamford, B. XIII. §. 7. 9. 12. p. 4. 8. 10, 11, 12.

He married Philippa daughter of John lord Mohun, who was re-married to Robert Fitzwalter, and dying 10 H. IV. was buried in St. Nicholas's chapel at Weft-minfter, where her monument remains, with her arms impaled by Fitz Walter, &c. Sandford, p. 382. Her will follows.

## PHILIPPA DE MOHUN DUCHESS OF YORK.

IN le nom de Dieu le piere, & de fitz, & de feint efpirit, & de noftre dame feinte Marie, Jeo Phelip, ducheffe de York, & dame de l'yfle de Wyght, le jour de feint Gregorie, l'an du grace MCCCXXX, a le chaftell de Carefbroke en l'ifle de Wyght, veullant tant come jeo fuy puiffant du corps & de memorie ordeiner ce que l'on ferra de moy & de mes biens apres mon deceffe, face mon teftament en la maner que s'enfuit. Primes, je recommand humblement ma alme a Dieu, fa benoite mere, & toutz les feintes, recreant [a] mercy de toutes mes pecchies. Et quelle part que ma leffe [b] morir jeo eflife fepulture de feinte efglife pur mon corps en l'efglife conventuell de Weftminfter. Auxint jeo voiel, que la ou jeo meorne [c] que la dirigie foit dicte a vefpre, & la meffe de requiem foit dite la matin apres en mefme lieu, & que chefcun preftre efteant a les dites fervices eit xiid. Item, jeo voille que mon corps foit cariè tanque a Weftminfter, repofant fur le voie a certeins lieues, jeo vole que exequies foient faitz, come dirigie a foir, & a metyn devant mon departir une meffe de requiem, & que mefme devoir [d] foit done & diftribue

[a] *craving.*
[b] Kelham has *felerramourir* shall die.
[c] Q. *meorge*, die.      [d] duty, ceremony.

tanque a ma veine ᵉ a Weſtminſter, come en meſſes, almoignes, & altres coſtages xx marcs, ou pleus, ou meinez come beſoigne i ſoit al diſcrecion de mes executours. Item jeo voille que aveine ᵉ Weſtminſter xiii povres homes ſoient veſtus, cheſcun home une hopelond ᶠ & une chaperon de noir, portant cheſcun deux un torche al dirige & al meſſe de requiem a matyn. Item, jeo voille que ſoit donne a cheſcun de les avaunditz homes xxd. de money. Item, jeo voille que le herce ſoit coveree de drap noir tout entour. Item, que une tres bele herce de cire de la mene ᵍ aſſiſe ſoit ſur la herce avandit. Item jeo voille que ſoit diſtribue le jour de enterement perentre M povres homes & femes vi marcs, xl d. come a cheſcun d'eux 1 d. Item, jeo voille & ordeigne pur avoir M dirigies en un jour, & lendemain apres ſoient dites M meſſes, & a cheſcun preſtre iiii d. apres ma mort en tout la haſt que bonement purroit eſtre pur ma alme & toux criſtiens. Item, jeo voille que xiii s. iiii d. ſoient paiez a deux homes pur lur traveyl portant les deniers entour les dirigies & les meſſes. Item, jeo deviſe al abbot de Weſtminſter xiii s. iiii d. & al priour de dit lieu le jour del dirigie & lendemain pur les ſervices vi s. viii d. Item a cheſcun moyne iii s. iiii d. Item jeo deviſe a cheſcun

---

ᵉ *venue*, coming.
ᶠ See before, n. ᵖ. p. 220.
ᵍ A curious hearſe of wax in a ſmall proportion placed upon it. Dugd. II. 158.

preſtre venant a ma enterement pur dirige & chanter meſſes xiid. Item, jeo deviſe xxli. pur chater[h] draps de ruſſet pur veſture de cent poures homes & femmes, cheſcun de eaux une hopelond & une chaperon. Item jeo de iſe a deux honeſtes preſtres pur chanter meſſes & pur dir le Trenthall del Gregory par un an entier pur ma alme & toutz criſtiens xx marcs. Item, jeo deviſe a quatre vincz povres homes & femmes bedredyn[i] xiii l. vi s. viii d. Item, jeo deviſe & ordeine pur les diſpences & coſtages entour ma enterement xx l. & pluis ſi beſoigne i ſoit per diſcrecion de mes executours. Item, jeo voille & ordeigne xx li. pur draps noire achater pur toutz ma meigne encouvertre[k] le jour de ma enterement. Item, jeo voille & ordeigne un chalis d'argent & un veſtement al autre de ſeint Nicholas a quel mon corps giſt. Item, jeo voille & ordeigne al priour de Crichurche & ſon covent de Cantirbury pur prier pur ma alme v marcs. Item, je voille & ordeigne al abbot de Charteſey & ſon covent pur prier pur ma alme xl s. Item, je voille & ordeigne al abbeſſe de Berkyng pur prier pur ma alme vi s. viii d. & al prioreſſe & le covent xxvi s. viii d. Item, al prioreſſe de Stratford[l] pur prier pur ma alme v s. & al covent xx s. Item, jeo voille & ordeigne al abbeſſe de

---

[h] *acketer*, to *buy*.   [i] bedridden.
[k] to cover (clothe) my whole houſhold.
[l] Stratford at Bow, a Benedictine nunnery, as old as the Conqueſt. Tan. 298.

Burnham

Burnham [m] xx s. & a la covent xx s. Item, jeo voille & ordeigne a la prioreſſe de Goryng [n] & ſa covent xx s. Item, jeo voille & ordeigne al college de Fodryngheye pur prier pur ma alme xL s. Item, jeo voille & ordeigne a cheſcun meſon & ſon covent de freres d deinz de [o] Londres de les IIII ordres pur venir a Weſtminſter a la dirige & le meſſe le matyn de mon enterement, a cheſcun covent de dictes freres xx s. Item, jeo voille & ordeigne a mon filtz Wauter, ſeignour filtz Waulter [p], pur aider & de perfourmer la voluntee de mon teſtament, une hanap dore coveres del faſſion de une eſtrille [q] chaſez [r] une anell dore ove une rubye, & un ſautier. Item, jeo voille & ordeigne a le Sieur Tiſtot pur eſtre mon ſerveieur [s] & pur eider & de perfourmer la voluntee de mon teſtament le meillour potté de les deux pottes graundes d'argent endorres. Item, jeo voille & ordeigne a Sire Johan Cornewall chevaler, pur eider & de perfourmer la voluntee de mon teſtament deux pottes d'argent endorrez paleez & pounſonnez [t] ove lilies ſur le covercle. Item, pur meſmes cauſes avanteres [u] cent marcs. Item, je voille & ordeigne a Johan Appilton eſquier cent marcs. Auxſint je voille & ordeigne a Aliſon Seint Paule

[m] Burnham, or Nun Burnham, a ſmall Benedictine nunnery in Yorkſhire, founded in the reign of H. III. Tan. 683.
[n] A ſmall Auſtin priory of nuns in Oxfordſhire, founded t. H. II. Ibid. 427.
[o] *dedans de*, within.
[p] Her ſon by her ſecond huſband Sir Walter Fitzwalter.
[q] *eſtrille* or *etrilie* is a currycomb: but how can a cup be of this ſhape.
[r] chaſed.  [s] ſuperviſor.  [t] ſtriped and ſpotted, or ſprinkled.  [u]

diz marcs. Item, je voille & ordeigne a Richard Wene & Anneyes Wene fa compaigne cent marcs, pur achatre a eulx une corrodie durant fes vies. Item, jeo devife & ordeigne le refiduez de toutz meis biens nient devant devifez que font diftribuez en quatre parties, ceft affavoir comme en meffes dictes, prifoneres releveez, povres fuftines, & male vies amendes, par bon advys & difcrecion de mes executours. Item, jeo voille & ordeigne mes executours Sir John Cornwall, Thomas Chaufer, John Hore, & Sire John Grafwell chapeleyn, & pur mefme le caufe pur eider & de perfurmer la voluntee de mon teftament, jeo voille & ordonne a Thomas Chawefer cent marcs, a Johan Hore & Sir John Cornewaall, a chefcun de eux xx.li. Don defubz notre feal de nos armez, jour, lieu, & an de notre feigneur avantditz.

Probatio dicti teftamenti coram domino Henrico (Chichele) in manerio fuo de Lamehith, 13 die Novembris, A. D. 1431.

Reg. Chichele, pars prima, fol. 428, a. b. in the archiepifcopal regiftry at Lambeth.

Philippa,

Philippa, second daughter and coheir of John lord Mohun of Dunster, was married first to Edward duke of York, whose will precedes this; and after his death to Sir Walter Fitz Walter, knt. by whom she had one son, Walter Fitz Walter, who died 10 H. VI. She died 1433, and was buried in St. Nicholas' chapel in Westminster abbey, where her monument and effigy still remain, with the arms of Mohun and Fitzwalter, engraved in Sandford, 382. and Dart. Dugd. II. 157.

THOMAS

## THOMAS DUKE OF CLARENCE.

IN Dei nomine, Amen. Decima die mensis Julii, Anno Domini millesimo cccc$^{mo}$ decimo septimo, nos Thomas filius regis, Dux Clarencie, Comes Albemarle, & Senescallus Anglie, sana mente, condimus testamentum nostrum in hunc modum. In primis, legamus animam nostram Deo omnipotenti, & beatissime Marie matri sue. Item, legamus corpus nostrum ad sepeliend' in ecclesia Christi Cantuar' ad pedes alte memorie domini & patris nostri, cujus anime propitietur Deus. Item legamus & ordinamus quod, debitis nostris plene persolutis, executores nostri emant, seu quoquo modo impetrent, jus patronatus alicujus ecclesie valoris XL li. per ann. & illam ecclesiam appropriare & unire faciant & procurent priori & conventui dicte ecclesie Christi Cantuar' sumptibus & expensis nostris recuperand' & levand' de summis nobis per dominum nostrum Regem, ac Duces Burie, Aurelian, Burbon, & Alancon [a], debitis, pro IIII$^{or}$ capellanis ydoneis s. cularibus inibi pro animabus prefati domini & patris nostri, ac matris nostre, & anima nostra, & Margarete consortis nostre, & animabus omnium progenitorum nostri Thome, & omnium fidelium defunctorum perpetuo celebraturis & divina officia facturis administraturis annuatim percipiendis pro omni suo servicio,

[a] Berry, Orleans, Bourbon, and Alencon; see p. 115.

quilibet

quilibet dictorum capellanorum decem marcas fterlingorum per manus prioris dicti conventus qui pro tempore fuerit, ita quod dicti prior & conventus faciant & inveniant fufficientem fecuritatem prefatis executoribus & heredibus noftris de dictos capellanos perpetuo, ut prefertur, fuftinendos, & inibi inveniendos, ac de femel in anno fpecialiter faciend' in dicta ecclefia per conventum predictum anniverfarium noftrum, ut moris eft, pro aliis principibus fieri folempniter pro perpetuo duratur'. Item, volumus & ordinamus quod iidem executores noftri emant, feu quoquo modo impetrent, patronatum alterius ecclefie valoris XI. marc' per annum, & eandem ecclefiam appropriandam decano, canonicis, & vicariis, ecclefie collegiate de Newerk apud Leyceftre, ad inveniend' duos ydoneos capellanos divina ibidem pro animabus predictis imperpetuum celebraturis modo & forma prenotatis. Item legamus duo milia librarum fterlingor' de dictis fummis levand' & recuperand' in forma predicta, debitis noftris plenarie perfolutis, ad diftribuend' & erogand' per manus executorum noftrorum, inter fervitores noftros fecundum ftatum & continuacionem in noftro officio per ipfos facto, in remuneracionem laborum fuorum nobis per ipfos impenforum. Refiduum vero omnium bonorum noftrorum fuperius non legatorum damus & legamus Margarete precariffime conforti noftre, ad difponend' & ordinand' de ipfis pro fe & falute anime noftre prout fibi melius videbitur expedire. Et ipfam Margaretam confortem noftram, noſtram, Dominum Johannem Pelham, Dominum Henricum Merſton clericum, Dominum Johannem Colvyle militem, & Willielmum Alyngton armigerum, noſtros facimus, ordinamus, & creamus hujus teſtamenti noſtri executores, ut ipſi illud exequantur in forma ſupraſcripta, prout prefate Margarete conſorti noſtre per aviſamentum predictorum Johannis, Henrici, Johannis, & Willielmi, melius videtur faciend' pro ſalute anime noſtre. In cujus rei teſtimonium preſentibus ſigillum noſtrum duximus apponendum die & anno predictis.

Hec eſt pura libera & ultima voluntas noſtri Thome filii Regis, Ducis Clarencie, Comitis Albemarl' & Seneſchalli Anglie, ex noſtra mera & ſpontanea voluntate, ac deliberacione & certa noſtra ſciencia facta, decima die Julii, anno regni Henrici quinti poſt conqueſtum quinto:

Premierment nous volons & ordonnons a l'onnour Dieu & pour la ſalvacion de noſtre alme, que immediate apres noſtre mort toutes les revenues & proffitz provenantz de noz chaſteaux, manoirs, ſervices, terres, tenementz, o toutz lours appurtenances, en Holderneſſe en le counte de Uerwyk[b], & aillours, ſi bien deins le reaume d'Angleterre come aillours, ſoient levez & receuz par Margarite noſtre treſchiere compaigne, & nos aultres feſſes & executours, d'an en an, aux termes deuz pour faire plain paiement de noz dettes: Et ency[c] a durer tant qe la ſomme de toutz nos dettes a noz creditours dues ſoyent plainement levez.

[b] York.     [c] ainſi.

levez. Et en outre, en plain declaracion de nostre volonte, nous volons & ordonnons que si les sommes a nous dues par nostre soverain seignour le Roy, et les Ducs de Berry, Orleans, Burbon, & Alancon, soient paiez apres nostre mort, nous volons qe le somme levee en la vie de nostre dit compaigne pour paier noz dettes de noz dits chasteaux, manoirs, services, terres ou tenements, soient repayes a nostre treschier compaigne, pour ce qe nous volons qe elle eit les chasteaux & services suisditz pour terme de sa vie de don & grant de nos feffees. Item nous volons & ordinons, qe touts les revenues & proffitz, provenantz de la garde de touz lours terres & tenements, si bien de nostre treschier fils Henri counte de Somerset, come de Thomas filz & heir a Monsʳ Morice Russel chevalier, ensemblement ovec les mariages d'icell, soient disposez & dispenduz en ayde du payement de noz dettes suisditz. Et si le dit Henri conte ou le dit Thomas Russell devie[d] deins aige, lours heirs deins age esteantz, adonques nous volons & ordonnons qe les gardes & marriages de lours heirs, terres, & tenements suisditz, de heir en heir, soient disposez & despendus de noz dettes suisdites, de & pour accomplir nostre testament & derraine volunte. Pourveu toutefoiz que les profits & les revenues de la garde des terres & tenements suisditz, de nostre dit filz, par deux ans entiers prochains devant le plain age du dit Henri nostre filz, soient deliveres al oeps & profit du mesme nostre filz le Counte pour mieulx son estat

[d] deceasé.

fuſtenir. Item, nous volons & ordonnons que tantoſt apres que noz dettes & noſtre derraine volunte ſoient payes & acomplies, que noz feffes de noz chaſteaux, manoirs, ſervices, terres, & tenements ſuiſditz, facent eſtate a Margarite noſtre treſchiere compaigne en les ditz chateaux, manoirs, ſervices, terres, & tenements, o ᵉ touts lours appurtenances ſuiſdits, pour terme de ſa vie; le remaindre, ſi nous devions ſans heir de noſtre corps, des dits chateaux, manoirs, ſervices, terres, & tenements, o ᵉ lours appurtenances, a Henri noſtre dit filz conte de Somerſet, et a ſes heirs maſles de ſon corps engendres: Et s'il aviegne que noſtre dit filz devie ſanz heir maſle de ſon corps engendres, nous volons & ordonnons que la reverſion des ditz chateaux, manoirs, ſervices, terres, & tenements, ovec touts lours appurtenances, remaigne a noſtre ſoverain ſeignour Henri le Roy d'Angleterre le quint, et a ſes heirs roys d'Angleterre, pour tous jours. En teſmoignance de la quel choſe a yceſte noſtre derraine volunte encloſe nous avons fait mettre noſtre ſeal. Donne comme deſſus.

Probatio dicti teſtamenti apud Lambeth coram Henrico Chichele Cant' archiep', die menſis xxiii° Novembris anno Domini 1423.

Regiſter Chichele pars prima, fol. 376. b. 377. a. b. in the Archiepiſcopal regiſtry at Lambeth.

ᵉ f. *ove*, with.

# THOMAS DUKE OF CLARENCE.

Thomas of Lancaster, second son of Henry IV. was created earl of Albemarle and duke of Clarence 1412, constable and lieutenant-general of the army in France and Normandy, lost his life on Easter-eve 1421, by incautiously encountering the French and Scots at Baugé, where he was borne down by a Scots lance, and with him fell several gallant officers, and 2000 private soldiers, besides many of both ranks made prisoners. His corps was brought over and buried at Canterbury in St. Michael's chapel in the South transept; but as his will directs that it be laid at the feet of his father, we must suppose the tomb whereon his image lies at Canterbury, was, with respect to him, only an honorary cenotaph. See it in Sandford, p. 310. and Dart. He married Margaret Holland widow of John Beaufort earl of Somerset, whose eldest son Henry he seems to have adopted, having no legitimate children of his own, Dugd. Bar. II. 196. Sandford, p. 309.

# HENRY V.

IN ye worſhip of ye bleſſed Trinite, of oure laide Saint Marie, and of alle ye bleſſed company of Heven: I Henry, by ye grace of God Kyng of Yngland and of France, lord of Irland, atte makyng of yes preſentes lettres, y ordeynet and diſpoſet to paſſe in to ye parties of France, to recover by help of God, my rightes yere to me longyng, have do write my wille and entente in manere aftir foloyng. For as much as before yis tyme I have enfeffed ſymplich and without condicion Henry[a] erchibiſshop of Cant'bury, Henry[b] biſshop of Wyncheſtre, Thomas[c] biſshop of Dureſme, Richard[d] biſshop of Northwich, Edward duc of York, Thomas erl of Aroundell, Thomas erl of Dorſet, Rauf erl of Weſtm'land, Henry lord filz Hugh, Roger Leche, Wautier Hung'ford, and Johan Phelip, knyghtes, Hugh Mortymer, Johan Wodehous, and Johan Leventhorp, eſcuiers, in ye caſtil and lordſhip of Hegham Ferrers[e], and in other lordſhips, ma-

[a] Chicheley.  [b] Beaufort.  [c] Langley.
[d] Courtney died at the ſiege of Harfleur, 1414.
[e] This eſtate was granted on the attainder of Robert earl of Ferrers, 50 H. III. to Edmund the king's younger ſon, created earl of Lancaſter, and after his attainder reſtored 17 E. II. to his brother Henry, by whoſe grand-daughter Blanche it devolved to John of Gaunt, and ſo paſt to his ſon and grandſon Henry IV and V. The latter ſettled it as above recited: E. IV. and ſucceeding kings, granted it to different perſons, and it now belongs to the honourable Thomas Wentworth, eſq. See Bridges's Northamptonſhire, II. 171—173.

noirs, landes, tenementz, and othir possessions, to me descended as to soon and heir aftir my lord my fadir Henry of Lancastre, last before me Kyng of Yngland and of France, Lord of Irland, ye whiche God assoille, as it is more specialy writen in my lettres patentes yerof maad: And also atte same tyme by myn othir Lettres patentes I enfeffed ye forsaid feffez in ye castils and manoirs of Halton[f] and Clyderhow[g], and in othir lordships, manoirs, landes, tenementz, rentes, services, and othir possessions, to me descended in manere aforesaid, als to soon and heir aftir ye forsaid my lord my fadir; and also in othir landes, tenementz, and possessions purchasset, as it is fully contenet in ye said myn othir lettres patentes: Alle ye whiche castils, lordships, manoirs, landes, tenementz, rentes, services, and othir possessions, been of ye value of $^{ml}_{vj}$li. yerely, whenne yai be descharged of fiez and annuytes with ye whiche yai be now charged: And now it is so, yat of ye forsaid feffez Richard yat was bisshop of Norwich, Edward yat was duc of York, Thomas yat was erl of Aroundell, Roger Leche and Johan Phelip, knyghtes, and Hugh Mortymer, escuier, be deed: Wherfore I wol and pray de forsaid Erchibisshop, bisshops of Wyncheftre and Duresme, Thomas now duc of Excestre and erl of Dorset, Rauf erl of Westm'land, Henry lord filz Hugh, Wautier Hung'ford knyght, Johan Wodehous, and Johan Leventhorp, escuiers, now beyng on lyve,

[f] in Cheshire.   [g] Clithero in Lancashire.

yat thogh yai with othir before nemet been fympfich and without condicion enfeffed in alle ye forfaid caftils, lordfhips, manoirs, landes, tenementz, rentes, fervices, and othir poffeffions; nethiryelees yat of all ye faid caftils, lordfhips, manoirs, landes, tenementz, rentes, fervices, and othir poffeffions, yai wil do fulfille my wille and entent aftir writen; but if it fo befalle yat or I paffe out of yis world, I change yis wille: And in yat cas I wol and pray ye forfaid feffez, yat yai do fulfille my latter wille, ye whiche yai may be certifiet of be my lettre fubfcribed with myn owen hand, and enfeelet with my feel: Firft, I wol and pray ye forfaid feffez, yat at what tyme in my lyve I do afk hem yai refeffe me agayn, or do make feffements to othir perfonne or perfonnes at my nominacion, in alle ye forfaid caftils, lordfhips, manoirs, landes, tenementz, rentes, fervices, and othir poffeffions, in bothe my forfaid lettres patentes efpecifiet, in fuche forme and manere as it fchal like me defire for ye tyme: And if before fuche refeffement or feffements it happeth yat I paffe out of yis world, yenne it is my wille, and I pray ye forfaid feffez, yat yai enformet by hem yat ar or fhal be nemet executors of my teftament, how fer my godes moeble may fuffice to ye paiement of my dettes, and fulfillyng of my laft wille; and if it fo be yat ye forfaid feffez may conceyve yat ye faid executors with my godes moeble may noght paie my dettes, and do playn execucion of my laft wille; Thanne it is my wille, yat of ye iffues, profitz, and revenues, of

alle

alle ye forſaid caſtils, lordſhips, manoirs, landes, tenementz, rentes, ſervices, and othir poſſeſſions, yat ſhal be receyvet by the forſaid feffez, or by any of hem, ſoms ſufficientz and neceſſaries by hem be paiet from tyme to tyme to my forſaid executours yerof, to paie my dettes, and do playn and entier execucion of my laſt wille: And I wol yat alle ye forſaid caſtils, lordſhips, manoirs, landes, tenementz, rentes, ſervices, and othir poſſeſſions, ye forſaid feffez hold in hir owen poſſeſſion til my dettes be playnly paiet, and my laſt wille entierely execut: And yat doen and performet, thanne I wol and pray ye forſaid feffez, yat if yer be at yat tyme on lyve any heir of my body goten, yai wil do enfeffe my ſame heir in alle ye forſaid caſtils, lordſhips, manoirs, landes, tenementz, rentes, ſervices, and othir poſſeſſions, in bothe my forſaid lettres patentes eſpecifiet, to have and to hold to my ſaid heir in ſuche eſtat as I had in ye ſame caſtils, lordſhips, manoirs, landes, tenementz, rentes, ſervices, and othir poſſeſſions, or I yerof mane any enfeffement in manere aforeſaid: And if ſo befalle yat without heir of my body comyng I paſſe out of yis world, or I aſk any ſuche refeffement or feffements as is beforeſaid, thanne I wol and pray ye forſaid feffez .. ye forſaid caſtil and lordſhip of Hegham Ferrers, and in alle othir lordſhips, manoirs, landes, tenementz, rentes, ſervices, and poſſeſſions, in my forſaid lettres patentes, with ye forſaid caſtil and lordſhip of Hegham Ferrers eſpecifiet, Yat, ſeen firſt and underſtanden ye chartiers, muniments and evidences, by force of whiche ye ſame caſtil and lordſhip of Hegham

Ferrers, and othir lordſhips, manoirs, landes, tenementz, rentes, ſervices and poſſeſſions expreſſet in ye ſame my lettres patentes deſcendit to me in heritage, ye ſaid feffez do enfeffe my right heirs in the ſame caſtil, lordſhips, manoirs, landes, tenementz, rentes, ſervices, and othir poſſeſſions, to have in ſuche and like eſtat as I had yereinne before my feffement aforeſaid; forthermore I wol and pray ye forſaid feffez, yat firſt my dettes paiet, and plain and entiere execucion of my laſt wille doen, ye forſaid feffez in ye forſaid caſtils and manoirs of Halton and Cliderhow, and in alle othir lordſhips, manoirs, landes, tenementz, rentes, ſervices, and othir poſſeſſions, in my forſaid lettres patentes, with ye forſaid caſtils of Halton and Clyderhow eſpecifiet, do departe as evenly as yay may in two parties egales ye ſame caſtils and lordſhips, manoirs, landes, tenementz, rentes, ſervices, and othir poſſeſſions, with ye ſaid caſtils of Halton and Cliderhow, expreſſet in ye ſame my lettres patentes: And in as much as yai may godely, ye forſaid feffez do aſſigne in ye toon of ye ſaid two parties, caſtils, lordſhips, manoirs, landes, tenementz, rentes, ſervices, and othir poſſeſſions, in ye South coſtees; and in ye tothir of ye ſaid two parties, ye ſaid feffez do aſſigne caſtils, lordſhips, manoirs, landes, tenementz, rentes, ſervices, and othir poſſeſſions in ye North coſtees of Yngland; and ſuche departiſon maad by ye ſaid feffez, I wol and pray hem yat in alle ye ſaid caſtils, manoirs, landes, tenementz, rentes, ſervices, and othir poſſeſſions, with alle yaire appurtenances yat ſhal in ye forme before ſaid be aſſignet in ſaid North coſtees of Yngland,

Yngland, ye faid feffez do enfeffe my brothir Johan duc of Bedford to have and to hold to hym and to his heirs mals of his body comyng: And if it fo befall yat my forfaid brothir Johan without heir mal of his body comyng departe out of yis world, thanne I wol yat alle fame caftils, lordfhips, manoirs, landes, tenementz, rentes, fervices, and othir poffeffions, fo geven to my faid brothir Johan after his deceffe, noon heir male of his body yenne beyng on lyve, remaigne to myn heirs kynges of Yngland, and be annexet to the corone of Yngland for evermore, in ye beft forme yat ye forfaid feffez, by avys of confeil of lawe, kan ordeigne or devyfe: And alffo I wol and pray ye forfaid feffez, yat in alle ye forfaid caftils, lordfhips, manoirs, landes, tenementz, rentes, fervices, and othir poffeffions, with alle yair appurtenances yat fhal in ye forme aforefaid be affignet in ye faid South coftees of Yngland, ye faid feffez do enfeffe my brothir Umfray duc of Glouceftre to have and to hold to hym and to his heirs mals of his body comyng: And if it fo befalle yat my forfaid brothir Umfrey without heir mal of his body comyng departe out of yis world, thanne I wol yat alle ye fame caftils, lordfhips, manoirs, landes, tenementz, rentes, fervices, and othir poffeffions fo geven to my faid brothir Umfray after his deceffe, noon heir mal of his body yenne beyng on lyve, remaigne to myn heirs kynges of Yngland, and be annexet to ye Corone of Yngland for evermore, in ye beft forme yat ye forfaid feffez, by avys of confeil of lawe, kan ordeigne or devife: And if it fo befalle yat or my dettes be fully paiet, and my laſt wille playnly execut, ye forſaid feffez dyee alle ſave thre, two, or oon, thanne I wol and pray the thre, two, or oon, yat yai in alle ye forſaid caſtils, lordſhips, manoirs, landes, tenementz, rentes, ſervices, and othir poſſeſſions, in bothe my forſaid lettres patentes expreſſet yai do enfeffe two of the xii perſonnes of ye which ye names been hereaftir writen, Robert[h] biſshop of Saleſbury, Johan[i] biſhop of Coventre and Lichefeld, Edward Courteney, Gilbert Talbot, Johan Neville, knyghtes, Robert lord of Wylughby[k], Edward Holand, Gilbert Umfraville, Johan Rodenhale, and Robert Babthorp, knyghtes, Roger Flore, and Johan Wilcotes, eſcuiers; and yat yenne in alle ye forſaid caſtils, lordſhips, manoirs, landes, tenementz, rentes, ſervices, and othir poſſeſſions, ye forſaid two do refeffe yaire feffours or feffour, and ye remaignant of ye ſaid xii perſonnes yat yenne ſhal happen to be on lyve, for to fulfille and execut all yat at yat tyme happeth to be unparformet of all my wille before writen. And in witneſſe yat this is my full wille and entente, I have ſet herto my grete ſeel, and my ſeel yat I uſe in ye governance of myn heritage of Lancaſtre: And I have ſubſcribed with myn owen hand yes preſentes lettres endentet and inpartit, and do cloſe hem undir my prive ſeel, ye xxi day of Juyl, ye yere of our Lord a thowſand foure hundred and ſeventene, and of my regne fift. This is my ful wille God knoweth.

[h] Robert Hallam, 1408—1417.
[i] John Keterich, 1415; tranſlated to Exeter 1419.
[k] Robert lord Willoughby of Ereſby, a gallant commander in this king's and his ſon's French wars; died 30 H. VI. Dugd. Bar. II. 85.

Voluntas

Voluntas metuendiffimi domini noftri regis intimanda feoffatis fuis in c'tis dominiis hereditatis Lancaftr'.

For a tranfcript of this will (from the original in the Chapter-houfe at Weftminfter) I am indebted to my worthy friend Abraham Farley, efq. deputy chamberlain of the receipt of his Majefty's Exchequer.

Henry V. the Conqueror of France, was born 1388; and, after a fhort but glorious reign of 9 years, 5 months, and 14 days, died in the 34th year of his age of a fever and flux, at Bois de Vincennes in France, Aug. 29, 1422; and was buried in the Confeffor's chapel at Weftminfter, in a little chapel, enlarged and beautified by Henry VII. and now kept lockt, where his monument and effigy, a headlefs defaced trunk of oak, remains. See Sandford, 289, 290.

See in Rymer, X. 506, a writ from Henry VI. to make good the payment of the legacy of £.200. to the clerks of Henry V's chapel, out of the lands and caftles in the hands of the archbifhop, &c. to be by them made over to the other executors, Walker Lord Hungerford, William Porter, Robert Babthorp, and John Leventhorp. Dated at Weftm. May 12, 1432. 10 Henry VI. Rot. Parl. IV. p. 393. A writ 3 Henry VI. 1425. in Rymér, X. 346. (tranfcribed in the Appendix to this volume, p. 407.) fpecifies veftments left by Henry V. to nine churches in France, which do not appear here.

## KATHERINE, QUEEN OF HENRY V.

THIS Princess, youngest daughter of Charles VI. king of France, born Oct. 27, 1400, was married June 3, 1420, to Henry V. by whom she had one son, afterwards king Henry VI. In 1428, she took to her second husband Owen Tudor, a Welsh gentleman of little fortune, though of illustrious birth, by whom she had three sons: 1. Edmund, created earl of Richmond, married to Margaret daughter of John Beaufort duke of Somerset, by whom he had king Henry VII. and dying 1456, was buried at St. David's, where his monument remains in the middle of the choir. 2. Jasper, created by H. VI. earl of Pembroke, which title he was twice deprived of by E. IV. but restored by Henry VII. and also created duke of Bedford. He married Catherine Rivers, and died 11 H. VII. and was buried in Keynsham abbey, Oxfordshire; his natural daughter Helen was mother of bishop Gardener. 3. Owen, a monk at Westminster.

She died at Bermondsea Jan. 2, 1437, and was buried at Westminster by her first husband. Her corps, being taken up when her grandson Henry VII. laid the foundation of his new chapel, remained above ground till it was pulled to pieces by the spectators and Westminster scholars; and what remains, being some masses of flesh dried as if tanned, is kept in a box within her husband's chapel.

It being notified to king Henry VI, in parliament, that his mother had made him executor of her will; the king appointed Robert Rolleston clerk, keeper of the great wardrobe, John Merston and Richard Alrede esquires, to execute the said queen's will, under the direction of Henry Beaufort bishop of Winchester, the duke of Gloucester, and the bishop of Lincoln, or any two of them, to whom they should account. The original will is not now to be found; but the commiſſion for executing it is as follows:

REX, omnibus ad quos, &c. Salutem. Sciatis, quod cum recolende memorie domina Katerina nuper regina Anglie, mater noſtra precariſſima, nos in teſtamento ſuo ſolum executorem ſuum ejuſdem teſtamenti nominaverit; ac nos conſiderantes, qualiter propter ardua & urgentia negotia, nos, ſtatum & utilitatem regni noſtri intime concernentia, taliter in preſenti occupati & prepediti ſumus, quod circa ea que pro debita & celeri expeditione executionis teſtamenti predicti pertinent faciend' & explend' commode & effectualiter intendere non poſſumus, ut vellemus; Volentes igitur, pro cura & adminiſtratione in hac parte fiend', ne executio ejuſdem teſtamenti in defectu noſtri ex cauſis predictis aliqualiter retardetur, ordinare & in quantum poſſumus, ut tenemur, providere; de aſſenſu dominorum ſpiritualium & temporalium, ac conſenſu communitatis regni noſtri Anglie, in preſenti parliamento noſtro exiſten', auctoritate ejuſdem parliamenti, ordinavimus & deputavimus, dilectos & fideles noſtros, Robertum Rolleſton

Rolleston clericum custodem magne garderobe nostre, Johannem Merston armigerum, & Ricardum Alred armigerum, ad omnia & singula jocalia, bona, catalla, & denariorum summas, ac debita, compota & arreragia firmarum, ac aliorum debitorum quorumcumque, que fuerunt predicte matris nostre, vel sibi quomodolibet spectantia sive pertinentia, infra regnum nostrum Anglie & extra, die confectionis testamenti predicti seu postea, de omnibus officiariis & ministris ipsius matris nostre, ac aliis personis quibuscumque, per indenturas inde inter ipsos Robertum, Johannem, & Ricardum, & predictos officiarios, ministros, seu personas debite conficiend'; necnon omnium summarum debitorum debita per quascumque personas, & a quibuscumque debita, que fuerunt prefate matris nostre, aut de jure legis nostre Anglicane eidem matri nostre qualitercumque esse aut accidere debuerunt, recipiend' & levand'. Volumus etiam, & auctoritate predicta ordinamus, quod predicti officiarii & ministri prefate matris nostre, ac alie persone predicte, omnia & singula jocalia, bona & catalla predicta, eisdem Roberto, Johanni, & Ricardo, per hujusmodi indenturas omnino reddere & liberare teneantur: quibuscumque adquisitionibus & proprietatis mutationibus, que de prefata matre nostra, post primum diem Januarii ultimo preteritum, ad instantiam servientum seu familiarium suorum vel alicujus eorum, ipsa in extremis languente, fieri pretenduntur, penitus cassatis & irritatis. Et quod predicti Robertus, Johannes,

singulares personas non in communitates ista legacio fiat. Item volo quod circa sepulturam meam, sive circa meas exequias principales, non sint nimis sumptuose seu pompose expense, nec alique nisi secundum discrecionem supervisorum testamenti mei, executorumque ejusdem, sed tantum quinque ordinentur cerei, stantes super quinque candelabra circa corpus meum, sine ampliori apparatu qui in talibus ordinari seu fieri consuebat. Item volo quod in die sepulture, sive exequiarum mearum principalium, sint tot torchei circa corpus meum continue ardentes ad Placebo et dirige, & in crastino ad missam, & toto tempore sepulture mee quot annos vixi, miserante Deo, in vita presenti, usque ad tempus illud, & remaneant dicti torchei omnes & singuli in eadem ecclesia, post sepulturam meam ubi corpus meum sepelietur ad illuminand' in elevacione corporis domini Ihesu Christi. Et volo quod tot sint pauperes viri quot erunt torchei qui eosdem torcheos toto prescripto tempore teneant, & habeat quilibet eorum unam togam, & unum capicium [a] de albo panno, & tot denarios quot annis vixi ut supradictum est. Item volo quod tot eligantur mulieres egene & bone fame & indigentes quot erunt viri pauperes tenentes torcheos predictos, & habeat quilibet earum unam togam & unum capicium de albo panno & tot denarios quot & pauperes prescripti. Et predicti omnes tam viri quam mulieres onerentur caritatis intuitu animam meam, animasque Margarete uxoris mee,

[a] *capuche*, hood.

parentum & progenitorum meorum, benefactorum ac omnium aliorum pro quibus teneor exorare vel exorari facere, & omnium fidelium defunctorum precibus suis devotis Deo & sanctor' patrociniis humiliter commendare. Item volo quod in die sepulture mee sive exequiarum mearum principalium generalis fiat distribucio sub hac forma, quod cuilibet venienti & in forma pauperis elemosinam petenti unus distribuatur denarius; & in quolibet anniversario tam mei, quam Margarete uxoris mee, volo quod abbas predicti monasterii si presens fuerit habeat VI s. VIII d. prior vero si presens fuerit habeat III s. IIII d. et quilibet ceterorum monachorum ejusdem monasterii qui in dictis anniversariis presens fuerit habeat xx d. Et pro custagiis, sumptibus, & expensis dictor' anniversarior' nostror' lego & assigno prefato monasterio sancti Edmundi cccc marc' usualis monete Anglie de bonis meis, & hac sub condicione, si videlicet ipse dominus abbas, cum ceteris monachis monasterii ejusdem, manucapere & suscipere super se voluerint, infra tempus certum, de consensu executor' & supervisorum meorum ipsis limitandum, ipsum monasterium in tantum dotare ecclesiarum appropriacione, vel terrarum empcione, earumdemque mortificacione, quod ex earum valore poterint onera predict' anniversarior' de cetero imperpetuum infallibiliter supportare, fideliterq' & effectualiter adimplere. Quod si predictus dominus abbas & monachi cum condicione & modificacione oneris predicti modo quo prefertur, recipere prefat' cccc marc' deliberate recusaverint, tunc volo quod

quod per avifamentum & difcrecionem fuperviforum & executorum teftamenti mei predicti, predicte cccc marc' deliberentur & erogentur in ufum operum mifericordie, videlicet in fuftentacionem & relevacionem tam monachorum, canonicorum, monialium, quam alior' pauperum ubi conveniencius ad Dei laudem, & honorem & falutem anime mee, magis predictis fuperviforibus & executoribus videbitur expedire; & quod hoc fiat cum feftinacione qua commode & racionabiliter poterit adempleri. Item volo & rogo quod fi predicti dominus abbas & monachi ejufdem monafterii fuper fe fufcipere voluerint onus predictum in forma, quod tunc in capitulis anniverfar' predict' prox' preordinatis fpecialiter recommendentur dicti monafterii monachorum precibus anima mea, Margarete uxoris mee & anime parentum noftrorum, ac benefactorum, ac omnium pro quibus tenemur exorare vel exorari facere, ac omnium fidelium defunctorum. Item lego domui Cartufien' de Monte Gracie [b] Eborac' dioc', quolibet anno a tempore mortis mee XL l. et hoc quamdiu dicta domus Cartufien' eft penfionaria vel penfione onerata Domine Johanne Regine Anglie pro prioratu de Hynkley [c] Lincolnien' dioc' dicte domui conceffo anno regni regis Henrici quinti tercio. Et volo quod ceffante penfione ceffet & legatum.

[b] The Carthufian priory of Mountgrace; c. York, founded 1396, by Thomas Holland duke of Surry and Kent (mentioned in note [e], p. 196). Tanner, p. 965.

[c] Hinckley was an alien priory of two Benedictine monks, belonging to Lyra abbey in Normandy, and given for a time to the Carthufian priory of Mountgrace, by R. II. wholly annexed to it by H. V. and after the diffolution, granted 34 H. VIII. to the dean and chapter of Weftminfter, who ftill enjoy it. Tanner, p. 241.

Item lego principali altari illius paroch' ecclesie infra cujus parochie limites continget me diem claudere extremum, nomine principalis five mortuarii, secundum quod consuetudo illius loci expofcit & a morientibus ibidem folvi folebat. Item lego fabrice five ornamentis ejusdem ecclesie cs. Item lego cuilibet facerdoti in eadem parochia mortis mee tempore existenti vi s. viii d. Item clerico parochiali ibidem iii s. iiii d. Item cuilibet domui Cartufien' in Anglia, domo Cartufien' de Monte Gracie folum except', v marc'. Item lego domino Johanni London in ecclefiæ Sancti Petri Weftmonafterii reclufo xli. Item lego mulieri recluse infra Bifhopefgate, London, xx s. Item lego domine Johanne recluse in ecclefia Sancti Clementis extra Temple Barre, xx s. Item lego domine Alicie recluse apud fanctum Albanum, xx s. Item lego cuilibet infirmo five invalitudinario infirmitatis, debilitatis, feu fenectutis caufa, in hiis quinque hofpitalibus exiftentibus, videlicet hofpitali fancte Marie, hofpitali fancti Bartholomei, hofpitali de Elfyng, hofpitali fancte Thome, et hofpitali fancti Egidii prope London, xii d. Item lego incarceratis hiis quinque carceribus, viz. Ludgate, Newgate, Fleete, Kyngesbenche, and Marchalfie, c li. diftribuend' pro eorum liberacione extra prifonam vel carceres, juxta difcrecionem executorum & fupervisorum meorum. Item lego ordini fratrum minorum in regno Anglie xl li. fecundum difcrecionem miniftri ejufdem ordinis & regni, ac diffinitorum[d] provincialis capituli in comunibus

[d] *Diffinitor* or *Definitor*, the vifitor of the order in general chapter. Du Cange.

ejufdem

ejufdem ordinis utilitatibus difponend'. Item lego ordini fratrum predicatorum ejufdem regni xxli. Item lego ordini fratrum Carmelitarum ejufdem regni xxli. Et volo quod fecundum difcrecionem provincialium ipforum ordinum ac diffinitorum capituli fuorum provincialium in communibus ordinum utilitatibus expendantur. Item lego ad honorem Dei omnipotentis, beate Marie femper virginis matris fue, fancti Gregorii martiris, & omnium fanctorum ejus, ecclefie collegialis de Wyndefore meam maximam crucem de argento deaurato cum armis meis fuper eandem. Item lego eidem ecclefie duas pelves de argento deaurato cum nativitate domini & annunciacione beate Marie [e] enamillat' in medio. Item lego eidem ecclefie unum par turribulorum de argento deaurato. Item lego eidem ecclefie unum veftimentum [f] integrum rubei coloris melius quod habeo de panno velveto aureo, id eft, unum cafulam cum II dalmaticis, III albis, III amictis, II ftolis, III manipulis, II towaillis, cum toto ornamento pro altare & unum corporas caas [g] uno panno pro pulpeto, VI capis, cum omnibus ceteris capis rubeis de panno aureo. Item lego

[e] This may help to folve the difficulty in note [r] p. 115. as it fhews the Nativity and Annunciation were common fubjects for enamelling.

[f] *veftimentum*, a whole fuit of church apparel, comprehending the *cafula* or cowl; the *dalmatica* or upper robe; the *alba* or albe, a kind of furplice; the *amictus* or amice, anfwering to the fcarf; the *ftola*, which, like the amice, went over the neck and hung down before, and was richly embroidered; the *manipulus* or handkerchief, worn over the left arm; the towels or napkins for the altar, which had alfo an altar cloth of linen, and another to hang down in front of the altar, the fontlet and curtains, the cafe for the pix, the pulpit cloth, and the *capæ* or copes. Du Cange in vocib.

[g] corporax cafe, or cafe for the pix.

eidem

eidem ecclefie meliorem calicem cum patena quem habeo de argento deaurato cum angelis thurificantibus fupra pedem ejufdem cum 11 melioribus cruettis pro vino & aqua de argento deaurat'. Item quia chriftianiffimus [h] princeps dominus meus Rex convenire intendit, & pro Deo pofuit [i], cum principali & capitali domo cui prioratus de Hincley fupradict' attinebat in Francia, quod de appropriacione quarundam domorum ejufdem religionis [k] ad prioratum de Sion [l] apud Shene per eundem chriftianiffimum principem noviter fundat' & dotat' una & pro appropriacione ejufdem prioratus de Hincley ad prefatam domum Cartufien' de Monte Gracie, quod eadem domus principalis merito & jufte ftarei content'[m] hinc, et pro recompenfa domui principali faciend' pro fepe dicto prioratu de Hyncley, lego & affigno quingent' marc'. Et fi poft concordiam factam inter dominum meum regem, & domum capitalem in fummam in quam convenient pro toto appropriando precio pertinente dicto prioratui de Hynkley, ad plus fe extendit quam ad quingent' marc', tunc volo quod fuppleatur de refiduo bonorum meorum. Item lego ecclefie Cartufien' de Monte Gracie unam crucem de argento deaurato cum lapide vocato berill in pede ad fervan-

[h] This title has been claimed by the kings of France from the beginning of that monarchy, and confirmed by Pope Pius II. to Lewis XI. who leaft of all deferved it: It feems to be given here more as a complimentary epithet to our Henry VI. on account of his piety.

[i] Quære, bound himfelf before God.

[k] of the fame *order*.

[l] This is the priory of *Jefus of Bethlem*, begun by H. V. 1414, for 40 Carthufian monks. Tanner, p. 544.

[m] Sic Orig.

dum

dum corpus Chrifti. Item lego prioratui de Wormyngey ⁿ unum veftimentum integrum blodii º pouderat' cum ftellis aureis, id eft, unam cafulam, cum II dalmaticis, III albis, III amictis, II ftolis, III manipulis, III capis, uno panno ad ponend' ante altare, uno panno ad ponend' fuper altare, & uno panno pro pulpeto, II towaillis pro altari cum frontela, ac uno corporas caas, & II ridellᴾ, de eodem, nec non II candelabris pro altari de argento, & meo majori Holiwater ftoppe-ᵠ de argento pro aqua benedicta cum afperforio de argento. Item lego capelle Beate Marie ʳ in ecclefia fancti Edmundi de Bury in cujus parte boriali difpono tumulari, unum veftimentum album de panno aureo, id eft, unam cafulam, unam albam, unam amictam, unam ftolam, unum manipulum, cum uno panno ad ponend' ante altare, uno panno ad ponend' fupra altare. Item unum calicem cum patena de argento deaurato, & II cruettis de argento deaurato, & eciam II candelabra de argento & unum miffale. Item lego monafterio monialium de Berkyng unum veftimentum de nigro & viridi velveto aureo cum

ⁿ Wormegay, a priory of black canons in Norfolk, founded t. R. I. united to Pentney, 1468. Tann. p. 354. The duke had a grant of the honor of Wyrmgay, 9 H. IV. Dugd. II. 125.

º blue.

ᴾ curtains.

ᵠ veffel for holy-water: this term occurs frequently in Blomefield's Hift. Norfolk.

ʳ The chapel of the Virgin here mentioned appears to have been, not where fuch chapels ufually were, at the E. end, but on the N. fide of the choir. As the duke directs his body to be buried on the *North* fide of the chapel, it may raife a doubt whether the body found, 1772, on the *South* fide could be his. See Archæol. IV. 312. and plan.

orphareis

orphareis ˢ de albo, id eſt, unum caſulam cum II dalmaticis, III albis, III amictis, duabus ſtolis, III manipulis, & III capis. Item lego ſorori mee Johanne ᵗ comitiſſe de Weſtmerland unum librum vocat Triſtram ᵘ. Item lego fratri meo Thome Swynford ˣ, unum ciphum cum coopertorio de argento deaurato ſecundum diſcrecionem executorum meorum nominand'. Item lego quaſdam ſummas auri inter armigeros meos, ceteroſque meos ſervientes diſtribuend' prout patet inferius, videlicet Thome Swynford, L marc'. Matildi Fulſhurſt, x marc'. Georgio Wighton, xx marc'. Johanni Walpoole, xL marc'. Willielmo Frenyngham, x marc'. Nicholao Porpoint, x li. Ricardo Togood, x li. Thome Swanton, c s. Johanni Smyth, v marc'. Johanni Kirton, x li. Willielmo Frere, x marc'. Roberto Bedelyngton, x li. Petro Walpole, c s. Johanni Northwode, xx li. Johanni Bermyngham, x li. Will. Bolton, xL li. Thome Sandon, xx marc'. Thome Boſwyle, x li. Johanni Aubrey, c s. Johanni Felix, c s. Johanni Neve, xL s. Thome Parys, c s. Johanni Lucas, xx marc'. Willielmo Burgh, xx marc'. Ricardo de Chaundrey, c s. Johanni Doucheman, x li. Johanni Maxey, c s. Will. Hert, v marc'. Alano Holme, c s. Johanni Gregory, xL s. Simoni Crokehorn, c s. Johanni Sumpterman, x marc'.

ˢ Fringes of gold thread. Du Cange in voc. *Aurifrigium. Orfrys,* Chaucer's Romant of the Roſe.

ᵗ Joan Beaufort married to her 2d huſband Ralph Neville firſt earl of Weſtmorland, and died 1440. See before, p. 176.

ᵘ A romance of that name.

ˣ His mother's ſon by her firſt huſband Sir Otes Swynford.

Roberto Norman, xl s. Rogero Brice, xl s. Henrico Haunſon, x li. Chriſtoforo Pulford, c s. Ric' Ryxton, v marc' Henrico Porter, xl s. Willielmo de Coquina, xl s. Willielmo Brone, x li. Ignaſio Cliſton, x li. Radulpho Wadeſwyk, xx mark'. Edmunde Thawer, x li. Item lego decano, preſbiteris, clericis & pueris qui mee modo capelle deſerviunt, c li. ſterling, pro qua ſumma c li. habend' & diſtribuend', ut prefertur, juxta diſcrecionem executorum meorum, volo omnes et ſingulos libros mee dicte capelle vendi meliori modo quo ſciverint mei predicti executores, quibus libris ſic venditis ſi quid de predicta ſumma c li. defuerit, id ſuppleri volo de reſiduo bonorum meorum. Item volo & ordino quod a die obitus mei uſque in diem ſepulture mee, & eodem die, domus & familia mea in tali modo infra prout eſſe cognoſcitur, pro preſenti, ad cuſtus & expenſas meas per viſum & diſcrecionem executorum meorum predict' cuſtodiatur. Item volo quod executores mei attendant diligenter quod omnes qui tempore mortis mee erunt michi ſervientes in familia domus mee, quibus in ſpeciale nichil legavi, nec aſſignavi, racionabiliter remunerentur de robis & equis meis ſecundum ſtatus & gradus perſonarum, per diſcrecionem dictorum executorum meorum. Item quia mutuum preſtare pro Deo & nichil temporale inde ſperare dinoſcitur acceptum, complacitum pariter, & ab eo preceptum, idcirco preſentibus lego & aſſigno c li. ad deponend' in ſecura ciſta infra collegium Regine in univerſitate Oxon', ut ſcolares indigentes

gentes per modum mutacionis inde releventur. Et volo quod de predicta pecunia in cista reposita, ut premittitur, statuta & confuetudines aliarum ciftarum in eadem univerfitate inviolabiter obferventur: & rogo quod mutuantes, intuitu caritatis & divini amoris pro quibus ifta facio, velint pro anima mea, & Margarete uxoris mee, ac pro animabus parentum & progenitorum meorum, benefactorum, & omnium fidelium defunctorum preces offerre devotas Deo. Item fub eifdem forma, modificacione, & modo, ac tenore verborum, lego & affigno cli. in fecura cifta ac fecura cuftodia in aula fancte Trinitatis in univerfitate Cantebrigg' deponend'. Item volo quod omnium premifforum legatorum execucio differatur ufque dum omnia mea propria debita, & ea que mihi incumbunt folvere pro aliquibus neceffariis ad opus proprium pertinent' foluta fuerint, except' folucione elemofine prius legate celebrantibus mille miffas pro anima mea ut prefertur in principio; non defiderando, neque volendo, quod predicta legacio in parte vel in toto differatur propter folucionem ftipendiorum domini mei regis, que nondum recepi, ymo cum hujufmodi ftipendia domini mei regis fuerint recept', volo quod cum omni expedicione qua fieri poterit folvantur & diftribuantur unicuique prout per compotum fecum racionabiliter fact' de jure debentur. Item lego & do omnia mea mobilia, ubicumque fuerint inventa, ad folucionem debitorum meorum, ac ultime hujus voluntatis mee perfectionem & legal' folucionem. Item rogo & requiro

quiro ex parte Dei omnipotentis feoffatos dominiorum, maneriorum, terrarum, & tenementorum meorum, jam in poffeffione, quod ipfi perimpleant & impleri faciant fine diffimulacione aliqua ultimam meam voluntatem de dominiis, terris, & tenementis meis fupradictis, prout in quadam cedula inde facta & in prefenti teftamento inclufa plenius continetur. Et in forma fupradicta debitis meis folutis, ultimaque voluntate mea hoc prefenti teftamento meo infcripta perimpleta & executa, fi quid de bonis meis fuperfit, illud totum ordino & difpono fecundum difcrecionem executorum meorum, per infpectionem fuperviforum meorum hujus teftamenti mei effe diftribuend' modo quo fequitur, ut viz. quingente marce iftorum bonorum meorum que fic fuperfunt in quinque partes equales dividantur & diftribuantur hoc modo, videlicet, prioratui de Wirmingey[x], abbathie de Weftdereham[y], monafterio monialium de Crabhows[z], monafterio monialium de Thetford[a] in com' Northfolch' & prioratui de fancto Dionifio juxta Southampton[b], monafterio monialium de Marham[c], & monafterio monialium de Blakeberwe[d] in com' Northff' c marc' eifdem diftribuend' equis porcionibus, alie vero c marc' pro miffis

[x] See before, note[n].
[y] Weft Dereham, an abbey of Premonftratenfian canons, founded 1186. Tan. 352.
[z] or Wigenhale. An Auftin nunnery founded 1181. Ib. 350.
[a] Thetford nunnery was founded by Hugh Norwold, and the convent of St. Edmund's Bury. Ib. 349. Martin's Hift. of Thetford, p. 98—110.
[b] A priory of Black Canons, founded by H. I. about 1124. Tan. 160.
[c] A Ciftertian nunnery, founded 1256. Ib. 361.
[d] Blackborough was made a Benedictine nunnery about 1200. Ib. 351.

pro anima mea & animabus fupradictis celebrand'. Item, c marce pro liberacione prifonariorum ubi magis neceffe fuerit, & precipue apud London'. Item c marc' pro lepra percuffis, & decubantibus in lectis, & c marc' pro factura & emendacione viarum ubi magis neceffe fuerit in com' Suff' & Effex. Et quamvis fuperius quibufdam meis fervientibus nominatim quafdam fummas legaverim ut fcriptum eft, nichilominus aliis fervientibus meis lego quafdam fummas, quibus fervientibus fuperius non legavi ut patet inferius. Nich'o Cheriton xli. Will'mo Harewode xl s. Waltero Sarjaunt x marc'. Thome Bouchier x marc'. Johanni Pyke v marc'. Ricardo Foteman v marc'. Ricardo Pondeman v marc'. Ricardo Barbour xl s. Thome de Halle xl s. Thome Chamber al' Lynk xl s. Henrico de Spicery al' Newerk c s. Thome Lewyn ii marc'. Johanni Hawflepe x marc'. Johanni Payn xl s. Roberto Hoode ii marc'. Thomas Bullok xl s. Johanni Elmer ii marc'. Ric'o Brewer xl s. Et de refiduo bonorum meorum lego domibus pauperum religioforum, nec non mendicancium, & pauperibus honeftis puellis maritand' que non habent amicos ad eafdem maritand' ubi videbitur predictis executoribus meis ac fuperviforibus magis proficere pro falute anime mee animarumque fupradictarum. Et iftius ultime voluntatis mee ordino, facio, & conftituo, executores meos dilectos michi in Chrifto dominum Willielmum Philip militem, dominum Thomam Walbere rectorem de Hadley, Willielmum Morley thefaurarium meum, Ricardum Aghton armigerum, & Johannem Bertram; & lego cuilibet executorum

## DUKE OF EXETER.

torum meorum predictorum XL li. sterling, eosdemque onerando, quod ad honorem Dei, ac anime mee salutem, pro hac mea ultima voluntate hoc presenti testamento meo inscript' adimplend' ordinent, procurent, disponant & administrent, prout omnipotenti Deo placere, ac anime mee saluti magis proficere eisdem videatur, sicut in extremo judicii examine se poterint excusare. Item volo quod una tumba fabricetur supra sepulturam, tam mei quam uxoris mee predicto loco, pro cujus fabrica lego c li. sterling si necesse fuerit meliori modo quo poterit in hoc opere disponend'. Hujus insuper testamenti mei administracionis supervisores ordino, facio, & constituo, dilectos michi in Christo magistrum Willielmum Alnewyk[e] episcopum Norwicen', magistr' Philippum Morgan[f] episc' Elien', dominum Ludovicum Robessart[g] militem, & dominum Walterum Hungerford[h] militem; & lego cuilibet eorundem super-

[e] 1426, translated to Lincoln, 1436.

[f] translated by bull from Worcester to Ely, 1426, died 1435.

[g] Lewis Robsert, a native of Hainault, standard-bearer to H. V. knight of the Bath and Garter, and created lord Bourchier 3 H. VI. in right of his wife Elizabeth, daughter and heir to Bartholomew lord Bourchier, died 1431, buried in St. Paul's chapel, Westminster-abbey. On his monument, among many other coats, are the arms of *Roet*, A. 3 wheels O. and also Roet's crest, which shews he was related to the testator's family, Catherine Swynford being daughter of Sir Payne Roet. See Dart's Westminster I. 181. Dugd. II. 202.

[h] Sir Walter de Hungerford succeeded his father Thomas 1412, was one of Henry the Fifth's executors (see before, p.   .) 6 H. VI. is styled lord of Heyhtsbury and Hemet, died Aug. 9, 1449, buried in Salisbury cathedral to which he had been once a great benefactor. Dugd. II. 204. His chapel on the N. side of the nave served as a pew for the mayor and archbishop to hear the sermon, till it was lately removed.

visorum

viforum mei teftamenti unum ciphum cum copertorio de argento deaurato; eofdemque rogando humiliter & fpecialiter ut hunc laborem, annuente Deo, meritorum in fe fufcipere non recufent. Volo eciam quod omnium in hoc prefenti teftamento premifforum & prefcriptorum difpoficio, ordinacio, & adminiftracio, fiat per executores meos, qui bis in anno prenominatis fuperviforibus meis fidelem compotum facere teneantur. Ac eciam volo quod executores mei inveniant per duos annos immediate fequentes diem obitus mei v capellanos feculares ad celebrand' pro anima mea, & anima uxoris mee, & pro quibus deprecari teneor, in monafterio Sancti Edmundi de Bury, ubi corpus meum fepelietur, videlicet, quod unus capellanorum predictorum celebrabit miffam de Trinitate, fecundus de Sancto Spiritu, tercius de fancta Maria, quartus de die, & quintus de requiem eternam. Et finaliter ipfam fanctam & individuam Trinitatem deprecor pro meis executoribus & eorum fuperviforibus, ut pro me ac mea ultima voluntate in prefenti teftamento meo content' perimplend' difponant, & adminiftrent, & adminiftracionem fupervideant, ut potiffime omnipotenti Deo adminiftracio placeat, & anime mee ad requiem & vitam eternam proficiat. Quodque Altiffimus concedat, qui fine fine vivit & regnat, Amen. Dat' apud manerium meum de Grenewych die & anno fupradictis; et anno regni metuendiffimi domini mei regis Henrici fexti poft conqueftum quinto.

Hec

Hec eſt ultima voluntas mei Thome ducis Exonie, videlicet, quod feoffati qui ad mei uſum feoffati ſunt in maneriis de Weſthorpalle Marſhalle in Weſtthorp, Wyverſton Keveles in Wyverſton, Over Rekynghale, Watleſfelde, Walſham, & Mutford; & advocacionibus eccleſiarum de Weſthorp, Wyverſton, Rekinhall, & Wateleſfelde, cum omnibus & ſingulis pertinenciis ſuis in com' Suff' ac in manerio de Crokeſeſton[1], cum ſuis pertinen' in comitat' Southampton, cum advocacionibus eccleſiarum ibidem, ac in reverſion' omnium meſuagiorum, terrarum, tenementorum, reddit' & ſervic' in civitate Norwic', ac eciam in manerio de Grenewych, & in omnibus & ſingulis terris, tenement', reddit', & ſervic', cum ſuis pertinenciis, que nuper adquiſimus in com' Kancie de Ricardo Tyrell & aliis feoffatis, permittant executores meos immediate poſt diem obitus mei percipere & recipere omnia exitus & proficua dictorum maneriorum, advocacionum eccleſiarum, reddit', reverſionum, ſervic', cum omnibus ſuis pertinenciis ſuperius ſpecificatorum & declaratorum, & quod eadem maneria, cum ceteris predict' cicius quo fieri poterit vendantur ad ſolvend' debita mea, & ad ultimam meam voluntatem in teſtamento meo ſpecificatam perimplend' prout meliori modo ſciverint executores mei, per diſcrecionem & aviſamentum ſuperviſorum in teſtamento meo predicto ſpecificatorum & nominatorum. In cujus rei teſtimonium preſentibus ſignetum meum apponi feci. Dat' apud Grenewych xxix<sup>no</sup> die

---

[1] Crux Eaſton.

menſis

mensis Decembris, anno regni metuendissimi domini regis Henrici sexti post conquestum quinto. Hiis Testibus; magistro Thoma Morstede, magistro Johanne Somersete, Thoma Hoo, Gilberto Debenham, magistro Roberto Wyot, magistro Willielmo Wode, Willielmo Bolton, Ignasio Clifton, Willielmo Bourg, Johanne Lucas, Johanne Aubrey, Christoforo Pulford, Johanne Neve, Johanne Smyth, Thoma Swanton, & Edmundo Tyler.

ITEM ultra testamentum & voluntatem meam predictam, lego Johanni de Veer [k] comiti Oxonie de vasis meis argenteis ad valorem xl li. secundum discrecionem executorum meorum limitand'. Item lego Ignasio Clifton ultra decem libras sibi in testamento meo legat' unum harnesium armorum [l], cum duobus equis, secundum discrecionem executorum meorum predictorum nominand. Item lego Thome Hoo armigero camere mee hostiario unum decursariis [m] meis vocat' Dunne. Item volo quod Willielmus Morley thesaurarius meus habeat, durante tota vita sua, omnia tenementa mea infra civitatem Norwicen' absque impedimento vasti. Et volo ulterius quod si predictus Willielmus Morley voluerit emere vel adquirere reversionem eorundem tenementorum, quod tunc ipse habeat eadem tenementa cum pertinenciis minori precio per cen-

---

[k] The second earl of Oxford of the name of *John*, beheaded with his eldest son Aubrey on Tower-hill, 1461. 1 E. IV. and buried in the Austin friars church, London. Vincent on Brook, 406.
[l] compleat suit of armour. [m] coursers.

tum marc' quam aliquis alius qui eadem emere vel adquirere voluerit. Item lego Ricardo Carbonell militi unum meum diploidem [f] longum de velveto defensinum [g]. Item volo quod Gilbertus Debenham armiger meus ab omni jure & clameo que ego seu executores mei in ipso exigere poterimus, liber existat & quietus. Item volo quod supervisores mei testamenti, ultra legacionem eis in dicto testamento meo assignat', prout aquariis, vel hujusmodi jocalibus secundum discrecionem executorum meorum predictorum remunerentur. Item lego Willielmo Philip militi unum ciphum, cum cooportorio de argento deaurato, secundum discrecionem dictorum executorum meorum nominand'. Item volo quod valetti, garciones, & pagetti, quibus in predicto testamento meo non est aliquid in certo legatum, secundum gradus ipsorum, & merita, per discrecionem dictorum executorum meorum remunerentur. Item volo quod in civitatibus regni Anglie notabilioribus publice proclametur quod si quiscumque infra dictum regnum moram trahens die mortis mee possit racionabiliter & de jure ostendere me racione empcionis victualium, marcandisarum, vel aliarum rerum quarumcumque, ad usum meum vel hospicii mei receptarum, & habitarum, sibi quicquam debuisse vel debere, dicti quibus quicquam debuero, ex causis predictis, ad certa loca mea parte limitand', diebus eciam ad hoc per avisamentum executorum meorum assignand', veniant debita hujusmodi prout de eisdem racionabiliter & de jure

[f] doublet.  [g] Q. faced with velve ?

oftendere poterint recepturi, & quod eifdem folvantur debita hujufmodi fideliter per executores meos prout juris fuerit & racionis.

Probatio dicti teftamenti coram Willielmo Lyndewode curie Cantuar' officiali, 28 Januarii, Anno Domini 1426.

Regifter Chichele pars prima, fol. 397. a. b. 398. a. b. 399. a. in the archiepifcopal regiftry at Lambeth.

Thomas Beaufort, third fon of John of Gaunt and Catherine Swinford, was created earl of Perch in Normandy, and made captain of Calais, and admiral of England, Aquitaine, and Ireland, 10 H. IV. chancellor of England 11 H. IV. earl of Dorfet 13 H. IV. lieutenant of Aquitain 1 H. V. one of the ambaffadors to treat of the marriage of that prince with Catherine of France, 2 H. V. governor of Harfleur, duke of Exeter for life, and knight of the garter, 4 H. V. He was taken prifoner in the battle wherein the duke of Clarence loft his life, 9 H. V. but next year defeated the earl of Armagnac before Melun. Befides feveral other gallant exploits, he had the leading of the rearward at the battle of Agincourt, and was appointed guardian of Henry VI. during his minority. He married Margaret daughter of Sir Thomas Neville of Hornby, knt. by whom he had no children; and died at his manor of Greenwich in Kent, Dec. 29, 1426, leaving his nephew John earl of Somerfet his heir. Vincent on Brooke, 104. Dugd. II. 125.

He

He was buried, agreeably to his directions, in the abbey church of St. Edmundſbury; in the ruins of which, ſome labourers digging for ſtone in the winter of the year 1772, diſcovered a body encloſed in lead, and preſerved in pickle. After it was opened, Mr. Cullum, an eminent ſurgeon in that town, examined it as minutely as circumſtances would permit, and his account of it was tranſmitted to the Royal Society (Phil. Tranſ. LXII. art. 33). He is poſſeſt of the right hand and the maſk of cere-cloth taken from the face, whoſe features were remarkably fair. This body, being preſumed to be that of the duke of Exeter, was interred in a wooden ſhell ſeven feet deep, at the foot of the north pillar of the centre tower, where an epitaph was intended to be affixt over it by Dr. Symonds, Profeſſor of Modern Hiſtory at Cambridge.

After the probabilities that have been urged by the learned in ſupport of their aſſignment of this body to the noble teſtator, it may ſeem preſumption to differ from them. But the duke's own direction in his will (which they had not before them) appears to be deciſive evidence that his body could not have been found on the *South* ſide, as repreſented in Mr. King's plan, Archæol. III. pl. 15. p. 313. All concluſions from likeneſs of features ſuppoſed to be retained in the maſk muſt fall to the ground on a view of the maſk, which by its thickneſs exhibits the eyes and noſe only *en creux*. Much of the dark hair of the forehead was torn off with it, and the haſte of the workmen deſtroyed the lower part. No other body was found with this as might have been expected.

## JOHN MOWBRAY, DUKE OF NORFOLK.

HEC est ultima voluntas domini Johannis ducis Norffolcie, comitis Mareschall' & de Notyngham, Anglie mareschalli, &c. facta apud Eppeworth, decimo nono die mensis Octobris, anno regni regis Henrici sexti undecimo, viz. In primis quod corpus suum sepelietur in ecclesia Carthus'[a] infra insulam de Axeholme in com' Lincoln', & quod omnia debita sua de bonis & catallis suis integris solvantur. Item, quod domina Katerina uxor dicti domini ducis habeat omnia vasa sua aurea, argentea, sive deaurata, ac omnia alia ornamenta, aurea, argentea, sive deaurata, ac omnia alia bona mobilia sua & catalla, debitis suis predictis plene persolutis, preter quod illud argentum sive aurum cunatum[b] existens infra manerium de Eppeworth tempore mortis predicti dominis ducis, quod inter servientes ejusdem domini ducis secundum discretionem dicte domine Katerine, post mortem dicti domini ducis participabitur, & preter quod omnes toge dicti domini ducis tempore mortis sue infra manerium predictum

[a] This house, called Epworth, was founded 19 R. II. by this earl's father Thomas Mowbray, earl of Nottingham, earl Marshal, and duke of Norfolk. Tann. 286.
[b] coined.

existent'

exiftent' diftribuantur inter fervientes prediftos, fecundum difcrecionem dictę domine Katerine; & quod predicta domina Katerina habeat ad terminum vite fue manerium de Eppeworth in com' predicto cum fuis pertinentiis, ac omnia alia terras, & tenementa, redditus, reverfiones, & fervicia, pafcua, pafturas, aquas, vivaria five pifcaria, chaceas, warennas, cum fuis pertinenciis, ac omnes alias commoditates predicto domino duci, five alio cuicumque nomine dicti domini ducis, five ad opus fuum infra infulam predictam pertinen' five fpectant'. Item, quod dicta domina Katerina habeat ad terminum vite fue omnia maneria dicti domini ducis, ac omnia alia terras & tenementa, redditus, reverfiones, & fervicia, pafcua, pafturas, aquas, vivaria five pifcaria, chaceas, warennas, cum fuis pertinen' ac omnes alias commoditates predicto domino duci five alio cuicumque nomine dicti domini ducis, five ad opus fuum infra comitat' Eborac' pertinent' five fpectant'. Item, quod dicta domina Katerina habeat ad terminum vite fue caftellum, honoris, five dominium de Brembre cum fuis pertinenciis ac omnibus commoditatibus fuis infra comitatem Suffex'. Item, quod dicta domina Katerina habeat ad terminum vite fue omnia caftella five maneria infra terram de Gower, in Wallia, cum fuis pertinenciis, ac dominium de Gower, cum fuis pertinenciis, ac cum omnibus aliis commoditatibus & proficuis fuis. Item, quod Thomas Newmarche habeat ad terminum vite fue officium fenefchalli manerii de Eppeworth cum vadiis antiquis. Et quod Johannes Dantre armiger habeat ad terminum vite fue decem libras

argenti

argenti annuatim percipiend' de manerio de Fornefette [c] in com' Norff' ad duos anni terminos. Item, quod Johannes Pecke habeat ad terminum vite fue cuftodiam parci de Lopham [d] in com' Norff' cum feodis antiquis. Item, quod Johannes Baffet armiger habeat ad terminum vite fue quatuor denarios per diem percipiendum *

& quod Thomas Hide habeat ad terminum vite fue tres denarios per diem percipiendum *

Item, quod omnes fervientes predicti domini ducis habentes literas fuas patentes de aliquibus officiis five feodis illis conceffis habendis ad voluntatem dicti domini ducis habeant, & quilibet eorum habeat eadem officia, five feoda, ad terminum vite eorundem. Item, quod dicta domina Katerina exiftat capitalis executrix teftamenti dicti domini ducis cum omnibus aliis perfonis executoribus in ultimo teftamento dicti domini ducis nominatis; excepto quod Edmundus Wynter non fe intromittat de racione executionis dicti ultimi teftamenti. In cujus rei teftimonium predictus dominus Johannes dux huic prefenti ultime voluntati fue figillum armorum fuorum appofuit.

Probatio dicti teftamenti apud Lambeth coram Henrico Chichele Cant' archiepifcopo, 14° Februarii, anno Domini 1432.

* Blanks left in the original.
[c] Forncet in Depwade hundred, Norfolk, ftill belongs to the duke of Norfolk. Blomef. III. 147.
[d] Lopham in Giltcrofs hundred, Norfolk, is ftill the property of the duke of Norfolk. Ib. I. 51.

## DUKE OF NORFOLK. 269

Register Chichele pars prima, fol. 435. a. b. in the archiepiscopal registry at Lambeth.

John Mowbray, born 1389, was restored 3 H. VI. to the title of duke of Norfolk, which had been forfeited by his brother Thomas's rebellion against Henry IV. He succeeded his brother 1406, 8 H. IV. being then 17 years of age; and though prevented from sharing in the victory at Agincourt by illness, yet continuing at the siege of Harfleur, he performed several important services in France. He married Catherine daughter of Ralph Nevil earl of Westmorland (remarried to Thomas Strangeways esq. John viscount Beaumont, and Sir John Widvile knt. brother to Anthony earl Rivers) and died October 19, 11 H. VI. 1432, leaving issue John, afterwards Duke of Norfolk. Dugdale[e] dates his will May 20, 7 H. VI. which is four years prior to this.

[e] Bar. I. 130. He adds that he ordained that the bones of his father should be brought from Venice to Epworth.

JOHN

# JOHN DUKE OF BEDFORD, REGENT OF FRANCE.

IN nomine Domini, Amen. Noverint univerſi hoc preſens publicum inſtrumentum inſpecturi, quod hoc eſt verum tranſcriptum ſive tranſcriptum quarundam literarum ſigillo venerabilis & circumſpecti viri magiſtri Alani Kyrketon decretorum doctoris, eccleſiarum Bath' ſancti Petri Ebor' & ſancti Pauli London' canonici, prebendatus rectoriſque ſeu curati eccleſie parochialis ſancti Petri de Oundell Lincoln' dioc' & capellani illuſtriſſimi principis domini Johannis gubernant' & regent' regni Francie, ducis Bedford' nuper decani, in cera rubea & tandem duplici ac ipſius ſigno manuali, ſignoque & ſubſcriptione venerabilis viri magiſtri Egidii de Ferreres clerici Ebron' dioc' oriundus publica auctoritate apoſtolica notarii, ut prima facie approbat' ſigillatar' ſignatar' & roboratur' ſanar' & integrar' non viciatar' non cancellatar' nec in aliqua ſui parte ſuſpectar' ſed omni prorſus vicio & ſuſpeccione carencium, nuncque notario publico ſubſcripto traditar' ad tranſcribend' anno ejuſdem domini milleſimo ccccº triceſimo quarto, indiccione decima quarta, menſis Novembris die nona, pontificatus ſanctiſſimi in Chriſto patris

patris & domini noſtri domini Eugenii divina providentia pape quarti anno quinto, quarum quidem literarum tenor de verbo ad verbum ſequit' & eſt talis: " Univerſis preſentes literas ſeu preſens inſtrumentum publicum inſpecturis Alanus Kyrketon decretorum doctor eccleſiarum Bath' ſancti Petri Ebor' & ſancti Pauli London' canonicus prebendatus, rectorque ſeu curatus eccleſie parochialis ſancti Petri de Oundell Lincoln' dioc', ac capellanus illuſtriſſimi principis domini Johannis gubernant' & regentis regni Francie ducis Bedfordie decanus, ſalutem in domino. Notum facimus quod in noſtra notariique publica & teſtium infra ſcriptorum preſencia perſonaliter conſtitutus prefatus illuſtriſſimus princeps dominus regens & gubernans, licet eger corpore ſanus tamen mente & in bona per Dei gratiam exiſtens memoria, conſiderans & attendens quod breves dies hominis ſunt, & quod nil eſt cercius morte, nec incercius ejus hora, nolens ab hoc ſeculo inteſtatus decedere, ymo tamquam verus catholicus, de bonis a Deo ſibi collatis cupiens, tam pro ſalute anime ſue quam alias uti melius poſſet, diſponere, fecit & ordinavit teſtamentum ſuum, ſeu ejus ultimam voluntatem in modum & formam qui ſequitur. Primo animam ſuam dum ipſa de corpore ſuo exierit devote & humiliter Deo creatori noſtro, & beatiſſime virgini Marie ejus matri, totique cetui curie celeſtis commendavit. Item ſepulturam ſuam eligit viz. in caſu quo ipſum decedere contigeret in partibus Normannie in eccleſia beate Marie Rothomagen'. Et ſi in

Picardia in ecclesia beate Mariae de Morivele, & in casu quod decederet in regno Anglie in abbathia seu monasterio de Waltham, London dioc'. Et voluit & ordinavit servicium, luminare, & alias ordinaciones inhumacionis, exequiarum, & sepulture suarum, fieri sicut decet pro principe sui status, juxta bonum avisiamentum, ordinacionem, & discrecionem suorum executorum inferius nominatorum, viz. illorum qui tempore decessus sui presentes in Francia erunt, si ibidem decedat; & si in Anglia decedat, ad voluntatem & ordinacionem illorum qui tunc ibidem erunt presentes. Item voluit & ordinavit quod debita sua solvantur, & forisfacta emendentur primitus, & ante omnia. Item dedit & legavit illi predictarum ecclesiarum in qua humabitur omnia integraliter ornamenta, & indumenta capelle, tam in tapis quam alias quae habet, brondata [a], & de radicibus auri [b] super velvetum rubeum, & unum calicem auri minutum lapidibus quem fecit fieri in hospicio suo de Turnell [c] Parisius per Stephen Allovus ejus aurifabrum. Item dedit & legavit prefate ecclesie unum par majorum turribulorum argenteorum & deauratorum que noviter fabricari fecit Parisius, & unam crucem argenteam deauratam

---

[a] embroidered.   [b] aurifrize as before, p. 254. n.

[c] The Palais des Tournelles at Paris, originally the house of a chancellor in 1390, was in 1422 the residence of the duke of Bedford, who enlarged and beautified it so much, that Charles VII. and succeeding kings of France preferred it to their palace opposite to it. After the unfortunate death of Henry II. at the tilting match, the list for which reacht from this palace to the Bastile along the Rue des Tournelles, Catherine of Medici disliked it so much, that she persuaded Charles to pull it down. It was completely demolished by Henry IV. who built the place Royal on its scite. St. Foix Essais Hist. sur Paris, I. 41.

## JOHN DUKE OF BEDFORD.

cum buretis [d], quas habuit de redemptione Johannis Alcurons. Item dedit & legavit illustrissime principisse domin. Jacobe ejus consorti omnes terras & tenementa, census, proventus, redditus, & dominia, cum omnibus suis juribus & pertinentiis universis, quas & que idem dominus testator haberet, possidet, sive ex conquestu, sive ex proprio, tam in Francia quam in Anglia, eis gavisus vita sua durante, solum exceptis castro, terra, & dominio de Hajaputa [e], que dedit & legavit Ricardo bastardo de Bedford, ejus filio naturali, cum omnibus juribus suis & pertinent' tenend' & habend' per ipsum Ricardum quoad vixerit dumtaxat. Item voluit & ordinavit quod post decessum dicte domine consortis sue ac dicti Ricardi, omnes terre, tenementa, census, redditus, & proventus, ac dominia predicta, cum suis juribus & pertinen' universis, pertineant & remaneant domino nostro Henrico, Francie & Anglie regi, quem fecit, nominavit, & ordinavit heredem suum. Item voluit & ordinavit quod executores sui habeant servitores suos specialiter in omnibus recommissos [f], eos in singulis favorabiliter & honeste tractando, ac eis favores exhibendo, & quod omni modo stipendia eis debita fideliter & integraliter cum omni diligencia eis persolvantur, quodque dictis servitoribus suis secundum discrecionem executorum suorum, meritis & qualitatibus personarum consideratis, fiat retribucio & recognicio servitiorum special' ad partem; de residuis autem bonorum non datorum nec legatorum, post debita soluta, forisfact' & legat' solut' & emendat', voluit idem dominus testator quod dicti executores sui

[d] Du Cange refers from *buretum* to *bruneta*, which he explains a species of money used in Italy during part of the 12th century. Sed q. if it has that sense here.
[e] Haraputa. Dugd. Bar. II. 202.
[f] *commendatos*, recommended. Du Cange in voc.

disponant, & provideant, ad salutem anime sue, juribus autem quorumcumque in omnibus hujusmodi residen' concernentibus in omnibus semper salvis; pro quibus omnibus exequend' & adimplend' ordinavit & elegit idem illustrissimus princeps testator executores suos reverendos & reverendum in Christo patres dominos Henricum Cardinalem [g] Anglie, vulgariter nuncupatum, Lodowicum episcopum Terouen' [h] cancellar' Francie ejus avunculum, Johannem [i] archiepiscopum Ebor'; Dominum Randulphum Cromwell dominum de Crombwell [k] thesaurarium Anglie; Dominum Johannem Falstolf [l] magistrum hospicii sui, Dominum Andream Ogard [m] ipsius camerarium, milites; Ricardum Boukeland the-

[g] Henry Beaufort bishop of Winchester, brother of H. IV. appointed cardinal of St. Eusebius by Pope Martin V. 1426, died 1447. Godwin ed. Rich. p. 795. He has the style of *Cardinal of England* in the public records and his own will.

[h] Lewis bishop of Terouenne (*Turvyne*, Dugd. *Turwin*, Sandford) 1417, chancellor of France, 1414; archbishop of Rouen, 1436; created by pope Eugenus IV. 1439, cardinal of the four crowns, and administrator of the see of Ely, where he was buried, 1448, having died at his palace at Hatfield. He was uncle to the duke's second wife, who was sister to Lewis de Luxenburg earl of St. Pol. Dugd. Bar. II. 202. The History of Charles VI. of France calls him a very cruel man, who was driven out of Paris with the partisans of H. VI. when it was reduced by Charles VII. His will may be seen in Du Chesne's Hist. des Chanceliers de France, p. 446.

[i] John Kemp, archbishop of York, 1425; cardinal of St. Balbina 1439, translated to Canterbury 1452, where he died 1453, and has a magnificent monument.

[k] Ralph Cromwell, lord Cromwell, was constituted treasurer of the king's exchequer, 11 H. VI. master of the king's mews and falconer in the room of the duke of Bedford 14 H. VI. He founded Tatshall college, c. Northampton, 17 H.VI. began a fair house at Colyweston in the same county, which as well as his castle at Tateshall, he ornamented with figures of purses alluding to his office, and dying 1455, 34 H. VI. was buried in the choir of his collegiate church, where his brass still remains in the beautiful chancel stript of its fine painted windows, and laid open to the weather. Dugd. Bar. II. 45.

[l] The famous knight and hero, who died 1459. See Biog. Brit. in his article.

[m] H. VI. granted licence to Andrew Ogard and others, to impark the manor of Rye, called also the island of Rye, in the parish of Stansted Abbots,

## JOHN DUKE OF BEDFORD,

thesaurarium de Calesio, & Robertum Whittyngham ejus receptorem generalem in Anglia, armigeros; quorum quatuor vel tres onus & executionem presentis testamenti, dum modo dictus dominus Cardinalis, vel prefatus dominus cancellarius Francie, sive memoratus dominus archiepiscopus Ebor' de illis quatuor vel tribus existat semper unus, possint perficere & adimplere adeo integre ac si omnes prenominati executores simul adessent; quos executores immediate aut tam cito post ejus decessum sicut commode fieri poterit, voluit seisiri de omnibus bonis suis, tam mobilibus quam immobilibus, & ipsa bona eis realiter tradi & liberari ad usum & complementum premissorum; & presentis testamenti voluit & ordinavit prefatum dominum regem esse & fore principium provisorem & principalem manutentorem; voluitque ac ordinavit quod hujusmodi testamentum teneat & valeat sic per modum testamenti vel codicelli aut ultime voluntatis melioribus modo & forma quibus fieri poterit; revocando & adnullando omnia alia testamenta seu ordinaciones ultime voluntatis per ipsum facta temporibus retroactis. Declaravit insuper prefatus princeps testator non esse voluntatis aut intencionis sui quod predicti executores sui, seu aliquis eorum, teneantur aut teneatur respondere de majori summa seu quantitate bonorum quam hujusmodi bona sua valeant, seu se pote-

c. Herts; to erect a castle with battlements and loop-holes; and to have free warren there, and in the vills of Stansted, Amwell, Hodesdon, Ware, and Wideford. [Cart. anno 34 H. VI. m. 6. Chauncey 195. Salmon's Hertf. p. 250.] The brick-gate of this mansion still subsists, known by the name of the Rye-house, and in the spandrils of the gate are the arms of Ogard, a mullet, with supporters and crest.

rint extendere. In quorum premifforum teftimonium & fidem prefentibus literis feu prefenti publico inftrumento figillum noftrum & fignum manuale una cum figno & fubfcriptione dicti notarii appofuimus. Dat' & act' in caftro Rothomagen' Anno Domini M° cccc. xxxv$^{to}$ die x$^{ma}$ menfis Septembris, Indiccione decima tercia, pont' fanctiffimi, &c Eugenii anno v$^{to}$; prefentibus nobilibus, ac circumfpectis viris Dominis Gerardo de Monfrant dicti domini teftatoris camerario, Nicholao Burdet militibus, M. Petro Yrforde facre theologie profeffore, confeffore, Roberto Warde elemofinario, magiftro Johanne de Rawmeris, & magiftro Philiberto Furnein, medicis predicti domini: Henr' Clyfford, Ricardo Leland thefaurar' domus, Johanne de Dupater, Reginald de Birfingham hoftiariis camere, Briano Stapilton, Johanne de Mortimer, chev. de Burnieby, Thome Dampore armigeris, Johanne Scruby, Roberto Martyn & aliis.

Notarius Willielmus Manchon, &c."

Probatio dicti teftamenti coram Henrico Chichele Cant. archiep'o apud Lambeth vii die menfis Octobr' Anno Domini M° cccc. xl. primo.

Regiftr. Chichele pars prima, fol. 475. a. b. 476. a. in the archiepifcopal regiftry at Lambeth.

John of Lancafter, third fon of H. IV. was, by his father, conftituted conftable of England, a. r. 4. by his brother H. V. a. r. 2. created earl of Kendal and duke of Bedford

# JOHN DUKE OF BEDFORD.

Bedford for life, which honours were confirmed to him by his nephew H. VI. a. r. 11. for ever. Henry V. appointed him protector and lieutenant of the kingdom of England, during his abfence in France 1415; and Henry VI. made him Regent of France 1425. After winning the battle of Verneuil he crowned his nephew king of France at Paris, Sept. 7, 1432, and not long after died there Sept. 14, 1435. He was buried in the cathedral at Rouen, where his monument was defaced by the Hugonots in 1462; but a brafs plate with his epitaph under his arms (torn away) between two oftrich feathers ftill remains affixt to a pillar. Lewis XI. when folicited to deface the monument of this illuftrious hero, magnanimoufly refufed.

He married, 1. 1423, Anne, daughter of John duke of Burgundy, who died in child-bed and her child with her 1432, and was buried in the Celeftines' church at Paris, where her epitaph remains, and a noble tomb of black marble. 2. Jacquette daughter of the earl of Luxemburgh, by whom he had no iffue, and who remarried Sir Richard Woodvile, afterwards earl Rivers, by whom fhe had Anthony his fucceffor, Elizabeth afterwards wife of Edward IV. and other children. She died 1472. Dugd. Bar. II. 200. Sandf. 312.

ANNE

## ANNE COUNTESS OF STAFFORD.

IN Dei nomine, Amen. I Anne countesse of Stafford, Bockingh' Herford' and Northampton[a], and lady of Breknoc, of hool and avised mynde, ordeyne and make my testament in English tonge, for my most profit, redyng, and understandyng in yis wise. First, I bequethe my soule to Almighty God, and my body to be buried in ye churche of L'Anthony byside Glouceftre, in ye place wher I have beforn ordeyned, and do mad my tombe. Also, I bequethe to the same churche a c marcs of money, or ye value thereof, of suche of my movable goodys as wole best seem to ye discrecjouns of myn executours: and also amongst all my detts, I wol that al my mesnial servants be paied furst of all her fees and wages, or of any other trewe proved dettes to hem dewe; and than all othir vitaillers, merchants, or artificers, that I owe any good, to be payed first, whereas most nede ys aftir ye good disposicion and demesnyng of my seyd executors: Also, I woll that any wronges or extorcions dewly proved byfor my executours, by me and my lyve don, that ye same myn executours satisfie hem agreablely as yer good discrecion wol seme best to discharge, and for the helth of my soule; and aftir ye acquietaill of my seyd detts, wrongs, and extorcions, I

[a] She had these titles from her mother's family, and that of Buckingham from her first husband's.

## ANNE COUNTESS OF STAFFORD. 279

wole yat my feyde executors, havyng tendir confideracion of fouche of my fervants, as well of women as men, as have longift don moft trewe and diligent fervife to me and litil veleuid [a] by me, or nought, yat yey aftir their wel avifed difcrecions rewarde eche of hem aftir yeire degre and defertes competently for their help and relyf, as ferforth as ye power of my feid executors wole ftretche in that partie. And alfo, my feyde detts, wrongis, and extorcions, and rewards of my fervants, paid and fatisfied; I bequethe xx li. yerly, to be paied by the hand of my feid executours for terme of xx yere, to the priftis of certen landis and tenements, beyng in ye handys of my feoffes, to do dyvyne fervife dayly for me during ye feide terme in ye college of Plecy [b], after the forme of my will [c], which I have before maad and writyn, feeled undir my feal. And for ye performyng of yis my laft will, bequefts, and ordinances, before reherfid, I make and ordeine my wel beloved fones Thomas byfshop of Worceftre [d], Henry erle of Eue, Will' Bourghchiers [e], Joh' Bourghchiers [f], Sir Nicol Wymbufsh clerk, Sir Roger Afton knyght, John Fray,

[a] i. e. little rewarded, or not at all.
[b] founded by her father Thomas of Woodftock.
[c] The former will, herein referred to, is not known to be *extant*.
[d] Thomas Bourchier bifhop of Worcefter 1435, Ely 1443, archbifhop of Canterbury 1454, which primacy he held 32 years; cardinal of St. Cyriac 1464, died 1486, buried on the north fide of the choir of his cathedral. See his tomb, Dart p. 163.
[e] her third fon, lord Fitz Warin in right of his firft wife. He died after 12 E. IV. Dugd. Bar. II. 131.
[f] her fourth fon lord Berners, in right of his wife, died 14 E. IV. Ib. 132.

## ANNE COUNTESS OF STAFFORD.

Robard Frampton, barons of ye Eftchecur, and Will' Palmer, myn executors, to execute and put in effect, as well ye primeffes, and to diftribue and difpofe in almeffe dede wher yey fhull feme moft niedeful and meritory for ye helte of my foule, befechyng and requirynge ye ryght reverent fadir in God Will'[g] byfsop of Lincoln, and my wel beloved fone Humfrey erle of Stafford, to have tendre furvieue of ye effect of ys my prefent teftament, duly and trewly to be performed. In witneffe whereof to yis my prefent teftament I fet my feal; wretyn the xvi day of Octobr' ye yeare of ye reigne of kyng Henry the VIth, after the Conqueft ye xviithe.

A blank left for the probate.

Regifter Chichele pars prima, fol. 479. a. in the archiepifcopal Regiftry at Lambeth.

Anne, eldeft daughter of Thomas of Woodftock duke of Gloucefter, 20 years old, 1 H. IV. (Dugd. I. 172). married firft to Thomas Stafford earl of Stafford, but he dying before confummation, fhe was married to his brother Edmund Stafford fifth earl Stafford, flain at the battle of Shrewfbury 4 H. IV. (fee before, p. 185.) by whom fhe had iffue Humfrey his fucceffor, flain at the battle of Northampton 38 H. VI; Philippa, who died young; and Anne, married firft to Edmund Mortimer earl of March; 2dly to

---

[g] William Alnwick bifhop of Lincoln 1436, tranflated from Norwich, died 1449.

# ANNE COUNTESS OF STAFFORD.

John Holland earl of Huntingdon and duke of Exeter, buried with him at St. Catharine's by the Tower. (Vincent on Brooke, p. 491. Dugd. Bar. I. 164. And see p. 290.) She was married secondly to William Bourchier earl of Ewe in Normandy, who died in France 8 H. V. and was buried at Lantoni by Gloucester, (Dugd. II. 129.) by whom she had Henry earl of Ewe and Essex, killed by a fall from his horse, 31 H. VIII.; Thomas bishop of Worcester, archbishop of Canterbury, and cardinal of St. Cyriac; William lord Fitz Warin, John lord Berners, and Anne (Eleanor, Dugd. I. 131.) wife of John Mowbray duke of Norfolk, whose father's will see before.

She died 17 H. VI. (Dugd. Bar. I. 164.) but where she was buried does not appear.

# JOHN HOLLAND DUKE OF EXETER.

IN the name of God, Amen. I John duke of Exceſtre, being in good heele and in good memory, ordeyne, diſpoſe, and make my teſtament in maner and ordre yat folweth. Firſt, y bequeth my ſoule to ye Fader, Son, and Holy Goſt, III perſons in Trinite, and oon ever-laſtyng God, he to do yerwith his beſt bleſſed wille; and my body, whan my ſoule is paſſed out of yis world to God, to be buryed in a chappell witin the chirch of Seynt Katryne beſyde the Toure of London, atte north-ende of the high auter, in a tombe yat is ordeyned for me, wit Anne my firſt wyff, and wit my ſiſter Cuſtaunce[a], and wit my wyff Anne yat now is, after the ordynance and diſpoſicion of myn executors, as it ſemeth hem moſt worſhip for myn eſtate. Alſo y bequeth to the high auter of ye ſaid chirch a cuppe of byroll garniſhed wit gold, perles, and precious ſtones, to put in the ſacrament; alſo a chalyce of gold wit al the hoole appareill of my cha-pell, and of the ſame ſtuffe and appareill y wol yat a chalyce, II baſyns, II candel-ſtykkes of ſylver, wit II peyre veſtementes, a maſſe book, a paxbred[b], wit a peire

[a] married firſt to Thomas Mowbray duke of Norfolk and earl of Nottingham, by whom ſhe had no iſſue; and ſecondly to John lord Grey of Ruthyn, by whom ſhe had two ſons, Edmund created earl of Kent, and Thomas Grey lord of Rugemont. Vincent on Brooke, p. 264.

[b] q. the ſame as the corporax caſe before mentioned.

cruettes

cruettes of fylver, be delyvered to the littell chappell where y fhal lye and my wyff, wit my fufter, for the preeftes yat fhall fynge there, and pray for oure foules. Alfo y bequeth to the preeftes and clerks, and other of the hous of Seynt Katryne, for the grete labour and obfervaunce, the day of myne obyte, and the day of myne burryyng quadraginta marc. Alfo y wol yat IIII honeft and cunnyng preefts be ordeyned yerly, perpetually to pray for my foule in the forfaid chappell; and for the foule of Anne my firft wyffe, the foule of my fufter Cuftaunce, and for the foule of Anne my wyffe yat now is, whan fhe paffeth oute of yis worlde, and for al the foules of my progenitours. Alfo y bequeth to the queer in the faid chirch certeyn peces of arras, fufficient and competent to honge the faid queer on both fydes, and there to abyde ftyll, and to be honged every principall feft in the worfhyp of God and Seynt Katryne in remembraunce of my foule. Alfo y bequeth III veftements, to be delyvered after my deth, that is to fay, on to the chirch of Stevynton[c], another to the chirch of Gaddefden[d], and another to the chirch of Dertyngton[e]. Item, y bequeth III mill marks, which is dew to me of my cofyn the duk of York[f], as it appereth by certeyn obligacions made betwene us of the fame, to pay my detts well and truly, and in as goodly hafte as myn executours may: and yat my creditours be fo entreted yat my foule be in

[c] Q. c. Bedford.  [d] Great Gaddefden, Hertfordfhire.
[e] Q. Dartington, c. Devon.  [f]

no perill, as it is conteyned in my laſt wille to this my teſtament annexed. Alſo y bequeth to Anne my wyff yat now is a bed of arras wit the ſcriptur of honnor[g], wit all the coſters [h] longyng to the ſame; and alſo yat ſhe have all her hoole ſtuffe lyke as y had wit her, and half the remanent not bequethen: Alſo y bequeth to my doughter Anne the white bed wit popynjayes [i], wit all the coſters longyng to the ſame: and to my ſaid doughter y bequeth the white bed wit egles embrawded, wit all the coſters longyng to the ſame; and as wel my litell white bed of damaſk wit coſters: Alſo y bequeth to my doughter halff my dyamounds, ſaffyres, rubyes, and precious ſtones, and halff my peerles: Alſo y bequeth to my ſon Sir Harry, all the remanent of my ſtuffe of my warderobe, and of myne arras not bequethed, and al myn armery and attry [k] hoole: Alſo y bequeth to my wyff Anne yt now is, a cupp of gold wit a facon, and an ewer of gold wit a facon taking a pertryche wit a rubye in his breſt: Alſo y bequeth to my doughter Anne xii white bolles of ſylver of a ſute, a cuppe of gold wit a George enameled with a boten [l]; and another cuppe of gold wit myne armes and firſt wyffs armes thereupon; ii baſyns, ii ewers, ii ſalt-ſellers gilt, with armes of Montgomery enameled in the topp: Alſo y bequeth to my wyff Anne yat now is, xii bolles of gold of a ſute, and an almeſdiſs the ſhipp [m]; and the grete baſyn of

[g] i. e. entitled or called: ſee hereafter.
[h] Q. the ſame as *coſtes*, p. 70. note [r].
[i] parrots.      [k] *artry*, p. 288. q. artillery.      [l] a button.
[m] Q. the baſon for alms enameled with a ſhip.

ſylver

fylver y bequeth to my doughter Anne: Alfo y bequeth XL marks, to be doon in almes the day of my burryyng, and of my moneth mynde to them yat be femeth moft pore and nedfull: Alfo y bequeth to my brother duk of Bukyngham[n] the playne cuppe of gold late made wit myn armes in the topp; and he to be my fupervifor: Than my detts paied, and my wille performed, and myne obite worfhipfully doon, as it longeth to myn eftate, y wol yat the refidew of all my goodes in this my teftament not bequeth be delyvered to my fon Sir Harry. Moreover y wol and charge my feoffeez of my manoirs of Stevynton, Berford Seynt Martyn[o], and Mannerbier[p], all thyngs in my teftament and wille performed, to make an eftate to my faid fonn Sir Harry of the faid manoirs. Provided alway, yat an annuyte of XL li. be referved for my II baftards fones William and Thomas. Thife y ordeyne and make myn executours, the reverent fader in God the archbifshopp and cardinal of York[q], my wyff Anne, the bifshopp of Chichefter, Adam[r], Richard Caudray clerk, Robert Whitingham knight, Wauter Moyle, and Thomas Mannyng clerk, to execute, performe, and fulfylle all thife articles and bequeftes above reherfed in this my teftement conteyned, and all othir pointes and articles of my laft wille, as it is con-

[n] Humfrey Stafford his wife's brother.
[o] Bereford St. Martin, c. Wilts. Dugd. Bar. II. 81.
[p] c. Pembroke.
[q] John Kemp.
[r] Adam Molins.

teyned

teyned in a cedule to this my teftament annexed, as they wol anfwere afore God. In witneffe of this my teftement and wille y have fett to my feall of myn armes and my fyne manuell. Thife witneffes, John Warde clerke, Thomas Yarom clerk, Thomas Wychard, Thomas Lovell, John Gaynesford, and other. Yeven the xvi daye of Julye, the xxvi yere of kyng Herry the Sixte, the yere of our Lord M CCCC XLVII.

Ultima voluntas domini Johannis ducis Exon.

This is the laft wille of me John duk of Exceftre, being in good heele and hoole mynde bleffed be God. Fyrft, y wol and charge my feoffeez of my manour and lordfhipp of Moche Gaddefden, in the countye of Hertford, yat they make an eftate of the fame by licence of the kyng, after fuch forme as myn executours and my lerned councell can beft devyfe, to be moft fuer for a chauntry to fuftene IIII honeft and cunnyng preeftes in the chappell, witin the chirch of Seynt Katryne befyde the Tour of London, where my body fhal reft, fo yat every preeft have yerely for his fallary and manfion xii marks, there to pray for my foule dayly; for the foule of my firft wyff Anne; for the foule of my fufter Cuftaunce; and for the foule of my wyff Anne yat now is, whan fhe is paffed out of this world; and for all my progenitours. And y wol yat the refidew of the faid manoir and lordfhipp yat remayneth over the fallary of the faide preefts be ordeyned

deyned and kept to make myn obite yerly therwith, and to diftribute the fame tyme amongs pore men and women of the hous of Seynte Katryne, in the remembraunce of my foule: Alfo y wol yat my fon Sir Harry and his heires be patrons of the faid chauntry, to prefente the faide preeftes whan any of them lakkyth by deth or by avauncement: provided alway, yat the faide preeftes fynge there in the faide chappell dayly as they be difpofed, and in non other place; and yat they be bounde to the queer in all dowble fefts of the yere. Alfo y wol the manoirs of Stevynton, Berford Seynt Martyn, Mannerbier, and Pennally[s], abyde ftill in my feoffeez hands to the tyme yat my detts be paied, and my wille and my teftament be performed; for y wol yat all the yffues and profytes comyng of the feide manoirs be receyved, and my detts therwith paied; and that don, and my wille performed, than y wol and charge my feoffeez to make an eftate to my fon Sir Harry and to his heires for evermore, wit condicion yat he graunt out an eftate of XL li. to my two baftard fones [t] ........ for terme of thaire lyves; yat is to fay, to eche of hem xx li. yerly out of faide manoirs: Alfo y wol yat my wyff Anne yat now is have a bed of arras called Honnour, wit all the cofters longing to the fame: Alfo y wol yat my doughter Anne have the white bed wit popynjayes, wit all the cofters longing to the fame: Alfo y wol yat my faid doughter

[s] Penaly, c. Pembroke.
[t] See their names before.

Anne have the white bed wit egylles embrawded, wit the cofters longing to the fame: Alfo y wol yat my faid doughter have the littell white bed of damafk, wit yat that longeth thereto: Alfo as touching my precious ftones, perles, dyamonds, rubyes, faffyres, and other, y wol yat my wyff have the on halff, and my doughter the other halff: Alfo y wol yat there be delyvered the day of my burryyng to the queer of the chirch of Seynt Katryne certayn peces of arras nedfull and competent to hange the queer a both fydes, and to be hanged there at every dowble or pryncipall feft, in remembraunce of my foule; and there to abyde ftill for ever to the worf-chipp of God and Seynt Katryne: Alfo y wol yat my fon Sir Harry have all the refidew of my warderobe and of myn arras nat bequethen, and all myn armery, and all my artry: Alfo y wol yat my wyff Anne have all her hoole ftuffe like as y had wit her: and halff the remanent of myn othr ftuffe, except yat is bequeth: Alfo y wol yat if my fon Sir Harry, or any of his heires, breke, lette or diftroble, any of the poyntes or articles conteyned in this my wille, that than he loofe and forgoo fro hym and fro his heires the faid manoirs of Steventon, Berford Seynt Martyn, Mannerbier, and Pennally; and than yat it be lawfull to my feoffeez, by th' avyfe of my execu-tours, to fille the feide manoirs, and the money thereof to be difpofed for my foule by myn executours: Alfo y wol yat my fervauntz yat have don to me continual fervice

## DUKE OF EXETER.

vice haive their feez for thaire lyves according to thaire patentez, yf they abyde upon thayre fervyce: Alfo y wol yat the $M^l$ $M^l$ $M^l$ mark, yat is dew to me of my cofyn the duk of York, as it appereth by certayne obligaciouns made betwene us of the fame, be ordeyned to pay my detts wel and truly, and to my fervaunts to rewarde the which yat hath no feez: Alfo y bequeth and wol yat my wyff have the xii bolles of gold of a fute, and an almefdiſhe the fhipp'. Dat. the yere of our Lord MCCCCXLVII, the xxvi yere of kyng Henry the Sixte, the xvi day of Juyll.

Probatio dicti teſtamenti coram Johanne (Stafford) Cant. archiep. apud Lamebith, 16 die Feb. A. D. 1447.

Regiſt. Stafford and Kemp. fol. 160. a. In the archiepifcopal regiſtry at Lambeth.

John (fecond fon of John Holland earl of Huntingdon and duke of Exeter, beheaded and buried at Pleſhey, 1 H. IV.) was reſtored to his eſtate 4 H. V. and was in feveral expeditions in France both in that and the fucceeding reign, having been taken prifoner when the duke of Clarence was ſlain. He was conſtituted lord high admiral of England, Ireland, and Aquitain, October 21, 14 H. VI. and next year conſtable of the Tower. He was created duke of Exeter 21 H. VI. with this fpecial privilege, that he and his heirs male ſhould have the feat in all parliaments and councils

councils next to the duke of York and his heirs male. He died Auguſt 5, 26 H. VI. and was buried on the North ſide of the chancel of St. Catherine's church by the Tower, where his monument with the figures of himſelf and his firſt wife remain much defaced.

He married firſt, Anne daughter of Edmund earl of Stafford, by whom he had one ſon Henry, who came to a violent end at ſea 13 E. IV. and a daughter Anne married firſt, to John lord Nevile, ſon and heir to Ralph 2d earl of Weſtmorland, by whom having no iſſue, ſhe married his uncle Sir John Nevile knight, and by him ſhe had Ralph third earl of Weſtmorland. His ſecond wife was Anne daughter of John Mountague earl of Saliſbury, who ſurvived him, and died 1457.

Dugdale has given an abſtract of the duke's will and that of his ſecond wife, Bar. II. 81.

HENRY

# HENRY THE SIXTH.

Copia ultime voluntatis Regis Henrici Sexti, pro Collegiis fuis Regalibus, viz. pro Collegio B. Marie de Etona, & pro Collegio B. Marie & S'ti Nicholai de Cantebr' perficiendis. [See a copy of part of this will in vitâ Gul. Waynfleti fcriptâ à Budderio.]

IN the name of the bleffed Trinity, the Father, the Sonne, and the Holy Ghoft, Oure Lady St. Marie mother of Chrift, and all the holy companie of heaven: I Henry by the grace of God king of England, and of France, and Lorde of Ireland, after the conqueft of England the Sixt, for diverfe great and notable caufes moveing me at the makeing of theife prefents, have do[a] my will and mine intent to be written in manner that followeth:

Forasmuch as I have enfeffed before this time John[b] Cardinall and archbifhop of Yorke, John[c] archbifhop of Canterbury, Robert[d] bifhop of London, William[e] bifhop of Lincoln, William[f] bifhop of Sarefbury, and Thomas[g] bifhop of Bathe and Welles, John Carpenter clarke of the churche of Worcefter, now bifhop of the fame, Adam Molyns clerck now bifhop of Chichefter, Walter Lyert clerck now

*Names of the feoffees.*

---

[a] a common phrafe for *have done*, or caufed.
[b] John Kemp, 1425—1454.     [c] John Stafford, 1443—1452.
[d] Robert Gilbert, 1431—1436, or his predeceffor Robert Fitzhugh mafter of King's-hall, and chancellor of Cambridge.
[e] Will. Alnwick, 1435—1450.     [f] Will. Aifcough, 1438—1450.
[g] Tho. Bekynton, 1443—1465.

## HENRY THE SIXTH.

bishop of Norwich, John Langton clerck late bishop of St. David, and now to God passed, John Dulaber clerk now bishop of St. David, William earle of Suff', now marques of Suff', Henry earle of Northumberland, John viscount Beaumont, Walter lorde of Hungerford, Rauf lorde Cromwell, Raufe lorde of Seudely, John Beauchampe knight, now lorde Beauchampe of Powicke, and James Fenes esq now lord of Say, John Somersett, Henry Sever, Richard Andrew, Walter Sherington, clerks; Edward Hungerford and Edward Hull knights; John Saintlo now to God passed, John Hampton, John Norres, William Tresham, John Vampage, and Richard Aldred, now to God passed, esqs. in divers castells, lordships, mannors, lands, tenements, rents, services, and other possessions, parcell of the duchy of Lancaster within England and Wales, as it is more specially and at large conteyned and written, in diverse my letters patents hereof made, of which letters the first beareth date the last day save one of Novembre, the year of my reign 22; the second beareth date the 7th day of Julie the same yeere; the third beareth date the 23d of Februari, the yeere of my reign 23; the fourthe beareth date the 29th of June in the same yeere; which castells, lordships, mannors, lands, tenements, rents, services, and other possessions, be of the yeerlie value of 3395 l. 11 s. 7 d. when they be discharged of the fees and annuities with which they be now charged, which letters patents and all things conteyned in them by the authority of my parlement last

*The lands all parcell of the duchye of Lancaster.*

*Date of the letters patents.*

# HENRY THE SIXTH.

last holden at Westminster, as by an acte of the same parlement plainly it appeareth, were authorized, approved, ratifyed, and confirmed, for to performe and fulfill my will, of and upon the disposition of said castells, lordships, mannors, lands, tenements, rents, services, and other possessions, by me to be made and ordeyned, and to my said feoffees, in my behalf to be declared and notifyed. I by these my present letters declare and notifie unto my said feffees, according to the said acte, that in these my letters is conteyned my said will, which I desire to be done and performed by my said feffees of the castells, lordships, mannors, lands, tenements, rents, services, and other possessions above sayd.

*The feoffment confirmed by act of parliament.*

First, forasmuch as it hath pleased our Lorde God for to suffer and grunte me grace for the primer [h] notable workes purposed by me after that I by his blessed sufferaunce tooke unto my self the rule of my said realmes, for to erect, found, and stablish unto the honour and worship of his name specially, and of the blessed Virgin our ladie St. Marie, encrease of virtues and dilatation of conning [i] and stablishment of Christian faith, my two colleges Roiall, one called the College Roiall of our Ladie of Eton beside Windesor, and the other called the College Roiall of our Ladie and St. Nicholas of Cambridge, the edifications of which colleges, now by me begoun, advised, and appointed, in manner and forme as hereafter followeth, may not be perfectly accomplished

*Causes that moved these two foundations.*

[h] Q. aforementioned.　　　[i] knowledge.

without

# HENRY THE SIXTH.

*The building to pass all other colleges in England.*

without great and notable workes affigned and purveied thereunto; I will, pray, and charge mine own feoffees, that unto the time that the faid edifications and other workes of bridges, conduicts, cloyfters, and others thinges begoun and advifed by me in either of the faid colleges, be fully performed and accomplifhed in notable wife then any of my faid realme of England; they fee that my faid colleges, according to the forme of generall graunts by me unto them made in that behalfe, have and perceive [k] yeerlie of yffues, profits, and revenues, coming of the aforefaid caftells, lordfhips, mannors, lands, tenements, rents, fervices, and other poffeffions, by the hands of the tenants, farmers, occupiers, and receivers of the fame

*A yearly fomme of 2000 lib. affigned, &c.*

2000 lib. for the edifications and workes abovefayd; that is to fay, to the provoft of my faid college of Eton, for the workes there yearlie 1000 lib. and to the provoft of my faid college of Cambridge, for the edifications and workes there yeerely 1000 lib. from the feaft of St. Michael laft paft unto the ende of the terme of twenty yeeres then next following, and fully and compleat; and if it be fo that the edifications of my faid colleges, or either of them, according unto my faid devife and ap-

*Order for the continuance of the edifications, &c.*

pointment herein conteyned, fhall not be fully accomplifhed and finifhed within the faid tearme of 20 years, I will then pray my faid feoffees that they do grant unto either of my faid colleges 1000 lib. to be taken yearlie from the ende of the faid tearme of twenty years, finifhed unto

[k] i. e. receive.

the

# HENRY THE SIXTH.

the time of the edifications of the one of my said colleges be fully accomplished and performed, of the yssues, profitts, and revenues abovesayd; and that after the finishment of the edifications of one of the said colleges, the said yearly 2000 lib. [1000] in semblable wise to be granted to the other of the same colleges whose edifications shall not be then finished, to have and perceive of the yssues, profits, and revenues abovesayd, unto the time of the edification of the same college, to be fully finished and performed; which edifications of my said college I have fully devised and appointed to be accomplished in this wise: that is to witt,

### The College of ETON.

I will that the quier of my said college of Eton shall conteyne in length 103 feet of assize[l], whereof behinde the high altare shall be 8 feete, and from the said altare to the quier dore 95 fete. Item, the same quier shall conteyn in breadth from side to side within the respondes[m] 22 fete. Item, the grounde of wall shall be enhanced higher then they be now on the utter side, ere it come to the layinge of the first stone of the clere wall 10 feet of assize. Item, the wall of the said quier shall conteyn in height fro the grounde workes unto the battlement 80 feet of assize. Item, in the East ende of the said quier shall be sat a great gable windowe of 7 bays and two butteraces, and either side of the said quier 7 windowes,

*Length and wideness of the quier.*

*Height of the said chappell.*

---

[l] statuteable feet.   [m] q. parallel correspondent walls or sides.

every windowe of foure bays and 8 butteraces, conteyning in height from the ground workes unto the overparts of the pinnacles 100 fete of affize. Item, that the faid grounds be fo taken, that the firft ftone lye in the middle of the high altare, which altare fhall conteyne in length 12 fete of affize, and in breadth 5 fete; and that the firft ftone be not removed, touched, nor ftirred, in any wife. Item, the veftry to be fet on the North fide of the fame quier, which fhall conteyne in length 50 fete of affize departed into two houfes, and in breadth 24 fete, and the wall in height 20 fete, with gable windowes, and fide windowes convenient thereto, and the grounde workes to be fette in the height of the grounde of the cloyfter. And I will that the edification of my faid college of Eton proceed in large forme, cleane and fubftantially, well replenifhed with goodly windowes and vaults, laying apart fuperfluities of too great curious workes of entaile and bufy mouldinge. Item, in the faid quier on every fide 32 ftalles and the roode lofte there, I will that they be made in manner and forme like the ftalles and roode loft in the chappell of St. Stephen at Weftminftr, and of the length of 32 feete, and in breadthe clear 12 feet of affize; and as touching the dimenfions of the church of my faid college of Eton, I have devifed and appointed that the body of the fame church between the yles fhall conteyn in breadth within the refponders 32 fete, and in length from the quier dore to the Weft dore of the faid church 104 feete of affize; and fo the faid body of the church

*Veftry.*

*No fuperfluity of curious building.*

church shall be longer then is the quier, from the reredosse[n] at the high altare unto the quier by 9 feete, which dimensions is thought to be a right, good, convenient, and due proportion. Item, I have devised and appointed that the yle on the otherside of the body of the church, shall conteyn in breadth fro respond to respond 15 feete, and in length 104 feete, according to the said body of the church. Item, in the South side of the body of the church a fair large dore with a porch, and the same for christeninge of children and weddinges. Item, I have devised and appointed six greces[o] to be before the high altare, with the grece called Gradus Chori, every of them conteyning in height 6 ynches, and of convenient breadth, every of them as due forme shall require. Item, in the breadth of the church-yarde, from the church dore unto the wall of the church-yarde within the wall of the West ende, which must be take of the streete beside the high waye, six foote of assize. Item, the grounde of the cloyster to be enhaunsed higher then the olde grounde 8 feete ere it come to the pavement, so that it be sett but two foote lower than the paving of the church, which cloyster shall conteyn in length Est and West 200 feete, and in breadth North and South 160 feete of assize. Item, the said cloister shall close unto the church on the North side at the West end, and at the North side at the East end of the church it shall be close unto the college, with a dore into the said college. Item, the said cloistre shall conteyne

*The south yle which is meant for the parish church.*

*The church porch for weddings.*

*Length and breadth of the cloister.*

---

[n] screen at the back of the high altar.
[o] steps, *gressus.*

in breadth within the walls 15 fete, and in height 20 fete, with clere ſtones round about inward, and vawted and embattled on both ſides. Item, the ſpace between the wall of the church and the wall of the cloyſter ſhall conteyne 38 feete, which is left for to ſett in certaine trees and flowers, behovable and convenient for the ſervice of the ſame church. Item, the cemitory of the ſame church ſhall be lower than the paving of the cloiſter 4 feete of aſſize, with as many greces up into the church dore as ſhall be convenient thereto. Item, in the middle of the Weſt of the ſaid cloiſter a great ſquare tower, with a faire dore into the cloyſter, which tower ſhall containe cleare within the wall 20 feete, and in height with the battlement and the pinnacles 140 feete. Item, from the highway on the South ſide unto the wall of the college a good high wall with towers convenient thereto; and in likewiſe from thence by the water ſide, and about the gardens, and all the precincte of the place round about by the highway, until it come to the cloyſter end on the Weſt ſide again. Item, that the water at Baldwyne bridge be turned over the warf into the river at Thamis, with a ditch of 40 foote of breadth, and the ground between the ſame ditch and the college ariſed of a great height, ſo that it may at all floods be plain and dry ground, where then will be in diſtance from the hall to the water at all times of day ground 80 feete; and as touching the dimenſions of the houſing of my ſaid college of Eton, I have deviſed and appointed that the South wall of the precincte of the ſaid college,

*Margin notes:*
- A ſpare ground for trees and flowers.
- The churchyard.
- Height and wideneſs of ſteeple.
- The water at Baldwyn bridge to be turned.

# HENRY THE SIXTH.

college, which shall extend from the tenement that Heugh Dyer now holdeth and occupieth, unto the Est ende of the gardens after long[p] the waters side, shall containe in length 1440 feete of assize, with a large doore in the same wall to the water side. Item, the Est wall of the same precincte, which shall extend fro the waters side to the high way at the newe bridge at the Est end of the gardens, shall containe in length 1200 feete of assize. Item, the North wall of the said precinct, which shall extend fro the Est end of the gardens after along the highway unto the North West corner of the same precincte, shall containe in length 1040 feete of assize, in which wall shall be a faier gate out of the utter court into the highway. Item, the west wall of the same precincte, which shall extend fro the said west corner of the same precincte unto the said tenement, which the said Hew Dyer now occupieth, shall containe in length 1010 feete; and so the utter walles of the said precincte shall containe in length about the same precincte 4690 feete of assize. Item, betwixt the said north wall of the said precincte, and the walls of the college in the utter court of the East part of the gate and the way into the college, shall be edifyed diverse houses necessare for the bake-howse, brew-howse, garners, stables, hey-howse, with chambers for the steward, auditor, and other learned counsell and ministers of the same college, and other lodgings necessarie for such persons of the same college as shall happ to be dis-

*South wall 1440 feet.*

*East wall 1200 feet.*

*North wall 1040 feet.*

*West wall 1010 feet.*

*The whole precinct of Eton college 4690 feet.*

*Houses of offices.*

[p] along.

eased

eased with infirmities. Item, in the west part of the same gate and the way into the college, on the north pane [q], 8 chambers for the poore men, and in the west pane 6 chambers, and behind the same a kitchin, buttry, pantry, and a ground for the said poor men. Item, the north pane of the college shall containe 155 feete within the walls, in the middle of the which shall be a faier tower and a gate howse, with two chambers on either side, and two chambers above, vauted, containing in length 40 feete, and in breadth 24 feete; and in the Est side of the same gate 4 chambers, 2 beneth and 2 above, every of them in length 35 feete, and in breadth 24 feete; and in the west side of the same gate a school-house beneath of 70 feete in length, and in breadth 24 feete. Item, the East pane in length within the walls 230 feete, in the middle whereof, directly against the entering at the cloister, a library containing in length 52 feete, and in breadth 24 feete, with three chambers above on the one side, and fower on the other side, and beneath nine chambers, every of them in length 26 feete, and in breadth 18 feete, with five outer towers and five inner towers. Item, the west pane of the said college 230 feete in length, in the which shall be directly against the library a doore into the cloister, and above eight chambers, and beneth other eight chambers, with three outer towers beyond the north side of the cloistre, and five inner towers, with a way into the quier for the ministers of the church between the vestry

[q] side.

*The library.*

and

and the same quier. Item the south pane in length 155 feete, in which shall stand the hall, with a vaute underneath for the buttery, a cellour, containing in length 82 feete, and in breadth 32 feete, with two bay windows, one inward and the other outward, with a tower over the hall-doore, and at the Est end of the hall a pantry, with a chamber beneath, and at the West end of the hall the provosts' lodgings above and beneath, containing in length 70 feete, with a corner tower inward, and another without; and on the South side of the hall a goodly kitchin, and in the middle of the quadrant[r] a goodly conduit within goodly devised, for the use and profit of the said college. Item, the height fro the streete to the enhansing of the ground of the cemetry seven feete diameter, and the same wall in height above that five feete diameter, with greeces out of the way into the same pane, as many as shall be convenient. Item, that the quadrant within the college, and the utter court be but a foote lower than the cloister. Item, all the walles of the said college of the utter court, and of the walles of the precinct about the gardens, and as far as the precinct shall goe, to be made of the hard stone of Kent; and the said gardens to be enhansed with earth to the heighth of a foote lower then the cemetory of the church.

The hall, buttry, and cellour.

The provost's lodging, &c.

quadrangle.

The

## HENRY THE SIXTH.

### The College of CAMBRIDGE.

And as touching the dimensions of the church of my said college of our Lady and St. Nicholas, at Cambridge, I have devised and appointed that the same church shall containe 288 feete of assise in length, without any yles, and all of the widenesse of 40 feete, and the length of the same church from the West end to the altare at the quier doore, shall containe 120 feete, and from the provost's stall unto the greece called Gradus Chori 90 feete, for 36 stalles on either side of the same quier, answering to 70 fellowes and ten priests, conducts, which must be de primâ formâ; and from the said stalles unto the est end of the said church 72 feete of assize: also a reredos[r] bearing the roodelofte departing the quier and the body of the church, containing in length 40 feete, and in breadth 14 feete; the walls of the same church to be in height 90 feete, imbattled, vawted[s], and chare roffed[t], sufficiently butteraced, and every butterace fined with finials[u]: and in the east end of the said church shall be a windowe of nine bayes[x], and betwixt every butterace a windowe of five bays, and betwixt every of the same butterace in the body of the church, on both sides of the same church, a closet with an altare therein, containing in length 20 feete and in breadth 10 feete, vauted and finished under the soyle of the yle windowes: and the pavement of the

*Marginal notes:* Length and widenesse of the chappell. Stalles. Height of the walles of the chappel. The side chappels.

---

[r] *Reredos* has here a different application from what it had before, p. 296. But it both places signifies a *screen*.     [s] vaulted.

[u] finisht.  *Finials* are the little spires ornamented with flower works that terminate the Gothic buttresses and turrets.

[x] Q. *d*aies, as in the copy of this will printed in Blomefield's Collect. Cantab. p. 125.

urch to be enhanced [y] four feete above the ground without, and height of the pavement of the quier one foote ameter above the pavement of the church, and the avement of the altare three feete above that. Item, on the north side of the quier a veſtry, containing in length o feete, and in breadth 22 feete, departed into two houſes eneath and two houſes above, which ſhall contain in eight 22 feete in all, with an entrie for the quier vawted. em, at the weſt end of the church a cloiſtre ſquare, ie eaſt pane containing in length 175 feete, and the weſt ane as much; and the north paine 200 feete, and the outh pane as much; of the which the deambulatory 3 feete wide, and in height 20 feete to the corbill table, ith cleare ſtories and buttrace, with finialls vawted and mbattled, and the ground thereof four feet lower than ie church ground; and in the middle of the weſt pane of ie cloiſtre a ſtrong tower ſquare, containing 24 feete ithin the walles, and in height 120 feete to the corbyl, ble, and fower, ſmall turrets over that, fined with pinacles, and a dore into the ſaid cloiſtre inward, and outward none; and as touching the dimenſions of the howſing f the ſaid college, I have deviſed and appointed in the outh ſide of the ſaid church, a quadrant cloſing to both ids of the ſame church, the laſt pane whereof ſhall conine 230 feete in length, and in breadth within the walls 2 feete: in the ſame panes middle a tower for a gatehowſe, containing in length 30 feete, and in breadth 22

*The veſtry.*

*The cloiſtre.*

*The ſteeple.*

*The quadrant court.*

*Gate-houſe.*

[y] raiſed.

feete

feete within the walls, and in height 60 feete, and thre[e]
chambers over the gate, every over other; and on eith[er]
fide of the fame gate four chambers, every containing i[n]
length 25 feete, and in breadth 22 feete; and over ever[y]
of thefe chambers two chambers above, of the fame mea[-]
fure or more, with two towers outward and two towe[rs]
inward. The fouth pane fhall contain in length 238 feet[e]
and in breadth 22 feete within, in which fhall be feve[n]
chambers, every containing in length 29 feete, and i[n]
breadth 22, with a chamber, parcell of the provoft's lodg[-]
ing, containing in length 35 feete, and with a chambe[r]
in the eaft corner of the fame pane, containing in lengt[h]
25 feete, and in breadth 22 feete; and over every of a[ll]
the fame chambers two chambers, and with five towe[rs]
owteward, and three towers inward: the weft pan[e]
fhall contain in length 230 feete, and in breadth withi[n]
24 feete; in which at the end toward the church fhall b[e]

**The library.**
a library, containing in length 110 feete, and in breadt[h]
24 feete, and under it a large howfe for reading and di[f]-
putations, containing in length 40 feete, and two cham[-]
bers under the fame library, every containing in lengt[h]
29 feete, and in breadth 24; and over the faid library a[n]
houfe of the fame largenefs for diverfe ftuffe of the college[.]

**Hall, celler, and buttry.**
in the other end of the fame pane an hall containing i[n]
length an 100 feete, upon a vault 12 feete high, ordaine[d]
for the celler and buttery, and the breadth of the hall 3[4]
feete, on every fide thereof a bay window, and in th[e]
nethe[r]

ether end of the same hall, toward the middle of the
ane a pantry and buttry, every of them in length 20  *The pantry.*
ete, and in breadth 17, and over that two chambers for
fficers, and at the nether end of the hall towards the
west a goodly kitchin: and the same pane shall have  *The kitchin.*
ward two towers ordained for the wayes into the hall
nd library, and in every corner of the quadrant shall be
wo corner towers, one inward and one outward, more
nen the towers above rehearsed; and at the upper end of
ne hall the provost's lodging; that is to wit, more then  *The provost's lodging.*
ne chambers for him above specifyed, a parler on the
round, containing 34 feete in length, and 22 in breadth,
wo chambers above of the same quantitie, and westward
losing thereto a kitchin for him, a larder, house, stable,
nd other necessary houses and grounds; and westward
eyond theise howses, and the said kitchin ordained for
ne hall, a bake-howse and brew-house, and other howses  *Bakehouse and brewhouse.*
f office, between which there is left a ground square
f 80 feete in every pane for woode and such stuff; and in
he middle of the said large quadrant shall be a conduict
oodly devised for the ease of the said college: And I will  *Water conduict.*
hat the edification proceed in large forme of my said
ollege cleane and substantiall, seting apart superfluity of  *No superfluity of curious works.*
oo great curious workes of entaile and busy moulding.
And I have devised and appointed that the precincte of
ny said college of our Lady and St. Nicholas, as well
n both sides of the garden from the said college unto the
water,

# HENRY THE SIXTH.

*The college to be enclosed with a wall 14 feet high.*

*The Street gate.*

*The parish church of St. John to be re-edified.*

water, as in all other places of the same precinct, [be] enclosed with a substantiall wall of the height of [14] feete, with a large tower at the principal entre again[st] the middle of the east pane out of the High streete; a[nd] in the same tower a large gate, and in the middle of t[he] west end of the New bridge; and the said wall to [be] crested, and embattled, and fortified with towers, [as] many as shall be thought convenient thereto. And [I] will that both my said colleges be edified of the mo[st] substantiall and best abiding stuffe of stone, lead, glass[e], and yron, that may be had and provided thereto: a[nd] that the church of St. John, which must be taken [for] the enlarging of my said college, be well and sufficient[ly] made againe in the grounde in which the provost a[nd] schollars abovesayd now be lodged or nigh by where [it] may be thought most convenient, to the intent th[at] Divine service shall mow be done therein worshi[p-] fully to the honour of God, our Blessed Lady Christ[s] mother, St. John Baptist, and all Saints: And also f[or] the expedition of the workes abovesayd, I will that m[y] said college of Cambridge have and receive yearely of t[he] yssues, profits, and revenues, coming of the said castell[s], lordships, manors, lands, tenements, rents, services, a[nd] other possessions abovesaid, 117 lib. 6 s. 10 d. during a[ll] the time of the edification of the said college, for t[he] yearly wages and rewards of officers and ministers longin[g] to the workes there; that is to wit, for the master [of] the workes, 50 lib. for the clerk of the workes, 13 lib. 6s. 8d. for the chiefe mason, 16 lib. 13 s. 4 d. for the chief carpenter 12 lib. 8 d. for the chief smith 6 lib. 13 s. 4 d.; and for the purveyors, either of them at 6 d. the day, 18 lib. 6 s. 8 d.; and in semblable wise, I will that my said college of Eton have and receive yearly, during the edification thereof, of the same yssues, profit, and revenues, 124 lib. for the yeerly wages and rewards of the officers and ministers belonging to the workes there; that is to wit, for the master of the workes there 50 lib, for the clerk of the workes 13 lib. 6 s. 8 d. for the chief mason 13 lib. 6 s. 8 d. for the chief carpenter 10 lib. for the chief smith 6 lib. 13 s. 4 d.; and for two purveyors either of them 6 d. by the day, 18 lib. 5 s. 6 d.: Moreover, for as much as I entirely desire that all the numbers of the persons ordeined, devised, and appointed by me, for to be in both my said colleges, be fulfilled in as hasty time as they goodly may, and so the numbers for the accomplisment of my devotion to be kept always perfect, and that certain of the liveloods with which I have endowed my said colleges be yet in reversion, so that the said numbers with other charges may not sufficiently be found and supported, unless that the same college be succored, otherwise I will, pray, and charge, my said feffees, that my said college have and receive yearly of the yssues, profits, and revenus, coming of the castells, lordships, mannors, lands, tenements, rents, services, and other possessions abovesayd,

*Fees granted to certain officers of the works.*

abovesayd, over the said yearly 2000 lib. to the same colleges, in the forme and for the cause abovesayd assigned, the summe of a thousand markes granted unto my said colleges during the lives of certain persons specified in my letters patents seweth [z], under the seale of my said duchy thereupon made, as it is in the said letters more clerely conteyned. Furthermore, I will, pray, and charge my said feffees for to be delivered to my said colleges 2000 lib. over the said yearly 2000 lib. and yearly 1000 markes unto them, in the formes abovesayd, assigned to be taken as soon as it goodly may be arreised and had by the same feasts, of the yssues, profits, and revenues, of the said castells, lordships, mannors, lands, tenements, rents, services, and other possessions; that is to say unto my provost and college roiall of Eton 1000 lib. and unto my provost and college royall of Cambridge 1000 lib. of sufficient and good gold, and of sufficient weight of my lawfull coine, which I have given for a treasure for them, to be kepte within them for diverse great causes, which be more plainly exprest in the statutes and ordinaunces of my said college, by me made in that behalf. And I will that my said college of Eton have of the said yssues, profits, and revenues, of the said castells, lordships, mannors, lands, tenements, rents, services, and possessions, 200 lib. in money, for to purvey them books to the pleasure of God and weale of my same college. And in semblable wise to my other college of Cambridge 200 lib.

*Gift of a 1000 lib. in money to each college, for a treasure to remain.*

[z] Q. following.

200 lib. for to ſtuff them with jewells for the ſervice of God, in the ſame college. And if it like unto God to call me out of this mortal life, before that my ſaid colleges be accompliſhed, and before they have ſuch as is to them here apointed, then I will and deſire that my will above rehearſed touching the ſame colleges and either of them, be ſpecially and principally accompliſhed, and in all points perfectly performed before all other things: And ſecondarilie, that my ſaid feoffees, informed by them that I ſhall ordain to be mine executors of my teſtament, ſo farr as my goods moveable may ſuffer for the payment of my debts, and fulfilling of my teſtament and laſt will, doe ſuch ſummes of mony ſufficient and neceſſarie in that behalf of the yſſues, profits, and revenus, coming of the lordſhips, caſtles, manors, lands, tenements, rents, ſervices, and other poſſeſſions aboveſayd, over that which is aſſigned to my ſaid college, to be payd from time to time to my foreſaid executors, they thereof for to doe and ſatisfie mine exequies, memorialls, and all things behoveable about my ſepulture in honorable wiſe, and to pay my debts of my howſe of my great wardrobe, and of my chambre, and to do plain and entire execution of my laſt will and teſtament, in the which I will that the debts of my howſehold be ſpecially preferred; and if it fortune me to deceaſe, after that the edifications, ordinances, and apointments of my ſaid colleges here before by me made, limited, deviſed, and aſſigned, be accompliſhed and performed,

*Theſe colleges to be performed before all other things.*

*After the colleges performed, order taken for the payment of houſehold debts, and then the overplus to revert to the crown.*

formed, I will then that my said feoffees do, in satisfaction of my debts with all the yssues, profits, and revenues of the said castles, lordships, manors, lands, tenements, rents, services, and other possessions, as is aforesayd. Moreover, I will that all the foresaid castles, lordships, manors, lands, tenements, rents, services, and other possessions, remain still in my feoffees hands untill the time that all this my will afore written, and every pointe of it, be entirely executed and perfectly accomplished; and that fully done and executed, then I will and pray my said feoffees, that the said castells, lordships, mannors, lands, tenements, rents, services, and other possessions, wholie remain to mine heirs and successours, kings of England, for ever more, and to be annexed to the crown of England for ever, in the best forme that the said feoffees, by advise of counsell of law, can order and devise; alway foreseen, that it be lawfull to me, dureing my life onely, by writing, to change this my will, and to the same for to adde, and therein for to muse in all thinges conteyned therein, except such ordinances and apointments as belong and concerne unto my said colleges which be above rehearsed, after my discretion; which changings, additions, and museings, if it fortune any to be, I will, charge, and pray my said feoffees duly to execute after my will; and if it fortune, that before my debts be fully payd, and my last will plainly executed, my said feoffees die all save three, or two, or one, then
I will

# HENRY THE SIXTH.

I will pray and charge them three, two, or one, that they in all the foresaid castles, lordships, mannors, lands, tenements, rents, services, and other possessions, in my foresaid letters patents expressed, do enfeoffe 14 persons, whose names be hereafter written, that is to wit, the reverend father in God William [a] bishop of Winchester, Reignald [b] bishop of St. Asaph, Thomas [c] earl of Devon, Richard [d] earl of Sarum, Henry [e] earl of Northumberland, John [f] earl of Shrewesbury, Thomas lord Clifford [g], Lion [h] lord of Weles, Mr. John Chadworth [i] provost of my said college of Cambridge, William Westbury, provost of my said college of Eton, Mr. William Say, Mr. Andrew Holts, Sir Robert Roose [k] knight, and Sir Thomas Stanley [l] knight: And if it fortune that the said fourteen persons, which the said three feoffees, two, or one of them, should so enfeoffee, as in the premisses before is rehearsed at

*A provision for new feoffees, in case the old die before the performance of the will.*

[a] William Wainfleet, 1447—1486.
[b] Reginald Peacock, 1444—1449.
[c] Thomas Courtney died 1 E. IV.
[d] Richard Nevil, who was also the famous earl of Warwick, slain at the battle of Barnet 1471.
[e] Henry Percie, third earl of Northumberland of that family, slain at Towton 1 E. IV.
[f] John Talbot slain in France 1453.
[g] Slain at the battle of St. Albans 33 H. VI. 1455, and buried in the abbey there.
[h] Third husband of Margaret Beaufort duchess of Somerset, grandmother to H. VII. He was slain at Towton 1 E. IV. Dugd. Bar. II. 12.
[i] Archdeacon of Wilts, prebendary of St. Paul's, bishop of Lincoln 1452, where he died, and was buried 1471. He was the second provost of King's College, elected 1446. Godwin.
[k] Great uncle to Thomas lord Roos of Hamlake. He died before 27 H. VI. Dugd. Bar. I. 553.
[l] Lieutenant of Ireland 9 H. VI. chamberlain to that king, and father of Thomas first lord Stanley. Ib. II. 248.

that time as such feoffment should be made, be not one alive but passed to God all fourteen, then I will that the said three, two, or one of my said feoffees, shall enfeoffe other fourteen persons spirituall and temporall, of good fame, faith, and credence, in all the said castles, lordships, mannors, lands, tenements, and rents, services, and other possessions: Forseen alway, that if any of the first fourteen persons be alive, when the said feofments should by the three feoffees, two, or one of them be made, I will that as many of the foresaid fourteen persons as then shall be alive, be put into the said feofment before any other persons of the same state and degree they be of: And forasmuch as for the good rule and profitable governance of the said castles, lordships, mannors, lands, tenements, rents, services, and other possessions, continually hereafter to be had, and for the effectuall and expedient levè of the yssues, profits, and revenues of the same, I have ordained, and made by my letters patents severall my well-beloved William Tresham esquire, chancellour, and Nich'us Willoughbie general receiver, and attorney of and for all the castells, lordships, manors, lands, tenements, rents, services, and other possessions abovesaid: And to the said office of chancellor have ordained, devised, and apointed, a seale to be used in that behalf, as in my said letters it plainly appeareth; I will, pray, and charge my said feffees, that they, by theere deeds sufficient in law, doe confirme and make sure the said William and Nich'as of and in the said offices to have and

*Officers constituted for the government of lands.*

# HENRY THE SIXTH.

and occupie feverally for terme of their lives. And furthermore, at my nomination made under the faid feale, during my life and after my deceefe, the nomination of the provofts of my faid college for the time being made under their feales; I will that my faid feoffees do order and make at all times hereafter needfull, as well fuch chancellour, generall receiver, and attorney, as ftewards, particular receivers, auditors, bailiffs, feoders, and all other particular officers and minifters of the faid caftles, lordfhips, lands, mannors, rents, tenements, fervices, and other poffeffions: alway forefeene that none of the officers or minifters of my faid duchy of Lancafter, during the time that he fhall ftand in the faid office, be hereafter ordained or made in any wife any officer or minifter of the faid caftells, lordfhips, mannors, lands, tenements, rents, fervices, and other poffeffions, which fhall come again into the hands of me, or mine heirs kinges of England: And that in every graunt which my faid feoffees hereafter by their letters and feale hereupon doe make, ther be put and conteined a claufe fpecially according unto this my will in this behalf. Furthermore, for the finall performing of my faid will to be put effectually in execution, I, confidering the great difcretion of the faid worfhipful father in God William now bifhop of Winchefter, his high truth and fervent zeale, which at all times he had and hath unto my weale, and which I have found and proved in him, and for the great and whole confidence which I have unto him, for thefe caufes will that he not only as furveiour

*The bifhop of Winchefter is ordeined furveyor and executor of the will upon fingular truft repofed in him.*

but also as executour and director of my said will be privy unto all and every execution of performing of my same will, and that his consent be had in any wise thereto; and if any execution of the performing of my said will, or if any part thereof, be done in any wise contrary to the tenor and effect thereof, I will that it stand void and for ever to be had for none; and if it befall that there be any diverse opinions, variance, or discord, betwixt my said feoffees and mine executours, in or for any execution of the performing of my said will or any part thereof, I give then and graunt to the said bishop of Winchester, by these presents, plain [m] power and auctorite; and finally, I will that he, as umpire in that behalfe, have at all times power and auctoritie for to call and take unto him such discreet persons of my said feoffees as unto him for the accomplishment of my will seeme most disposed; and that after their advise heard, do make the finall conclusion in that part: And I will that the power, state, title, and interest of that person, and the persons of my said feoffees, in whom the cause of such variance and discord, by the said bishop of Winchester, and two other of my said feoffees, shall be founde, cease and be void, as well in all things touching my said feofment, as in all things touching my said will; and if it be soe that the said bishop of Winchester passe unto God out of this mortall life, I being alive, then I will that this auctoritie and power by me unto him in the forme abovesaid, given and graunted, re-

*If any quarrel rise between the feoffees and executors, the bishop of Winchester shall decide the doubt.*

[m] full, *plein.*

turn again wholly unto me, and abide in mine own disposition: And in case I be called out of this mortall life, the said bishop of Winchester me overliving, I will then that at such time as God shall give him knowledge by likelihoode o' this brief passage out of this world, my said will at that time not fully accomplished, he remembre him of the most discreet, faithfull, and true person, a lord spirituall and temporall, which the said bishop of Winchester, by experience had the mean time, shall finde and prove for to be best and most godly disposed, and most fervent in zeale, to the performing of my said will: and as well unto the same lord, without inordinate affection or acception of person, as he shall in breef time streightly answere herein before the tribunall seate of Christ oure alder[n] saviour and terrible judge, as unto the provosts of both my said colleges for the time being, committee wholy under his letters and seale the said power and auctoritie, which he hath in the same forme abovesayd, of my guift and graunt made unto him in this behalfe. And if it soe be that the said lorde unto whome the said power and auctoritie shall in the forme abovesaid by the said bishop of Winchester be committed, be not profitable unto the performing of my said will; I will that the provosts of my said colleges for the time being, have full power and auctoritie for to discharge the said lord of all power and auctority unto him committed in this behalfe; and thereupon the same provosts being remembred in the manner and

*A provision of a surveior, in case the bishop of Winton die before the king; another provision in case the bishop die after the king.*

*If the surveior upon trust be not profitable for the college, he may be removed by the provosts, and a new one placed by them.*

---

[n] al͞ðep, Sax. elder, i.e. the first. Bailey.—Q. *al der*, most dear. Dr. Johnson explains *alderlievest* (Shakspeare, 2 H. VI.) by *most beloved*.

forme, as it is above rehearsed, have full power and auctoritie for to commit under lettres and seales such power and auctoritie in this partie unto another lord, and from time to time, as by me is here in the forme abovesaid committed unto the said bishop of Winchester, in every pointe according unto the same: And semblaby[o], if the said lord decease, my said will not accomplished, the said provosts in likewise remembred and advised, shall commit the said power and auctoritie unto another lorde, and fro time to time, as often as any of those cases shall fall unto the time that my said will and every part thereof be plainly and entirely accomplished and performed; and in case that any of my heirs and successours, kings of England, disturb, let, or in any wise interrupt my said executours, feffees, surveiour or surveiours, it shall be lawfull for my said feffees to sell and alienate all the said castles, lordships, mannors, lands, tenements, rents, services, and other possessions for [fro] my said heirs and successours, so letting the execution of my said will, to such as shall be thought to my said executours, surveiour, or surveiours, expedient. The mony thereof arising to be employed by the same executours, surveiour, or surveiours, upon the fullfilling of my said will, and surplus (if any be) to be employed upon the holie workes of pietie. And that this my said will in every pointe before rehearsed may the more effectually be executed, I not onlye praye and desire, but also in Christ require and charge all and every of my said feoffees, mine execu-

*Marginal note:* If the executors be interrupted by any of the king's heirs, &c. the feffees may sell the lands to certain uses.

[o] In like manner.

tours, and surveiour and surveiours, in the vertue of the aspersion of Christ's blood and of his paineful passion, that they having God and mine entente only before their eyne, not leteing[p] for dread or favour, of any person living of what estate, degree, or condition, that he bee truly, faithfully, and diligently execute my said will, and every part thereof, as they will answer before the blessed and dreadfull visage of oure Lorde Jhesu, in his most fearfull and last day, when every man shall be most straightly examined and dealt with after his merits. And furthermore, for the more sure accomplishment of this my said will, I in the most entire and most fervent wise pray my said heirs and executours, and successours and every of them, that they shew themselves well willing, faithful, and tender lovers of my desire in this behalf; and in the bowells of Christ our alder, just, and straite[q] judge, I exhorte them to remember the terrible comminations and full fearfull imprecations of holy scripture against the breakers of the law of God, and the letters of good and holy workes. *Quod si audire nolueris, venient super te omnes maledictiones istæ, et apprehendent te. Maledictus eris in civitate, maledictus in agro: maledictus fructus ventris tui, & fructus terræ tuæ. Maledictus eris egrediens, & maledictus ingrediens. Mittet tibi dominus famem & esuriem, & increpationem in omnia opera tua quæ tu facies, donec conterat te & perdat velociter, propter inventiones tuas pessimas. Adjungat tibi pestilentiam: percutiat te dominus*

*A dreadful charge given to the executors, &c.*

*The like charge given to his heirs and Successors.*

Deut. xxviii.

[p] letting, hindering.   [q] strict.

*egestate,*

*egeſtate, febri & frigore, ardore & æſtu, & aere corrupto ac rubigine & perſequatur donec pereas. Tradat te dominus corruentem ante hoſtes, &c.*

I alſo, in amiable wiſe, exhort my ſaid heires and ſucceſſors in Chriſt Jeſu, the liberall rewarder of good deeds, to remember the deſireable bleſſings and moſt bounteous grace, promitted to all ſuch as obſerve the lawes of Chriſt, being helpers and promoters of good and vertuous deſire; Scripture in the ſame ſaying to ſuch: *Venient ſuper te univerſæ benedictiones iſtæ. Et apprehendent te. Benedictus tu in civitate, & benedictus in agro: benedictus fructus ventris tui, & benedictus fructus terræ tuæ; benedictus eris egrediens & benedictus ingrediens. Dabit dominus inimicos tuos qui conſurgent adverſum te corruentes in conſpectu tuo. Per unam viam venient contra te, & per ſeptem fugient a facie tuâ. Mittet dominus benedictionem ſuper cellaria tua & ſuper omnia opera manuum tuarum; ſuſcitabit te dominus ſibi in populum ſanctum, videbuntque omnes terrarum populi, quod nomen domini invocatum ſit ſuper te, & timebunt te gentes terrarum: abundare te faciet dominus omnibus bonis, &c.*

And in witneſs that this is my full will and intent, I have ſett hereto my great ſeale, and the ſeale of my ſaid duchy, and my ſeale apointed and aſſigned by me for the ſaid caſtles, lordſhips, mannors, lands, tenements, rents, ſervices, and other poſſeſſions put into the ſaid feoffment: and alſo as well the ſignet I uſe in mine owne governance for the ſame duchie, as the ſignet of mine armes. And I have ſigned with mine owne handes

theſe

thefe prefent letters indented and tripartite, and doe them to be inclofed under my privy feale at my faid college of Eton, the 12th of March, Anno Domini 1447, and of my reign the 26th.

Harleian MS. 7032. Nº 11. p 289. to 304. both inclufive, being one of Mr. Baker's MSS. ex manufcripto Cajo-Gonvill cui titulus, Mifcellaneæ Collectiones Magiftri Roberti Hare, vol. II.

Henry VI. was only child to Henry V. whofe prophetic expreffions at his birth he literally fulfilled; being more a monk than a monarch. He fucceeded his father at nine months old, 1422, was crowned at Weftminfter 1429, and in Paris 1431; and before he had reigned 25 years, was difpoffeffed of all his territories in France. In the year 1452 the rebellion which had been fomenting in England broke out; and Henry, after having been twice depofed and imprifoned in the Tower, was, in 1472, there affaffinated in the 51ft year of his age, by Richard duke of Gloucefter, afterwards king Richard III. He was firft buried at Chertfey abbey, and then removed by order of Edward IV. to Windfor, and there interred under a fair monument in St. George's chapel, of which there are at prefent no remains, whilft that of his competitor and his fucceffor Edward IV. ftill exifts.

He married 1445 Margaret daughter of Renè duke of Anjou, a lady of a fpirit as oppofite to that o her

her father, as her husband's was to his father's. By her he had an only child Edward, born 1453, married to Anne daughter of Edward Neville earl of Salisbury and Warwick, and murdered after the battle of Tewksbury, by Richard duke of Gloucester, who married his widow.

# CARDINAL BEAUFORT, BISHOP OF WINTON.

IN nomine sancte & individue Trinitatis, patris & filii & spiritus sancti, ac gloriosissime virginis Marie, & tocius curie celestis, Amen. Ego Henricus miseracione divina titulo sancti Eusebii, sacrosancte Romane ecclesie presbiter, cardinalis de Anglia vulgariter nuncupatus[a] episcopus Winton. indignus, gratias Deo, compos mentis, & sane memorie, ac in sinceritate catholice fidei integer & indubius existens, considerans interiori acie mentis mee quam fallax, quam transitoria, mutabilis, & immutabiliter caduca sit hec vita, quam pocius umbram que cito evanescit seu spectaculum fore conspicio quam perhennitatem dierum, idcirco volens, cum Dei paciencia, bona mea terrestria in celestia commutare, & eadem bona mea que michi divina disposicione collata fore cognosco pro anime mee salute disponere in pios usus, condo testamentum meum & hanc meam voluntatem in hunc modum.

In primis, lego animam meum omnipotenti Deo plasmatori[b] meo, & sue misericordie, ipsiusque matri virgini gloriose, & corpus meum humand' in ecclesia mea Winton' in eo videl't loco quem pro sepultura mea elegi & assignavi. Et volo quod omni die imperpetuum celebrantur tres misse pro anima mea per tres monachos ejusdem ecclesie, in

---

[a] He has this style in the public records. Rymer. Rapin, V. 268.
[b] maker.

capella

capella dicte sepulture mee, una videl't de requiem, alia de die, tercia de annunciacione virginis gloriose, videl't cum officio " rorate celi desuper" & aliis singulis eidem officio pertinen'. Et in qualibet missa volo quod cum secreto & post communi dicatur ista oracio " Deus qui " inter apostolicos sacerdotes," &c. exprimendo nomen Henricum Cardinalem, et quod quilibet sic celebrans habeat in speciali memoria in missa sua animas Johannis ducis Lancastrie & Katerine conjugis sue genitorum meorum, animas Henrici quarti, & Henrici quinti regum Anglie, Johannis comitis Somerset, Thome ducis Exon, fratrum meorum, Johanne comitisse Westmerlandie sororis mee, & Johannis ducis Bedford; & volo quod fiat assecuracio, secundum discrecionem executorum meorum & jurisperitorum, pro continuacione istarum missarum, & pro obitu meo solempniter in predicta ecclesia singulis annis imperpetuum tenendo meliori & securiori modo quo fieri poterit. Item volo quod quilibet sic celebrans habeat & percipiat singulis septimanis II d. per diem per manus prioris seu sui deputati. Et volo quod septimanatim mutentur isti sic celebraturi, & intitulentur in tabula conventuali sub isto titulo, fre.... [c] celebraturi proxima septimana pro anima Henrici cardinalis Anglie; pro quibus quidem missis & obitu sic imperpetuum celebrand' volo quod executores mei concordent cum priore & capitulo predict' & pro onere VI d. solvend' tribus monachis dict' missas singulis diebus celebraturis. Item volo quod exequie mee

[c] Q. fratres.

celebrentur

celebrentur non nimis fumptuofo modo, fed fecundum ftatum in quo Deus voluerit me decedere, & hoc fecundum difcrecionem executorum meorum. Item volo quod diftribuantur in die fepulture mee ccli. pauperibus ibidem congregand' fecundum maius vel minus juxta difcrecionem executorum meorum. Et fi contigerit me obire in aliquo loco diftanti ab ecclefia mea Wynton predict' volo quod ultra fumptus neceffarios pro conductu corporis mei ad locum fepulture, diftribuantur dietim xli. pauperibus elemofinam petentibus fecundum maius vel minus juxta difcretionem executorum meorum. Et fi contigerit corpus meum pernoctare in aliquo loco, volo quod pro anima mea fiant exequie mortuorum de nocte, & miffa de requiem de mane, in ecclefia ubi fic continget corpus meum pro illa nocte commorari, et quilibet prefbiter ibidem celebrans habeat viiid. et quod offerantur in fingulis ecclefiis tres panni aurei de meis propriis majoris precii vel minoris, juxta difcrecionem executorum meorum & fecundum exigenciam locorum. Item volo quod quanta celeritate fieri poterit poft deceffum meum decem millia miffarum, fcilicet tria milia de requiem, III milia de "rorate celi de fuper," III milia de fancto fpiritu, & mille de trinitate: et poft oracionem officii in qualibet miffa dicatur oracio, " Deus qui inter apoftolicos facerdotes," &c. exprimendo nomen ut fupra, & volo quod quilibet celebrans miffam habeat vid. Item volo quod fufficienter provideatur per executores meos in omnibus ornamentis honeftis & neceffariis pro capella & altari in loco fepulture mee ut videl't ordinent pro eodem altari II veftimenta communia pro
diebus

diebus feriatis & 11 vestimenta meliora pro festis majoribus cum una cruce deaurata secundum discretionem executorum meorum & cum ymaginibus meis de salutacione, viz. una ymagine beate Marie virginis, & alia archangeli Gabrielis cum olla & lilio [d]. Item, unum calicem aureum cum uno pari urceolorum [e], uno pari candelabrorum cum tintinabulo, & deosculatorio pacis [f] de auro. Item lego eidem altari unum par candelabrorum argenteorum & deauratorum, cum una calice argenteo & deaurato cum urceolis, campana, & deosculatorio pacis deauratis. Item 11 paria pelvium deauratorum, viz. unum par melius & aliud minoris valoris. Item unum vas aque benedict' argenteum ad minus valoris x marc'. Item lego eidem altari unum par candelabrorum argenteorum quod est in oratorio meo, in diebus feriatis ad serviend' eidem altari singulis diebus, 11 missalia mea, secundum discretionem executorum meorum, & unum breviarium meum majus, non notatum quod quondam erat episcopi Bathon'; que omnia volo remanere eidem altari imperpetuum, & in nullo alio loco deservire. Et quod prior & conventus dicte ecclesie obligentur quod dictis vestimentis consumptis, seu alias in tantum usitatis quod cum honestate non possint ulterius deservire, ipsi providebunt dicti altari de aliis vestimentis competentibus eorum sumptibus & expensis, & prout po-

[d] All the representations of the salutation, introduce a *lily* in the angel's hand, and a *flower-pot* on the floor between him and the Virgin; the latter may be only a piece of furniture, the former answer to a caduceus or palm-branch.

[e] poti. [f] a pax.

terit concordari inter executores meos & ipsos. Item volo quod prior dicte ecclesie mee Winton' & conventus ejusdem habeant de me cc li. & calicem meum meliorem cum patena, & vestimentum meum integrum totaliter inbrondatum quod emi ab Hugone Dyke; ita tamen quod nullus isto vestimento utatur si non episcopus Winton' pro tempore existens in ecclesia tum quando voluerit, vel aliquis qui debet officiari in presencia regis, regine, vel regis primogeniti. Item lego priori ejusdem ecclesie unum ciphum deauratum ad minus valoris xli. cum II ollis argent' & deaurat' galoniers [g], & IIII ollis argent' non deaurat' galoners, ad finem quod rex, regina, quandocumque vel episcopus Winton' pro tempore existens fuerit in civitate seu suburbiis ejusdem, ubi eis debet deserviri de prebenda [h] panis & vini in presentacione cujus servitor prioris tenetur dicere "Saint Pier & Saint Pol vous envoient," eo tunc predict' unum portetur in eisdem cum quatuor ollis galoners non deaurat'. Et ultra hoc volo quod prior habeat quatuor ollas argenteas potellers [i] cum uno pari pelvium coopertarum & II pelvibus simplicibus cum duobus aquareis [k]. Item duas duodenas discorum, duas duodenas salvariorum, VI chargeours, II saleria [l] deaurata; que omnia volo imperpetuum deservire prioribus ejusdem ecclesie temporibus congruis

[g] of gallon measure.
[h] a portion: a feed when applied to horses.
[i] Q. of *pint* measure. Du Cange explains *olla potteller* a porringer.
[k] ewers.
[l] salt-sellers. This English word is a redundancy. Salerium, Saliere, implying the same, as *sellar*, in one word.

&

& debitis. Et quod prior obligetur, sub pena privacionis, ista non alienare, neque impignorare, nec extra monasterium ducere. Et quod pondus omnium istorum vasorum per me legatorum remaneant penes conventum. Et quod semel in anno supprior & octo seniores tocius conventus videant quod ista bona remaneant in manibns dicti prioris. Et volo quod ista remaneant priori & conventui ecclesie mee predicte; sic tamen quod ipsi obligentur & quod fiat assecuracio ut predictum est per advisamentum & discrecionem executorum meorum de observando solempniter obitum meum singulis annis imperpetuum. Et quod quilibet monachus celebraturus diebus obitus & anniversarii mei, dicat in missa post officium cum secreto & postcommunione, "Deus qui inter apostolicos sacerdotes," &c. nomen Henricum Cardinalem ut supra. Item do eidem priori viginti marcas, et cuilibet confratrum meorum ibidem XL s. ut ipsi pro anima mea orent; & ministris ecclesie c s. distribuend' secundum discrecionem dictorum prioris & conventus. Item lego priori, suppriori, & conventui ejusdem ecclesie mee, VI duodenas discorum de argento, quilibet discus ad valoris XL s. V duodenas tassiarum [m] de argento, unaquaque tassia ponderis II marc' de pondere Troiano [n] cum

---

[m] *tasses*, cups.

[n] Troy weight. None of the glossaries give a satisfactory etymology of this word. Spelman and Du Cange after him content themselves with saying that *Trojæ pondus apud Anglos dicitur quod 12 uncias in libra numerat.* Somner supposes it the same with *Trona* or *Trone* in Scotland, but the authorities alledged prove the latter to be only the weighing engine and not the weight.

majori

majori cipho meo cooperto, & vi ollis argenteis, videl't ii galoneys, & iiii<sup>or</sup> pottellers, que omnia volo deservire in refectorio, & nullo modo alibi. Et quod prior pro tempore existens, cum octo senioribus capituli, in festo sancti Michaelis videant omnia ista cum ponder'.[o] remanere in refectorio: et quod de istis vasis deserviatur conventui in refectorio existen' diebus nativitatis domini, pasche, penthacostes, assumpcionis, & annunciacionis beate virginis, omnium sanctorum, apostolorum Petri & Pauli, sancti Swithini, & in die anniversarii mei; quo die volo quod confratres mei habeant pitanciam ad valorem xl s. Item, remitto abbati & conventui sancti Augustini extra Cantuariam ccclxvi li. xiii s. iiii d. in quibus ipsi michi obligantur, ita quod pro ista summa ipsi obligentur secundum discrecionem executorum meorum quod dietim imperpetuum in tribus missis, viz. in una de virgine gloriosa & in missa celebranda ante feretrum beati Augustini, necnon in missa capitulari immediate post primam collectam dicetur in singulis dictarum missarum suo per d'nm [p] collecta " Deus qui inter apostolicos sacerdotes, &c." exprimendo nomen Henricum Cardinalem ut supra dictum est: et una cum hoc quod singulis annis imperpetuum diem obitus mei solempniter observabunt cum exequiis ix. li. [q] de nocte & missa solempni in die. Item, do et lego abbati predict' unum ciphum deauratum valoris x li. cum sex simplicibus peciis deaurat' ii ollas deauratas, ii ollas argenteas potellers, xii discos, xii salsaria [r] & iiii char-

[o] Quere according to their full weight.
[p] These words being unintelligible in the original, quere if *supradicta*.
[q] Sic Orig.
[r] Saltsellers, as before *Salaria*, note [l].

geours, 11 pelves argenteas cum 11 aquariis, que volo imperpetuum remanere eifdem abbati et conventui in forma qua alia per me data & legata remanent priori & conventui dicte ecclefie mee Winton. Item, lego eidem abbati x marc' & cuilibet monacho ejufdem monafterii xx s. ut ipfi pro anima mea orent. Item, volo quod diftribuantur cccc li. incarceratis, five pro tranfgreffione, five pro debito, in utroque computatorio [s] London' in Newgate, Ludgate, Flete, Marefcalcia, Banco Regis, & in carceribus infra manerium meum in Suthwerk, pro liberacione eorundem per manus aliquorum virorum bone confcience quos executores mei voluerint eligere & nominare; ita quod quatuor eorundem executorum meorum in nominacione hujufmodi perfonarum quibus iftam diftribucionem debuerunt facere fint concordes. Item, volo quod diftribuantur duo milia marcarum inter pauperes tenentes meos in comitatibus Hampfhire, Wilts, Surr', Somerf', Oxon', Barks, & Bucks. Et fiat ifta diftribucio vel in pecuniis, vel in aliis rebus que magis videbuntur tendere ad utilitatem eorundem fecundum formam in articulo proxime preceden' expreffat' viz. per manus aliquorum virorum bone confciencie juxta difcretionem executorum meorum fic ut premittitur nominand'. Et quod ipfi habeant pro labore eorum illud quod dict' executoribus videbitur racionabile et conveniens. Item, lego fratribus predicatoribus London XL. li. ut ipfi pro anima mea orent. Item, tribus aliis domibus & ordinibus mendicancium in

[s] Compter.

eadem civitate, viz. cuilibet domui x. li. Item, lego cuilibet conventui fratrum mendicancium infra dioc' meam x marc'. Item, lego domino meo regi Henrico tabulettum cum reliquiis qui vocatur Tablet de Bourbon, & unum ciphum de auro cum aquario qui erat illustrissimi principis recolendeque memorie patris sui, fact' de auro per eundem principem in die Parasceves oblato, de quo cipho ipse solebat usualiter potare & ultimo potavit, supplicando & humillime intercedendo apud ejus serenitatem quatinus velit succurrere & subvenire executoribus meis in hiis que possunt tendere ad salutis anime mee prout sibi, ut Deus novit, semper fui fidelis, & affectans prosperitatem status sui, optansque & desiderans ea que possent tangere ad salutem sui in anima & in corpore. Item, lego Johanne[t] uxori Edwardi Stradlyng milit. II duodenas discorum, IIII chargeours, XII salsaria, II pelves cum II aquariis, II ollas pottellers, & XII pecias de argento. Item, unum ciphum deauratum valoris x li. Item, unum lectum de albo serico enbrondat' cum rosis, cum tapitis & cussinis eidem pertinen' & centum libras in auro. Item, lego Hans Nulles XL li. Item, volo quod clerici capelle mee existentes in servicio meo tempore mortis mee, & ad locum sepulture mee corpus meum ducentes, habeant de regardo[u] c marcas inter eos dividendas, secundum discrecionem executorum meorum, attendendo promociones eorum & tempora quibus michi servierunt. Item, volo quod si pro aliqua solucione denario-

[t] The bishop's natural daughter. See hereafter.     [u] Reward.

rum faɛt' ante dat' prefencium, pro quibus eram obligatus, aliqua erat defalcacio facta veri debiti, quod fiat reftitucio perfone feu ejus executoribus cui talis defalcacio facta fuerit de tali fumma fic defalcata; que quidem fumma defalcacionis hujufmodi apparere poterit per libros compotorum thefauri de Wolvefey. Item, fi aliquas denariorum fummas recepi ab aliqua venacione facta infra chafeas, parcos, vel garennas meas, volo quod fiat reftitutio de fumma fic recepta in quantum legitime conftare poterit de aliqua fumma fic recepta. Item, volo quod debita mea fi que fuerint ante omnia perfolvantur. Item, quod fiqui fint qui velint & poffint jufte conqueri de aliqua oppreffione, feu aliquo malo per me eis injufte illato quod fiant eis reftitucio & emenda, petendo veniam & mifericordiam prout ipfi unan . . . . . confequi volunt. Item, remitto dictis tenentibus meis quafcumque denariorum fummas quas ipfi, aut eorum aliquis, debeat michi in die obitus mei. Item, volo quod per difcrecionem dict' executorum meorum diftribuantur duo milia librarum inter fervitores meos domefticos ac familiares, habito refpectu ad quantitatem temporis quo fteterint in fervicio meo, ad qualitatem fuorum graduum & perfonarum, & ad eorum in me merita in cafu quod eifdem executoribus meis ante obitum meum non declaravero, vel fcriptis dimifero modum & formam diftribucionis hujufmodi faciende; volo tamen quod Hans Nulles fit contentus de eo quod fibi legatum eft, & quod non comprehendatur quoad iftum articulum inter alios fervitores meos. Item, volo quod refiduum bonorum

meorum

meorum non legatorum juxta difcreciones & confciencias dict' executorum meorum difponatur & convertatur in opera caritatis & in pios ufus, utpote in relevandis pauperibus domibus religioforum five religiofarum ere alieno oppreffis, in maritandis puellis pauperibus, in fuccurrendo pauperibus egeftatem & neceffitatem evidentem pacientibus, & in alia fimilia opera pietatis, prout ipfi crediderint faluti anime mee magis poffe expedire. Hujus autem teftamenti mei ac ultime voluntatis ordino & conftituo reverendum in Chrifto Patrem Dominum Cardinalem & Archiepifcopum Eboracen.' [x] nepotem meum [y] Marchionem Dorfet, Fratrem Ricardum Vyell priorem ecclefie de Witham [z] ordinis Cartufien. Magiftrum Stephanum Wilton archidiaconum Winton cancellarium meum, Ricardum Waller, armigerum, magiftrum hofpitii mei, Willielmum Whaplode fenefcallum terrarum epifcopatus mei Willielm' Mareys thefaurarium meum de Wolvefeye, Will'm Toly, & Will'm Port; rogans eos cum omni finceritate cordi atq' exhortans in vifceribus caritatis, quatinus in exequendo & adimplendo iftum teftamentum meum & hanc ultimam voluntatem meam fidelitatem, & diligenciam adhibeant quam fibi in cafu fimili adhiberi & preftari vellent, & prout velint

[x] John Kemp, 1425—1452.

[y] Edmund third fon of John Beaufort, fon of John of Gaunt, created marqüis of Dorfet, 21 Hen. VI. flain at St. Albans, 1455, fee before, p. 211. He married Eleanor fecond daughter of Beauchamp earl of Warwick, by whom he had four fons and feven daughters. She died 1467. Sandford, p. 331, 332.

[z] In Selwood, c. Somerfet; fee before, p. 218. note [c].

ante

ante tribunal tremendi judicis in extremo examine respondere. Et lego cuilibet dictorum executorum meorum onus executionis hujus testamenti mei, & administracionis bonorum meorum in se assumenti pro labore suo, videlicet, dicto Reverendissimo Patri ducentas libras, et unum ciphum aureum valoris quadraginta librarum, & dicto nepoti meo marchioni ducentas libras & unum ciphum aureum valoris XL librarum, & unicuiq' aliorum executorum meorum predict' centum libras. In cujus rei testimonium hoc testamentum meum sub sigillo armorum meorum clausi atq' signavi. Dat. in palacio meo de Wolveseye, vicesimo die mensis Januarii Anno Domini millesimo cccc$^{mo}$ XLVI$^{to}$.

## CODICILLUS PRIMUS.

IN Dei nomine, Amen. Ego Henricus miseracione divina Cardinalis de Anglia, ac Episcopus Winton, post testamentum meum scriptum et sigillo meo XX die Januarii, anno Domini Mill. cccc°. XLVI$^{to}$. signatum, altissimi gracia mediante, senciens me compotem mentis, Volendo ultra ea que continentur in eodem testamento aliqua ad salutem anime mee de residuo bonorum meorum in testamento meo non legatorum certo modo disponere, que non occurrebant menti dum testamentum meum hujusmodi conficeretur, facio hunc presentem Codicillum hujusmodi voluntatis mee disposicionem in se distincte continentem. Et volo quod ea que continentur in isto eodem codicillo meo ejusdem sint momenti,

momenti, vigoris, et efficacie, ac si in dicto testamento meo conscripta & comprehensa essent, & nichilominus quod ibidem testamentum meum quoad omnia & singula que in eo continentur suum roborem retinere & sortiri intelligatur, preterquam in hiis que per me signantur, et in speciale et per terminos expressos in hoc codicillo forsan mutari continget; in quo casu intencionis mee est, & volo quod stetur terminis & verbis hujus codicille & non testamenti mei supradicti, et quod voluntas mea quantum ad hoc observetur secundum formam hic insertam et expressatam. Itaque in primis lego priori et conventui ecclesie Christi Cant' mille libras, de qua summa volo quod v$^c$ marc. convertantur et applicentur ad solucionem faciend' pro manerio & dominio de Bekesbourne prope Cantuar' et reliqua pars dicte summe mille li. ad fabricam ejusdem ecclesie. Ita tamen quod quidem prior et conventus ordinent & faciant securitatem executoribus meis in dicto testamento meo nominatis quod singulis diebus imperpetuum facient tres missas celebrari pro anima mea per tres monachos ejusdem ecclesie secundum formam illarum trium missarum que continuis diebus imperpetuum celebrabunt pro anima mea in ecclesia mea Winton in dicto testamento meo expressatam, et obitum meum singulis annis imperpetuum solempniter observabunt. Item, lego ad opus et fabricam ecclesie Lincoln' cc li. ita tamen quod decanus & canonici ejusdem ecclesie diem obitus mei singulis annis imperpetuum observari promittant, et pro anima mea eodem die missam de requiem celebrent solempnem,

lempnem, et nocte precedente vigilias mortuorum exequantur folempniter & ficut confueverunt facere pro fundatoribus ejufdem ecclefie, dando fecuritatem executoribus meis fupradictis pro fe & fuccefforibus fuis de hoc debite faciendo. Item, lego domino meo Regi difcum five plattam meam auream pro fpicebus, & ciphum meum aureum enamellatum per totum cum ymaginibus, cum uno aquario ejufdem operis eidem cipho pertinente.

Item, cum alia certa jocalia et vafa aurea & argentea per dominum meum regem et officiales fuos autoritate fua ac parliamenti fui in ea parte utentes anno regni fui fecundo michi impignorata fuerunt pro certis pecuniarum fummis [a] extendentibus fe ad eftimacionem & valorem eorundem pignorum, fibi ad fuam, & dominorum de fuo concilio inftanciam mutuo per me conceffis, fub ea viz. condicione quod fi de eifdem fummis non fieret michi plenaria folucio in termino feu terminis hinc inde concordat' quod extunc

[a] The Bifhop lent the King at one time *pour l'efploit de v're prefent voyage vers les parties de France & Normandie a v're tres grande befoigne et neceffite & pur l'aife de v're povre communalte de Engleterre*, £. 14,000; and £. 8306. 18s. 8d. was then due *u fa auncien creance a vous fait, come piert par vos honurables letters patentz a luy ent faitz, et a vos ditz Communes miniftres,* fay the Commons in their petition, 9 Hen. V. 1414. defiring to have it confirmed, and the letters patents inrolled in parliament. For the £. 14,000. the King made over, in the fifth year of his reign, the duties and cuftoms on certain imports at Southampton; and when the bifhop had reimburft himfelf to the amount of £. 8306. 18s. 8d. he lent the King another £. 14000. making in all £. 22306. 18s. 8d. for which the faid cuftoms were again mortgaged to him, and the cocket of the faid port and its dependencies; which grant was confirmed in the above parliament. Rot. Parl. vol. IV. p. 132—135. But a good deal of the loan remained unpaid at the time of the bifhops death, as appears by this codicil. The King redeemed, 1432, the *fword of Spain*, and other jewels, which had been pledged to the Cardinal for £. 493. 6s. 8d. Rymer, X. 502.

bene

bene liceret michi eifdem jocalibus & vafis uti & gaudere tamquam propriis ita ut eadem bona de natura pignorum tranfirent in meram naturam proprietatis mee & mea effent & remanerent, prout in literis regiis et indenturis inde confectis plenius liquere poterit; Nichilominus quamquam hec ita fint, & quod ipfa jocalia et vafa pro non obfervacione dicte condicionis ex parte Domini Regis, et non folucione dictarum fummarum jure optimo mea fint, volo tamen quod de illis eifdem jocalibus & vafis omnia illa que in manibus meis tempore obitus mei remanferint Dominus Rex fi ferenitati fue placuerit habeat, dum tamen folvat dict' executoribus meis omnes illas fummas pecuniarum pro quibus prius impignorata fuerant; except' tabuletto de Burbon & illo cipho & aquario aureo fact' per Dominum Regem pie memorie de auro in die Parafceves oblato, de quibus eft facta mencio in dicto teftamento meo, que volo clare remanere Domino meo Regi tanquam fibi legata per vim dicti teftamenti mei fine aliqua folucione pecuniarum pro eifdem fienda. Et volo quod pro folucione facienda pro dictis olim pignoribus concedatur Domino Regi per eofdem executores meos fpacium unius anni, & fi infra idem tempus vel in fine ejufdem non fiat ifta folucio, quod tunc vere liceat executoribus meis de eifdem rebus ad falutem anime mee difponere ficut de ceteris bonis meis. Item, quamvis fatis effet expediens in omni actu predicti teftamenti mei, necnon hujus codicilli execucionem concernente omnes execۃutores meos fimul prefentes fieri, cum tamen poffet contingere quod non omnes

X x       femper

semper in hujufmodi actu perficiendo propter alias eorum occupaciones & impedimenta fimul convenire poffent; volo quod ex eifdem executoribus meis faltem quinque in omni actu execucionis hujufmodi fint concordes fine quibus ad omne minus in unum confentientibus nichil fiat quod de jure effectum aut vim executionis confequi poffit. Item, volo quod difponatur per executores meos ut a die obitus mei ufque ad finem unius anni integri, omnes fervitores familiares mei teneant fe fimul, commorentur, & cohabitent in aliquo loco et hofpicio honefto & congruo per executores meos ordinando; Et quod per executores ipfos provideatur omnibus eifdem fervitoribus familiaribus meis in hofpicio hujufmodi ftare & fimul expectare volentibus, unicuiq' viz. fecundum ftatum fuum competenter et honefte tam in efculentis & poculentis quam in vadiis[b] et ceteris rebus, fecundum formam & regulam ordinariam in domo mea confuetam & per me hactenus obfervatam. Item, lego rectori & confratribus domus de Afhrigge ad fabricam novi operis dicte domus c li.; dum tamen fecuritatem executoribus meis faciant ad obfervand' ea pro anima mea que alias a me erant ordinata et eis declarata, necnon per eofdem michi conceffa. Item, lego abbati & conventui de Hyda juxta Winton ad reparacionem ecclefie ejufdem cc li. dummodo fingulis annis imperpetuum ipfi teneant & obfervent diem obitus mei, & de hoc folempniter faciendo fecuritatem executoribus meis faciant pro fe et fucceffloribus fuis. Item, lego fervitori meo antiquo Ricardo Petteworth c li. ut ipfe pro ani-

[b] Wages.

ma mea oret. In quorum premifforum teftimonium hunc prefentem codicillum meum figneto meo fignavi. Dat' in palacio meo de Wolvefeye VII^mo die menfis Aprilis, Anno Domini millefimo cccc^mo XLVII^mo.

## CODICILLUS SECUNDUS.

IN Dei nomine, Amen. Ego Henricus miferacione divina Cardinalis de Anglia ac Epifcopus Winton, poft teftamentum meum fcriptum & figillo meo XX° die Januarii, anno Domini millefimo cccc^mo XLVI^to. fignatum, & quendam codicillum de poft per me VII° die menfis Aprilis, anno Domini millefimo cccc^mo XLVII° editum, fenciens eciam nunc ficut tunc me, gratie Altiffimo, compotem mentis mee, volenfque ultra ea que continentur in eifdem teftamento meo & codicillo aliqua difponere de refiduo bonorum meorum in dict' teftamento & codicillo non legatorum fpecialiter nec difpofitorum, facio jam nunc & condo hunc prefentem codicillum meum ultimam voluntatem meam quoad que in eodem diftribuuntur diftincte continentem, decernens quod ea que in ifto eodem codicillo meo deftribuuntur ejufdem fint roboris et efficacie ac fi in dicto teftamento meo confcripta feu comprehenfa fuiffent. Et quod quatenus prefens difpoficio mea in hoc codicillo contenta obviat five difcordat aliquibus in dict' teftamento meo & codicillo meis defcriptis, illa que in prefenti codicillo meo continentur forciantur & habeant effectum et vigorem, & quod nichilominus dict' testament' & codicillus quoad omnia alia & singula, que in eisdem continentur sint & maneant rata atque firma. In primis igitur in illo priori codicillo meo disposuero quantum ad certa jocalia & vasa aurea & argentea per Dominum meum Regem & officiales suos autoritate sua ac parliamenti sui in ea parte utentes, anno secundo regni sui impignorata pro certis pecuniarum summis per me tunc mutuatis ad estimacionem & valorem eorumdem pignorum se extendentibus, que quidem jocalia atque vasa postea racione non solucionis dict' pecuniarum in termino hinc inde concordat' ex speciali concessione & concordia dicti Domini mei Regis per literas suas patentes expressis inproprietatem meam transierunt, quod hujusmodi non solucione non obstant, et eo quod dicta jocalia & vasa sic in proprietatem meam transierunt, & jure optimo mea facta sint, prefatus Dominus meus Rex omnia illa que de eisdem tempore obitus mei in manibus meis remanserunt si sibi placeret haberet ; dum tamen prius solveret executoribus meis omnes illas pecuniarum summas pro quibus impignorata fuerunt. Jam tamen reminiscens illorum notabilium & insignium collegiorum ; viz. Beate Marie de Eton juxta Windesor, & Sancti Nicholai Cantabrigg', per dictum Dominum meum Regem ex singulari & precipua sua devocione ad divini cultus augmentum catholiceque fidei exaltacionem sancte ac salubriter fundatorum, desiderans que pro salute anime mee de gracia ipsius Domini mei Regis ejusque benevolencia & assensu concurrentibus particeps fieri oracionum & aliorum omnium suffragiorum

fragiorum ac pietatis operum in dictis suis collegiis Deo offerendis, & specialiter quod singulis diebus ab eo qui officium alte & principisse in quolibet dict' collegiorum celebraturus est, exceptis majoribus duplicibus festis ac parasceves, ab Sabbato Sancte Pasche dicatur pro me & pro salute anime mee una specialis collecta, & quod in utroque dictorum collegiorum singulis annis imperpetuum commemoretur & observetur solemniter dies anniversarius obitus mei, cum missa de requiem, & cum exequiis mortuorum, die immediate precedente. Et cum premissis confidens & humillime supplicans eidem Domino meo regi quatinus dignetur & velit exhibere se favorabilem & graciosum executoribus dicti testamenti mei, & eosdem in execucione ultime mee voluntatis supportare atque defendere, lego atque dispono utrique dictorum collegiorum summam mille librarum recipiend' & deducend' de illa majori summa per dictum dominum meum Regem persolvend' prefatis executoribus meis pro jocalibus & vasis supradict' serenitate sue rehabend' secundum modum & formam in dicto priore codicillo meo contento expressat': Quas quidem summas, sic ut prefertur prefatis collegiis dispositas, converti volo in utilitates eorundem collegiorum, tales videliz' que servicium eximiam circumspeccionem dicti domini mei regis videbuntur magis opportune. Item, lego Domine mee Regine lectum blodium de panno aureo de Damasco que pendebat in camera illa in manerio meo de Waltham[c], in qua eadem Domina mea Regina cu-

[c] A stately palace of the bishops of Winchester, S. of Winchester, demolisht during the civil wars. Wykeham died here 1404. All its remains consist of the West side of the hall, and a South West tower.

babat illo tempore quo fuit in dicto manerio, una cum tribus tapetis d'arras in eadem camera tunc pendentibus.

Item, lego atque remitto domino de Tiptoft [a] illas cccxxxiii li. vi s. viii d. in quibus idem dominus de Tiptoft per suum scriptum obligatorium michi tenetur et obligatur. Item, simili modo lego et remitto Willielmo Stafford totum illud in quo ipse per literas suas obligatorias que sunt de summa cc li. michi tenetur et obligatur: ita tamen et non aliter, quod idem Willielmus per literas suas sufficientes & legitimas in ea parte conficiend' acquietet tam executores meos quam eciam magistrum Thomam Forest, magistrum sive custodem hospitalis Sancte Crucis juxta Winton, & confratres ejusdem de summa xl li. in quibus sibi teneor racione cujusdam annuitatis xx li. sibi pro feodo suo concesse, una cum facultate distringendo pro eisdem in manerio de Heynstrigge [e] dict' hospitali nunc appropriat. Item, lego Johanni bastardo [f] de Somerset cccc li. cum certa quantitate vasorum argenteorum secundum discrecionem dictorum executorum meorum eidem assignand. Item, lego simili modo Willielmo [g] Swynford nepoti meo cccc li. cum certa quantitate vasorum sibi assig-

---

[d] John Tiptoft, second Lord Tiptoft, succeeded his father beforementioned, p. 205. note ᵉ, and was beheaded on Towerhill, and buried in Blackfriars, London, 1470. He was the patron of Caxton, and one of the revivers of learning in England, Dugd. Bar. II. 41.

[e] Henstridge, c. Somerset.

[f] Perhaps John of Gaunt's eldest son by Catherine Swinford, who was born a bastard, though legitimated by act of parliament, 20 Ric. II.

[g] Q. Some grandson of Catharine, the bishop's mother, by her first husband.

BISHOP OF WINTON.

nand' secundum discrecionem eorundem executorum meorum. Item, lego Thome Burneby scutifero familiari Domine mee Regine xx li. & unum ciphum de argento deaurato secundum eorundem executorum meorum discrecionem sibi liberand. Item, lego Edwardo Stradling [h] militi certum porcionem vasorum argenteorum juxta disposicionem dict' executorum meorum sibi liberand' & tradend'. Item, lego Johanni Yend seniori, xii discos argenteos per discrecionem executorum meorum limitand. In quorum omnium premissorum fidem & testimonium huic presenti codicillo meo signetum meum est appensum. Dat. in palacio meo de Wolveseye [i], nono die mensis Aprilis, Anno Domini millesimo ccccmo xlvii°.

Commissio ad proband' dictum testamentum & codicillos 11 die mensis Septembris, 1447.

Registr. Stafford & Kemp, fol. 111. a. b. 112. a. b. 113. a. b. in the Archiepiscopal Registry at Lambeth.

[h] Who had married the Bishop's natural daughter; see before, p. 329, note q, and p. 343.
[i] Wolvesey-house (or castle, as Bp. Pontisara styles it, 1300.) built by Bp. Blois about 1138, was in Camden's time very spacious, and surrounded with many towers; but being demolisht in the civil wars, Bp. Morley built a handsome house near it, in which he included its chapel. Its ruins are extensive and magnificent. Warton's Description of Winchester, p. 82.

Henry

## CARDINAL BEAUFORT,

Henry Beaufort, second son of John of Gaunt, studied first at Peterhouse, Cambridge; afterwards at Oxford, of which latter university he was chancellor, 1399; but he compleated his studies at Aix le Chapelle. He was prebend of Thame and Bokingham in Lincolnshire diocese, consecrated bishop of Lincoln, 1397, when very young, and seven years after, on the death of Wykeham, translated to Winchester 1404. 4 Hen. VI. He assisted at the council of Constance, 1417, and June 23, 1426, was created Cardinal of St. Eusebius [k], by Pope Martin V. who appointed him his legate, or rather general of his forces against Bohemia [l], which he invaded 1429, with 4000 men, raised by the contributions of the English clergy, and who under him served in France before, on the loss of the battle of Patay. In the decline of life he applied himself sedulously to the care of his diocese, and, among other acts of munificence, founded near St. Cross's hospital, another, for a master, two chaplains, thirty-five poor men, and three nurses; by the name of " the almshouse of noble poverty," whose annual revenue amounted to £. 188. He was four times Chancellor of England, 1404, 1414, 1417, 1424; and in 1417 undertook a voyage to the Holy Land. He died April 11, 1447, Rapin says [m], in despair, that his riches could not

---

[k] Godwin de præf. ed. Rich. p. 231. n. See an attempt to deprive him of his bishopric of Winchester on this promotion, 1431. Rymer, X. 1497.
[l] See the Cardinal's petition to the King, for leave to levy and carry over these troops, and the King's answer, the Cardinal's Commission, &c. 1429. 1431. Rymer, X. 419—427. 491.
[m] V. 357.

exempt

exempt him from death. Shakſpeare has beautifully improved the thought [m]. He lies buried under a noble monument in the preſbytery, behind the high altar of his cathedral. His figure in his Cardinal's habit lies on an altar-tomb, on the verge of which remained of his epitaph, in biſhop Godwin's time only theſe words: *Tribularer ſi neſcirem miſericordias tuas.* He was a prelate of exceſſive frugality, whereby he amaſſed ſo much wealth, that when Henry V. a little before his death, propoſed to convert the revenues of the clergy into ſupplies for his foreign wars, the biſhop his uncle lent him £.20,000. out of his own coffers, on the ſecurity of the crown jewels. The influence which his wealth gave him, and a good ſhare of political prudence, ſoon gave him an aſcendency over his nephew the Duke of Glouceſter, Protector in the abſence of the Duke of Bedford. The Duke of Glouceſter came at laſt to an open rupture with him, and brought him to a trial, in which he was acquitted, but the Great Seal taken from him. As Henry VI grew up he gained great authority over him, and obtained ſeveral pardons, 1437, and 1442. He had juſt turned the tables on his rival the Duke of Glouceſter, who was found dead in his bed at Bury a month before the biſhop died. In his youth-

---

[m] " If thou beeſt Death, I'll give thee England's treaſure,
" Enough to purchaſe ſuch another Iſland,
" So thou wilt let me live, and feel no pain."
   Second Part of Hen. VI. Act iii. Sc. ult.

ful days, before he took orders, he had by Alice daughter of Richard Earl of Arundel, fifter of the Abp. of Canterbury, a daughter Jane, whom he married to Sir Edward Stradling, Knt. of Glamorganfhire. It is remarkable of this bifhop that he, as well as his immediate predeceffor and fucceffor in this fee, held the epifcopal dignity longer than any other of our prelates [n], except Thomas Bourchier Abp. of Canterbury.

Godwin, ed. Rich. p. 231. 296. Sandford, p. 260. See alfo Rymer, X. 419, 420, &c. 497. 516.

[n] His immediate predeceffor Wyckham enjoyed the fee of Winchefter, from 1365 to 1405; the Cardinal, from 1405 to 1447; and his fucceffor Wainfleet, from 1447 to 1486; making 121 years; and each of them about 40. If we add the time that Beaufort held Lincoln, he will have been a bifhop 50 years.

# KING

# KING EDWARD IV.

BY the following extracts, communicated by Dr. Ducarel from the Regifters at Lambeth, it clearly appears this king had made a will; but where it is now depofited is unknown. Probably it was intentionally deftroyed during the ufurpation of his brother Richard III.

Sequeftracio bonor' Regis Edwardi IIII$^{ti}$.

Anno Dñi milleſimo cccc$^{mo}$ octuageſimo tercio, indiccõe prima, pontificatus S. in Xp̄o patris et Dñi Dñi Sixti divina providencia Pape quarti anno xii$^{mo}$ menſis Maii die vii$^{mo}$, infra domum [a] ſolite habitacõis magnifice preclareque Dñe Domine Cecilie Duciſſe Ebor' infra poch' Sc̄i Petri juxta Powliswharf civitatis London' ſituat'; Preſentibus ibidem Reverendiſſimo in Xp̄o Patre & Dño Thoma [b] Dei g̃ra Ebor' Archiep̄o, Reverendiſque Patribus Thoma [c] London', Willmo [d] Winton', Roberto [e] Bathonien' & Wellen', Johne [f] Wigorn', Edwardo [g] Ciceſtren', Johne [h] Lincoln', Johne [i] Elien', & Edmundo [k] Roffen' eadem g̃ra Ep̄is, ac magnificis p̄potentiſbuſque dñis Ric̃o

---

[a] No mention of this houſe in Stowe.
[b] Thomas Rotheram, 1480—1501.
[c] Thomas Kemp, 1448—1489.
[d] William Wainfleet, 1447—1486.
[e] Robert Stillington, 1465—1491. He was chancellor of England from 1465 to 1473.
[f] John Alcock, 1476—1486. He was chancellor 1473 and 1486.
[g] Edward Story, 1477—1504.
[h] John Ruſſel, 1480—1495.
[i] John Morton, 1478—1486.
[k] Edmund Audley, 1480—1492.

346                EDWARD THE FOURTH.

Duce Glouceſtr', Henrico ¹Duce Buk', Willmo ᵐComite Arundell, Will o Haſtyngs ⁿ d̄no de Haſtyngs, Tho' Stanley ᵒ d̄no de Stanley, & aliis pceribus regni q̄mplurib'; Reverendiſſimus in Xp̄o Pater & Dn̄s Dn̄s Thomas Dei gracia tit' sc̄i Curaci ᵖ in Thermis ſacrosc̄e Romane eccl̄ie p̄ſbit' Cardinalis ᑫ, Cant' Archiep̄us, tocius Anglie Primas & Apoſtolice ſedis Legatus, poſt obitū felicis memorie Edwardi quarti nup Regis Anglie & Francie, ac d̄ni Hib̄nie, pro eo, & ex eo, q̄d executores in ſuo teſtamento nōiati onus execucōis ejuſdē ſeu adminiſtracionē bonoꝝ' dicti defuncti in ſe aſſumere diſtulerunt; et ne a quoq̄m illicite diſtrahant' aut conſumant'; & ex aliis legitimis cauſis ip̄m ad tunc movent'; virtute prerogative ſue, & eccl̄ie ſue Cant'; omnia & ſingula bona & jocalia ejuſdem d̄ni nuper Regis legitime ſequeſtravit, ac cuſtodiā h̄mōi ſequeſtr' in omnib' & ſingulis jocalib' predict' int' poſit', dilect' filiis Willmo Dawbeney, Rico Laurence, & Roberto Forſter, in forma juris commiſſ'. Et deinde tunc ib̄m idem Reverendiſſimus in Xp̄o pater Cardinalis & Archiep̄us Cant'; ad quem, virtute prerogative ſue & eccl̄ie ſue Cant' p̄dict', mortuo p̄fat' Rege, cuſtodia ſigillor' quorumcumq' ejuſdem nuper Regis notor' ptinere dinoſcit', Sigillum magnū, Sigillū privatū, & Signetū ad p̄fat' Regē dum vivebat ptinent'; ad manus ſuas recepit, & penes ſe cuſtodivit.ʳ.

                                                                    Comiſſio

¹ Henry Stafford duke of Buckingham, beheaded at Saliſbury by Richard III. whom he had ſet up.

ᵐ William Fitz-Alan, eighth earl of Arundel, died 3 Hen. VII.

ⁿ William Lord Haſtings, beheaded by Richard III. prior to his uſurpation, and buried at Windſor, near Edward IV.

ᵒ Created earl of Derby, 1 Hen. VII.

ᵖ Cyriaci.

ᑫ Thomas Bourchier, 1454—1486.

ʳ It is very remarkable that the next inſtrument to this ſequeſtration, in the Lambeth Regiſter, and immediately preceding the following commiſſion for paying the expences of the king's funeral, contains the following ſummons
                                                                         of

# EDWARD THE FOURTH.

Comiſſio p: Funeralib': Regis ſolvend'.

Thomas miſeracōe divina, &c. Reverendiſſimo confr̄i n̄ro Thomę Dei gr̄a Ebor' Archiep̄o, et venerabilibus fratribus n̄ris Joh̄i Lync', Edwardo Cyceſtren', et Joh̄i Elien', eadē gr̄a Epiſcopis; necnon dilect' filiis Dn̄is Will' Haſtynges Dn̄o de Haſtynges, Thome Stanley Dn̄o de Stanley, ac Thome Mongomery militi, executoribus in teſtamento et ultima voluntate felicis memorie Ed-

of Edward V. for calling a parliament on the 25th day of June then next following; which ſummons, though foreign to the purpoſe, it is apprehended will be acceptable, as it is not known to have ever yet appeared in print.

Breve pro Parliamento.

Edwardus, Dei gratia, Rex Anglie & Francie, & Dn's Hib'nie, venerabili in Chriſto Patri Thome eadem gratia Archiep'o Cantuar' tocius Anglię Primati, Salutem. Quia, de aviſamento & aſſenſu conſilii noſtri pro quibuſdam arduis & urgentibus negociis, nos, ſtatum & defenſionem Regni noſtri Anglie ac eccleſie Anglicane concernentibus, quoddam Parliamentum noſtrum apud Weſtm' viceſimo quinto die Junii prox' futur' teneri ordinavimus, & ibidem, vobiſcum, ac cum ceteris prelatis, magnatibus, & proceribus dicti Regni noſtri colloquium habere & tractatum; vobis, in fide & dilectione quibus nobis tenemini, firmiter injungendo mandamus, quod, conſideratis dictorum negotiorum arduitate, et periculis imminentibus; ceſſante excuſatione quacumque, dict' die & loco perſonaliter interſitis, nobiſcum, ac cum prelatis, magnatibus, & proceribus predictis, ſuper dict' negociis tractatur' veſtrumque conſilium impenſur'. Et hoc, ſicut nos & honorem noſtram ac ſalvationem & defenſionem Regni & Eccleſie predictor' expeditionemque dictorum negotior' diligit', nullatenus omittatis. Premunientes Priorem & Capitulum Eccl'ie veſtre Cantuar'; ac Archidiaconos totumque Clerum veſtre Dioc', quod iidem Prior & Archidiaconi in propriis perſonis, ac dictum Capitulum per unum, idemque Clerus per duos procuratores idoneos plenam & ſufficientem poteſtatem ab ipſis Capitulo & Clero diviſim habentes, p'dict' die & loco perſonaliter interſint, ad conſenciend' hiis que tunc ibidem de communi conſilio d'ci Regni noſtri, divina favente clemencia, contigerit ordinari. T. meipſo apud Weſtm' XIII die Maii, Anno Regni noſtri primo.

Regiſtr' Morton, Dene, Bourchier & Courtney, fol. 175. b.

wardi quarti nuper Regis Anglie et Francie, ut afferitur, nominat', Saltem in oīni Salvator'. Cum nos omnia & fingla bona prefati nuper Regis ubicunq' infra provinciā ñram Cantuar' ac in quorumcunq̄ manibus exiftent', pro eo, & ex eo, q̃d vos onus execucionis teftamenti ejufdē in vos affumere diftuliftis, prout differt' in p̄fent', & ne a quoq̃m illicite diftrahantur aut confumantur, exq' aliis legitimis caufis nos in ea p̱te moventibus, legitime fequeftraverimus. Ex p̱te tamen v̄ra nobis extunc intimatū, q̃d expenfe funerales confuete & omnino de jure in hoc cafu requifit', que ad eftimac̄oem MCCCCLXXXXVI lib' XVII fol' II den' fe extendunt, fuper cujus eftimacionis veritate a vobis plene inftructi fumus, nondum funt folute, nec de illis hactenus fint aut eft que primo & principalit' folvi deberent aliqualit' fatisfact' : Ne perfone quib' debetur fatisfaccōi hmōi debitam expectarent folucōem aut quicquam circa folucōem hmōi di . . . am foret abfq̄ auctoritate noftra quomodolibet attemptatū, nobis fupplicari fecift', ut bona ipfius defuncti in eftimacōe predict' conftantia & p̱ appreciatores ñros juratos primitus jufte appreciatos propterea vendicōi trader', & cū pecunia ex vendicōe hmōi proveniente folucōem facere expenfarū funeralium predict' libere poffit, fequeftracōe ñra p̄dict' non obftan'; vobis plenā, tenore prefenciū, committimus poteftatem. Dat' fub figillo Archiep̄atus ñri in mañio ñro de Knoll, XXIII die menfis Maii, A. D. MCCCCLXXXIII, & ñre tranfl' anno XXIX.

Regiftr. Morton, Dene, Bourchier, and Courtney, fol. 175. a. b. in the Archiepifcopal Regiftry at Lambeth.

Edward

## EDWARD THE FOURTH.

Edward IV. died of a quartane ague, at his palace of Westminster, on the 9th of April, A. D. 1483, in the forty-second year of his age, and twenty-second of his reign, just on the eve of a war with France; and lies buried at Windsor, in the new chapel he had there founded, where his magnificent monument of brass, gilt, (engraven in Sandford, p. 413.) remains entire to this day.

An imperfect account of his funeral is printed in the Archæologia, vol. I. p. 348.

# ELIZABETH

## ELIZABETH WIFE OF EDWARD IV.

IN Dei nomine, Amen. The xth daie of Aprill, the yere of our Lord Gode MCCCCLXXXXII. I Elifabeth by the grace of God Quene of England, late wif to the moſt victoroiuſe Prince of bleſſed memorie Edward the Fourth, being of hole mynde, ſeying the worlde ſo traunſitorie, and no creature certayne whanne they ſhall departe frome hence, havyng Almyghty Gode freſh in mynde, in whome is all mercy and grace, bequeith my ſowle into his handes, beſeechyng him, of the ſame mercy, to accept it graciouſly, and oure bleſſed Lady Quene of comforte, and all the holy company of hevyn, to be good meanes for me. It'm, I bequeith my body to be buried with the bodie of my Lord at Windeſſore, according to the will of my ſaide Lorde and myne, without pompes entreing or coſtlie expenſis donne thereabought. It'm, where I have no wordely goodes to do the Quene's Grace, my dereſt doughter, a pleaſer with, nether to reward any of my children, according to my hart and mynde, I beſech Almyghty Gode to bliſſe here Grace, with all her noble iſſue, and with as good hart and mynde as is to me poſſible, I geve her Grace my bleſſing, and all the forſaide my children. It'm, I will that ſuche ſmale ſtufe and goodes that I have be diſpoſed truly in the contentac'on of

my

my dettes and for the helth of my fowle, as farre as they will extende. It'm, yf any of my bloode wille any of my faide ftufe or goodes to me perteyning, I will that they have the prefermente before any other. And of this my prefent teftament I make and ordeyne myne Executores, that is to fey, John Ingilby, Priour of the Chartour-houfe of Shene, William Sutton and Thomas Brente, Doctors. And I befech my faid dereft doughter, the Quene's grace, and my fone Thomas, Marques Dorfett, to putte there good willes and help for the performans of this my teftamente. In witneffe wherof, to this my prefent teftament I have fett my feale, thefe witneffes, John Abbot of the monaftry of Sainte Saviour of Bermondefley, and Benedictus Cun, Doctor of Fyfyk. Yeven the day and yere abovefaid.

Extracted from the Regiftry of the Prerogative Court of Canterbury.

Doggett. 9. fol. 74. a.

Henry Stevens,
George Goftling, jun<sup>r</sup>. } Deputy Regifters.
John Grene,

EDWARD IV. soon after his coronation, propofed a marriage with a daughter of Lewis duke of Savoy, fifter to the Queen of France, for which purpofe the earl of Warwick was fent to France. In the mean time, the King hunting in Wickfield foreft, and coming to the manor of Grafton, in Northamptonfhire, fell paffionately in love with Elizabeth, widow of Sir John Grey of Groby, and daughter of Sir Richard Woodvile, Knt. afterwards created Earl Rivers, by Jaquetta, relict of John Duke of Bedford, and daughter of Peter of Luxemburg, Earl of St. Paul. He was married to her at the above manor, May 1, 1464; and on the 26th of May, in the year following, fhe was folemnly crowned at Weftminfter. She was his wife near 19 years; during which her father and fourth brother were beheaded in his caufe, by the Northamptonfhire men, 1468, and herfelf forced to take fanctuary at Weftminfter, 1470, where her eldeft fon Edward was born. After her hufband's death, her elder brother, Anthony [a], and her fon by her firft hufband,

---

[a] The following abftract of his will is from Dugd. Bar. II. p. 233. made 23 June, 1483. in Sherif Hutton caftle, Yorkfhire, not long before his execution: "He bequeathed his heart to be carried to our Lady of Pue, adjoining to St. Stephen's College, Weftminfter, there to be buried, by the advice of the dean and his brethren; and in cafe he fhould die fouth of Trent to be alfo buried before our Lady of Pue aforefaid: appointing that all the lands which were his father's fhould remain to his right heirs, with his cup of gold of Columbine; and that fuch lands as were the Lady Scales, his firft wife, fhould come to his brother, Sir Edward Wydvill, and to his heirs male, and for lack of fuch heirs male unto the right heirs of his father; but he to whom it fhould fo come, before he took poffeffion thereof,

to

## ELIZABETH WIFE OF EDWARD IV.

being beheaded at Pontefract by Richard, she took refuge a second time at Westminster, which she quitted not till after Richard III's death. Henry VII. having seized on all her possessions, she retired to Bermondsey abbey, where she soon after died, and was buried near her husband Edward. She obtained his licence, in the 6th year of his reign, to complete the foundation of Queen's College, Cambridge, begun by Henry VI's Queen. Sandford, p. 407.

By her first husband, who was slain in the battle of St. Alban's, 39 Hen. VI. she had issue, 1. Sir Thomas Grey, created by Edward IV. in the eleventh year of his reign, earl of Huntingdon, and four years after marquis of Dorset. He fled from Richard III's tyranny to the Duke of Richmond, and died 17 Hen. VII. 2. Richard, beheaded as above [b].

By the King she was mother of, 1. Edward, born 1470, proclaimed King, and murdered with his brother. 2. Richard duke of York, born 1474, married to Anne only daughter of John Mowbray, Duke of Norfolk. 3. George, Duke of Bedford, died an infant. 4. Elizabeth, born 1466, married to Henry VII. 5. Cecily, married 1st, to John Lord Viscount Welles, son of Margaret Beauchamp,

to deduct 500 marks, to be employed for the souls of the said Lady Scales, and Thomas her brother, and the souls of all the Scale's blood, in helping and refreshing hospitals, and other deeds charitable. Also to find a priest one year at our Lady of Pue, to pray for the souls of those brothers and all Christian soules. Likewise to find another priest to sing at the chapel of of the Rodes in Greenwich, to pray for his own soul, and all Christian souls. Farther directing, that all his apparell for his body and horse-harness should be sold, and with the money thereof shirts and smocks for poor folk to be bought."

[b] Dugd. Bar. II. 719, 720.

dutchefs of Somerfet, (mother of Margaret Beaufort, countefs of Richmond, mother of Henry VII.) by her fecond hufband Lionel Lord Welles; and he dying 1498, leaving by her one daughter, Anne [c], fhe was married, 2dly, to Kyme of Lincolnfhire, and buried at Quarrera, in the Ifle of Wight. 6. Anne, married to Thomas Howard third Duke of Norfolk, and buried at Framlingham, having had one fon, who died young, and was buried, at Lambeth [d]. 7. Bridget, born at Eltham, 1480, became a nun at Dartford, where fhe died about 1517 [e]. 8. Mary, died at Greenwich, 1482, buried at Windfor. 9. Margaret, born 1472, died the fame year, buried at Weftminfter, on the north fide of the Confeffor, where a fmall altar tomb remains, with part of the epitaph given by Sandford. 10. Catherine, married to William Courtney earl of Devon, died and was buried at Tiverton, where fhe has a monument, with her effigies, on the fide of the altar [f]. Sandford, p. 415—420.

[c] Dugd. Bar. II. 13.
[d] Ibid. II. 274.
[e] Ibid. I. 642.
[f] See mention of her in the wardrobe-account, in Mr. Walpole's Hiftoric Doubts, p. 67.

THE unfortunate EDWARD V. was barely proclaimed King when he was murdered by his ufurping uncle RICHARD III *. who, after a turbulent reign of two years and two months, came to a deferved end in Bofworth field.

The will of HENRY VII. having been printed at length, with a judicious preface and appendix, by Thomas Aftle, Efq. F. R. and A. S. S. 1775, 4to. it would be unneceffary to reprint it here. We fhall therefore clofe the prefent feries with the will of Margaret Countefs of Richmond, mother of Henry VII.

* It is not generally known that, in July 1483, King Richard III. with his Queen and their attendants, were received and entertained at Oxford by Wainfleet, the founder of Magdalen College, as appears from the regifter books of that college. See Wood's Hiftoria & Antiquitates Oxon. L. p. 233.

## MARGARATE COUNTESS OF RICHMOND.

IN the name of ALMIGHTY GOD, Amen. We Margarete Countes of Richmond and Derby, Moder to the moſt excellent Prince King Henry the VIIth, by the g'ce of GOD King of Englond and of Fraunce, and Lorde of Irlande, our moſt dere Son, have called to our remembrance the unſtabilneſſe of this tranſitory worlde, and that ev'ry creatur here lyving is mortall, and the tyme and place of deth to ev'y creatur uncerteyn. And alſo calling to o'r remembrance the great rewards of eternall lif that ev'y Criſten creatur' in ſtedfaſt faith of holy church ſhal have for their goode deeds doon by theym in their preſent lif, We therefore beyng of hole and goode mynde, &c. the VI day of Juyn, the yere of our LORD GOD a thouſand five hundreth and eight, and in the XXIII yere of the reigne of our ſaide moſt dere ſon the King, make, ordeyn, and declare, our teſtament and laſt will, in man' and forme folowing, that is to ſaye, Firſt, we gif and bequeth our ſoule to Almighty GOD, to o'r bliſſed Lady Seynt Mary the Virgyn, and to all the holy company in heven. And our body to be buried in the monaſtery of Seynt Peter of Weſtm',

Weſtm', in ſuche convenable place as we in o'r lif, or our executors aftir our deceſſe, ſhall provide for the ſame within the Chapell of o'r Lady, which is nowe begon by the ſaid o'r moſt deer ſon. It'm, we woll, that placebo and dirige w't lauds and w't all divine ſ'vices, prayers, and obſervants belongyng thereunto be ſolemply and devoutly ſongen and ſaid in the daye of o'r deceſſe, by all the preeſts, myniſters, and children, of o'r chapell, and maſſe of requiem, w't note, in the mornyng nexte enſuyng, with all divine ſ'vice, prayers,. and obſervants belonging thereunto, in as ſolempe and devoute wiſe as they can doo or deviſe : and ſo to contynue to ſynge and ſay daily ev'y day fro daye, as long as o'r body ſhall reſte there unremoeved toward the ſaid place of our interment ; and that ev'y preeſt and leyman of o'r ſaid chapell have for his labor in that behalf for ev'y daye for ev'y ſuche placebo, dirige, and lauds, w't maſſe of requiem, xii d. and ev'y child of the chapell iiii d. It'm, we will that like placebo and dirige, with lawdes, and maſſe of requiem, be ſolemply and devoutly ſaid and ſongen daiely ev'y day during all the ſaide tyme in the pariſhe church of the place where it ſhall pleaſe Almighty God to call us owte of this tranſitory lif to his infynite m'cy and grace by all the preeſts and clerks of the ſame church ; and by other preeſts to the nowmber of lx or under, and clerks to the nowmbre of xxx, or under, reſortyng to the ſaid church. And that ev'y of the ſame preeſts beyng p'ſent, and helping to ſuche placebo and
dirige

dirige w't lawdes and maſſe of requiem, and ſaying alſo ther maſſe for our ſoule have for his labor and reward in that behalf for ev'y ſuche time xii d. And ev'y of the ſaid clerks beyng preſent and helping at ſuche ſ'vice of ev'y ſuch placebo and lawdes with high maſſe of requiem have for his reward iiii d. and ſoo to contynue daiely till o'r body be remoeved, and to have like reward for ev'y daye. It'm, we will, that o'r executors aſſone as they convenyently may aftir our deceſſe, cauſe ſolemply and devoutly to be ſongen or ſaid for our ſoule in ev'y of xv pariſhe churches next adjoyning to the place of our deceſſe, by all the preeſts, clerks, and myniſters, of ev'y ſuch churche, placebo, dirige, with lawdes and maſſe of requiem with all divine prayers and obſerv'nces belonging thereunto. And our excutors cauſe to be geven and deliv'ed therefore to the church-wardeyns of ev'y ſuche church x s. to be diſtributed, that is to ſaye, to ev'y preſt beyng p'ſent, and helping all divine ſ'vice of the ſame, and alſo ther ſaying maſſe of requiem, xii d. and to ev'y clerk iiii d. and the reſidew of the ſame, if any remayn, to be diſpoſed to the reparacions or ornaments of the ſaid church. It', we will, that ev'y preeſt, to the nowmbre of lx, beyng preſent in the pariſhe church where our body ſhall reſte eny nyght betwene the place of o'r deceſſe and the place of our interment that ſhal be helping at all divine ſ'vices of placebo and dirige with lawdes and maſſe of requiem, with note, and there ſaye placebo, dirige with lawdes, and maſſe of requiem,

ſhall

shall have for his labor viiid. And ev'y clerk, to the nowmbr' of xxx clerks, beyng p'fent, and helping to sing and say placebo and dirige, with lawdes and masse of requiem, or seying there placebo and dirige, with lawdes, iiii d. It', we bequeth to the curate of ev'y church where our body shall reste at nyght iii s. iiii d. And to the wardeyns and parishoners of ev'y suche church to th'use of the same church xs. in money, and ii torches. And to the ryngars of the bells of ev'y suche church iii s. iiii d. And we will that ev'y preeft, laymen and childern of our chapell have for their reward for the same daie like somez as is appoynted to be gefen to theym in our chapell, as is bifore said. And we will that all the said masses and other masses that shalbe said for our soule aft' our decesse unto the tyme of o'r enterment excepte the high masse of requiem shalbe orderd and said as can be aft' the forme and order of a trantall. It'm, we will that o'r executors geve and deliver to the church-wardeyns of ev'y other parishe that our body shall passe through toward the said place of our enterment, other then in the said citie of London, xvii s. viii d. and a torche, to cause placebo and dirige with lawdes, and messe of requiem, to be solemply and devoutely songen or said in ev'y suche churche by the preefts and clerks of the same. And to geve therof to ev'y preeft for his labor vi d. and to ev'y clerk iiii d. and the residew therof to be disposed for the reparacion of the ornament and church of the same parishe. It'm, we will that in like wise our executours yeve and deliver to the church-wardeyns of ev'y church that our body fhall paffe through within the faid citie of London xs. and a torche to caufe like placebo and dirige with lawds, and maffe of requiem, to be folemply and devoutly faid and fongen by the preefts, miniftres, and clerks, of ev'y fuche churche, and to geve to ev'y preft for his labor vi d. and to ev'y clerk iiii d. and the refidew thereof to difpofe to the reparacions of the ornaments and church of the fame parifshe. It'm, we will that our executors yeve and deliver to the freres of ev'y of the iiii orders of freers in the faid citie of London, for their labour to geve their attendaunce upon the comyng of our body through the fame citie and for placebo and dirige, with lawds and maffe of requiem, to be folemply fongen and faid in ev'y of the churches of the faid freers xl s. It', to the prior and covents of Crift's churche in London, Seynt Mary Spitell, Seynt Barthilmewes, and to the abbotts and covents of Tower-hill [a] and Bermondfey, for a folempne dirige, and maffe to be hadde and kepte in ev'y of the fame place to ev'y of them, xx s. It'm, to the Crowche Freers, and to the prior and covent of Elfyngfpitell for a like dirige and maffe to either of them xiii s. iiii d. It'm, we bequeth to th'abbot and covent of the monaftery of Seynt Peter of Weftmynfter, for placebo and dirige, with lawds and maffe of requiem, and other divine fervice and obfervances to be had and doon in the fame monaftery at the daie and in the tyme of our enterment, as followeth,

[a] i. e. St. Mary Mountgrace.

that

that is to faye, to the abbott of the fame monaftery, if he be there prefent, xx s. to the prior if he be prefent, x s. to ev'y monke prefent there, beyng a preeft, II s. to ev'y monke beyng profeffed and noo preeft, XII d. to ev'y monke beyng novice and not profefte, VIII d. And at our moneths daye to every of the perfones of the fame monaftery above reherfed for like placebo and dirige, with lawds and maffe of requiem, with all divine fervice and obfervaunce belongyng therunto the like fomes of money as above is fpecified. And to the bells ryngars the tyme of our enterment, XVI s. VIII d. And at our monethes daie VI s. VIII d. And to the Deane and Chanons of the College of Seynt Stephen, for a like folempne dirige, with lawdes and maffe of requiem, there by theym to be faid and fongen in the tyme, and in the daie of our faide enterment LX s. to be diftributed by the difcrecion of the deane and treforer of the fame place for the tyme beyng for al maner of charges to be doon aboute our faide enterment. And to the deane and chapiter of the college of Wynburn[b], for a like folempne dirige, with lawdes, and maffe there to be faid and fongen at the tyme and in the daie of our enterment XL s. It', we will, that our executours geve and deliver to the churche-wardeyns of the parifshe church of Seynt Margarets of Weftm' XL s. and a torche, to caufe a like folempne dirige, with lawdes and maffe of requiem, there to be folemply and devoutly faid and fongen, in the fame churche,

---

[b] Where her father and mother John and Margaret duke and duchefs of Somerfet are buried.

by the prests, ministres, and clerks, of the same churche, at the tyme and in the daie of the enterment of our body. And to geve to every preeft therof for his labor XII d. and to ev'y clerk VI d. and the refidew of the fame XL s. to be difpofed to the reparacions of the ornaments and churche of the fame parifshe. It'm, we will that in the daye that it fhall pleafe Almighty GOD to call us from this p'fent and tranfitory lif to his infynite mercy and grace, and in the daie of o'r enterment there to be diftributed in almes amongs poore people by the difcrecion of our executour CXXXIII li. VI s. VIII d. or more, as fhall be thought convenyent by their difcrecions. And CC li. to be difpofed in bying of clothe for our executors and fervants, men and women, or other perfones, by the difcrecions of our executours that fhall give their attendance upon the conveyaunce of our body, and our faid enterment, and at our moneths daie. It', we will, that o'r executors provide and ordeyne a convenyent herfe, by their difcrecion to be fett and occupied in the place where we fhall deceffe, in our chapell, during all the tyme that our body fhall refte there. It', we will that our executors provide and ordeyn by their difcrecion another convenyent herfe, in the parifshe church where we fhall deceffe, there to be fett and occupied during all the faid tyme. It', we will that our executours provide and ordeyn a convenyent herfe by there difcrecion in the faid monaftery of Seynt Peter of Weftm', where our body, with Godd's grace, fhalbe interred. It'm, we will that o'r executours provide and ordeyn by their difcrecion torches

con-

convenyent to be occupied and spent in the place where we shall decesse; and in the parisshe church of the same, till our body shalbe removed; and also to be occupied and geven by the wey in conveying of our body unto the citie of London, and through the same citie unto the same monastery at the tyme of our enterment. It'm, to the torches holders in the said chapell and parisshe church for ev'y day till the body be removed to ev'y of them IIII d. It', for the wages of the torche bearers fro the place of our decesse unto the said monastery of Westm', and in the same monastery, to ev'y of theym, by the day XII d. It'm, we will, that our executours content and paye the costs and charges of our household servants and officers, and of suche other convenyent and necessary persones that shall geve their attendance in conveying of our bodye from the place where we shall decesse unto the said monastery of Westm', and geve to every persone for his costs for every daye VIII d. It'm, we will, that our executors content and paye to every of the same p'sones for their costs for II daies lying at Westm', and in the citie of London, the tyme of our interment, for every of them XII d. by the daye. It'm, we will, that our executors geve to every of our household servaunts VIII d. for every day, for their costs, to bringe them fro' Westm' unto the place where our household shall be kepte aftir our decesse, by the space of a quarter of a yere. It'm, we will that our executors cause placebo and dirige, with lawdes, and masse of requiem, with divine services, prayers, and observaunces,

belonging

belonging thereunto, to be folemply and devoutly faid and
fongen by the prefts, myniftres, and children of our chapell
in the place where our chapell fhal be kepte at the tyme of
our deceffe bifore the enterment of the fame, and in fome
other convenyent place, by the difcrecion of our executors,
by the terme of xxx daies nexte enfuyng our faid enterment;
and to geve to every preeft and layman of our chapell beyng
prefent and helping thereunto for his labour for every day that
he fhalbe fo prefent and helping therinto iiij d. and to every
child of the chapell 1 d. It'm, we will that our executors,
in as goodly hafte and breff tyme as they can or maye aftir
our deceffe, content and paye all our detts. And we will,
that our faid executors caufe all our houfehold fervants to be
kepte togider, and houfehold kepte in all things convenyent
for theym at and in fuche convenyent place as fhalbe
thought by o'r executors moft neceffarye for the fame from
the tyme of our deceffe by the fpace of oon quarter of a yere
at the lefte. And that our executors, by all the fame time,
fhall provide and ordeyn, or caufe to be provided and ordeyned for all our faid houfehold fervaunts; that is to faye,
for as many of theym as will there foo tarrey and abide by
all the faid tyme, mete, drynke, and other thing convenyent
for houfehold, as they have ufed and accuftomed to have
had heretofore in oure houfeholde. And alfo to content
and pay to every of our houfehold fervaunts, bothe man and
woman, their wages for oon halfe yere next after our deceffe, as well to them that will departe within the quarter of
oon

## COUNTESS OF RICHMOND.    365

oon yere aftir our deceſſe, as to theym that will tarry and abide togider in houſehold during all the ſame quarter. It', we will, that our executors, aftir our funeralls and detts contented and paid, ſhall truely deliver, content, and paye, all other legacies conteyned and ſpecified in a ſcedull to this our preſent teſtament and laſt will annexed. All whiche legacies conteyned in the ſame ſcedull we will and ordeyn that they ſhalbe had, reputed, and taken as parcell of this our preſent teſtament and laſt will, according to the true entent and meanyng of the ſame. Nev'theleſſe we will, that if at any time hereaftir we for any cauſe reaſonable doo alterate or chaunge any thing conteyned or ſpecified in this our preſent teſtament and laſt will, or in the ſaid ſcedull therunto annexed, or ellys adde any thing in writting ſcedull or codicell, the whiche ſhalbe heraftir in this our preſent teſtament and laſt will annexed, we will and declare, that the ſame writting, ſcedull, or codicell, and every thing in them, and in ev'y of theym conteyned and written, ſhalbe taken, reputed, executed, and fulfilled as parcell of this our preſent teſtament and laſt will, according to the true entente and effecte of the ſame. And of this p'ſent our teſtament and laſt will, we make and ordeyn our executors Richard [c] Biſshop of Wyncheſter, John [d] Biſshop of Rocheſ-

[c] Richard Fox, Bp. of Wincheſter, from 1502 to 1530.

[d] John Fiſher, her confeſſor, maſter of Queen's College, Cambridge, chancellor of the Univerſity, and cardinal, beheaded by Henry VIII. 1536. An altar-tomb, with flowerings and ſuch ornaments, diſcovered on ſome late repairs in a ſmall chapel adjoining to the chapel of St. John's College, Cambridge, was ſuppoſed to be his monument, or one intended for him by himſelf in his life-time.

ter;

ter, my Lord Herbert [e] the King's Chamberlayn, Sir Thomas Lovell [f] Tresuror of the King's houshold. Sir Henry Marney [g] Chauncellar of the Duchie of Lancester, Sir John Seynt John [h] our Chamberlayn, Henry Horneby our Chauncellor, Sir Hugh Asshton Comptroller of oure houshold.

[e] Charles Somerset Lord Herbert of Gower and Chepstow, natural son of Henry Beaufort, Duke of Somerset, son of Edmund Duke of Somerset, uncle to the testatrix. From his relationship to Henry VII. and his many excellent qualities, he was much in that Prince's favour, and was chamberlain of his houshold: having married Elizabeth daughter and heir of William Herbert, Earl of Huntingdon, he became, in her right, Lord Herbert, and was created Earl of Worcester. He died April 15, 1526, and lies buried with his said Countess in a chapel which he erected in the royal chapel at Windsor, where a fine monument remains over them. From him descends his Grace Henry Somerset now duke of Beaufort, 1780.

[f] Sir Thomas Lovell, Knt. of the Garter, was an active man in Henry VII's reign. When only an Esquire he was, in 1485, made Chancellor of the Exchequer, and Esquire of the King's body, knighted at the battle of Stoke, and Knight of the Garter. In 1502 Treasurer of the Houshold, and President of the Council, and one of Henry VII's Executors, Constable of the Tower, Surveyor of the Court of Wards, Steward and Marshall of the Houshold to Henry VIII. He built the gate-house at Lincoln's-Inn, and East Harling-hall, Norfolk, refounded Haliwell Nunnery, Shoreditch, where he was buried 1528. dying at his house called Elsyngs, at Enfield. Blomf. Norf. I. 219.

[g] Henry Marney, Privy-councillor to Henry VII. and VIII. Knight of the Garter, Captain of the Guard, Keeper of the Privy Seal, was created Lord Marney, April 9, 14 Hen. VIII. 1523. Of his holding the above office I find no other mention except in Tanner's Bib. Brit. p. 752, where William Walter, a poetical writer is called servant of Henry Lord Marney, Chancellor of the Dutchy of Lancaster. He died May 24, 1523. and was buried in the chancel of Layer Marney church, Essex, where he has a monument. Salm. Essex. 449. Dugd. II. 301. where see his will.

[h] Q. eldest son of Sir Oliver St. John, half brother to the testatrix, and son of her mother by her second husband, Sir Oliver St. John of Bletsoe. Collins's Peerage, V. p. 104. There is still in the Bletsoe family a carpet, with the arms and matches of the family, worked by the testatrix.

And

And we, in our moſt humble wiſe, hartly pray and beſeche the King our ſovereigne Lord and mooſt deere ſon, that it wold pleaſe his highnes to be ſup'viſors of this our p'ſent teſtament and laſt will, and to be goode and gracious Lord, and to ſhewe his ſpeciall favor, helpe, and aſſiſtance, to our ſaid executors, and to ev'y of them, in executing and performing of this our preſent teſtament and laſt will. And alſo that it would pleaſe his Highneſs to ſee and cauſe as well all the premiſſez afore reherſed as all that hereafter is ſpecified in this our preſent teſtament and laſt will, or in the ſaid ſcedull therunto annexed, or that ſhalbe conteyned in any other writting or codicill to be hereafter herunto annexed to be well and truely executed and performed in every behalf for the ſingular love that we bare and ever have borne unto his Highneſs, as he will have our bleſſing, and be diſcharged before GOD and for the ſingular truſt we have in the ſame. And alſo we ſpecially will and deſire the moſt Reverend Fader in God William[i] Archbiſshop of Canterbury to be and cauſe as moche as in hym is or may be, all our ſaid teſtament and laſt will, and every article therof, to be truly executed and performed, according to the true entent and effect of the ſame, as we putt in hym our ſingular truſt.

Ultima voluntas ejuſdem d'ne Margarete.

And foraſmoche as the ſingular lawde, praiſe, and pleaſur of Allmighty GOD reſtith moſt in this tranſitory world in

[i] Warham, 1504—1532.

admyniftracion of facrifice, and divine fervices, by the miniftres of holy churche for remyffion of our fynnes, and in the encreas of vertue, cunnyng[k], and of all criften faith, and in doyng of goode almes-deeds, and werks caritatifs; therefore we entending, with the grace of Almighty God, to caufe hym to be the more honored and ferved with facrifice and divine fervices, by the myniftres of holy churche, as well within the faid monaftery where we intende, with Godd's grace, our body to be enterred, as in the univerfitees of Oxenford and Cambrigge, and other places where the lawes of God be more fpecially lernyd, taught, and prechid, and fcolers to the fame entent to be brought up in vertue and cunnyng[k] for the increafe of Crift's faith have provided, ordeyned, and eftablifshed, as followith; that is to fay, three perpetuall daiely maffez, with divine fervices and obfervaunts, to be daiely faid by three fadde[l] and difcrete monks of the faid monaftery, and oon perpetuall anniverfary, to be yerely, folemply, and devoutly, holden and kepte, with LXX lights, and with the diftribucion of x li. in almes at every fuche anniverfary in the fame monaftery, for the helthe of our foule perpetually, while the world fhall endure; and oon perpetuall brother, called a converfe to be perpetually kepte in the fame monaftery, fpecially to ferve the fame monks at their maffes, and all other preefts that fhall fay their maffes at the aulters whereat II of the faid II chauntries maffez fhall be faid. And alfo have pro-

[k] Knowledge.     [l] Sober.

vided

vided, eſtabliſhed, and founden, by the Kyng's licence II perpetuall reders in holy theologie, oon off theym in the univerſitie of Cambrigge, and another of theym in the univerſitie of Oxforde, and oon perpetuall precher of the worde of God in the ſaid univerſitie of Cambrigge. And have licence to founde a perpetuall chauntry in the churche off Wynburn of oon perpetuall preſt to teche gramer frely to all theym that will come thereunto perpetually while the world ſhall endure; and licence to geve to either of the ſaid II reders, and their ſucceſſors, lands and tenements to the yerely value of xx li. and to the ſaid precheor and his ſucceſſors x li.; and to the ſaide chauntery preſt of Wynburn x li. And alſo whereas King Henry the VIth of bleſſed memory was in mynde and purpoſe to have provided and ordeyned in a place in Cambrigge called than Godd's-houſe, ſcolers, to the nowmbre of LX there to lerne and ſtudy in all liberall ſcience, in which place was never ſcolars, felowes of the ſame place above the nombr' of IIII, for lakk of exhibicion and fynding we have nowe of late purchaced and obteyned licence of the ſaid King our moſt deere ſon, and by reaſon thereof have founded and eſtabliſhed in the ſame place a college, called Criſt's college, of a maiſter, XII ſcolers felowes [m], and XLVII ſcolers diſciples there, to be perpetually founden and brought up in lernyng, vertue, and connyng according to ſuch ſtatuts and ordyn-

---

[m] Edward VI. to avoid a ſuperſtitious alluſion to Chriſt's twelve diſciples, added a thirteenth fellow. Fuller's Hiſt. of Cambr. p. 91.

naunces as we have made, and shall make, for the same. And for the fynding of one of the said three chauntery masses, to be saide in the saide monastery of Westm', we have purchased and obteyned a graunte of the abbot, prior, and co'vent, of the saide monastery, by whiche they have bounden theym and their successors to us, our heirs and executors, by their deed sealed, with their covent seale, to cause oon daiely masse to be said by a monke of the said monastery, at the aulter of the shryne of Seynt Edward in the same monastery perpetually while the world shall endure. And we the saide Princesse, for the singuler love, favor, confidence, and trust that we do bere, and of long tyme have born to the said monastery, and to the governors and mynisters of the same; and trusting that the abbot, prior, and the governors and mynistres of the same monastery for the tyme beyng, of their true substanciall and vertuouse disposicion, will well and truely kepe and performe, in their behalf, the will, mynde, and entent, of us the said Princesse, in keeping of the other twoo of the said three chaunteryes masses, and of our said anniversary, with the said LXX lights, and distribucion of x li. in almes, at every such anniversary, and of the saide converse; and also content and paye yerely to every off the said reders, and their successors, XIII li. VI s. VIII d, and to the said prechor, and his successors, x li. perpetually while the worlde shall endure. Therefore we, by reason of letters patents of licence of the said King our Soverain Lorde and moost deere

son,

## COUNTESS OF RICHMOND.

son, beryng date the xth day of Maye, the xiiiith yere of his reigne, have geven and graunted to the abbott, prior, and convent, of the said monastery, the advowsons of the church of Swynneshede[n], in the county of Lincoln, and of the church of Cheshunt[o], in the countie of Hertf', than of our patronage, and also caused the same churches to be lawfully appropried to the abbot, prior, and convent of the same monastery, and their successors, at our propre costs and charges; whiche personages, th'abbot, prior, and convent, of the same monastery, at their speciall desire, and by their entire assents and consents, have accepted and taken at the yerely value of liii li. vi s. viii d. over all charges; that is to saye, either of the same churches, at the yerely value of xxvi li. xiii s. iiii d. over all charges whiche be in deede at this day of gretter valowe. And also by reason of the said licence geven unto us by the King[p] our

---

[n] Given at the dissolution to Trinity College, Cambridge.

[o] Edward IV. seized the advowson of Cheshunt, as parcel of the Earldom of Richmond; and gave it to the Dean and Canons of Windsor. But the testatrix recovered it, and presented to it, 1492 and 1494, two eminent personages, afterwards Bishops, William Smyth of Litchfield, and Hugh Oldham of Exeter. She gave it to the abbot and convent of Westminster; who presented to the vicarage, 1502, 1526. On the suppression the Dean and Chapter sold the rectory to Anthony Dering, and after several purchasers, it is now the property of Mr. Martin. The advowson of the vicarage was granted by Mary to Bp. Bonner, whose successor, before 1610, conveyed it to Robert Cecil, afterwards Earl of Salisbury, whose descendants possess it at present.

[p] In Mortmain, for £.150. per annum. Widmore's Hist. of Westm. Ab. p. 122. ex archiv. He says, she conveyed £.90. of it to the convent; but the total of the three sums here above specified amounts to £.86. 12s. 4d.

Soverain

Soverain Lord and moſt dere Son, we have geven and graunted unto the ſaid abbot, prior, and convent, and their ſucceſſors, the manors of Drayton, with the appertenaunces, in the county of Midd'x, and divers londs and tenements in Weſt Drayton, Hillyngdon, Colham [q], Woxbrig [r], and Drayton; and alſo divers londs and tenements in Willeſdon, Padington, Weſtburn, and Kenſyngton, in the county of Midd'x, which the ſaid abbot, prior, and convent, at their owne deſire, and by their entire aſſents and conſents, have accepted and taken of us, for and at the yerely valow of xxvii li. xiii s. iiii d. and all charges. And alſo by reaſon of the ſame licence, we have geven and graunted to the ſaid now abbot, prior. and convent, and their ſucceſſours, divers londs and tenements in grete Cheſterford [s], in the countie of Eſſex, which the ſame abbot, prior, and convent, of their owne aſſent and conſents, have accepted and taken, at the yerely valow of vi li. over all charges; all which manors, londs, and tenements, ſo geven and graunted by us to the abbot, prior, and convent, and their ſucceſſors. And the ſaid churches and benefices of Swynneſhede and Cheſtehunte, now appropried, as is aforeſaid, amounten all to the yerely valow of lxxxvii li. over all charges. And all the yerely charges of the ſaid ii chaun-

---

[q] Q. Copham,         [r] Uxbridge.
[s] Mr. Morant (Eſſex, II. 555.) mentions lands in Great Cheſterford granted by Maurice Berkeley, with the advowſon of the church to the convent of Weſtminſter, 18 Henry VII. but the Counteſs's benefaction in the ſame place has eſcaped him.

tery maffes perpetually to be kepte in the faid monaftery, and the faid yerely charges of the faid anniverfary, with the faid lights of LXX tapers, and diftribucion of almes of x li. yerely be affeffed by the affent and confent of the faid abbot, prior, and convent, at xxx li. And the yerely charges for the fynding of the faid converfe at c s. which xxx li. and c s. yerely, for all the fame charges we the faid Princeffe have geven and graunted to the fame abbot, prior, and covent, and their fucceffors, for the fame fynding of the fame II chauntery maffes and perpetuall anniverfary, with the faid lights, almes, and converfe perpetually while the world fhall endure. And for the exhibicion and perpetuall fynding of the faid II perpetuall reders in the faid univerfities of Oxenford and Cambrig, the faide abbot, prior, and covent, at our defire and requeft, and according to the faid confidence and truft, have geven and graunted by thefe feveral deeds, bering the date the firft day of July, the yere of our LORD M$^l$ v$^c$ and three, and of my faid Soverain Lord and Son XVIII. to either of the fame II reders an annuytie of XIII li. VI s. VIII d. yerely. And alfo by another deede, beryng the date the fixte day of November, the yere of our LORD GOD M$^l$ v$^c$. v. and of my faid Soverain Lord and Son XXI. to the faid perpetuall prechor an annuytie of x li. for his exhibicion and perpetuall fynding in fuche manor and forme as in the fame deeds more playnly apperith. All which cofts and charges for the perpetuall fynding of the faid II chauntery maffes,

and

and of the said perpetuall anniversary, with the said lights and yerely almes, and of the said oon converse, and of the said II perpetuall reders, and of the said perpetuall prechar as is afore rehersed, extende to the yerely some of LXXI li. XIII s. IIII d. And soo the said yerely value of the said churches geven and appropried, and of the said temporall lond geven and graunted by us to the saide monastery extende and amount yerely over the said yerely charge to the some of XV li. VI s. VIII d. whiche XV li. VI s. VIII d. we have geven and graunted to the said abbot, prior, and covent, and their successours in reward, and to and for the entent that they shall the more surely, truely, and devoutly observe, kepe, and performe, our said devout will, mynde, and entent, in the premissez, in keping of the said perpetuall chauntry masses, and of the said perpetuall anniversary and converse, and content and paye the said annuyties to the said II reders and prechors, and their successors. And for the charge of wyn, wax, vestments, and ornaments, to be daiely occupied at the said three chauntery masses, or any other masse there to be saide; and for suche casuelties and charge as may fortune to fall by reason of the said londs and tenements, by aydes, subsidees, or otherwise. And also we have, bifor this tyme, yeven to the said abbot, prior, and convent, divers books, chalices, and vestyments, and other ornaments, to be used and occupied oonly aboute the aulters where the said III chauntery masses shalbe said. And over, that we att our greate

costs

costs and charge have purchased and obteyned bulls of greate indulgencies and pardon of holy faders popes of Rome unto the said monastery for all persons saying or hering any of the said 11 chauntery masses, or any other masse, to be said by any preest at the aulter provided, or the aulters to be provided by us, or our executors, in the saide monastery there, as the same 11 daiely masses shalbe said, as grete as be in the place called Scala celi, without the walls of the citie of Rome, which is daiely, as is supposed, playn[t] remission, to the grete comforte and relief of the said monastery, and of all Christen people resorting thereunto, as in the same bulles more playnly at large apperith of record. And where the foresaid abbot, prior, and covent, have bounden theym and their successours to us the said Princes, our heyres and executors, by indentur, sealed with the common seale, beryng date the secunde day of March, in the yere of our LORD GOD M$^l$. v$^c$. v. and of my said Soverain Lord and Son the xxi. enrolled in the Kyng's Court of Chauncery, to cause the said three masses daiely to be said by three monks preests of the saide monastery, beyng of goode and honest conversacion, well and sufficiently lernyd, and of goode and vertuouse disposicion, with all suche speciall collects, divine services, prayers, and observances, and also to kepe and holde our said anniversary solemply, with divine services, prayers, and observances, and with the said lights and distribucion

[t] full, *plain.*

of almes of x li. yerely; and also fynde and kepe oon converse for us in the said monastery perpetually, while the world shall endur, in suche maner and forme as in the same endenturs is conteyned and specified: and also have, by their severall dedes, sealed with their common seale, and graunted to either of the said II reders, and their successors, an annuytie of XIII li. VI s. VIII d. And to the said prechor, and his successors, x li. We will and specially requyre the said abbott, prior, and covent, and their successours, in speciall confidence and truste, and as they will therfore aunswere afore Almighty God, at the dredfull daie of fynall jugeament, to see and cause the said three daiely masses, with the prayers, observances, and serymonyes, to to be daily saide; and the said anniversary, with the said lights and distribucion of almes yerely to be truely holden and kepte; and to provide, have, and kepe, oon converse for us in the saide monastery perpetually while the world shall endur according to the true entent of the said indenture; and also to content and paye to either of the said II reders and their successours, yerely, XIII li. VI s. VIII d. and to the said prechor, and his successors, yerely, x li. according to the said graunts. And whereas we the said Princesse, by reason and vertue of lettres patents made to us by the said King our Sovrain Lord and most deere Son, beryng date the first daye of Maye, the xx yere of his reigne last paste, have established and founded the said college called Crist's College, in the said universitie of Cam-

COUNTESS OF RICHMOND.

Cambridge, to the hole nowmbre of LX perſons, with ſervants to theym convenyent and neceſſary; and, by reaſon of the ſame licence, have geven and graunted to the maiſter and ſcolers of the ſame college, and their ſucceſſours, for their exhibicion and ſuſtentacion, the manors of Malketon [u], Melreth [x], and Beache [y], with dyvers londs, tenements, rents, reverſions, and ſervices, in Malton, Melreth, Beache, Whaddon, Kneſworth [z], Hogynton [a], Orwell, and Baryngton [b], in the countie of Cambrigge; the maner of Diteſworth [c], with th'appertenaunces, with divers londs and tenements in Diteſworth, Kegworth, Hathern, and Watton, with the advouſons of the churches of Malketon, Kegworth, and Sutton de Bonyngton [d], in the countie of Leyceſter, and the manor of Roydon [e] in the countie of Eſſex, to have to theym and their ſucceſſours, for evermore; and alſo obteyned licenſe to the ſame maiſter and ſcolers, and their ſucceſſors, to appropre to theym and their ſucceſſours the ſaide church of Malketon, and alſo

[u] Malton. This is a decayed pariſh, now included in that of Orwell, where the church, antiently a rectory, ſtill remains in ruins. The rectory of Orwell belongs to Trinity College. Ecton, p. 98.
[x] Meldreth.   [y] Waterbeach.
[z] Kneeſworth.   [a] Q. Oakington.
[b] Barrington.   [c] Diſeworth.
[d] The Villare places Sutton Bonington in Nottinghamſhire; but it is not in Ecton.
[e] In 1522, the Maſter and Fellows of Chriſt's College in Cambridge are recorded to have had the manor of Roydons, Inq. 14 H. VIII. Oct. 30. But what manor is meant, and how they loſt it, I cannot learn. Morant's Eſſex. II. 490.

the

the churches of Fendrayton, Helpeston[f], and Navenby[g], as in the same lettres patents more playnly apperith; which churches of Malketon, Fendrayton, and Helpeston, we have causid actually to be impropried by assent and consent of the ordynaries, and of all other havyng therin interest unto the same maister and scolers, and their successours, aftir due forme and processe of the lawe in that parte requisite: also we have, by the Kyng's licence, and by auctoritie, assent, and consent, of the ordinary, and of all other having interest, united, annexed, and appropried, for ever the parifshe churche of Manberer[h], in Wales, within the diocese of Seynt David, to the said maister, scolers, and their successors. Item, we have, by the Pope's auctoritie, and the King's special graunte and licence, yeven unto the same maister, scolers, and their successors, the abbey of Creyke[i], in the diocese of Norwich, with the purtenances, which was in the King's hands, as dissolvyd and extincte. All which maners, londs, and tenements, and other the

[f] Both in Cambridgeshire.
[g] Naumby, c. Lincoln.
[h] Manwrbwr, c. Pembroke. "This lady being of Welsh affinity, a Teuther by marriage, and having long lived in Wales (where her son, king Henry VII. was born in Pembroke) thought fitting, in commemoration thereof, to leave some Welsh land to this her foundation." Fuller ubi sup.
[i] This priory of Austin Canons (made an abbey by Henry III.) was, about 22 Henry VII. looked upon as dissolved, becaufe the abbot died without a convent to errect another; whereupon the lands and revenues, by the procurement of the King's mother, the lady Margaret, Countess of Richmond, were settled upon Christ's College, Cambridge, being of her foundation, who are still possest of them. Tan. Not. Mon. p. 356. Blomf. Norf. III. 776.

premisses, we late purchased and provided to the same entent: and will therfore, and specially desir and requyre the said maister and scolers, and their successours, to cause and see our foundacion of our said college to be truely observed and kepte, according to the statuts and ordynances by us therof made, and to be made, and according to our will, mynde, and entent, as they will therfore answere bifore Almighty God at the dredefull daye of fynall jugeament [k]. And also we specially desire and requyre our executors, and every of them, that they, according to the confidence and truste that we have putt in them, and in every of them, to see and cause, as ferr as in theym is, or shalbe, saide III daily masses to be said and doon, and the anniversary, with the said lights, distribucion of almes, to be holden and kepte, and the said converse to be provided and kepte in the said monastery, and the said annuities to be truely content and paid to every of the said reders and prechars, according to our will, mynde, and entent, aforesaid, and also to see and cause the maister and scolers of the said college, called Crist's College, to be orderid, rewlid, and governed according to our saide will,

---

[k] In the North vestry windows are the effigies of Henry VII. and his mother the Countess of Derby and Richmond, with her first and second husbands, in armour, with their helmets by them; also John Beaufort her father, and Margaret her mother; but they are now much broken and defaced, and the inscriptions spoilt. There may still be read,

" . . . *Komitissa Rychemondie et Derbei* . . . *tis pro quibus* . . . . *suo*
" *verbo* . . . . . *tam magni* . . . . . ." Blomefield, Collect. Cantab. p. 216.

mynde, and entent, and, according to the said statuts and ordinaunces; and also to see and cause all our testament, and last will to be truely executed and performyd in every behalf, as they will answer before Almighty God at the dredfull daie of finall jugement. And also we, in moost humble and hertie wise, praye and beseche the said King our Soverain Lord, and moost deere Son, for the most tendre and singular love that we bear, and would have born to hym, to see and cause our said will therein, and in all other things, to be truely executed and performed. And whereas we the said Princesse, by our deede bering date the first day of Aprill last past, the xx yere of the reigne of our most dere Sonne King Henry the VIIth, have enfeoffed the right reverend Fader in God John[1] Bishop of Rochester, Hugh[m] Bishop of Excester, and other of and in our maners of Maxey[n] and Torpell, in the countie of North', to have to theym, and their heyres, upon confidence thereof to performe our last will; and whereas the said Bisshoppes, and their cofeoffez, sithen that at our speciall request and desire have divised and graunted to William Ratcliff, David Cecile, and Thomas Williams of Stamford a felde, and a close by side Crakelolme, late in the tenure of James Mandesley, within the Lordship of Maxey, to have and to holde, to theym and to their

---

[1] Fisher.   [m] Oldham, 1504—1520.
[n] Maxey is in Nassaburgh Hundred, Northamptonshire. The manor now belongs to the dean and chapter of Peterborough. Magn. Brit. III. 469.

assignes,

assignes, during the lif of Margaret White, anchores in the House of Nones ° beside Stamford, to th'use and entent that the same William Ratcliff, David, and Thomas, and their assignes, shall take and dispose th'issues and profitts therof to and for the exhibucion and fynding of the said anchores, and of a honest woman to attende upon hir during her lif. And also we have geven and graunted to our servant Edithe Fowler, late the wif of Thomas Fowler, widow, certyn parcells of the said manors, londs, and tenements, to the yerely valow by estimacion of x li. And also we have geven and graunted to our servant Elizabeth Massey divers other parcells of the said maners, londs, and tenements, to the yerely valow, by estimacion, of vi li. xiii s. iiii d. And also to our servant Richard Stukley and Margarete his wif, to the lenger lyver of theym, certeyn other parcells of the saide maners, londs, and tenements, to the yerely valow, by estimacion, of iiii li. And also have geven and graunted to our servant Henry Ludley certeyn other parcels of the said maners, londs, and tenements, to the yerely valow, by estimacion, of iiii li. as by their severall graunts therof more playnly apperith. All which dimises and graunts made by the said Bisshopps, and other their co-feoffez, to all the said persones, we the saide Princesse, by our severall deeds, sealed with the seale.

---

° A Benedictine Nunnery in Stamford-baron, founded an abbot of Peterborough 6 Henry II. greatly reduced at the dissolution, when the site was graunted to Richard Cecil. Tan. Not. Mon. p. 382.

of our armes, have ratified, approved, and conferred, as in the fame deeds more playnely apperith. And for the further fuertie of the parties to whom the faide graunts and confirmacions be made, we will and declare by this our prefent teftament and laft will, that all and every of the fame perfones have and enjoye feverally all the faid londs and tenements conteyned and fpecified in the fame graunts and confirmacions according to the tenors and effects of the fame. And we in moft humble wife praye and befeche the King our Soverain Lorde and moft deere Son to give his gracious affente to the fame; and to fuffre them, and every of them, to have and enjoye the fame, according to our faid will, mynde, and entent. Item, we will, that our executors, affone as they convenyently maye aftir our deceffe, doo make, or caufe to be made, in the chapell there, as our body fhalbe interred, a convenyent tombe, by their difcrecions; and oon aulter, or II, in the fame chapell, for the faid II chauntery maffes there perpetually to be faid at the howres and tymes and with all fuche prayers and obfervaunces as is afore reherfed. Item, where we have licence of the faid King our moft deere Son, by his lettres patents graunten unto us, and our executors, to eftablifshe and founde a perpetuall chauntery of oon preeft in the college of Wymborn, and to geve to hym and to his fucceffors londs and tenements to the yerely [value] of x·li. We will, that if we founde not the faid chauntery in our lif that then our executors, affone as they conveny-

ently

ently maye aftir our deceſſe, ſhall eſtabliſh and founde the ſame chauntery of oon perpetuall preeſt in the ſame college, there to kepe contynuall reſidence, and to teche frely gramer. And we will, that all the londs and tenements called Foſters, which be purchaced in Currey-Revell, which be of the yerely valow of vııı li. be ſold by our executors, to pay our detts or laſt will, and to be diſpoſid in charitable works of pitie and mercy for the wele of our ſoule. And whereas we the ſaid Princeſſe in the tyme of the reigne of King Edward the IIIIth, obteyned his Lettres Patents of licence to put in feoffament, and by reaſon of the ſame licence, dide put in feoffament our maners of Martok, Currey-Ryvell, Kyngeſbury, and Quene-Camell, in the ſame countie of Somerſet, with the hundred of Bulſton, Abdike, and Horethorn, in the ſame countie, and our bourghes of Samford, Peverell, and the hundreth of Allerton, with th'appertenances in the countie of Devon, to Robert [p] biſhop of Bathe, Sir Raynold Bray, knyght, and others, to have to theym and their heyres, to th'uſe and entent therof to performe our laſt will, which Biſhop, and his co-feoffes, by reaſon of the licence which the ſaid King our Soverain Lord and moſt deere Son graunted unto theym at our deſire by his lettres patents the vith yere of his reigne, made aſtate of all the ſaid maners and other the premiſſes to Richard [q] biſhop of Lon-

[p] Stillington, 1465—1491.
[q] Fitz James, 1506—1522.

don, and Richard Skipton, Clerke, to have to theym and their heyres, in fee; which bishop and Richard Skipton, by reason of the same lettres patents, made astate of all the same maners, and other the premisses, to the right reverend fader in God Richard [r] than bishop of Excester, now Bishop of Wynchester, Elies Daubeney of Dawbeney, knyght, William Smyth [s] than deane of Seynt Stephens, nowe bishop of Lincoln, Thomas Lovell, knyght, William Hodie, knyght, and Richard Emson [t], yet lyving, and other deceffed, in fee, to th'entent therof, to performe our laft will, by vertue wherof the said bishop of Wynchester, and his co-feoffez be thereof feafid in fee to the same use and entent: We the said Princeffe will and declare, by thies presents, that where our moevable goods which we shall have at our deceffe, be not fufficient, aftir our funerall had and don, to content and paye all our detts and legacies, and to performe our teftament and laft will, in every behalf; that therefore our executors and affignes shall have and take all th'yssues and profitts and revenues of all the same maners, and other the premisses, unto the tyme that they with the same yssues, profitts, and revenues,

---

[r] Fox, translated to Wells, 1492; Durham, 1494; Winchester, 1502; died 1530.

[s] Bp. of Coventry and Litchfield, 1492; Lincoln, 1495.

[t] This son of a sieve maker, as Lord Bacon calls him, the fit instrument of Henry VII's peculations in the close of his life, and the famous coadjutor with Dudley, was created a baron of the exchequer, and received the honour of knighthood. Henry VIII. who, with greater profusion, came not a whit behind his father in rapacity, made them both the first sacrifice of his reign.

have

have contented and paid our faid detts and legacies, and throughly and perfitely performed our teftament and laft will; and that the faid bifshop of Wynchefter and his co-feoffes, their heyres and affignes, fhall ftand and be feoffed of the fame maners and other the premiffes to the fame ufe and entent, and fuffer and not lett our faid executors and affignes fo to doo. And we, in our mooft humble wife, alfo praye the faid King our moft deere Son to geve his gracious affent thereto to fuffer and affifte our executors and affignes fo to do, as we putt our finguler truft in his Highnefs. And we the faid Princeffe, aftir our detts paid, and aftir our legacies and bequefts fpecified in this our prefent teftament and laft will, and in the fcedulles therunto annexed, fully and truely in every thinge executed and performed, will, that our executors, calling into their inward mynds and remembraunce Almighty God, and the dutie of executors, for diftribucion of goods to them in. fuche caas committed to diftribute the refidue of all our faid goods for the welth of our foule, in fuche wife as by their difcrecion fhal be thought mooft beft, meritorious and convenyent. In wittnefs wherof, to thies prefents we have fet to our figne manuell and feale of arms the daie and yere abovefaid.

Ultima voluntas ejufdem D. Marg

Be it remembred, That it was alſo the laſt will of the ſaide Princeſſe to diſſolve th'oſpitall of Seynt Joh'nis in Cambrigge[u], and to alter and to founde therof a college of ſeculer perſones; that is to ſay, a maiſter and fifty ſcolers, with divers ſervants; and newe to bielde the ſaid college, and ſufficiently to endowe the ſame, with londs and tenements, aftir the maner and forme of other colleges in Cambridge; and to furnyſshe the ſame, as well in the chapell, library, pantre, and kechen, with books and all other things neceſſary for the ſame. And to the performans whereof the ſaide Princeſſe willed, among other things, that hir executors ſhuld take the yſſues, revenues, and profitts of hir londs and tenements put in feoffament in the counties of Devonſhire, Someiſettſhire, and North-

---

[u] Founded by Nigellus biſhop of Ely, or rather by Henry Froſt burgeſs of Cambridge in his time, in honour of St. John the Evangeliſt, for a ſecular maſter and brethren, ſaid to be endowed with £.140. *per ann.* but at its ſuppreſſion the revenues amounted only to £.80. Tanner. Not. Mon. p.43. The Counteſs had been ſolicited by ſome men of character in the other univerſity to place her remaining charities upon Oxford, at St. Frideſwide's; but Bp. Fiſher, by more powerful arguments, and particularly by pointing out the melancholy ſtate and diſſolute lives of the brethren of Old St. John's Houſe, turned her thoughts back again to Cambridge. Their prodigality and exceſſes had occaſioned them to mortgage all their lands and ſettled eſtates beyond their worth, and at laſt the houſe itſelf was abandoned. The beſt thing that could be done was to diſſolve it, and ingraft a college on the old ſtock. The conſent of the biſhop of Ely, as reputed founder and dioceſan, was eaſily obtained of James Stanley, and the King's licence as eaſily. But before this could be done in due and legal form, the King died; and before much more could be done to the purpoſe, the foundreſs likewiſe died; and had ſhe not lodged this truſt in faithful hands, this great and good deſign had died with her. Baker's Pref. to her Funeral Sermon by Biſhop Fiſher, p. xv.

amptonſhire,

amptonshire, &c. Also the saide Princesse willed, that with the revenues comyng of the said londs putt in feoffament that the said late hospitall shulde be made clere of all olde detts dewly provid, and also that the londs and tenements to the same late hospitall belonging, shuld be sufficiently repayred and maynteyned. Also the said Princesse willed, that hir householde servants whiche had long contynued and done to hir goode servyce shoulde be rewarded with parte of hir goods, by the discrecion of the Reverend Fader in God Richard Bishop of Wynchester, upon informacion geven unto him of their goode service and merits; and in likewise she wold, that by his discrecion hir executors shuld be rewarded. Also the said Princesse willed, that the nowmbre of xii poore men and women that hir grace kepte and founded at Hatfeld in hir liftyme shulde be kepte and maynteyned, at hir costs, during all the lyves of the saide poore men and women. Also the saide Princesse willed, that over and above x li. londs by yere which she wold shuld be purchased and geven unto hir chauntry and free scole of gramer in Wynborn Mynster, she wold, that other vi li. shuld be purchased, and the King's licence to be obteigned for the same. Also the saide Princesse willed, that the maister and felowes of Crist's College of Cambridge should have provided for them and their successours londs and tenements to the yerely value of xvi li. over and besids other londs that the said college hath in possession. Also the saide Princesse willed, that the said Crist's College shuld, at hir costs and charge,

charge, be perfitly fynifhed in all reparacions, bielding, and garnyfhing of the fame. Alfo the faid Princeffe willed, that faide maner of Malton, in the fhire of Cambrige, whiche belongeth to the faid Crift's College fhould be fufficiently bielded and repayred, at hir cofte and charge; foo that the faid maifter and fcolers may refort thidder, and there to tary in tyme of contagioufe feknes at Cambrige, and exercife their lernyng and ftudies. Alfo the faid Princeffe willed, that a ftrong coffer fhould be provyded in the faid Crift's College, at hir cofts and charge. Alfo that hir faid executors fhulde putt in the fame a c li of money, or more, to the ufe of the faid college, to be fpended as they fhall nede. Alfo the faid Princeffe willed, that all hir plate, juells, veftments, aulterclothes, books, hangyngs, and other neceffarys belonging to hir chapell in the tyme of hir deceffe, and not otherwife bequethed, fhuld be divided betwene hir faid colleges of Crifte and Seynt John, by the difcrecion of hir executors. Alfo the faide Princeffe willed, the IIII daye before hir deceffe, that the Reverend Fader in God Richard bifshop of Wynchefter and maifter Henry Hornby, hir Chauncellor, fhuld the fame day have the overfight of hir faid will and teftament; and by theire fadneffe and goode difcrecions fhulde have full auctoritie and power to alter, adde to, and demynifhe, fuche articles in hir faid will and teftament, as they thought moft convenyent, and according to the will of the faid Princeffe.

Probat' dict' teftamenti apud Lamhith, xvii die Menfis Octobris, Anno Domini Mill'imo Quingenteffimo xii°.

MAR-

## COUNTESS OF RICHMOND.

MARGARET, only daughter of John Beaufort duke of Somerset (grandson of John of Gaunt) by Margaret daughter of John Beauchamp of Bletsoe, was married to Edmund de Hadham, second son of Owen Tudor the second husband of Catherine Queen of Henry V. created 31 Henry VI. earl of Richmond, with precedence before all other earls. He died 35 Henry VI. 1456. and was buried in the middle of the choir of St. David's cathedral, under an altar tomb yet remaining, with an inscription, styling him, " Father and Brother to Kings." His widow married Henry a younger son of Humphrey Stafford duke of Buckingham, slain at the battle of Northampton, 38 Henry VI. whose will bears date 1481, 21 Edward IV [x]. She took to her third husband Thomas Lord Stanley, who narrowly escaping death from a blow of a halberd at the arrest of Lord Hastings, joined the Countess's son at the battle of Bosworth, and had the honour of placing the usurper's crown on his head, and was the same year created

---

[x] He bequeathed his body to be buried in the college of Pleshy, in Essex, and gave £. 160. to buy twelve marks of livelode by the year, to be amortized for the finding an honest fittting priest to sing for his soul, in the said college of Plafshe, for evermore. And to his son-in-law the Earl of Richmond a trappur of four new horse-harness of velvet. To his brother John Earl of Wiltshire his bay courser; and to Reynold Bray [*], his receiver-general, his grizzled horse. Of which testament he appointed Margaret Countess of Richmond his wife his Executrix. Dugd. Bar. I. 167.

[*] This trusty servant of the Countess of Richmond was one instrument in bringing about the Revolution in favour of her son, being sent by the Duke of Buckingham and Morton Bishop of Ely to concert measures with her and Edward IV's dowager. Dugd. Bar. II. 239. ex Polyd. Verg. p. 553.

Earl of Derby, which title has been held to this day by his lineal descendants, of whom our histories recite a glorious series.

She had no children by her two last husbands, and only one son by her first.

Having lived to see the coronation of her grandson Henry VIII. she departed this life just thirteen months after the date of her testament, June 29, 1509, and is buried, according to her appointment, in the South side of the chapel of Our Lady at Westminster, begun to be built by her son, and commonly called Henry VIIth's chapel. Her effigies of copper gilt, habited in an ermine mantle, with a coronet on her head, and a hind at her feet, lies on a tomb of black marble, at whose head are her arms impaled by those of the Earl of Richmond, as at the feet by those of the Earl of Derby. On the South side Henry VII. impaling Elizabeth of York, Henry V. impaling Catherine of France, and Arthur Prince of Wales. On the North side Henry VIII. impaling Catherine of Arragon; John Duke of Somerset, impaling Margaret Holland, her grandfather and grandmother. Her simple epitaph, reciting her charities, was drawn up by Erasmus, who received twenty shillings for it. See it, and the monument, in Sandford, 328. in Dart I. 148. and in Baker's Preface to Fisher's Funeral Sermon, where is also an engraving of the arms used in her seal, and now borne by the colleges of Christ and St. John in Cambridge; And see Dugd. Bar. II. 237, 238.

THE

THE several great benefactions of this good lady for the promotion of learning, which had been gradually emerging in this kingdom during the distractions of the wars between the houses of York and Lancaster, render it necessary to give a more particular account of her foundations than could be divided into notes.

The Countess had letters patents, 12 Henry VII. to purchase lands of the yearly value of £. 10. to found and endow at Winborn a perpetual chantry of one priest, in honour of the blessed Jesus, the Annuntiation of the Blessed Virgin Mary, and for the health of her soul, and the souls of her parents. But dying before it was endowed, her executors obtained letters patents, 1 Henry VIII. ratifying the former, and empowering them to purchase lands to the value of £. 6. per annum, over and above the others, by indenture, tripartite, 2 Henry VIII. between them, the Dean and Chapter of Wimborn, and the sacrist, or keeper of Brembre's chantry there. The executors founded a chantry at the altar on the South side of the tomb of John duke of Somerset, and Margaret his wife, father and mother of the testatrix, and appointed Richard Hodgekynnes, B. A. to be first chaplain, continually resident in the college of Wimborn, in a house appointed by the dean and chapter there to teach grammar to all comers as in Eton and Westminster schools, without any other perquisites than were appointed by the executors; and to celebrate daily mass at the said altar, for the souls of the foundress, King Henry VII. her parents and ancestors; the collects and other ceremonies are particularly prescribed. He was to keep her anniversary July 9, and after it to distribute twenty shillings, as follows; to the sacrist of the college if present at her mass sixteen pence, to every chaplain devoutly singing eight pence, to every secondary and parish clerk four pence, to the sacrist for five wax candles to be burnt about the bier, and two on the altar, and for bell ropes, sixteen pence; to the ringers eight pence; the residue among the poor of the parish, at one penny or twopence each. His stipend was ten pound per annum, and his door-keeper's forty-shillings, and he was to give an account of his expences each Michaelmas, to the sacrist, and one of the senior chaplains of Brembre's chantry; and the surplus money was to be kept in a chest under three keys, one in the hands of the Dean or his sacrist, another in those of the senior chaplain, and the third in those of the chaplain of this chantry; or to be taken out as wanted. In 1511 Richard Hodgekyns was chantry priest, and received six pounds per annum. At the dissolution this chauntry fell with the college of Winborn and all its revenues into the King's hands; part was leased out, and part continued as a precarious maintenance to the ministers of the church, till 5 Eliz. certain of the parishioners, by means of Lord Montjoy, obtained the Queen's letters patents to found the free grammar-school now subsisting at Winborn, in which

which the munificence of the pious testatrix is absorbed; and instead of one priest a schoolmaster is maintained by an income of £. 34. per annum, and an usher at £. 25. per annum. Hutchins's Dorset, II. 81. 83.

The Cambridge public lecture in divinity she instituted in the 13th year of her son's reign, on the feast of the Nativity of the Blessed Virgin, and by her original foundation appointed John Fisher, S. T. P. her first reader, who was succeeded by Dr. Cosin, Master of Benet, and he by William Burgoyn, afterwards Master of Peter-house; and he by Erasmus. She likewise gave rules and statutes for the choice of her reader, and for the discharge and performance of the duties of his place, and endowed her lecture with 20 marks per annum, payable by the abbot and convent of Westminster. The same day and year she instituted the like reader at Oxford, with allowance of the same salary, and almost under the same rules with that at Cambridge, and nominated one John Roper, S. T. P. her first reader.

In the 20th year of the same reign she founded a perpetual public preacher at Cambridge, with a stipend of £. 10. per annum, payable by the abbot and convent of Westminster, whose duty was to preach at least six sermons every year at several churches specified in the foundation in the dioceses of London, Ely, and Lincoln; and one John Fawn, S. T. P. is appointed her first preacher, by the original foundation.

This foundation of a public preacher is peculiar to Cambridge, for Mr. Wood's suspicion of the like at Oxford has no foundation.

The foundation of Christ's college was undertaken by the advice and persuasion of Bp. Fisher; who, by her statutes, was appointed visitor for life after the foundress. The foundation has been placed in the year 1505, but the statutes were not given, nor the foundation perfected, till the year following. The original obligation of John Syclyng, last master of God's house, and first master of Christ's college, for observing the foundress's statutes, bears date Sept. 5, 22 Henry VII. from which day and year, I suppose, and not sooner, the government and statutes of that college took place and begun to be in force. And because the bishops of Ely had yet kept up some claim or shew of power, a grant was obtained from James [Stanley] bishop of Ely, son in law to the foundress, 1506, whereby he gave leave to the Master, Fellows, and Scholars, to celebrate divine offices in their college chapel, which had been already consecrated; and by another grant of the same date, at the instance of the foundress, he exempted the college from episcopal and ordinary visitations for himself and successors for ever. The endowments of the college are all specified in the foundress's will, and though it appears from thence that she herself was very liberal, having bestowed good lands and manors of her own, yet the abbey of Creyke given her by Henry VII. and God's House,

which

which was of the foundation of Henry VI. did go a good way, and pretty deep, in the foundation.

In regard to the foundation of St. John's College, she did indeed leave a will and lands in feoffment for the performance thereof, and thefe were very fufficient, had they been fecured againft the next heir the King her grandfon; and though her will (as far as appears) was very good, and duly attefted, yet that part of it which concerned her foundation of a new college, having been done by way of codicil, before it could be fealed, the good lady departed this life, and left fome ground for cavil. This might have been borne with had they been fure of the old houfe, but that was yet ftanding undiffolved, fo that all that had been done towards it was to begin anew, with lefs power, and under greater difadvantages. King Henry VII. was now wanting; the King reigning, as he had not the fame ties of duty and affection, fo he was under no obligation to make good his father's promifes; and having an eye upon the eftate, he had no very ftrong inclination to favor a defign that muft fwallow up a part of his inheritance. The bifhop of Ely, who was eafy and complying enough whilft the foundrefs was living, fhe being gone, began to fhew his nature, and was full of difficulties, and withheld his confent for half a year.

His firft bufinefs ought to have been to have vifited and reformed the houfe, and to have prevented thofe enormities that occafioned its diffolution; but having rather

cooucountenanced their loofenefs, by his ill example, it is no wonder if he had fome tendernefs and feeling of the infirmities of his brethren, or was unwilling to confent to a thing that fo plainly reproached him with his own great neglect and worfe example.

Great application was to be made both at court and at Ely; the affair was likewife to be folicited at Rome, and where Julius II. being then pope, nothing was to be done without addrefs and management, and all the other requifites to expedite fuch an affair. The expences of the bulls are put down upon the executor's accounts (figned and allowed by Polydore Vergil), which are very high for a thing fo much in courfe and of no greater confequence than the diffolving an old ruinous houfe, that might have been done without afking the pope's leave, had it been thought expedient; and yet, when the bull came, it was found defective, and was to be renewed at a new trouble and expence. The latter indeed was not loft; for when the decretory bull was fent it ftruck the old houfe at one blow, without confent either of the King or of the bifhop of Ely.

The King's licence was granted Aug. 7. ann. reg. primo. It fets forth the defolate ftate and condition of the houfe, though not in fo difmal a manner; gives leave to the executors, upon its fuppreffion, to convert it into a college *unius magiftri, ac fociorum, et fcholarium ad numerum* 50 *vel circa, in fcientiis liberalibus, jure civili & canonica, et theologiâ ftudentium,* to be ftiled *St. John's College*;

to unite, incorporate, and annex, all the lands of the old house to the college so erected; and further grants leave to the college when erected to hold £. 50. per annum. over and above the lands of the house, the statute of *mortmain* notwithstanding.

This licence was granted at the request of the foundress (though then deceased) as well as of her executors; for there is an old draught or original of the King's licence, signed Henry, but not sealed, whereto is prefixed the petition of his *humble graunt dame*, in a form there put down: so it seems, her petition was either preferred, or left to be preferred, after her death; and the King's licence under seal, refers to her petition.

The bishop of Ely's first grant is dated March 7, 1509. after the King's licence, and before the papal bull came, whereby he first makes conditions for himself and successors, by reserving to himself a power of naming three persons during his life, and to his successors a power of naming one, to be elected fellows of the college, *si habiles et idonei sint*, a clog that yet remains upon the society; and then grants, that the college, when erected, shall enjoy the jewels, goods, &c. belonging to the house, and obliges himself, that, the papal bulls first had, he would give leave and allow the house to be incorporated to the college. And he empowered Richard Wiot, S. T. P. Master of Christ's college, John Fotehede B. D. and William Thornborough, to take a full and perfect inventory of all the jewels, muniments,

ments, and other moveables of the houfe, and to have them in fafe cuftody till the college fhould be erected.

When the pope's bulls came, the bifhop of Ely paffed another grant, dated Dec. 31. ann. reg. fecundo, whereby he conveyed over to the executors all the fcite and manfion, and all the houfes, churches, chapels, and edifices, belonging to the houfe, together with all manors, lands, rents, tenements, and other poffeffions appertaining thereunto, and all his right as founder in the fame; which houfe being fuppreft, diffolv'd, and extinguifhed, by apoftolical authority, by the King's licence, and by his confent, devolving to him as founder, being of the foundation of him and his predeceffors, he grants to them, to the end and intention, that they might change, found, create, and erect it into a college of fecular ftudents, to endure for ever; ordinary jurifdiction always referved to him and his fucceffors. And he appointed and conftituted Richard Henrifon, clerk, and others, his proctors or attornies, to enter and take feifin and poffeffion of the houfe; and being feized, to deliver full, plenary, and peaceable poffeffion thereof to the foundrefs's executors.

By virtue of this grant, on the 20th of January, the fame year full and peaceable poffeffion of the houfe, &c. was delivered by Richard Henrifon, the bifhop's commiffary to Henry Hornby S. T. P. one of the executors, in the name and ftead of the reft; in the prefence of William Woderove S. T. P. mafter of Clare-hall, and deputy vice-

vice-chancellor, William Burgoign S. T. P. John Fotehede S. T. B. master of Michael-house, Oliver Scalis public notary, and many other students and burgesses.

And so the old house, after much solicitation and long delay, after a tedious process at Rome, at court, and at Ely, under an imperious pope, a forbidding prince, and a mercenary prelate, with great application and industry, and at no less expence, was at last dissolved and utterly extinguished, on the 20th day of January, A. D. 1510. and fell a lasting monument to all future ages, and to all charitable and religious foundations, not to neglect the rules or abuse the institutions of their founders, least they fall under the same fate.

Though all this was transacted in the name of the executors, it ought never to be forgot, that the bishop of Rochester was the sole or principal agent.

The house being thus dissolved, the next thing the executors were to think of, was to set about their new foundation; which they were now empowered to do by a full authority. Somewhat they were now sure of, and we have a college in view, but as yet a very poor one: for the revenues of the old house were small, according to an authentic account amounting only to £. 80. 1*s*. 10*d*. *ob. per ann.* And it is pretty plain, from the King's licence of *mortmain*, he did not intend the foundation should be over large, it being thereby limited to £. 50 *per annum,* besides the revenues of the old house.

It is true, the foundress had done her part, having left the issues, profits, and revenues, of her estate and lands, to the value of £. 400. and upwards, to that purpose, and for the uses of her will; but surely the King, when he granted such a mortmain, did not intend the executors should enjoy them long. However, being unwilling to understand his meaning, or being willing to push things as far as they would go, or presaging already the future growth of the college, though from unhopeful beginnings, they went on with good assurance; and having cleared the debts of the old house, according to the direction of the foundress in her will, as well as the rubbish of the old buildings, which in great part were very ruinous, they proceeded to the foundation, both of the fabric and body politic of the college.

The charter of foundation was given April 9, 1511, in the name and by the authority of all the executors.

In all this charter, which is a very long one, there is no mention made of the large revenues left by the foundress, for the uses of her will; but the King's licence of *mortmain* is there recited, whereby the college is limited to £. 50. *per annum* besides the lands and revenues of the house. About the same time the fabric of the house was undertaken, which was made equal to the design.

The expence of the whole building amounted in all (after some deductions for other uses) to betwixt four and five thousand pounds, a round sum in that age! for so much

much was paid by the executors towards the building to Robert Shorton mafter of the college, and fo much was paid by him to Oliver Scalis, clerk of the works, at feveral payments, as appears by their feveral accounts.

All this while the executors had to do with a greater man, the King, as heir at law to the foundrefs's eftate. All due care had been taken to fecure their intereft therein, by proving her will, both in the Prerogative Court and in the Court of Chancery, by advice of the judges, wherein archbifhop Warham was very ufeful and favourable, both as Archbifhop and Chancellor of England; who, after a long, tedious, and expenfive hearing, witneffes examined, the King's council heard, and judges confulted (all which was neceffary to guard him againft the King) at laft approved and allowed the will as good. Upon this ground the profits of her lands were received for fome years, firft by Bifhop Fifher, and afterwards by Dr. Hornby; but this was not to continue long; for what by the clamours of the Countefs's officers and fervants, who, becaufe they could not have all themfelves, were willing to give all to the King; what by the advice of fome potent courtiers, of which number Wolfey is faid to be one; and what by the frefh fuit of the King's auditors and council, who are ufually ready to fecond the courtiers in fuch defigns, the executors were fo hard preffed, and fo ftraitly handled, that they were forced to let go the lands, notwithftanding all the claim they had to them.

The lands being gone, they were to look out and sue for a compensation, otherwise all was at a stand. Somewhat of that kind was easily obtained; but that at first granted, as it was small in itself, so it was soon defeated by unexpected accidents, and an untimely death. Somewhat more durable was to be had, and there being an old decayed *Maison Dieu* or hospital at Ospring in Kent worth having, this falling under the Bishop of Rochester's view, was quickly thought of, and being by devolution in the King, by the Bishop's application at court, with the mediation of the Queen, Wolsey, and other courtiers, it was at last obtained.

This, with the lands of the old house, together with the foundress's estate at Fordham, which was charged with debts by her will, with some other little things purchased with her monies, was the original foundation upon which the college was first opened; and whoever dreams of vast revenues, or larger endowments, will be mightily mistaken. Her lands put in feoffment for the performance of her will, lay in the counties of Devon, Somerset, and Northampton; and though I should be very glad to meet with lands of the foundation in any of these three counties, yet I despair much of such a discovery. But whoever now enjoys the manors of Maxey and Torpell, in the county of Northampton, or the manors of Martock, Currey-Ryvell, Kynsbury, and Queen-Camel, with the hundreds of Bulston, Abdike, and Horethorne, in the county

of

of Somerſet; or the manor of Sandford Peverell, with the hundred of Alberton, in the county of Devon; though they may have a very good title to them, which I will not queſtion, yet whenever they ſhall be piouſly and charitably difpofed, they cannot beſtow them more equitably than by leaving them to St. John's college, Cambridge.

Mr. Thomas Baker's preface to the Counteſs's funeral ſermon, preached by biſhop Fiſher at her moneth minde: p. viii—xliv.

APPENDIX.

# APPENDIX.

## N° I. p. 207.

Rot. Parl. 1 Hen. V. n. 13. vol. IV. p. 5.

Pur les Executeurs de darrien Roy Henry [IV.]

ITEM, certeines Lres patentes feurent faites pur les Executours du Roy Henry, pier ñre Sr le Roy q'or eſt, en la fourme q'enſeute.——Henricus, Dei gra, Rex Angl' & Franc', & Dñus Hibnie, Omnibus ad quos preſentes Lre pervenerint, Salutem. Sciatis, qd cum recolende memorie Dñus Henricus, nuper Rex Anglie, pater ñr, cogitans diem exitus ſui appropinquare, ac pie deſiderans dum adhuc ageret in humanis, precipue pauperibus ligeis ſuis, quibus in diverſis pecuniarum ſummis erat aſtrictus, ſatisfacere, & aliis pietatis operibus ſaluti anime ſue ſalubriter providere, Teſtamentum ſuum condiderit, in quo, de bonis & catallis ſibi a Deo collatis creditoribus ſuis primo ſatisfieri, ac certa legata ſolvi, & nonnulla pietatis opera exerceri & impleri, diſpoſuit venerabilib' patribus, Henrico [a] archiepo Eborum, Thoma [b] epo Dunolm', ac Johanne Pelham, Roberto Waterton, & Johanne Leventhorp, nominatis Executoribus; necnon Nobis, & Conſanguineo ñro Thoma [c] archiepo Cantuar', ſuperviſoribus ad hoc deputatis; Qui quidem archiepus Ebor', epiſcopus, Johes, Robtus, & Johes, advertentes bona & catalla ipſius patris ñri ad perſolucoem debitorum ſuor' & alior' in Teſtamento pdco diſpoſitor' non ſufficere,

---

[a] Thomas Fitz Alan, ſon of the earl of Arundel, biſhop of Ely, 1374—1388; archbiſhop of York, 1388—1396; of Canterbury, 1396—1414. He was alſo lord chancellor.

[b] Thomas Langley. See above, p. 205.

[c] Thomas Arundel.

# APPENDIX.

Executionem Teſtamenti hujuſmodi admittere renuunt & recuſant, & ſic diſpoſitio Teſtamenti bonor' & catallor' hujuſmodi ad dc̄m conſanguineum n̄rm, tanquam ad ordinarium de jure p̱tineret, ac bona & catalla p̄dc̄a pro ſatisfacc̄ōe & ſoluc̄ōe, & aliis p̄dc̄is implendis, venditioni publice exponi deberent; Nos, attendentes bona & catalla p̄dc̄a Nobis & n̄ris uſibus fore accom̄oda, ac honeſtius eſſe bona & catalla illa penes Nos remanere, quam venditioni publice aliqualiter, ut premittitur, exponi, eadem bona & catalla ab ipſis qui tempore dc̄i patris n̄ri cuſtodiam eorundem habuerint recepimus, & penes Nos retinemus; eorumq; valorem per veram eſtimac̄ōem inde fc̄am, qui ad viginti & quinque milia marcarum ſe extendit, ut diſpōſitio p̄fati patris n̄ri in quantum ſumma illa ſufficere poſſit exinde perſiciatur, ejuſq; anima miſericordiam Altiſſimi facilius promereatur, ac Nos de bonis & catallis p̄dc̄is penes Deum & homines ſimus penitus excuſati, prefatis archiep̄o Eborum, ep̄o, Joh̄i, Roberto & Joh̄i, concedimus & aſſignamus p̱ preſentes; Habend' & percipiend' ſummam p̄dc̄am infra quatuor annos prox' ſequentes poſt dat' preſentium, videlt ad feſta Sc̄i Mich̄is & Paſche extunc prox' tribuen' equis portionibus quatuor milia librar'; & ad feſta Sc̄i Mich̄is & Paſche extunc prox' ſequen' equis porc̄ōibus quatuor milia librar; & ad feſta Sc̄i Mich̄is & Paſche extunc prox' ſequen' quis porc̄ōibus quatuor milia librar'; & ad feſta Sc̄i Mich̄is & Paſche extunc prox' ſequen' equis porc̄ōibus Quatuor milia ſexcentas ſexaginta & ſex libras, treſdecim ſolidos, & quatuor denarios; deinde primo creditoribus ipſius patris n̄ri pro victualibus & expenſis hoſpitii ſui, ac neceſſariis camere, ac garderobe ſuar', ab eis empt'; necnon p̱ pecuniarum ſummis eidem patri n̄ro p̱ ipſos creditores mutuatis, juxta ſanas difrec̄ōes ſuas ſatisfaciend'; ac deinde alia pietatis opera juxta diſpoſic̄ōem ipſius patris n̄ri p̄dc̄am, ſi ſumma hujuſmodi ad hoc ſufficiat, per ſuperviſum n̄rum ac ipſius conſanguinei n̄ri, ſeu deputatorum n̄ror' faciend' & exercend'. Volentes

lentes ulterius & concedentes, de aſſenſu dñorum ſpiritualium & temporalium, ac cõitatis regni ñri Anglie in p̃ſenti Parliamento ñro exiſten', quod tam idem conſanguineus ñr, quam p̃fatus archiep̃us Eborum, ep̃us, Joħes, Roƀtus, & Joħes, de omnimodis p̃litis, querelis, actionibus, & demandis, que p̃ p̃fatos creditores, vel alios quoſcumque, verſus p̃fatum conſanguineum ñrum, ratione commiſſionis adminiſtrationis ſumme p̃dc̃e p̃fatis archiep̃o Ebor', ep̃o, Joħi, Roƀto, & Joħi, per ipſum faciend'; aut verſus ipſos archiep̃um Ebor', ep̃um, Joħem, Roƀtum, & Joħem, r̃one admiſſionis Adminiſtrationis hujuſmodi, ſeu occupationis, receptionis, ſeu deliberationis ſumme p̃dc̃e, vel alior' bonor' ſeu catallor' que fuerunt p̃dc̃i patris ñri quorumcumq̃, capi, proſequi, vel moveri poſſint, in futur' quieti ſint, & penitus exonerati imperpetuum; aliquo ſtatuto in contrarium fc̃o non obſtante. Volumus tamen, qd̃ iidem archiep̃us Ebor', ep̃us, Joħes, Roƀtus, & Joħes, omnes denarios quos ipſos de ſumã p̃dc̃a recipere & habere continget, circa ſatisfactionem debitor' p̃dc̃or', ac alia pietatis opera p̃dc̃a, in forma p̃dc̃a faciend', fideliter ſolvant & expendant, p̃ ſuperviſum ſuprad̃em: Et qd̃ ad compotum ſive ratiocinium inde reddend' niſi coram p̃fato conſanguineo ñro, vel ejus ſucceſſoribus, nullatenus teneantur; aliquo ſtatuto vel ordinac̃õe in contrarium factis, vel alia cauſa quacumque non obſtante. In cujus rei teſtimonium has l̃ras ñras fieri fecimus patentes. Teſte Meipſo apud Weſtm', xv die Maii, anno regni ñri primo.

Nº II.

## N° II. p. 243.

### Rot. Parl. 2 H. VI. m. 30. Vol. IV. p. 213.

#### Pur Johan Stafford, Treforer d'Engleterre.

ITEM, une autre Petition en papier fuift baille en le dit Parlement, p̱ Maiftre John Stafford Treforer d'Engleterre, ovec une endenture faite p̱entre luy, & Henry Sire Fitz Hugh, Walter Hungreford, Walter Beauchamp, Lowys Robeffart, William Porter, & Robert Babthorp, Chivalers; John Wodehous, & John Leventhorp, Efquiers; Executours del teftament de le tres noble Prince Sr̃ Henry, jadis Roy d'Engleterre, piere a ñre tres foverein Sr̃ le Roy q'or eft, nomez des certeins biens, chateux, joialx, & fummes de deniers, q̃ feurent a dit nadgairs Roy, deliverez as ditz nomez Executours, p̱ le dit Treforer, p̱ vertu des lettres patentes de ñre dit Sr̃ le Roy au dit Treforer faitez celle partie; folonc la forme & effect d'une acte en le darrein Parlement ñre Sr̃ le Roy q'or eft, enrolles, le tenour de quell Petition cy enfuit.

Au Roy ñre foveraigne & tres graciouſe Sr̃, & as Seigñrs Spirituelx & Temporelx de ceft prefent Parlement, fupplie humblement vre fervitour Meftre John Stafford Treforer d'Engleterre, q̃ come ñre foveraigne Sr̃ le Roy qe or eft, de l'advys fon grand Counfaill, & affent des Seigñrs Efpirituelx & Temporelx, & fon Communalte de fon Roialme d'Engleterre, en fon darreyn Parlement, p̱ auctorite du dit Parlement, voudra ordiner & graunta q̃ ñre dit Sr̃ le Roy ferra delyverer & affigner p̱ fon depute ou fes deputes a fes tres chiers & loialx Henry Sr̃ Filz Hugh, Sr̃ Lowes Robeffard, Wauter Hungerford, Wauter Beauchamp, William Porter, and Robert Babthorp, Chivalers; John Wodehous, & John Leventhorp, Efquiers;

Efquiers; Executours nomez del teftament de tres haut & tres puiffant Prince Sr̃ Henry le Quint, nadgairs Roy d'Engleterre, piere ñre dit Sr̃ le Roy q'or eft, des biens, chateux, joialx, & fommes des deniers, queux furent le dit nadgairs Roy, a le value de XL M. marcz, come p un acte en le dit Parlement eint fait pluis pleinement appiert; p force de quell acte, ñre dit Sr̃ le Roy, p advys de fon dit Counfaill p fes lettres patentz fift affign' & conftit' le dit fuppl' fon depute a delyverer & affigner pur le dit ñre Sr̃ le Roy & en fon noun a lez nomez Executours du dit nadgairs Roy fuifditz diverf' biens, chateux, joialx, & fommes des deniers, en les ditz lettres patentz contenuz; & autres biens, chateux, joialx, & fommes des denirs, a le value du dit fomme de XL M. marz atteignauntz, des biens, chateux, joialx, & fommes des deniers queux furent le dit nadgairs Roy; p endentures ent affairs pentre le dit fuppliant, & les nomez Executours fuifditz; p force de quellx lettres patentz & acte avauntditz, le dit fuppl' ad delyvere les ditz biens, chateux, joialx, & fommes des deniers, en les ditz lettres patentz contenuz; & autres biens, chateux, joialx, & fommes des deniers, queux furent en la garde & mayns des diverf' officers le dit jadis Roy a les ditz nomez Executours, ficome p les endentures pentre le dit fuppl', & les ditz nomez Executours, ent faitz pluis pleynement appiert; folunc la forme & effect du dit acte, & les lettres patentz fuifditz.

Que pleafe a Vous, tres gracioufe Sr̃, de faire enacter & enroller en le Rolle du ceft Parlement les fuifditz endentures. Et outre ceo de ordeigner p auctorite de ceft prefent Parlement, q̃ le dit fuppl', fez heirs, affignes, terre tenauntz, & executours, de cy en avaunt, de toutz les ditz biens, chateux, joialx, & fommes des deniers, & de chefcun parcell d'ycellez, fi bien devers Vous, voz heirs, fucceffours, & executours, come devers chefcun autre perfon qeconqe, foient quietez & difchargez a toutz jours. Et q̃ de

chefcun

chefcun maner d'action & empefchement, fi bien p̄ Vous, voz heirs, fucceffours, ou executours, come p̄ autre perfon q̄comq̄, envers le dit fuppliant, fez heirs, affignez, executours, ou terre tenauntz, pris ou purfuez, a prendrez ou a purfuers, p̄ caufe d'afcun poffeffion, adminiftration, ou lyvere des ditz biens, chateux, joialx, & fommes des deniers, ou d'afcun parcell d'ycelles, ou autre caufe q̄comqe; le dit fuppliant, fez heirs, affignes, executours, & terre tenauntz fuifditz, foient auxint quitez & difchargez, & les ditz pleynauntz, empefchuauntz & purfuantz, ent foient barrez & excludez a toutz jours; pur Dieu & en oevere de charite.

La quelle Petition leeu & entendu, ordine fuift & accorde p̄ les Seigñrs Efpirituelx & Temporelx de ceft prefent Parlement, p̄ l'affent des Communes en icell affemblez, q̄ les ditz endentures foient enactez & enrollez en le Rolle du dit Parlement; le tenour des queux endentures cy enfuit.

Hec Indentura facta apud London', Vicefimo fexto die menfis Augufti, Anno regni Regis Henrici fexti primo: Inter Magiftrum Johannem Stafford Thef' Anglie, & deputat' per literas ejufdem Domini Regis patentes affignat', ex parte una. Et Henricum Dñum Filz Hugh, Walter' Hungreford, Walter' Beauchamp, Lodowic' Robeffart, Willielmum Porter, & Robertum Babthorp, Milit'; ac Johannem Wodehous, & Johannem Leventhorp, Armiger'; Executores Teftamenti recolende memorie illuftriffimi Principis & Domini Domini Henrici Quinti, nuper Regis Anglie, Patris p̄dicti Dñi Regis nunc, nominat', ex parte altera. Teftatur, quod predictus Magifter Johannes Stafford deputat', deliveravit & affignavit pro dicto Domino Rege nunc & nomine fuo; prefat' Henrico Domino Filz Hugh, Waltero, Waltero, Lodowico, Willielmo, Roberto; Johanni Wodehous, & Johanni Leventhorp, de bonis, catallis, & jocalibus, ac denar' fummis, que fuerunt ipfius nuper Regis,

Regis, citra prox' Parliament' expend', applicand', convertend' & fideliter adminiſtrand', juxta formam & effectum cujuſdam acti in ultimo Parliamento dicti Dñi ñri Regis, nunc prox' ante dat' confectionis preſentium habiti; & in Rotulo ejuſdem Parliamenti irrotulati; diverſ' bona, catalla, & jocalia, ac denar' ſummas ſubſcriptas; videlicet, (vid. Rot. Parl. vol. IV. p. 214—241.).

Et preſens Indentura teſtatur, quod predicti Henricus Dominus Filz Hugh, Walterus Hungreford, Walterus Beauchamp, Lodowicus Robeſſart, Willielmus Porter, & Robertus Babthorp, Milites; ac Johannes Wodehous, & Johannes Leventhorp, Armigeri; Executores Teſtamenti Domini Henrici Quinti nuper Regis Anglie defuncti nominat'; receperunt die & anno predictis de dict' Magiſtro Johanne Stafford, Theſ' Anglie, & deputat' Domini Regis nunc, diverſa bona, catalla & jocalia, ac denar' ſummas preſcript', que fuerunt predicti nuper Regis, ad valentiam xviiiM.ccccIIIIli. IIIIſ. xđ. appretiat', per Johannem Palyng, & Johannem Wynne, aurifabr'; Hugonem Dike, & Johannem Chirche, mercer'; & Johannem Bullok, tapicer'[a], de London', ad hoc jurat'; in partem ſolutionis Quadraginta Millium marcarum dict' Execut' nominat' aſſignat', ſecundum formam & effectum acti ſupradicti, que comprehenduntur in preſent' indent' in viginti una paginis pergameni de eiſdem ſuperius ſcript'; quarum prima pagin' cont' ſummam IXM.CIIIIli. xIſ. IXđ.—Secunda pagin', McxIIli. xIxſ. vIIđ. ob. —Tertia pagin', MccxIxli. IIIIſ. vIIđ. ob.—Quartà pagin', ccccLxli. xvIIſ. IIIđ.—v$^{ta}$ pagin', c$^{xx}_{IIII}$IIIIli. IIIIſ. vIđ. q̃.— vI$^{ta}$ pagin', DcLxxIIli. xvIIſ. q̃.—vII$^{ma}$ pagin', McLxvIli. vIIđ. ob.—vIII$^{va}$ pag', cccLvIli. xvſ. vIIIđ. ob.—Ix$^{na}$ pag', ccxxIxli. xIxſ. xIđ.—x$^{a}$ pag', cccLvIli. Ixſ. vIIđ. ob.—xI$^{ma}$ pagin', ccccxLIIIIli. IIIſ. IIđ. ob.—xII$^{ma}$ pagin', cccxIli. vIIſ. vIIIđ.— xIII$^{t\,a}$ pagin' cxIxli. IIſ. xIđ. ob.—xIIII$^{ta}$ pagin', DcccvIIli.

[a] Weaver.

IIſ.

11 ſ. 1 đ.—xvᵗᵃ pagin', cc$^{xx}_{iiii}$xviii ɬi. xiiii ſ. vi đ.—xviᵗᵃ pagin', cccc$^{xx}_{iiii}$xiii ɬi. vii ſ. iii đ. q̃.—xviiᵐᵃ pagin', ccxviii ɬi. xix ſ.—xviiiᵛᵃ pag', dl ɬi. vi ſ. ii đ.—xixⁿᵃ pagin', $^{xx}_{iiii}$viii ɬi. vii đ. oƀ.—xxᵐᵃ pagin', xliii ɬi. xvi ſ.—xxiᵐᵃ pag', clxx ɬi. iiii ſ. viii đ. q̃.

In cujus rei teſtimonium, huic parti Indentur', penes prefat' Magiſtrum Johannem Stafford, Theſ' Anglie, & Deputat' Domini Regis nunc remanenti, prediƈt' Henricus Dominus Filz Hugh, Walterus, Walterus, Lodowicus, Willielmus, Robertus, Johannes Wodehous & Johannes Leventhorp, Execut' prediƈti nuper Regis nominat', ſigilla ſua appoſuerunt. Dat' die & anno ſupradiƈtis.

---

### Nº III. p. 243.

### Rot. Parl. 1 Hen. VI. m. 14. vol. IV. p. 172.

Pur l'Execution de la darrain volunte de piere du Roy.

FAIT aſſavoir, q'en ceſte Parlement furent baillez une Petition & une Cedule conſuitz enſemble, tachez ore a le dorſe de ceſte rolle de Parlement, de la quell Petition le tenure cy enſuit.

Pleaſe au Roi ñre Sr̃ ſoverain, p aſſent des Seigñrs Eſpirituelx & Temporelx en ceſte preſent Parlement, & p auƈtorite de meſme le Parlement, grauntier & ordeiner tout ceo q'eſt contenuz en une Cedule a yceſte Bille annexee, & q̃ lettres patentz de n̄ɾe Sr̃ le Roi, p auƈtorite de meſme le Parlement, ſoient faitz, ſelonc les fourme & contenue de ycelle Cedule, pur Dieu & en oevere de ch̃ite. Et le tenure de la dite Cedule cy enſuit.

REX,

REX, Omnibus ad quos &c. Salutem.

Sciatis, quod de avifamento Concilii ñri, & affenfu Dominorum Spiritualium & Temporalium, ac confenfu Communitatis Regni ñri Anglie, in prefenti Parliamento ñro exiftentium, auctoritate ejufdem Parliamenti, volumus, ordinamus, & concedimus, quod nos deliberari & affignari faciemus per deputatum ñrum aut deputatos ñros dilectis & fidelibus noftris Henrico Dño Filzhugh, Waltero Hungreford, Waltero Beauchamp, Lodowico Robeffart, Willielmo Porter, & Roberto Babthorp, Militibus; ac Johanni Wodehous, & Johanni Leventhorp, Armigeris; Executoribus una cum aliis, in Teftamento cariffimi Dñi & Patris ñri Dñi H. nuper Regis Anglie defuncti nominatis; bona, catalla, & jocalia, ac pecuniarum fummas valorem Quadraginta Milium Marcarum attingentia de bonis, catallis, & jocalibus, ac denariorum fummis, que fuerunt prefati Patris ñri. Et quod iidem Henricus Dñus Filzhugh, Walterus, Walterus, Lodowicus, Willielmus, Robertus, Johannes, & Johannes, omnia & fingula eis in hac parte fic deliberand' & affignand' circa folutionem cujufdam fumme Decem & Novem Milium Marcarum, in quibus dictus Pater nofter, tempore obitus fui, illis qui Executores Teftamenti recolende memorie Dñi H. nuper Regis Anglie, Avi ñri fimiliter defuncti, nominati fuerunt, indebitatus fuit, pro certis bonis & catallis, que fuerunt ejufdem Avi ñri receptis, & penes ipfum Patrem ñrum retentis, quam aliarum fummarum pro expenfis hofpitii, ac neceffariis camere & garderobe ipfius Patris ñri, ac diverfarum fummarum fibi mutuatarum, & alias, in partem executionis & complementi ultime voluntatis prefati Patris ñri, per avifamentum, fupervifum, & contrarotulationem tam fupervifornm in dicto Teftamento p̄dicti Patris ñri nominatorum, quam cariffimi avunculi ñri Humfridi Ducis Glouceftr', & cariffimi confanguinei ñri Thome Ducis Exon', ac venerabilium patrum Henrici Wynton' confanguinei ñri cariffimi, & Thome Dunelmen'

Dunelmen' Cancellarii ñri, epifcoporum, feu deputatorum fuorum in hac parte, expendant, applicent, convertant, & fideliter adminiftrent, in quantum commode poterint, citra prox' Parliamentum ñrum exnunc tenend': Et quod ipfi, cum fuper hoc debite requifiti fuerint, fidelem compotum inde reddant prefatis fupervifioribus, ducibus & epifcopis, feu eorum deputatis, quodque Parliamento illo finito, deinceps ab ulteriori compoto five ratiocinio inde reddendo penitus exonerentur, ac adeo liberi fint & illefe conditionis, tam erga nos, quam prefatos fupervifores, duces & epifcopos, ac alios quofcumque, ficut ipfi aliquam receptionem, occupationem, folutionem, five adminiftrationem hujufmodi bonorum, catallorum, & jocalium, aut pecuniarum fummarum, eis fic affignatorum & liberatorum, fuper fe nufquam affumpfiffent. Volumus etiam, ac de avifamento, affenfu, confenfu, & auctoritate p̃dictis, ordinamus, concedimus, & ftatuimus, quod tam p̃dicti Henricus Dñus Filzhugh, Walterus, Walterus, Lodowicus, Willielmus, Robertus, Johannes, & Johannes, quam omnes alii Executores in Teftamentis p̃dictis nominati, ac eorum heredes, executores, attornati, fervientes, & deputati, de omnimodis placitis, querelis, actionibus, & demandis, per creditores tam dicti avi ñri, quam prefati patris ñri, aut alias feu aliam perfonas vel perfonam, verfus p̃dictos Henricum Dominum Filzhugh, Walterum, Walterum, Lodowicum, Willielmum, Robertum, Johannem, & Johannem, aut prefatos alios executores, in Teftamentis p̃dictis nominatos, heredes, executores, deputatos, attornatos, & fervientes, feu eorum aliquem, occafione adminiftrationis, occupationis, perceptionis, receptionis, folutionis, aut liberationis dictorum bonorum, catallorum, & jocalium, aut denariorum fummarum, eifdem Henrico Domino Filzhugh, Waltero, Waltero, Lodowico, Willielmo, Roberto, Johanni, & Johanni, fic affignand' vel liberand', feu alicujus parcelle eorumdem, profecutis aut motis, capiend', profequend', aut movend', in futur' quieti &

exoncrati

exonerati exiſtant imperpetuum, ac querentes & impſitantes, de oīni actione precluſibiles, & precluſi, in hac parte; et quod Cancellarius Anglie, aut cuſtos magni ſigilli ñri, vel heredum, aut ſucceſſorum noſtrorum, pro tempore exiſtens, auctoritate p̄dicta, fieri facere & liberare teneatur, tam prefatis Henrico Dño Filzhugh, Waltero, Waltero, Lodowico, Willielmo, Roberto, Johanni, & Johanni, quam dictis aliis executoribus, in teſtamentis p̄dictis nominatis, & eorum cuilibet, ac heredibus, executoribus, deputatis, attornatis, & ſervientibus ſuis, & cujuſlibet eorumdem, tot & talia brevia de ſuperſedeas, in quibuſcumque placitis & querelis, verſus ipſos, ſeu ipſorum aliquem, contra formam & effectum preſentium, motis vel movendis, quot & qualia, eis & eorum cuilibet, in hac parte fuerint neceſſaria, ſeu quomodolibet oportuna, aliquo ſtatuto in contrarium facto, ſeu alia cauſa quacumque non obſtante. In cujus &c.

Les queux Petition & Cedule leeuz en ceo meſme Parlement, & les matiers compriſez en ycelles bien entenduz, le Roi de l'aſſent & aviſement des Seigñrs Eſpirituelx & Temporelx eſteantz en le dit Parlement, & de l'aſſent auxi de les communes eſteantz en meſme, voet & ad ordeinee & grauntee toutz les articles, choſes, & maters contenuz en la cedule avauntdite, & q̃ lettres patentz du Roi ſoient ent faitz deſoutz ſon graunde ſeale en due fourme ſelonc l'effect & le tenure de meſme la cedule en toutz points, & ceo p̱ l'auctorite de ceſte Parlement.

N° IV. p. 243.

Rot. Pat. 3 H. VI. p. 2. m. 10. Rymer, vol. X. p. 346.

Super Liberatione diversis Franciæ ecclesiis, juxta Testamentum Henrici nuper Regis.

REX, omnibus ad quos, &c. Salutem. Sciatis quod cum dilectus Clericus noster, Magister Robertus Gilbert, nuper Decanus Capellæ carissimi Domini & Patris nostri Regis defuncti, per præceptum carissimi consanguinei nostri Ducis Exonie, & dilectorum & fidelium nostrorum Domini de Bourgchier, Walteri Hungerford, & Willielmi Porter, militum, ac Domini Fitz-Hugh jam defuncti, Executorum nominatorum in Testamento dicti Patris nostri, liberari fecerit diversis ecclesiis in partibus regni nostri Franciæ res & parcellas subscriptas, pro exonerationibus animæ dicti Patris nostri fiendis; videlicet,

Abbatiæ Sancti Dionisii unam Crucem argenteam deauratam, cum uno magno pede stante, ponderis viginti & octo librarum Troye;

Unam altam Frontellam [a], & unam bassam Frontellam, de velvet rubeas, cum foliis aureis brouderatas;

Unam Paruram [b] positam cum perreia [c] & armis Angliæ;

Tres Capas de velvet rubeas, cum rosis aureis, leonibus, & floribus de liciarum, brouderatas;

Duas Tunicas, & unam Casulam, de eisdem panno & colore.

Tres Albas cum Paruris, Stolis, & Favones [d] de eisdem panno & colore.

Et etiam unum par Curtinarum de tartryn rubearum.

[a] Frontel to the altar.  
[b] *Parure*, ornament.  
[c] *Pierrerie*, precious stones. Du Cange in voc.  
[d] Or *fanones*, banners. Id. in voc. *Favo* & *Fano*.

Item, apud Maunte, unum Veſtimentum aureum panni viridis, cum foliis aureis, & unam altam Frontellam cum una baſſa Frontella ejuſdem panni.

Item, apud Vernon, unum Veſtimentum ejuſdem panni viridis aurei.

Et ſimiliter apud Rothomagum, duos pannos blodei coloris, cum falconibus aureis, pro veſtimentis inde faciendis;

Et unum Pannum rubei coloris aureum pro orfrais inde faciendis.

Item, apud Offay, unum Pannum aureum, blodei coloris, cum falconibus & heronis.

Item, apud Arkes, unum Pannum aureum ejuſdem coloris.

Et conſimiliter apud Ewe, unum Pannum, blodei coloris, cum foliis aureis.

Item, apud Heſdyn, unum Pannum aureum rubei coloris, cum foliis aureis.

Et apud Tirewyn, unum Pannum aureum rubei coloris, cum foliis aureis.

Nos, de aſſenſu Concilii noſtri, conſideratione præmiſſorum, volumus quod præfatus Robertus de omnibus rebus & parcellis prædictis, per ipſum ut præmittitur liberatis, erga nos, hæredes & executores noſtros, in Scaccario noſtro ſeu alibi, quietus ſit & exoneratus imperpetuum per præſentes.

In cujus, &c.

  Teſte Rege, apud Weſtmonaſterium, xxviii die Junii.
    Per Breve de privato ſigillo.

# GLOSSARY.

## A.

ABBEYE *de Lysnes*, Lesne abbey at Erith in Kent, 107.
*Acordaunt come affiert*, as like as it can be made, 92.
*Adaquaria*, ewers, 195.
*Aderere*, tout du suite, Lacombe; in arrear, 124.
*Chescun person de l'afferant*, every one according to what he can afford, 159.
*Affiaunce*, confidence, 129.
*Affie*, confide, 164.
*Affres (averia)*, beasts, 34.
*Afforsaunt*, strengthening, 141.
*Aillours*, ailleurs, otherwise, 157.
*Alant, alen*, a dog, 157.
*Album.* See *Vestimentum*.
*Alder*, most dear, 315. Dr. Johnson explains *alderliveft* (Shakspeare, 2 H. VI.) by *most beloved*.
*Alme*, soul, 172.
*Almesdis the shipp*, q. the dish or bason for alms enameled with a ship, 284.
*Amaille, emaille*, enamelled, 24.
*Amenuser*, to diminish, 102.
*Amien, Amienx*, Amiens, 152.
*An (l') renoef darrein passiz, renuef, reneuef, renouvelle.* The last past, or the last new year, 156.

*Anees*, q. *anels*, rings, 100.
*Anel, Anelx*, rings, 106, 154.
*Angleseye*, Anglesey abbey, c. Cambridge, 110.
*Anthoneny (l')*, Lantony, Llanhodeni, or Lantonia prima, in Monmouthshire, 107.
*Anthony (priorie de l')*, Lantoni priory, 48.
*Anyntiz*, aneantie, undone, destroyed, 123.
*Aournementz*, ornaments, 85.
*Apper*, Q. *a prier*, 55.
*Aquaeris*, ewers, 325.
*Arare*, arrear; as *aderere*, 54.
*Arerissement*, backwarding, hinderance, 122.
*Arme*, army, 148.
*Assherugge*, Ashridge priory, c. Bucks, 71.
*Assize de perie*, set with stones, 105.
*Assize (feet of)*, statutable feet, 295.
*Atant*, autant, so much, 121.
*Attantz*, for as much, 122.
*Attry, artry*, q. artillery, 284. 288.
*Avaunt*, so far as, 136.
*Aveine*, venue, coming, 225.
*Augnell de perill*, ring, or perhaps angell, of pearl, 151.
*Auxint*, aussi, sometimes *ausinc*, 45.
*Aynx*, aisne, eldest, 158.

*Balois,*

## GLOSSARY.

### B.

*Balois,* a species of rubies of a vermeil rose colour. Chambers's Dict. 71.
*Barrez,* bars, 99.
*Baryngton,* Barrington, 377.
*Baſſinet,* basnet, helmet, 221.
*Baudik,* belt, 113.
*Baukyn, Baldekynus,* pannus omnium ditiſſimus, of silk and gold thread. Du C. 179.
*Bayes,* Q. daies, 302.
*Beache,* Waterbeach, 377.
*Beauval en Shirwode,* a house of Carthusians, founded by Nich. de Cantilupe, 218.
*Bedhampton,* in Hants, 214.
*Bedridyn,* bedridden, 226.
*Benegerer,* q. *Bignor,* in Arundel rape, 131.
*Benoit' ove eſperge,* holy water-pot, with a sprinkler, 25.
*Berdefelde,* Q. Berdwell, c. Suffolk, 33.
*Berford Seynt Martin,* Bereford St. Martin, c. Wilts. 285.
*Bernoldſwyk,* Barnoldsweek in Stancliffe hundred, in the West Riding of Yorkshire, 151.
*Bervynes, babeines,* levres de certains animaux. Lacombe. q. faces or heads, 132.
*Bien poy,* very near, 127.
*Blakeberwe,* Blackborough priory, c. Norf. 257.
*Blendeworth,* in Hampshire, 213.
*Blodio & viridi colore enamalet',* enameled with red and green, 89.
*Blodius,* color sanguineus. Du C. blue, 253.
*Bloy,* blue, 219.
*Bobaunce, bobans, bobanité,* ſumptuoſité. Lacombe. extravagance, 84. 121.
*Bodekeſham,* Q. Botteſham, c. Cambridge, 33.
*Boten,* a button, 284.
*Bremmesfeld,* Brimsfield, c. Glouc. 89.
*Brigaudiers,* brigandine, a fashion of ancient armour, consisting of many jointed and scale-like plates, pliant and easy for the body. Cotgrave. 221.
*Brondatum,* embroidered, 88. 272.
*Bruggerak,* Brigerak, a town in Gaſcoigne, 83.
*Brugwater,* Bridgewater, 110.
*Brune,* Bourne in Lincolnshire, 118.
*Bruſkyn; bruſq* is old French for green, 37.
*Bruſyerd,* Bruſyard, c. Suffolk, 111.
*Buretis,* Du Cange refers from *buretum* to *bruneta,* which he explains a species of money uſed in Italy during part of the 12th century. Sed q. if it has that ſenſe here? 273.
*Buiſſeaux,* bushels, 35.
*Burbon,* Bourbon, 230.
*Buris,* Berry, 229.
*Burnham,* or Nun-Burnham, a small Benedictine nunnery in Yorkshire, 227.
*Buſteleſham Mountagu,* Biſham abbey, founded by William Montacute earl of Salisbury, 98.

### C.

*Caen (noneynes de)* nuns of Caen, 50.
*Cameca, camoka, camuca, camucum, camaca, pannus de comoca, vell camocas,* ſo often mentioned in antient wills, is explained by Du Cange as a kind of rich ſtuff or silk, 25. 150.
*Cantirbirs,*

# GLOSSARY.

*Cantirbirs*, Canterbury, 135.
*Capæ*. See *Vestimentum*.
*Capicium, capuce*, hood, 147.
*Capitz*, tester, 72.
*Cariant illocques*, carrying thither, 218.
*Carves*, carts, whence *carvage*, 34.
*Casula*. See *Vestimentum*.
*Celure*, coverlet. Kelham. Q. if not rather *teaster* from *ciel*, 73.
*Cercliis* (circulis), circles, 195.
*Cest'*, f. *sept* for *septiesme*, 177.
*Chambre toute entiere*, the furniture of the chamber, 112.
*Champ (le) piers overez*, the field partly wrought, 157.
*Chansure pur les moignes*, q. song-money, or allowance for singing masters, 26.
*Chaperon de fere*, iron scull-cap or morion, 221.
*Chargeours*, chargers, 24.
*Charlton*, there are two places of this name in Sussex, in the rapes of Bramber and Chichester, 213.
*Charthous de Londres*, Charter-house or Carthusians, 218.
*Chasez*, chased, 227.
*Chater*, acheter, to buy, 226.
*Chateux*, chattels, 121.
*Chekere*, F. chequer'd, 25.
*Chirbury (priorie de)*, priory of Black canons at Snede, 108.
*Chirpelere (meson de)*, Q. Chipley, a priory of Austin canons in Suffolk, 52.
*Christianissimus princeps*, a title long claimed by the kings of France, and given to our Henry VI, in compliment to his piety, 252.
*Cixtes*. Q. *cistes*, little boxes, 72.
*Clanfeld*, in Hampshire, 213.
*Clere memoir (de)*, of famous memory, 161.

*Clifford en Gales* a Cluniac priory in Herefordshire, 111.
*Clyderhow*, Clitherow in Lancashire, 237.
*Coellers, Coillers*, spoons, 100. 112.
*Coers*, hearts. Dugdale translates it cover, 134.
*Coler*, collar, 155.
*Combien que de present ne cognoisse nulle en especiale meintenaines*, though at present I know of none in special maintenance, 148.
*Coes (les) de la ville*, les communs de la ville, 84.
*Colham*, Q. *Copham*, 372.
*Comhir*, Cumhyre, a Cistertian abbey in Radnorshire, 110.
*Compas*, 219. Q. if a circle.
*Compasse*, circle, 155.
*Computatorio*, compter, 328.
*Conning*, knowledge, 293.
*Contra ioustee*, contradiction, 139.
*Coronne*, coronet, 139.
*Coronacioun en la summite d'un petite tablet d'or*, 134. Q. a representation of some coronation of the Virgin or other person.
*Corporas caas*, corporax case, or case for the pix, 251.
*Costeles*, Q. costly, 30.
*Costages*, cost, expenses, 46.
*Costies, costes, costers*, side pieces, 70. 234.
*Covere*, q. corners, 178.
*Cov'ture*, coverlet, 72.
*Coungie*, congé, leave, 170.
*Crabhows*, or Wigenhale, in Norfolk, an Austin nunnery, 257.
*Crokeston*, Crux Easton, 261.
*Croys Roys*, Roisia's cross, the Austin priory at Royston, founded by Roisia de Vere, 110.

*Cunatum*,

*Cunatum*, coined, 266.
*Cunnyng*, knowledge, 360.
*Cureez (le) dite eglise aient n're melior chivall ou le prix en nom de principal,* the curates of that church to have our best horse, or his value, in the name of the principal, 84.
*Cursarii,* coursers, 262.

### D.

*D'alisaundre,* of Alexandria, 114.
*Dalmatica.* See *Vestimentum.*
*Dameiux (a),* q. *ad Amieux,* at Amiens, 151.
*Damortiez,* amortize, 93.
*Darreinere,* dernier, 38.
*Darreynement,* lately, 128.
*Dassher (ove un),* with a sprinkler, 106.
*D'autre part,* on the other side, 83.
*Decovrez,* uncovered, 158.
*D'egles,* with eagles, 74.
*Debues,* due, 74.
*Dedeinz, deinz, da deinz, de dedans de,* within, 34. 146. 227.
*Deliberacio,* delivery, 89.
*Demeore, demorance, demoree, demeorge,* delay, 98.
*Demoerant,* remainder, 93.
*Demy gros,* half groats, 218.
*Deosculatorium pacis,* a pax to put the host in, 324.
*Depden,* Debden, 184.
*Dertyngton,* Q. Dartington, c. Devon.
*Desaise,* Q. disease, illness, 183.
*Destrez, destriers,* horses, 68.
*Desyve,* decease, 180.
*D'evelyn,* Dublin, 116.
*Devie,* die, 113. decease, 233.
*Devions, devier,* or *devoyer,* to die; 83.

*Devoir,* duty, ceremony, 224.
*Diffinitor,* or definitor, the visitor of the order in general chapter, 250.
*Diploidem,* doublet, 263.
*Ditesworth,* Diseworth, 377.
*Dissipacio,* spending, 89.
*Donwiz,* Dunwich, 33.
*Door,* d'or, of gold, 30.
*D'orge et draget,* monk, meslin, or mixt corn, 34.
*Dorra,* shall give, 126.
*Dossier,* back piece, 74.
*Dossier (un), et huyt pieces pur les costs et dieux banqueres,* a back piece, and eight pieces for the sides and two benches, 69.
*Donne,* donnez, given, 123.
*Doune en charge,* give in charge, 146.
*Doutant,* q. *redoutanz,* fearing, 178.
*Draget, dragere,* meslin, mixtcorn, 35.
*Drapest,* Q. *d'aprest,* loans, 37.
*Duytee, duitz,* duty, obligation, 138.
*Dymenge,* Dimanche, Sunday, 44.
*Dynde,* blue, 51.

### E.

*Eez,* Essex, 44.
*Effeffez,* feoffees, 172.
*Ebu,* eu, had, 148.
*Eident,* aiding, 101.
*Ely (measoun de)* the Benedictine priory at Ely, 135.
*Emprendre,* borrow, 109.
*Empriaunt,* praying or requesting, 126.
*Enbeseiller,* q. embezzle, 155.
*Enaseres,* hereafter, 106.
*En busoigne,* be necessary, 165.
*Encouvertre,* to cover, clothes, 226.
*Ency,* ainsi, 230.

*En*

# GLOSSARY.

*En greyn*, in grain, 37.
*Enguerdonnent*, reward, 74.
*Enhanced*, raised, 303.
*En mye le quer*, in the middle of the choir, 217.
*Ennorez*, gilded, 121.
*Enseßiblement*, ensemblement, together, 35.
*Ent*, thereon, 162.
*Entour*, entre, among, 220.
*Epitumum, Epitimium*, 2. a field of battle, a term peculiar to Ordericus Vitalis.
*Erge*, orge, barley, 35.
*Escheiez*, eschus, escheated, 131.
*Eschette*, q. *escheque*, chequered, 156.
*Esmon*, Edmund, 100, 113.
*Especial choistre*, of especial choice or succession, 178.
*Epeie*, sword, 112.
*Esploitable*, profitable, 127.
*Espois*, pois, pease, 36.
*Esportable*, q. *esploitable*, profitable, 121.
*Esqueles*, poringers, 24.
*Estatut merchant*. A bond of record, acknowledged by the *clerk of the statutes merchant* and the lord mayor of the city of London, or two merchants assigned for that purpose; and before the mayors of other cities and towns, or the bailiff of any borough, &c. 104.
*Estelle*, estoile, a star, 114.
*Estlinges*, sterling, 70.
*Estoise*, subject, *estoiser a la ley*, subir à la loi, 37.
*Estoisent*, *estoier*, to stand to, to abide. Kelham. 75.
*Estoor*, store, 121.
*Estore, estovoir*, necessity; estoyer, *estre*, 45.
*Estrange de jent*, de gent estrange, of strange people, 121.

*Estre*, propre, own, 55.
*Estre ce*, *estre ceo*, besides this, 94.
*Estrille*, or *etrille*, a currycomb, 227.
*Eues*, had, 38.
*Ewerot*, Q. a little ewer, 27.
*Exequiis ix. li. (cum)*, sic orig. 327.
*Exploitez*, expended, 127.

## F.

*Faiz*, made, *i. e.* work, 151.
*Fanon*, manipule, towel, 71.
*Farlyngton*, q. Farringdon, c. Hants, 213.
*Favones*, or *Fanones*, banners, 415.
*Feez*, fees, wages, 135.
*Ferniculs, fermilet*, clasp, buckle, 154.
*Ferures*, fetter-locks, 155.
*Feur et paille*. Lacombe makes *feur* synonymous with *paille*, elsewhere, hay, forage, 34.
*Feurer, fuere*, artisan, ouvrier, 53. It is not easy to explain the office of the several domestics, such as *Ferour, Hastiler*, &c. 53.
*Fesaunce d'ecestes (a la)*, at the making of these, 133.
*Fiertre, fierte*, feretory, shrine, 32.
*Finols, finials*, a term of Gothic architecture for the little ornaments that terminate pinnacles, 47. 302.
*Firmayl*, chain, 100.
*Flounce*, rim, 182.
*Foer a, al foer*, in the shape of, 133.
*Foill*, q. breadth, from feuille, 181.
*Forcell*, q. strong box. *Forcerett* or *forchiere*, is explained by Lacombe petit coffre, 139.
*Forneeette*, Forncet in Deepwade hundred, Norfolk, 268.
*Founce*, fond, bottom, 114.
*Frontella*, frontel to the altar, 415.

*Gaddesden*,

# GLOSSARY.

## G.

*Gaddesden*, Great Gaddesden, Hertfordshire, 283.
*Galoniers*, of gallon measure, 325.
*Garenne*, Warren, 37. 69.
*Gartiers, lokers, & faucons*, garters, fetter-locks, and falcons, the badges of the house of York, 219.
*Gaudes*, trinkets, gawdies, 5. 160. 180.
*Gaudes de get*, trinkets of jet.
*Gemelex*, double, or pair of, 108.
*Gerfacon'*, Gerfalcon, a courser, 88.
*Gesier*, to lye, 44.
*Gesnie, gesine*, l'etat d'une femme en couche, 115. See *Jhazen*.
*Gessine*, le ceremonie et le festin des relevailles, 115. See *Jhazen*.
*Gipwy*, Ipswich, 33.
*Godet*, a mug, cup, 24.
*Goleclyve*, Goldcliff in Monmouthshire, 110.
*Goryng*, a small Austin priory of nuns in Oxfordshire, 227.
*Graunts*, q. large beads, 180.
*Grauntz de n're saunk*, great people of our blood or lineage, 84.
*Gre*, allowance, 54.
*Greces*, steps (*gressus*), 297.
*Greindre*, plus grande, largest, 38, 108.
*Guerdon*, guerdon, reward, 75.
*Guerdoner*, to reward, 85.

## H.

*Habergeon*, a coat of mail, 181, *ove un crois de laton merchie sur le pis encontre le cuer*, with a cross of Latin markt or wrought on the spot opposite to the heart (of the wearer).
*Haberjon*, habergeon, coat of mail, 221.
*Halton*, in Cheshire, 237.
*Hamound (l' abbey de)*, the abbey of Haghmond, c. Salop, 127.
*Hanap'*, coupe à boire, cup, 24.
*Have do*, have done, 291.
*Heenton jouste Bathe*, Hinton; a foundation for Carthusians by Ela countess of Salisbury, 218.
*Henxmen*, henchmen, 220. * This is an old English word for a *page* or *equerry*, derived from the Saxon hengert, a *horse*. Spelman. *Hanchman*, in the Highlands of Scotland, is a close attendant on a chief in quality of secretary or servant, from *hanch*, quasi *qui claudit latus*. See Letters from the North of Scotland, II. 156.
*Herce*, herse, or frame of wood-work to put over the body while it lay in state, 45, 68.
*Herce de cire*, a curious hearse of wax in a small proportion placed upon it, 225.
*H'noise, harnoise*, mounted, 24.
*Hernoise*, furniture, 31.
*Heynstigge*, Henstridge, c. Somerset, 340.
*Hogynton*, Q. Oakingham, 377.
*Holi-water stoppe*, vessel for holy-water, 253.
*Hopolande, hopelande, hopulandes, houpelands*, long cloaks. L. 220. 225.
*Hosbandre*, of husbandry, 214.
*Hostel*, house, 131.
*Hou mont*, the black Prince's motto, in German signifies a *haughty spirit*, 67.
*Housell, houces*, housings, 221.
*Huche*. Lacombe explains this word *couvrechef, voile, coffre, coeffe*. Here it means a pall over an empty coffin representing the real one, 45.

*Hugucion*,

# GLOSSARY.

*Hugucion*, Hugutio or Hugh de Vercellis bishop of Ferrara, a great writer on the Decretals, 31.
*Hurlle (priorie de)*, Hurley priory, c. Hants, 49.
*Huykes*, q. if not *huque*, a huke, or Dutch mantle, 220.

## I.

*Jernem'*, Yarmouth, 33.
*Jhazen*, une nouvelle accouchée. Laccombe. q. the labour or the purification of our Lady. 115. See *Gessnie* and *Gessine*.
*Illoeq'*, there, 32.
*Joefne, joene*, jeune, young, 35.
*Joeux des enfantz*, jeux des enfans, childrens sports, 112.
*Joust (juxta)*, near, 171.
*Isoit*, should be, 93.
*Issint*, ainsi, so, 84.

## K.

*Katryngton*, Katherington, in Hampshire, 213.
*Knesworth*, Kneesworth, c. Cambridge, 377.

## L.

*Lanternan*, Llantarnan in Monmouthshire, 110.
*Laynes*, q. wool, 121.
*Lee*, broad, 26.
*Leger*, slightly, 136.
*Lerra morir*, shall die, 101.
*Lesse morir*, Kelham has *se lerra mourir*, shall die, 224.
*Lessez*, omitted, 166.
*Leteing*, letting, hindering, 317.

*Lettron*, q. *lettrin*, catafalque, 152.
*Leve de latoun suzorrex*, i. e. washed over with Latyn, &c. 67.
*Leu*, Q. l'on, 67.
*Linges*, Q. sheets, 84.
*Lintaux*, sheets, 72.
*Lit estandard*, q. a *standing* bed, or one whose tester rested on pillars, 131.
*Lite*, lit, 154.
*Litel veleuid*, little or not at all rewarded, 279.
*Long*, along, 299.
*Lonquets*, q. wild vine-branches. *Langos*, les coursons de la vigne. 180.
*Lore, lors*, then, 159.
*Luminour*, administrateur ou marguillier de l'eglise. Laccombe. Q. chaplain, or chapel-clerk, 50.
*Lyncheux*, sheets, 100.
*Lyngbrok'*, a priory of Austin nuns on the river Lug in Herefordshire, 99.

## M.

*Maes, mais*, pas, excepté, plus, dès que. but, only, 120.
*Male talent*, resentment, 147.
*Malison*, or *malichon*, malediction, 75.
*Malketon*. Malton. This is a decayed parish now included in that of Orwell, where the church, antiently a rectory, still remains in ruins. The rectory of Orwell belongs to Trinity College, Cambridge, 377.
*Manberer*, Manûrbûr, c. Pembroke, 378.
*Manere (en) d'une cheon*, in the shape of a dog, 112.

*Manipulus.* See *Vestimentum.*
*Mannerbier,* Mannûrbûr, c. Pembroke, 285.
*Marcher, marquer,* to mark, 76.
*Marches de terre* or *marche,* land valued at one mark, 113.
*Maser.* Lacombe explains *mazer* the material of which were made drinking vessels, thence called *mazelins, mazesins,* or *mazetins:* and Kelham explains *hanap de mazer,* a bowl made of mazer. Du Cange says, *mazer, mazerinus, maza'um, mazdrinum,* are the name of precious cups; of what material he does not determine, but inclines to think them the *pocula murrhina* of the antients, called in later writers, *hanaps de madre:* and then they will be made of precious stones, which, from the many instances of their being mounted in silver, recited by Dugdale, is much more probable than that they were of *maple wood,* as Somner thought.— And in some other instances, the material is put for the vessel, 25. 142
*Massez,* q. *masles,* male; or rather massive, 139.
*Materat',* mattrass, 79.
*Materes,* matters, 141.
*Meignalx,* menial, 219.
*Meigne,* houshold, 98.
*Meignee,* famille, menage, 38.
*Melreth,* Meldreth, c. Cambridge, 377.
*Melx,* mieux, best, 121.
*Meorne,* Q. *meorge,* die, 224.
*Merchez,* marques, marked, 182.
*Mermyns de mier,* mermaids of the sea, 73.
*Mesnez,* remaining, 102.

*Messalx,* missals, 153.
*Mialty, mialtz, mieultz, multz,* best, 154.
*Miden',* Meath, 90.
*Miegnals,* menials, 116.
*Mieltz,* mieux, 41.
*M l'res de perles,* Dugdale translates this a thousand pearls, 30.
*Mixtilon,* monk, meslin, or mixt corn, 34.
*Molets,* mullets, 181.
*Monstre,* q. for montee, set forth, or amounting, 112.
*Mors,* f. morceau, 24.
*Mort estor',* dead stock or store, 34.
*Mortiers,* lamps, 84.
*Moun aun doun,* my new-year's gift, 129.
*Multz, mialtz, mieultz, multz,* best, 154.

## N.

*Naturelx,* kind, 134.
*Naturesse,* kindness, 221.
*Navenby,* Naumby, c. Lincoln, 378.
*Nichol, Nichole,* Lincoln, 42. 83.
*Nief pur encens,* ship for incense, 31.
*Nient,* not, 102.
*Noche, ouch,* or *nouche,* a gold stud, or setting for jewels, 50.
*Noir traille,* q. black lattice work, 155.
*Noneignes,* nuns, 153.
*Noneynes de Caam,* nuns of Caen, 50.
*Nones beside Stamford.* 381. A Benedictine Nunnery in Stamford-Baron, founded by an abbot of Peterborough, 6 Henry II. greatly reduced at the dissolution, when the site was granted to Richard Cecil.

*Notele*

## GLOSSARY.                                425

*Notele (priorie de)*, Notley abbey, c. Bucks, 49.
*Nounchalure*, indifference, 147.

### O.

*O*, f. *ove*, with, 234.
*Oeps*, use, work, 30. 69.
*Oevres*, oeuvres, works, 146.
*Olla & lilio* All the representations of the Salutation introduce a *lily* in the angel's hand, and a *flower-pot* on the floor between him and the angel; the latter may be only a piece of furniture, the former answers to a caduceus or palm-branch, 324.
*Or de Cipre*, gold of Cyprus, Cyprus work, 179.
*Ordenns*, 148. commands.
*Oreford*, Orford, 33.
*Orphareis*, fringes of gold, 254. 272.
*Os*, a bone, 106.
*Ov'eigne leve de latoun fuzorrez*, work in relief of copper gilt, 67.
*Overaigne*, work, 32.
*Ovrage*, work or pattern, 151.
*Oustell*, maison. L. houshold, 133.
*Oustez, ostes*, taken from, 130.
*Owelment*, equally, 130.

### P.

*Paane, pane*, parcel, skirt, 35.
*Palorz*, paled, 107.
*Pance*, q. belly-piece, from *pance*, gros ventre. L. *pance*, a great-bellied doublet. Cotgrave, 221.
*Pane*, side, 300.
*Paone*, purple, 25.
*Papejayes*, popinjays, parrots, 35.
*Paramont la tombe*, on the top of the tomb, 67.
——— *les stallez*, above the stalls, 70.
*Parentre*, q. among, 127.
*Parochiell*, to the parish, 145.
*Patens*, the paten, 152.
*Pauleatum*, paled, 88.
*Paxbred*, the same as *corporas caas*, 282.
*Pennally*, Penaly, c. Pembroke, 287.
*Pepyrying*, Peppering in Arundell rape, 124.
*Perceive*, i. e. receive, 294.
*Pere*, piere, stone, 217.
*Perfaire*, finish, 85.
*Perie (ove)*, with stones. Dugdale not understanding it leaves a blank, 114.
*Perill*, q. *perle*, 151.
*Perount, peront*, wherefore. K. whereby, 122.
*Perriea*, 415.  } q. pierres, pre-
*Perrie*, 25. 106. } cious stones.
*Piers*, partly, parcel, 149.
*Piert*, appears, 122.
*Pipes*, q. pipes or tuns, or staves: Lacombe gives both these senses, 149.
*Pitea grante*, quære, *ptie*, i. e. *partie grante*, in part granted, 93.
*Plain, plein*, full, 214.
*Plasmator*, maker, 321.
*Playn*, full, 375.
*Plomstede*, probably Plumstead in Kent, 103.
*Ponder' (cum)*, quere, according to their full weight, 327.
*Ponsonez*, pinkt, 180.
*Pootz*, pots, 24.
*Popynsayes*, parrots, 284.
*Port (le quel) mon mesnes desus moy ensmble*, which I wear myself about me, 154.
*Portehors*, portiforium, with which the French word is synonymous, 71.
*Portiforium melius meum notatum*,

my best portiforium with musical notes, 88.
*Poffeffion*, q. *profeffion*, 112.
*Poffeffioners*, q. housekeepers, 40.
*Paft com*. post communionem, a part of the service of the church, 180.
*Povres naifs de mes manoirs*, poor servants born on my estates, 94.
*Potager*, officier qui a soin du potage du Roi, 52.
*Potellers*, q. of *pint* measure. Du Cange explains *olla potteller* a porringer, 325.
*Pounfonnez*, striped and spotted, or sprinkled, 227.
*Pounts et caufes*, bridges and causeways, 41.
*Pour*, power, 75.
*Prebenda*, a portion: a feed, when applied to horses, 325.
*Primer*, Q. aforementioned, 293.
*Prioratus de Sion apud Shene*, the priory of *Jefus* of Bethlem, for 40 Carthusian monks, c. Surrey, 252.
*Premiez*, q. proviez, provided, 217.
*Pro Deo pofuit*, quære, bound himself before God, 252.
*Profcheinement*, next, from *profchain*, 105.
*Pur nul mifchiefs*, to prevent prejudice being done to them; or, on no account, 69.
*Pur fopur*, for supper, 129.

## Q.

*Qar*, car, for, L. 127.
*Q. erex*, Q. quarres, 51.
*Qe eftre*, f. *jeo eftre*, I will, 187.
*Quadrant*, quadrangle, 301.
*Quaremele*, Lent, 34.
*Quillers*, Q. esquiles, bells, 25. *Cuilier*, a spoon or ladle. *Howell*.
*Quillies*, receuillez, 53.
*Quilte*. This is not a modern French word, and yet occurs not in old glossaries, 74.
*Quir*, cuir, 31.
*Quiffins*, cushions, 72.
*Quyre*, *cuir*, leather, 134.

## R.

*De Radicibus auri*. See *Orphareis*.
*Raffata*, q. Taffeta, 32.
*Rebatement*, abatement, 149.
*Rebatuz*, abated, 132.
*Recommiffos, commendatos*, recomended, 273.
*Recreant*, craving, 224.
*Regardes*, rewards, fees, salaries, 148.
*Regardia*, rewards, 247.
*Regardum*, reward, 329.
*Reguerdonez*, rewarded, 116.
*Rere doffe at the high altar*, screen at the back of the high altar, 297. 302.
*Refpondes*, q. parallel correspondent walls or sides, 295.
*Refones d'averell*, 182.
*Retrettz*, withdrawn, 123.
*Ridell*, curtains, 253.
*Riems, rien*: in old French this word has a positive sense, and means *any thing*, 45.
*Rimeie*, poetry, 181.
*Robertefbrugge*, Robertsbridge abbey in Sussex, 135.
*Roeis*, Royston, 32.
*Roffe*, rose, 101.

## S.

*Sadde*, sober, 368.
*Salaria, Saleria*, salt-sellars. This English word is a redundancy; Salerium, Saleire, implying the same as *fellar*, in one word. 325.

*Sale*,

# GLOSSARY.

*Sale*, seems to be used for the *hangings* of a hall, 72. 128.
*Saler*, salt-seller, 24. 112.
*Samyt*, fine stuff or linen, 31.
*Stens, sens*, senses, 147.
*Schapewyk*, Shapwick, c. Somerset, 131.
*Seele entier*, whole tester, distinguished from half tester, 132.
*Seint Esmon*, q. *St. Edmond's*, scil. Bury, 32.
*Seint Marie*, Lincoln minster, or cathedral, dedicated to the Virgin Mary, 152.
*Semail*, seed corn, 34.
*Semblably*, in like manner, 316.
*Sen lac*, or *Sang Lac*, the spot where the decisive battle was fought between Harold and William, 2.
*Sepulchre*, 155. The sepulchre of our Lord, which was on the N. side of the altar in many churches. See a curious description of it at Northwold in Norfolk. Blomef. I. 157, who refers to others in the churches of Hurstmonceaux, c. Sussex, and Stepney. See also Ib. p. 487.
*Sensures*, censers, 220.
*Serveieur*, supervisor, 227.
*Serverve*, supervisaunce, 105.
*Et ad le Surveue de toutz terriens faitz & pensez pur quelx il rendra guerdon a chescun solom son desert*, and has the over-sight of all earthly deeds and thoughts, for which he will render a reward to every one according to his deserts, 166.
*Qi si ele soy seut d'avoir autre marry*, q. *seure*, sure; or perhaps *sente*, if she should be *inclined* to marry again, 130.

*Sevelier, ensevelir*, 92.
*Seweth*, q. following, 308.
*Seyn, cloche*, bell, 25.
*Seynt*, girt, or *ceint*, a bell. K. 106.
*Soeffre*, suffer, 75.
*Solers, souliers*, shoes, 178.
*Solom l'affairement*, in proportion, or what it will make, 127.
*Soudre, souder, surder*, to arise. Kelham, 74.
*Soucstoke*, q. Southwick in Bramber rape, 124.
*Soulez, solz*, or *souz*, pence, 116.
*South priour*, q. *soubs priour*, sub prior, 99.
*Stanndon*, Standon, c. Herts, 33.
*Stevynton*, Q. c. Bedford, 283.
*Stokes*. There were three religious houses of this name. Stoke Cursey, c. Devon; another in c. Somerset; and the college in Suffolk, 110.
*Stola*. See *Vestimentum*.
*Stop (un)*, a holy water *stoup* or vessel, 106. 253.
*Straite*, strict, 317.
*Stratford* at Bow, a Benedictine nunnery, as old as the Conquest, 226.
*Suages*, q. *servages*, services, 129.
*Subirs*, Sudbury, 33.
*Suelleshales jouste Whaddon*, Snelleshall in Whaddon parish, 111.
*Sullyngton*, q. Sulton in Arundel rape, 131.
*Surorre, surdorre*, gilt, 24.
*Surveoirs*, supervisor, 227.
*Sutton de Bonyngton*. 377. The Villare places Sutton Bonington in Northamptonshire; but it is not in Ecton.

4 T.

## GLOSSARY.

### T.

*Tache*, faftened, *attache*; *tache* in old French and Spanifh is a nail, 31.
*Tantq'*, unto, until, 68.
*Taffiæ*, *taffes*, cups, 326.
*Ten'tz*, tenements, 148.
*Terrien*, earthly, 164.
*Tertaryn*, Tattarian, 182.
*Textes*, woven, 149.
*Tilteye*, an abbey of White monks in Effex, 110.
*Torcenous*, wrongful, 39.
*Tortelez*, wreathed work, 114. Dugdale tranflates it of a *tortois*, (Bar. I. 150).
*Tottyngton*. Tottington. There is a place of this name both in Arundel and Bramber rape, 124.
*Trav'fin*, *traverfin*, crofs-piece, 73.
*Treftouts*, all; in the fulleft fenfe of the word; all and every, 149.
*Tripere*, tripod, 114.
*Triftram*, a romance of that name, 254.
*Troiano (pondere)* Troy weight, 326. None of the Gloffaries give a fatisfactory etymology of this word. Spelman and Du Cange after him content themfelves with faying that *Trojæ pondus apud Anglos dicitur quod 12 uncias in libra numerat*. Somner fuppofes it the fame with *Trona* or *Trone* in Scotland, but the authorities alledged prove the latter to be only the weighing engine and not the weight.
*Truffe*, found, K. fed q. 128.
*Tuelie*, *tuyau*, *conduit*, pipe, 24.
*Tyrteyne*, 25. *forte de mauvaife etoffe qui a pris fon nom de Tyre, et dont on habille la milice*. Laccombe.

### V.

*Vadlet*, valet, 116.
*Velveto defenfinum (de)*, q. faced with velvet? 263.
*Vernicie*. q. a Veronica, 152.
*Uerwyk*, York, 232.
*Veftement*, furniture, 149.
*Veftes*, *veffes*, vetches, 36.
*Veftes de aras*, q. garments of arras, 195.
*Veftimentum*, 251. a whole fuit of church apparel, comprehendi g the *cafula*, or cowl; the *dalmatica*, or upper robe; the *alba*, or albe, a kind of furplice; the *amictus* or amice, anfwering to the fcarf; the *ftola*, which, like the amice, went over the neck, and hung down before, and was richly embroidered; the *manipulus*, or handkerchief, worn over the left arm; the towels or napkins for the altar, which had alfo an altar-cloth of linen, and another to hang down in front of the altar, the frontlet and curtains, the cafe for the pix, the pulpit cloth, and the *capæ* or copes.
*Vadiis*, wages, 336.
*Ulture*, quære Ulfter, 111.
*Ulveftier*, Ulfter, 34.
*Unc*, *oncques*, by no means, 84.
*Ungore*, encore, 85.
*Voine*, vain, 84.
*Voifent*, q. fhall walk before our Lady, 68.
*Upmerdon*, Upper Merden in Chichefter rape, 124.
*Urceoli*, pots, 324.
*Ufqe*, Vfk, or Cairufk in Monmouthfhire, 108.
*Ufque*, verfus, 196.

# GLOSSARY.

### W.

*Waltham, manerium de,* a stately palace of the bishop of Winchester in Hampshire, demolished during the civil wars, 339.
*Wallyng encountre le mer,* sea walls, 135.
*Warbyngton,* Warbleton, 213.
*Warnecamp,* quære *Warnham* in Bramber rape, 124.
*Waſſaill,* waſſell or grace-cup. A corrupt pronunciation of *waes hael,* be of health, 115.
*Witham, Wytham en Selwode,* a Carthuſian monaſtery in Selwood, c. Somerſet, 218. 331.
*Wodehous,* near Clebury Mortimer, c. Salop, 110.
*Wormyngey,* Wormegay, a priory of black canons in Norfolk, 253. 257.
*Woxbrig,* Uxbrig, 372.

### Y.

*Yeovil, Yevil, Evill,* in Somerſetſhire, 137.
*Ymage (un) de la incarnacioun de notre dame,* a picture of the incarnation of the Virgin Mary, 133.
*Ynde,* blue, 25. 115.
*Yverne en,* in winter, 129.
*Yvele,* q. Ewell vicarage, Surry, 137.

## DOUBTFUL WORDS.

*Accuby,* 182. accubes, reſting-places, Howel; lits, Borel.
*Anal,* 182. q. *amail,* enamel.
*Ariez,* 182.
*Avanteres,* 227. q. avant hier, formerly.
*Averill,* 182.
*Avis.* 183. q. *a vie,* for en vie, in his life.
*Batuz.* 105.
*Beal,* 182. q. *bel,* handſome.
*Bittiz,* 132.
Chare roff'd, 302.
*Eſpiner,* 182.
*Ferour,* 53. q. blackſmith.
*Haſtiler,* 53. q. ſpearman or ſpearmaker.
*Parkes,* 114. *perk* is uſed in Blomfield for a *pedeſtal.*
*Plonket,* 100.
*Raille,* 149.

## ERRATUM.

P. 120. r. note, Elizabeth daughter of William de Bohun earl of Northampton.

# NEW BOOKS lately printed by and for J. NICHOLS.

British Topography, or an Historical Account of what has been done for illustrating the Topographical Antiquities of Great Britain and Ireland. In two volumes, quarto. Price Two Guineas and a Half in boards.

The History of the Town of Thetford, in the Counties of Norfolk and Suffolk, from the earliest accounts to the present time. By the late Mr. Thomas Martin, of Palgrave, Suffolk, F. A. S. Quarto. Price in boards 1l. 4s.

Medals, Coins, Great Seals, and other Works of Thomas Simon; engraved and described by George Vertue. The second edition, with additional plates and notes, and an appendix by the editor. Quarto. Price one guinea in boards.

The Connexion of the Roman, Saxon, and English Coins; deducing the antiquities, customs, and manners of each people to modern times, particularly the origin of feudal tenures, and of Parliaments. Illustrated throughout with critical and historical remarks on various authors, both sacred and prophane. By W. Clarke, A. M. Chancellor of the Church of Chichester. Quarto. Price one guinea in boards.

Mr. Pegge on the Coins of Cunobelin. 4to. Price 5s. sewed.

Four new editions of the Supplement to Swift's Works; with explanatory notes on all the former volumes, and an Index, by J. Nichols. In quarto, large octavo, small octavo, and 18mo.

Russia: Or, a Complete Historical Account of all the Nations which compose that Empire. Two volumes, octavo, price 10s. 6d. in boards.

Hymns to the Supreme Being: In imitation of the Eastern Songs. Octavo. Price 3s. 6d. in boards.

A complete and elegant Edition of the English Poets, in sixty volumes, with Prefaces biographical and critical to each Author, by Samuel Johnson, LL.D.

A Select Collection of Poems, with Notes Biographical and Historical by J. Nichols. Four volumes, small octavo, adorned with four portraits by Kneller, Lely, &c. Price 10s. 6d. in boards.—Four more volumes are in the press.

The Original Works of William King, LL.D. Advocate of Doctors Commons, &c. with Memoirs of the Author and Historical Notes, by J. Nichols, in three volumes, octavo. Price 10s. 6d. sewed.

The Origin of Printing, in Two Essays, by W. Bowyer and J. Nichols. Octavo. Price 3s. sewed.

Some Account of the Alien Priories, and of such Lands as they are known to have possessed in England and Wales. Two volumes, crown octavo, adorned with a Map of Normandy, and eight other elegant Engravings. Price 7s. sewed.

The History of the Royal Abbey of Bec in Normandy, translated from a French MS. presented to Dr. Ducarel by Dom. Bourget. Price 3s. sewed.

Heylin's Help to English History; continued to the present time by Paul Wright, D. D. F. S. A. Adorned with copper-plates. Price 8s. sewed.

Letters from an English Traveller [Martin Sherlock, Esq.]. Translated from the French Original, printed at Geneva; with Notes; quarto. Price 3s.

# ADDITIONAL OBSERVATIONS

## AND

## CORRECTIONS,

COMMUNICATED BY SOME LEARNED FRIENDS.

Page ix. *After* l. 7, add, "Eleanor Queen of Henry II. — — — 13*."
———— x. l. 2. r. "*Mohun*."
———— l. 15. r. "Edward V."
———— 3. In the 3d metrical line, Hearne gives it "*mevable*." See his Robert of Gloucester, p. 586.
———— 5. l. *antepen.* for 4 read 2. See Sandford, p. 27.
———— 12. *lin. ult.* r. Mans.
———— 17. note, l. 1. for ".own" r. "half." L. 5 of the text, r. "capellani mei."
———— 21. l. 6. Leland (Collect. I. 554.) from the Scala Chronica, says, "Edward I. gave to his son Edmund *yn his testament* 4000 markes by yere of landes to be performid by his son Edward upon his benediction. In party whereof Edmund had afte' che counte of Kent, but he had not the hole sum afore Edward the Third's days." This implies a will after Edward I. came to the crown.
———— 31. note *h*. r. "Ferrara."— Text, l. 5 from the bottom, "de causa Dei adversus Pelagianos," by *Thomas Bradwardine*.
———— 41. notes, r. "husband's."
———— 49. note *o*, r. "Hurley."
———— 49. l. *antep.* "*priorie* de Notéle." But the house in note *p* was from the first an *abbey*.
———— two last lines, "n're priorie de *Scoule*."— Finding no such religious house any where, Stonle perhaps may be the true reading; for at *Stonely* in Huntingdonshire was a priory, connected with the Mandeviles and the Bohuns; for which see *Tanner*, p. 194. See also p. 55. *lin. ult. infra*.
———— 54. note *g*. r. "*arare*, arrear."

# ADDITIONAL OBSERVATIONS

Page 55. note *i.* " a prier" in Italics.
— 59. l. 9. Perhaps " pat*i*retur."
— 86. note *a*, " William, *de Cloune.*" Br. Willis. [By comparing Br. *Willis's* two accounts of *William Knight*, as given in his Abbies, and at the end of Notit. Monast. it will appear that in the latter place, for " 1322" we should read " 1522."]
— 109. l. 11. *emprendre*, to undertake. *Cotgrave.* See also p. 420. col. 2.
— 110. note *a.* r. " LLantarna*m*," and again in the Glossary.
———— *b.* r. " 1143."
— 121. note *e*, read " 127."
— 126. note *c.* r. " college."
— 136. ——— *m.* r. " Not."
— 155. ——— *a.* r. " Brotherton."
— 161. ——— *x.* l. 11. for " *minis*." r. " *nimis.*"
— 165. and 198. dele notes *i*, and say *Roger* Walden, dean of York, and high treasurer of England, was archbishop of Canterbury the two last years of Richard II's reign, and was afterwards, for the last year of his life, bishop of London. See Richardson's Godwin, p. 123, 124. 187.
— 180. ——— *m.* r. " vigne."
— 181. l. 14. Concerning *Ægidius de Columna* see Cave's Hist. Lit. ii. 339.—edit. *Oxon.*
— 184. note *l.* " Nic. Mile——28 July."
— 186. l. 4, 5. " but—iv." should be erased.
— 189. l. 16, 17. omit " since the time of R. I." Sandford, p. 376, will clear up this.
———— l. 22. r. " 377."
— 199. notes. *lin. ult.* r. " Plesh*y.*"
— 201. note *b*, line 2. for " x " r. " y."
— 204. l. 10 from the bottom, r. " prey my."
— 207. lines 4, 5, 6. the inverted commas omitted.
———— l. 8. r. " Baugé." and " 1421."
— 211. l. 5. " Moriton" or " Mortain ?"
— 216. l. 9. r. " once."
— 218. note *e*, r. " 470."
— 222. l. 13. should it not be " Of his dukedom of Aumarle he "?
— 224. note *b*, r. " *se lerra mourir.*"
———— l. 6. r. " MCCCCXXX."
— 244. l. 16. r. " *Somerset*shire."
———— line 9 from the bottom, Sandford, p. 293, writes that Helen had issue *Stephen* Gardiner, Prior of Tinmouth, afterwards Bishop of Winchester. But the Prior's christian name was *Thomas*; see Willis's

## AND CORRECTIONS

Willis's Abbies, ii. 165; and he was probably Helen's son. As to the Bishop's parents see the note in Richardson's Godwin, p. 236, from Ric. Parkeri Sceletos Cantabrigiensis, as published in the 5th volume of Leland's Collectanea.

Page 249. (2) note *b*, line 2. r. " and *earl of* Kent."—for " e " r. " f."
——————— 3. r. " 695."
—— 250. (2) l. 11. " ecclesia."
—— 251. l. 9. " collegialia."
—— 251. note *f, lin. antep.* r. "*frontlet*," as at p. 428. col. 2.
—— 253. notes. *lin. ult.* for " IV." r. " III."
—— 256. l. 1. " mutuacionis."
—— 259. notes. *lin. ult.* " bishop."
—— 263. note *g*, " faced;" literally " guarded."
—— 267. l. 10 from the bottom, " castellum honoris sive dominii."
—— 270. l. 8, 9. Quære " canonici prebendati." See p. 271. l. 6, 7.
—— 272. 5, 6. " habet et possidet."
—— 274. note *h*, l. 3. r. " Eugenius." " crowns." The Latin is " SS. coronatorum;" see Bentham's Ely, from Anglia Sacra. Of the four crowned with Martyrdom, see Bede in his Martyrologium, p. 443, and Hospinian, Festa Christianorum, p. 101.
—— ibid. note *k*, lines 3, 4. for " Northampton" r. " Lincoln." L. 4. for " in the same county" r. " c. Northampton."
—— ibid. l. 4. r. " 1443."
—— 275. l. 14, for " principium," perhaps " precipuum."
—— 280. l. 5 from the bottom, r. " earl *of*."
—— 291. l. 6. r. " Budde*n*o."
—— 298. *lin. antep.* " dry."
—— 302. note *r*. l. 1. r. " 297."
—— 315. l. 5. for *this* r. his; and l. 8. for *and* r. or. l. 15. " oure *alder* Saviour," our common Saviour, the Saviour of us all. See in the Glossaries to Urry's and Tyrwhitt's Chaucer. So p. 317. l. 16. where erase the commas.
—— l. 16. perhaps " committe," with a silent *e.* See Budden.
—— 317. l. 4. clearer, if the comma were erased after *favour*, and in the next line placed after *bee.*
—— 321. *lin. penult.* " celebrentur," as in p. 323. l. 1.
—— 322. l. 5. " post communione," as in p. 326. l. 13, 14.
—— 324. *lin. penult.* " dicto." note *e*, r. " pots."
—— 325. l. 16. " unum." Q ? " vinum."
—— note *i*. Rather " of *pottle* measure," the half of the gallon measure.
—— 329. l. 11. " salutem."
—— 331. l. 5 from the bottom, " cordis."

# ADDITIONAL OBSERVATIONS.

Page 338. l. 13. "Q ? *obstant*."
—— 341. note *b*. line 2. for "q" read "t."
—— 342. l. 4. r. "prebendary."
—— 349. l. 6. for "brass" r. "steel."
—— 350. l. 8. from the bottom, Q ? "worldely."
—— 352. l. 5. *Carte* says "the forest of Whitlebury."
—— 354. —— "Quarrer."
—— 358. l. 10 from the bottom, "at all."—*Lin. ult.* "placebo *and* dirige."
—— 359. lin. penult. "ornaments."
—— 365. Lin. antepen. Q ? "our p'sent," as in p. 367.
——— note *d*, lin. 2. r. "1535."
—— 367. l. 7 from the bottom, "to *se* and cause." Compare p. 379. l. 3, 4, 12; p. 380. l. 2.
—— 375. note *r*. "*plein*."
—— 378. note *i*, l. 3. "elect."
—— 381. note *e*, l. 1. r. "founded *by*."
—— 385. l. 7 from the bottom. Q ? "do distribute." Clearer, if the comma were erased in the foregoing line; and placed in this after "committed."
—— 396. last line r. "canonico."
—— 403. l. 1. r. Samford.
—— 404. note *a*, r. "Henry Bowett, bishop of Bath and Wells 1401, archbishop of York 1406—1423." The first note should be made *c*, and the present note *c* erased.
—— ibid. l. 4 from the bottom, r. "diserec'oes."
—— 405. l. 10 from the bottom, r. "equis."
—— 419. col. 1. l. 5 from the bottom, for "252" r. "232."
—— 419. under *Coellers*, for "100" r. "102." Under *Costres*, for "234" r. "284." Under *Corporas caas*, add "*Paxbrede* is the Pix." See Dugdale's Bar. II. 208.
—— 421. col. 2. l. 10. "towel" surely should be omitted; as in the page there referred to, we read "fanon avec towaill." See *Fanon* & *Manipulon* in Cotgrave. The word at p. 415, seems from the context to be restricted to the same sense as that at p. 71 ; and if so, note *d*, at p 415, might be spared, as also the article "*Favones*," in the Glossary.
—— 423. col. 1. l. 5. for "Hants" r. "Berks."
—— 425. col. 2. r. "Perrcia." Under *Plain*, r. "314."
—— 426. last article, *lin. penult.* r. "Saliere."

www.ingramcontent.com/pod-product-compliance
Lightning Source LLC
Chambersburg PA
CBHW021847230426
43671CB00006B/293